GAME GRAPHICS PROGRAMMING

ALLEN SHERROD

Charles River Media
A part of Course Technology, Cengage Learning

Australia, Brazil, Japan, Korea, Mexico, Singapore, Spain, United Kingdom, United States

COURSE TECHNOLOGY
CENGAGE Learning™

Game Graphics Programming

Allen Sherrod

Publisher and General Manager,
Course Technology PTR:
Stacy L. Hiquet

Associate Director of Marketing:
Sarah Panella

Manager of Editorial Services:
Heather Talbot

Marketing Manager: Jordan Casey

Senior Acquisitions Editor: Emi Smith

Project Editor: Kate Shoup

Technical Reviewer: Michael Duggan

CRM Editorial Services Coordinator:
Jen Blaney

Copy Editor: Ruth Saavedra

Interior Layout: Jill Flores

Cover Designer: Mike Tanamachi

CD-ROM Producer: Brandon Penticuff

Indexer: Valerie Haynes Perry

Proofreader: Michael Beady

Library of Congress Control Number: 2007935957

ISBN-13: 978-1-58450-516-7

ISBN-10: 1-58450-516-8

Course Technology
25 Thomson Place
Boston, MA 02210
USA

Cengage Learning is a leading provider of customized learning solutions with office locations around the globe, including Singapore, the United Kingdom, Australia, Mexico, Brazil, and Japan. Locate your local office at: **international. cengage.com/region**

Cengage Learning products are represented in Canada by Nelson Education, Ltd.

For your lifelong learning solutions, visit **courseptr.com**

Visit our corporate website at **cengage.com**

Printed in the United States of America
1 2 3 4 5 6 7 11 10 09 08

DEDICATION

This book is dedicated to my friends and family, who have always believed in me and wished me well. This is also dedicated to you, the reader, for honoring me by showing your support.

ACKNOWLEDGMENTS

I would like to thank my friends and family for supporting me in my efforts to get into the field of game development and to make something out of my life that I can enjoy and be proud of. The path I've taken has not been an easy one, but it is one that I believe in and one that I will succeed in.

I would like to give thanks to Jenifer Niles, who was the first to give me a chance after receiving the proposal for my first book, *Ultimate Game Programming with DirectX* and for also being the first one to bring up and initiate the opportunity for me to write this book on game graphics. I also want to give many thanks to Heather Hurley, Emi Smith, Jennifer Blaney, Lance Morganelli, Kate Shoup, and the rest of the men and women of Charles River Media/Course Technology PTR/Cengage Learning for working so hard to make all of this possible.

Also, I would like to thank you, the reader, for purchasing this book. I hope you have as much fun reading it as I had writing it.

ABOUT THE AUTHOR

Allen Sherrod, a DeVry University graduate in the Computer Information Systems program, has authored games and graphics-related books including *Ultimate Game Programming with DirectX* (first and second editions), *Ultimate 3D Game Engine Design and Architecture*, and *Data Structures for Game Developers*. Allen is also the host of www.UltimateGameProgramming.com. He has written for *Game Developer* magazine and Gamasutra.com, and is the founder of Re-Inventing Games & Graphics, Inc.

CONTENTS

CHAPTER 9   ADVANCED LIGHTING AND SHADOWS   393

CHAPTER 10   GLOBAL ILLUMINATION TECHNIQUES   421

INTRODUCTION

OVERVIEW TO THIS BOOK

To say that the graphical imagery in video games is very important to the games industry is a bit of an understatement. The graphics in games are so important that they often can make or break a game's success. It is true that all other aspects of a game are important, but the visuals are at times the main selling point along with game play, brand recognition, and so forth. This has been true for a long time in the games industry, where 3D games have been known for their visuals.

In this book, we will examine many graphical techniques that are used in the games industry to create cutting-edge, modern applications. The graphics used in games are real-time computer graphics. This means a lot of the information discussed in this book also applies to other graphical-related industries that use either real-time or non-real-time graphics, but our focus will be primarily on video games. Since this book focuses on game graphics, we will examine many different real-time techniques as well as some non-real-time techniques that can be preprocessed and used in games, which is very common in video games today.

By the time you reach the end of this book, you will have a firm understanding of many of the more popular effects and techniques used in modern video games and how to implement them. This book discusses a lot of theory and makes heavy use of both pseudo code and illustrations to help make it easier for you to learn the information regardless of what programming language, graphical tools, and so on you choose to use. There will also be C++ code samples throughout this book, but the information provided is generally not specific to any one language or tool.

WHAT'S DIFFERENT ABOUT THIS BOOK

This book takes a detailed look at computer graphics on all levels. Throughout this book, detailed and informative C++ source code and pseudo code is used to gain an understanding of how the different algorithms and effects are structured and how they are executed to create a rendered result. One of the things that makes this book different from many others on the market is that this book delivers its information in a straightforward manner and in a way that is not dependent on any one programming language, graphical tool, operating system, and so on. Although this book is geared toward programmers, it is impossible to talk about a book on graphics without talking about art and assets as well.

Another feature that makes this book different from the rest is that the information is not presented in a manner that assumes you will learn a technique or algorithm by reading the author's code with no further or more detailed explanation (i.e., explanation of the code but not the "what" or "why"). In programming, there is rarely only one way to do something, and in a book like this, it is important to discuss what a technique is, how a technique can be done, optimizations that can be done to improve its performance, and alternatives, with further discussion of why the technique exists and detailed explanations of how it works. Code will be presented after a technique has been thoroughly discussed and has been viewed and examined from many different angles. The code samples are examples of implementation. It is my hope that you will gain enough detailed information before getting to the code that you don't actually need the code samples to implement the information yourself. Of course, the code samples are there to help and to serve as an example.

This book does not focus only on beginner techniques or only on advanced techniques but on game graphics as a whole. Everything from complex lighting and shadowing techniques and algorithms to colors, pixels, and bits are discussed. The biggest question that will be answered throughout this book is "Why?". Why would developers want to use this technique? Why is this specific algorithm for this effect better than others and in what situations? Being able to answer these questions can take you a long way toward efficiently and effectively creating stunning graphical scenes in your games. For many techniques, the specific algorithms and steps taken to create the effect depend on many factors that make the choice difficult to determine at times.

WHO THIS BOOK IS FOR

This book is for anyone looking to take their knowledge of computer graphics to a more advanced level. Although this book is pretty lengthy, it does not discuss in great detail everything that a complete beginner would need to go from novice to expert, but it does review a bit of information that all readers should not only know but have a firm understanding of. Because this is only one book with a finite size, it is assumed that you are coming to it with at least some prior knowledge and experience with the fundamentals. Even if this knowledge comes from working with OpenGL or Direct3D to draw a few triangles to the screen, it helps to have some experience.

The samples in this book use the C++ programming language. They also use either OpenGL, Direct3D, or both for graphics rendering, or they use ray tracing (using C++) and even, to a degree, software rendering to create output. If you have a graphical rendering system and programming language of your choice, you can still get a lot out of this book because the information presented is not dependent on any one of these technologies. The sample code will use them but only as examples of implementation after a technique has been discussed in great detail.

This book is for the following:

- Computer graphics students
- Computer graphics enthusiasts
- Programmers who are beginners at computer graphics but not complete novices (i.e., have at least some experience rendering geometric shapes and primitives to a window)
- Intermediate and advanced computer graphics programmers looking for an easy–to-read reference
- Computer graphics artists (with some knowledge of programming, at least with programmable shaders) looking for a reference to add to their library on computer graphics

WHAT YOU WILL NEED TO KNOW FOR THIS BOOK

In this book, it is assumed that you are familiar with a programming language such as C++ and that you are capable of writing applications for the operating system and platform of your choice. It is also assumed that you have some experience, even if it is not a lot, rendering geometry to a window using OpenGL, Direct3D, or your own rendering routines (e.g., a software rendering system or ray tracer), and it is assumed that you have some mathematics background, either high school or university level, as well. Because games rely heavily on mathematics, it is assumed that you are familiar with concepts such as vectors, matrices, transformations, and so on. We will review the common game mathematics used throughout this book, but the review will not be a complete introduction, which could easily span a book or two of its own.

This book is targeted toward programmers, so you do not need to be an artist or have a high level of artistic ability. If you have the ability to create images and geometry, that would be a plus since you can create your own content and test your code against it (but it is not necessary since the focus is on programming, theory, and the algorithms that make up various effects).

To follow the code on the CD-ROM. it is necessary for you to be familiar with C++. All code samples use the C++ programming language and some of them also use high-level programmable shaders, which are based on the C programming language syntax. Shaders will be discussed in great detail so you do not need to be an expert or have much experience with them, although for a book of this level it is assumed that you have at least done the basics with shaders on a novice level.

HOW THIS BOOK IS ORGANIZED

This book is composed of 16 chapters. The first five chapters fall under the "Introduction" section and serve as a quick review of the various bits of information readers should already be somewhat familiar with. The following two chapters, Chapter 6 and Chapter 7, fall under the "Shading and Surfaces" section. Chapters 8, 9, and 10 are under the section "Direct and Global Illumination," and Chapters 11 and 12 are under "Special Effects." Chapters 13 and 14 discuss rendering nature, which includes water, terrains, and skies. The last two chapters, Chapters 15 and 16, are the optimization and conclusions chapters. Below, we will discuss what information can be expected out of each chapter.

- Chapter 1, "Introduction to Game Graphics," sets the tone for what readers can expect from the remainder of the book. This chapter discusses the tools that are used to create some of the art assets and resources such as textures, environments, and geometric models.

- Chapter 2, "2D and 3D Graphics," covers the basics of 2D and 3D computer graphics. The information covered in this chapter includes common game mathematics, colors and pixels, computer memory, and geometry and primitives. This chapter lays the foundation for the rest of the book and serves as a review on many topics that readers are expected to be familiar with.
- Chapter 3, "Ray Tracing," covers the basics of CPU ray tracing using C++. Ray tracing is an important rendering technique that is used throughout computer graphics and is very important in learning about computer graphics in general. The information covered in this chapter can also be applied to nongraphical areas of a video game such as collision detection using lines of sight and even to some rendering graphical effects, which are discussed. Since ray tracing can be done in both offline and real-time applications, it is beneficial to discuss it in this book on game graphics since games do use, to an extent, ray-tracing ideas and techniques in a few different areas. Also, ray tracing is used in games for preprocessed effects that have been popular for almost as long as 3D games have been around.
- Chapter 4, "Rasterization," covers the rasterization technique for creating computer-generated images. The topics covered in this chapter include software rendering, the OpenGL graphics API, and the Direct3D graphics API. Each of these graphical rendering tools uses rasterization, and this chapter will give readers a detailed explanation of how rasterization works and how to implement it.
- Chapter 5, "Programmable Shaders," looks at programmable shaders and high-level shading languages in computer graphics. In this chapter, we'll discuss shaders in general and their use in both OpenGL and Direct3D. This chapter is very important because many of the graphical techniques that are used in modern video games can only be done using programmable graphics hardware.
- Chapter 6, "Mapping Surfaces," discusses texture mapping. Additionally, texture compression using graphics hardware is discussed in detail as well as additional techniques that can be done with textures and images such as billboards and various image filters. Textures take up a lot of system resources and storage in modern video games, and using them correctly and efficiently is not always trivial.
- Chapter 7, "Additional Surface Mapping," picks up where Chapter 6 leaves off. The techniques discussed in this chapter include alpha mapping, dynamic cube mapping, reflections, refractions, and off-screen rendering, to name a few.
- Chapter 8, "Lighting and Materials," discusses surface materials, light sources in virtual environments, and reflection models. Lighting in games is very important, and this chapter will introduce the topic to you and how to represent it in a game using per-vertex and per-pixel lighting.

- Chapter 9, "Advanced Lighting and Shadows," builds off of the information covered in Chapter 8 and covers more advanced lighting techniques. Among these techniques are deferred shading, light mapping, and various shadowing techniques. Shadowing techniques are commonly used in computer graphics to add more realism to 3D scenes. A scene without shadows does not look as realistic, even if lit, because the absence of that detail stands out in the human mind. Shadows are just as important as lighting itself and are covered in great detail in this chapter by using common techniques that can be found in modern 3D games.

- Chapter 10, "Global Illumination Techniques," discusses global illumination techniques that are used in computer graphics to achieve greater levels of realism and detail that cannot be done otherwise using the direct illumination lighting and shadowing techniques that are common in computer graphics. Global illumination is used heavily in realistic renderings and is extremely useful in computer graphics. Global illumination gives even simple scenes a profound look of realism.

- Chapter 11, "Special Effects: High Dynamic Range," covers the topic of high–dynamic-range rendering (HDR). HDR has become very popular in recent years and is seen in many video games, movies, and so forth. This chapter covers what HDR is, why it is so important in computer graphics, and how it is performed.

- Chapter 12, "Special Effects: Additional Effects," discusses various special effects that are commonly seen in video games and that have yet to be discussed. Among the topics discussed in this chapter are particle systems, motion blur, depth-of-field, weapon special effects, and arbitrary decals.

- Chapter 13, "Sky and Terrain Rendering," covers the rendering of skies and clouds in video games, as well as terrains. Though the topic seems trivial, it is very important and can become quite complex when you are trying to realistically render an outdoor scene.

- Chapter 14, "Water Rendering," discusses how to render realistic water in games. Water rendering is becoming a bigger topic in the games industry, and the ability to render water realistically can increase a scene's realism a lot.

- Chapter 15, "Optimization," discusses optimizations that can be performed to gain the best performance when rendering scenes. In video games, this is very important because time is everything, and the faster a scene can render, the more time can be dedicated to other resources such as physics, artificial intelligence, scene management, and so forth.

- Chapter 16, "Conclusions," is the final chapter in this book. We will look at the future and the next steps you can take once you have completed this book. Although this book covers a lot of useful information, the field of computer graphics will expand and evolve as time passes and as technology becomes more powerful and efficient. Also, even though this book is quite lengthy, it cannot cover everything in the large field of computer graphics.

SOURCE CODE FOR THIS BOOK

ON THE CD

On the CD-ROM that accompanies this book, you can find all the chapter samples that are discussed. The samples are organized by chapter and have programming projects for Microsoft's Visual Studio .NET 2005 and XCode for Mac OS X and files for Linux users. As mentioned previously, the source code for the samples in this book are written using C++.

ERRATA

The men and women of Charles River Media, a part of Cengage Learning, as well as myself, have worked very hard to ensure that this book is error-free and of the highest quality. Sometimes errors do slip by our radar and make it into the final print. If you notice any errors please feel free to send us your feedback at http://www.UltimateGameProgramming.com or at http://www.charlesriver.com. There you can take a look at the current errata and, if you don't see your error on the list, please let us know of it as soon as you can. These errors can include typos, mislabeled figures or listings, or anything else that you notice that you feel is not quite right. Reporting any errors will allow us to make the necessary changes and to allow future readers to avoid any confusion if they come across the same issue in their texts.

INTRODUCTION TO GAME GRAPHICS

INTRODUCTION TO GAME GRAPHICS

In This Chapter

- Computer Graphics in Media
- Computer Graphics in Print
- Computer Graphics in Video Games
- About this Book

Computer graphics can be seen in many different areas of various media and entertainment fields. The topic of computer graphics is huge and can become very technical when dealing with advanced rendering topics. Having an understanding of computer graphics is the key to being able to create the types of visuals that are becoming commonplace across the various industries. Today, visuals are very important in the entertainment industry, whether these visuals are realistic, nonrealistic, or artistic in some manner.

The focus of this book is computer graphics in modern video games. The effects and visuals seen in today's games require artistic talent as well as technical knowledge about the software and the hardware technology being utilized. What makes video games and other interactive applications special is that they are indeed interactive products that operate in real time. Video games are progressing in a direction that is getting them closer to the visuals in movies, but, unfortunately, the power of computer hardware still has a ways to go. Also, video games have other resource-consuming systems such as artificial intelligence, networking, sound, input detection and response, physics, and so forth, each having to operate in real time. This in itself makes creating impressive visuals difficult because games are required to render a number of times per second instead of one frame in X amount of time, which the movie and TV industries can afford when preprocessing visuals. With so many different areas of a game requiring resources, there is often a balance between all systems, where quality, performance, and practicality must be traded around and balanced to complete the project.

COMPUTER GRAPHICS IN MEDIA

Computer graphics can be seen everywhere from magazines, to video games, movies, television, and so forth. Visuals are often a huge selling point for many products and services. It is the beautiful graphics that often draw consumers to video games, similar to how special effects, among other things, can be used to draw audiences to a movie theater. Often, the visual representation is mistaken for a representation of the quality of the work. Because what people see is so important to their first impression, computer graphics is a highly important and sought after field of study. It is no wonder that movie and video game trailers often attempt to show off the visuals of a movie or game while giving only a brief look at the story instead of the other way around. Today, gamers have learned to look past just the graphics when purchasing a game, but there was a time in the history of video games when some games truly did sell based on their looks alone.

COMPUTER GRAPHICS IN PRINT

In magazines, ads often must sell themselves on a visual alone. This visual has many purposes, the most important being to draw readers' attention to the page and to inform them about some type of product or service in a meaningful way. When it comes to computer-generated images in a print publication, the layout, style, art, and so forth must say a lot to the reader in one or two pages, often using few words. In other words, an image must say a thousand words in an attempt to be as efficient and effective as possible.

Graphics in Movies and TV

Movies and television are rich sources of computer-generated special effects. Some movies are made using computer generation, as seen in animated films such as *Shrek 3* by DreamWorks Animation, *Finding Nemo* by Pixar, *Teenage Mutant Ninja Turtles* by Imagi Studios, and many others. In computer-generated animations such as those seen in movies the images are generated offline, meaning they are not done in real time, which is unlike the major requirement of a video game. Since computer-generated movies are not in real time, the level of quality and detail are often much higher than that of a video game because video games must make scarifies in performance versus detail and quality, whereas offline-rendered products such as animated movies allow the time to compute the detail we have grown accustomed to seeing. The quality seen in animated movies, at this time, is something that cannot be done in real time. In the future this will change as technology becomes more powerful and efficient. Offline-rendered content will always be able to compute more complex results than real-time content because of the luxury of time.

 Video games can use a combination of preprocessing rendering effects along with real-time rendering, as shown throughout this book. This allows for complex rendered content to be used in a real-time application.

Other films and TV programs use computer-generated content to create special effects and scenes that blend with live action actors and actresses, which can be seen in the movie *300* and *Sin City*, which are based on the works of Frank Miller. In the movie *300* the visuals were so impressive that they were a major reason why audiences, both fans of Frank Miller and newcomers to his work, flocked to see the film when it made its debut in movie theaters in 2007. Using computer graphics and live actors, the makers of the movie were able to deliver a story in a unique and creative way. The same can be said of the movie Sin City, in which live actors were used together with computer-generated scenes and special effects.

COMPUTER GRAPHICS IN VIDEO GAMES

Computer graphics in video games is a huge area of study and will continue to grow as time goes on. Over the past few generations the graphics in games have increased considerably in technical terms, quality, and art style. With this increase in graphical quality also came an increase in what gamers expect from the games they buy. Every time a new game makes a leap in graphical quality, it raises the bar for the entire industry. For many years video games have been sold based on their graphical representation. Today, this is accompanied by increased physics, artificial intelligence, and other areas that in the past took a back seat to the visuals. With games becoming higher in quality, they are starting to gain ground against other entertainment media such as the motion picture industry.

 Not all games have to look photo-realistic to look great and to have great visual appeal.

In this book we will examine not only various areas of computer graphics, but we will focus on some modern and upcoming effects and algorithms used to create cutting-edge games. These areas of focus cover both 2D and 3D graphics as well as real-time and preprocessed rendering effects. The information covered in this book can be used outside of the games industry as well as in it, although the game aspects of these effects and their implementations will be discussed.

2D Graphics

2D graphics have been around in some form since the beginning of game graphics. In the early days of video games, 2D side-scrolling games were popular. Later, 3D games started to emerge and became the standard in the industry. Although 3D graphics have taken a huge role in video games, 2D gaming applications are still very popular. This can be seen on handheld gaming systems such as the Nintendo DS and Sony's PSP. It can also be seen on Microsoft's Xbox 360, Sony's PlayStation 3, and Nintendo's Wii video game consoles, where past arcade and console games are making a comeback as downloadable games. Along with bringing back old-school games, new 2D games are also being made available for download on each of these systems. One very popular 2D video game is *Geometry Wars Evolved* for the Xbox 360, which is shown in Figure 1.1.

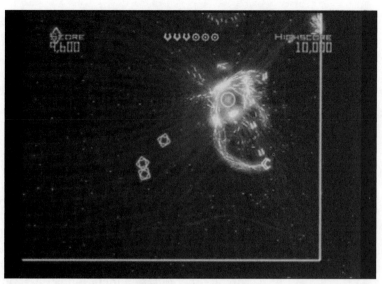

FIGURE 1.1   *Geometry Wars.*

The rise of the casual gamer and casual gaming market is allowing easy-to-use and fun 2D games to become quite successful. At one time, video games were more for the hard-core gaming audience. The success of the Nintendo Wii has been proven that non–hard-core gamers are also looking to have fun with video games.

There is still a place for 2D-based games in the marketplace, and they can prove to be a very valuable way into the games industry for enthusiasts, students, and those looking to make their way into professional game development. Not only are past arcade and console games doing quite well on the newer generation consoles, but new games based in or partially in 2D are also becoming very successful. An example of this can be seen with Nintendo's *Super Paper Mario* on the Nintendo Wii, which uses both 2D and 3D game play to deliver a unique experience. Some gamers, often casual gamers, want to play fun yet simple games, which are at times done in 2D.

Not all games that are simple have to be 2D, just like not all 2D games are simple.

In this book, 2D graphics are discussed along with their 3D counterpart. 2D graphics are essential and can be used as a stepping stone to moving toward the 3D realm for beginners. With the success 2D games enjoy today, it is important to discuss the topics that concern those types of applications since not all topics that apply to 2D games apply to 3D games and vice versa. Also, even in 3D games 2D elements are often used for user interfaces, menus elements, particles, and so forth.

3D Graphics

3D graphics really started to take a strong hold in the mid 1990s on the PC and have been used extensively ever since. Today's 3D games have evolved and now include not only 3D graphics but also 3D interactions through realistic physics, much more advanced and realistic artificial intelligence, and much more complex engineering designs, to name a few. Each of these areas are highly technical professions on their own. As computer processing power increases, so does our ability to create more complex gaming applications through many of these different areas.

3D games offer a new level of realism. In 3D games, lighting and shadows can be simulated to appear more realistic, objects can have dynamic and complex animations that are physics based, reflections can appear on surfaces in real time, and the overall difference between interactive and noninteractive entertainment, such as animated movies, is starting to decrease greatly in terms of popularity and sales. The popularity of 3D games and the evolution of gaming as a whole have allowed video games to compete with all other entertainment industries, and they are worth billions.

 Preprocessing effects are computed ahead of time, and the results are used later during run time. Postprocessing effects are added to a rendered scene after the scene has been rendered, and effects are calculated in real time during an application's execution.

One of the first types of popular 3D game genres where graphics pushed what is cutting-edge was the first-person shooter. First-person shooters have always been very popular styles of games on the PC, and, thanks to games like Rare's *Goldeneye 007* for the Nintendo 64 and Bungie's *Halo* for the Xbox, those types of games are also very popular on the home consoles as well. First-person shooters have redefined the games industry on more than one occasion (e.g., *Quake*, *Goldeneye 007*, *Half-Life*, *Halo*, the upcoming *Crysis*, and so forth). One of the biggest games of recent times is the *Halo* series from Bungie, which have sold numbers in the millions over the years. *Halo 3*, the first *Halo* game on the Xbox 360, is one of the console's biggest brands, with a following of millions of fans worldwide and was considered by many to be one of the most, if not the most, anticipated game releases of 2007. First-person shooters are known for both their game-play and their graphics. Some of the biggest game engines, the Quake engine and the Unreal engine, started out as frameworks for first-person shooting games on the PC. The CryEngine, used to power the game *Crysis* from Crytex, is among the first games to run using DirectX 10 and shader model 4.0 technology. We discuss shaders a little more throughout this book.

Many, but not all, game engines are developed around first-person shooters. Some of these engines include the Quake Engine, Doom 3 Engine, Crysis Engine, Far Cry Engine, Offset Engine, Unreal Engine, Half-Life Engine (which was originally a variation of the Quake 2 Engine), and others.

ON THE CD

Throughout this book we examine the many different graphical techniques and effects seen in modern, cutting-edge video games such as *Halo 3* and *Crysis*. Along with this discussion, implementations are provided on the book's accompanying CD-ROM, complete with source code. Understanding what professional game studios are using and knowing how they work can allow you to create your own rich and detailed game worlds that can visually compete in the marketplace.

Rasterization and the Rendering Pipeline

Rasterization is the rendering technique used to display virtual scenes in real-time applications and is the technique commonly used in PCs, home consoles, and mobile video game systems. Rasterization is fast, whereas other techniques, such as ray tracing, are not as fast to process in real time using available hardware. Ray tracing is generally not as fast due to the amount of processing power and the number of computations needed to render a complex scene at a high resolution, especially at high definition, but rasterization offers an efficient alternative for games. Although rasterization is fast, it is more complex to implement than ray tracing. On PCs, the top two graphics application programming interfaces (graphics APIs) are OpenGL and Direct3D. These graphics APIs are standard methods used to talk directly to the hardware on PCs, and they perform rasterization to create rendered scenes.

Ray tracing for real-time applications has become a reality on today's hardware (GPU, cell processors, multicore processors, etc.) but is not quite at the point where commercial games have been able to use it for real-time rendering of complex scenes at resolutions we are used to seeing in games. In the era of high-definition gaming, real-time ray tracing is not quite practical yet as a complete rendering solution for modern video games. In time this will change.

Rasterization works by taking a 3D scene made up of polygons and primitives and generating a 2D image out of it. Generally, a polygon in an application such as a video game describes a triangle made up of three points (Figure 1.2). A stream of triangles is passed to the graphics hardware, is transformed into 2D form, and is displayed to the screen. Transformations are done using various mathematical matrices that describe the view, the scene, and object positions and orientations, which we discuss in more detail later throughout this book. The points of the polygons are known as vertices. Polygons that are transformed to 2D but are partially outside of the bounds of the screen are clipped to the rendering area. Clipping is a way to truncate polygons that are outside of the rendering area, which is often the window's screen, as shown in Figure 1.3 (discussed in Chapter 4, "Rasterization"). Once polygons have been transformed to 2D and have been clipped to the screen bounds, the color information is stored and the surfaces that make up the polygon are filled in line-by-line, where each line is known as a scan-line.

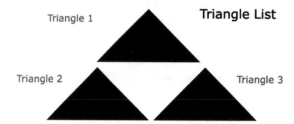

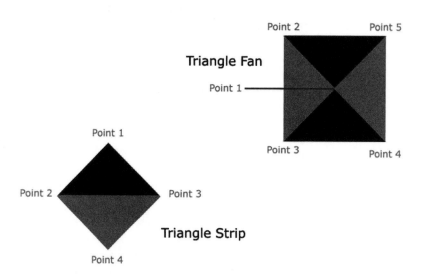

FIGURE 1.2   Various types of triangles.

Unclipped Polygon to the Viewport

Clipped Polygon to the Viewport

FIGURE 1.3 Clipping polygons.

 A polygon is a geometric shape made up of three or more connected points. In games, polygons often refer to three-point polygons, also known as triangles.

In the early days of 3D graphics, APIs such as OpenGL and Direct3D used fixed algorithms that were executed during the rendering process. These series of fixed algorithms are known as the fixed-function pipeline. Today we use programmable shaders, which are custom-written algorithms that we can create and use in our applications instead of the fixed-function pipeline. We discuss programmable shaders in more detail later. Programmable shaders are the future for many reasons, one being that they are not restricting like the fixed-function pipeline, which could not be customized but instead could generally only have fixed features enabled or disabled. By being able to write our own algorithms we are able to create just about any effect that we can dream of.

 Graphics APIs are starting to embrace shader-only approaches and are getting rid of the fixed-function pipeline. This has already been achieved in Direct3D with Direct3D 10, which is part of DirectX 10 from Microsoft.

In common graphics APIs such as OpenGL and Direct3D the information generated for a frame to be displayed includes not just color information but also depth, stencil flags, and anything else that can be used to perform rendering tasks (discussed in Chapter 4). Throughout this book we will see how many different pieces of information are needed to perform one or more rendering passes to create complex and advanced graphical effects.

With rasterization, polygons are transformed and clipped, and then the volume that makes up the shape is filled in. This happens with all polygons, and to boost performance optimizations other techniques are usually used to prevent rendering of polygons that are not visible or are occluded by others pieces of geometry.

XNA

The XNA Game Studio is a development tool created by Microsoft to allow developers of all levels to create video games on their Windows-based operating systems and their Xbox 360 video game consoles. XNA Game Studio is composed of the XNA framework along with a content pipeline tool and is based on Microsoft's Visual Studio toolset. By using this framework and the C# programming language development teams can more quickly develop their gaming projects. The XNA framework is made up of the following items and more:

- Content pipeline
- Rendering libraries
- Input libraries (which include Xbox 360 controllers)
- Sound libraries
- Starter kits

XNA has become a great way for hobbyists, students, and independent game developers to create not only games on Microsoft's Windows operating system but also Microsoft home consoles. XNA marked a major step forward in game development by supplying anyone who is interested with a free set of professional tools and utilities. The release of XNA was quite an event in the independent game-development scene. Although Microsoft is not the first to allow development on their consoles outside of licensed developers, they are the first to do it in a way that has really helped the game development scene with easy-to-use and free tools supported and documented by a major development company. By giving the tools away for free, Microsoft is truly allowing anyone and any team to start making games immediately.

XNA is available for Windows XP, Windows Vista, and the Xbox 360, making it multiplatform.

Because XNA uses the same shader language as Direct3D, a lot of the information and code seen throughout this book can also be used by anyone using the XNA framework. Shaders are discussed in more detail in Chapter 5, "Programmable Shaders." Anyone who is new to computer graphics and development can consider using XNA as a way to get started in the field and as a way to gain experience. Figure 1.4 shows an example 3D scene being rendered using the XNA framework.

 XNA is the name of the framework and is not an acronym for anything.

FIGURE 1.4   An example of an XNA game, *Spacewar.*

 Each of Sony's PlayStation game consoles allowed for indie development with the PlayStation 1 using Net Yaroza, the PlayStation 2 using the official PS2 Linux Kit, and the PlayStation 3 using Linux as well. The PlayStation 3 indie support is quite limited but is much cheaper than the kits for the previous PlayStations.

ABOUT THIS BOOK

Computer graphics is a huge part of video games and is an expanding area of study. This book discusses and examines game graphics used in modern video games. At the end of this book you will have learned a lot about topics dealing with lighting, shadows, shading, special effects, and much more. This book is intended for those who have some experience with computer graphics, but it also covers some of the fundamentals to help make everything clear from the beginning. As you progress through the book, the topics will become more complex, and a strong understanding of the fundamentals will come in handy. The main purpose of this book is to serve as a reference to intermediate-level graphics programmers.

Purpose of this Book

This book is on computer graphics used in modern video games. The goal of this book is to give you the information necessary to create the type of visuals and effects that you see in modern video games. Throughout this book a lot of detailed information is presented that covers both the basics and more advanced topics. This understanding will allow you to learn techniques and information not presented in this book much easier because of the level of background information you'll be given.

Video game graphics are a challenge, and this book aims to demystify many of the techniques and effects that are becoming standard in video games. The presented information includes the following:

- Theory
- Mathematics
- Pseudo-code
- Code samples
- Visuals aids

The book progresses to more advanced topics with each chapter. At the end of this book you should have a firm understanding about modern game graphics, their algorithms, and how they can be implemented. After reading this book, you will be prepared to learn and implement new techniques as they become practical to perform in real-time applications. The video games industry is a fast-moving industry and will require developers to evolve with the times.

Prerequisites and Prior Knowledge

This book covers a lot of information on advanced graphical techniques that are used in video games. Because of this, it is not possible to cover every bit of information in great detail. In other words, although this book does go into great detail and does take some time to cover the fundamentals, it is necessary to have some background knowledge so you can focus on the advanced techniques that modern games are known for. The information you should be familiar with includes the following:

- The basics of creating a window using the graphical API of your choice (e.g., OpenGL, Direct3D, etc.)
- A basic understanding of game mathematics
- Experience creating texture images with the editor of your choice or a source of such content (you can also use the content that comes with this book for your personal use)

- Experience creating 2D shapes and 3D models with the modeler of your choice or a source of such content (again, you can also use the content that comes with this book for your personal use)
- Experience with modern video games

This book makes heavy use of shader technology in a number of chapters, so it is necessary to have access to hardware that supports that technology, which we talk about more in Chapter 5.

The topics discussed throughout this book are presented in pseudo-code before covering an implementation in C++. If you are using technology other than the technology this book uses (OpenGL, Direct3D, etc.) or you use a different programming language, then you must be comfortable enough with those technologies to implement the theory and pseudo-code presented in this book. Pseudo-code is very important because it lays out a road map of how an algorithm can be coded (one way) in the language of your choice as well as being easy to read without any special knowledge of an individual language. Along with the pseudo-code, C++ is also used throughout this book because it is currently the main language of choice in game development and it serves as an example of turning pseudo-code into actual code. You can think of the C++ code as an extra to each of the topics discussed in this book, while the focus on learning will be done with background information through theory, mathematical equations, and through pseudo-code of the algorithms.

Every topic is discussed in great detail throughout this book, but if you come into this text with at least a basic understanding of the various points mentioned earlier in this section, you will have a better chance of fully understanding the more difficult and advanced topics as well as being able to implement them in your own projects. In each chapter some sections offer recommendations to resources that can be used to gain any background information that you need to have. For example, if you have never worked with OpenGL or DirectX and would like to, Appendix C, "Recommended Resources," has a few resources you can check out to get the detailed introduction you need in order to move to more advanced rendering topics.

ON THE CD

This section assumed that you will be coding along with the topics in this book or will at least be reading the sample code off of the accompanying CD-ROM. If you are not a programmer, you can still use the information in this book to gain a deeper understanding of the different graphical techniques and algorithms seen in video games, although it might be harder to follow in some sections without knowing how to program.

Tools Used in this Book

This book is all about computer graphics for programmers, but to display content to the screen, we need to use the art and assets that are available to us. As you may already know, a huge amount of information is used in a virtual scene. This information typically consists of the following and more:

- Static geometry
- Dynamic models
- Environment geometry
- Shaders
- Decal textures
- Normal maps
- Environment maps (cube and sphere maps)
- Additional textures (gloss, height, alpha, and so forth)

The content that is often rendered in a scene is created by artists. To create the effects discussed in this book you do not need to be an artist because you can either use the content that comes on the book's CD-ROM for your personal use, you can download free content over the Internet, or you can purchase content.

This section is a discussion of the various tools I have available to me. You do not need these tools for this book, and you do not have to use or purchase them.

For this book I used Lightwave and ZBrush for the creation of the 3D geometry. I don't consider myself an artist, but using these two tools I've been able to create geometry and texture high-polygon geometric models fairly effectively. If you are not an artist and would like to create 3D models, even as a hobby, I recommend ZBrush 3 for its ease of use, affordable price, and powerful tool set. I also enjoy using Lightwave applications, but it does have more of a learning curve than ZBrush for beginners new to modeling, much like 3D Studio Max, Maya, Softimage, and other modeling and animation packages. ZBrush takes a different approach to 3D modeling and texturing, and many newcomers might find it interesting to work with.

Shaders are very powerful. Although not necessary, a few free tools are available to help make creating shaders easier and more productive. One such tool is NVIDIA's FX Composer. This tool allows for the creation of shaders (more on this in Chapter 5) and offers a live preview and syntax checks to detect and report errors in your shader files, to name a few functions. Using the FX Composer IDE (integrated development environment), it is easy to detect errors in shader code as you code instead of encountering them during run time when you try to load and execute your shader. The FX Composer is free and might be worth checking out for shader programmers. Check out NVIDIA's developer Web site (http://developer.nvidia.com) for more information on this and other free tools that are available.

3D environments are complex in many ways. They often have numerous static and dynamic geometric models, each with their own textures, shaders, scripts, and so forth. The geometry that composes the environment itself can be separate from the objects that populate them and require its own management systems to effectively render them.

In Chapter 15, we will discuss optimizations that can be performed to improve the performance of a complex 3D scene. Among these optimizations are various scene management data structures and algorithms that make it possible to render a complex scene in real time. This is the key to efficient rendering because scenes, even scenes that might not seem complex, can easily contain more information than the hardware can handle at one time at an acceptable rate. In addition, other systems require resources such as the physics system, artificial intelligence, networking, sound, scripting, and so forth. We discuss optimizations in more detail in Chapter 15.

A few of the scenes seen in this book were created using a tool called 3D World Studio (see Figure 1.5) from Leadwerks (http://www.leadwerks.com). This tool is a constructive solid geometry editor, much like Valve's Hammer Editor and Id's Quake 3 map editor, and can allow for easy and fast creation of complex environments and objects using simple shapes such as boxes, cylinders, spheres, and so forth. The advantage to this tool is that it can be used to create full-blown game levels using an editor that is flexible enough to be used in just about any game. The downside is that it exports to a limited number of file formats, or you have to read the tool's native format directly and either create your own exporter or use the editor's format. In this book, the geometry created using this tool has been exported to the OBJ file format, which is discussed in Appendix D, "OBJ File Format." Using this tool is not necessary, but if you already have it, plan on getting it, or are looking for a tool that you can use in your own or commercial projects, it can be very beneficial.

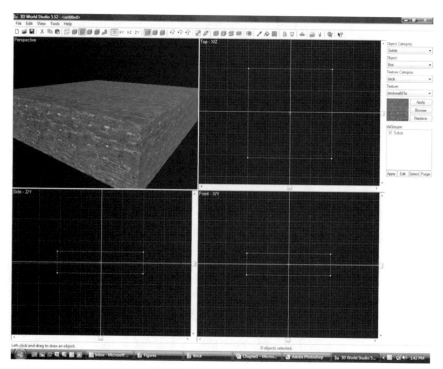

FIGURE 1.5   3D World Studio.

The last tool, which was used for the content creation of textures for this book, is Adobe's Photoshop CS 2 (see Figure 1.6). Textures are a huge part of game graphics, and a good editor is very important for anyone who wants to create their own textures or to modify existing ones. I find Photoshop CS 2 to be a great tool to use and have been using Photoshop products for years. With Photoshop you can create just about anything you can imagine as long as you have the skill to do so. Although the learning curve is steep, if you are looking for a tool to create textures, you might want to check out Adobe's Photoshop. An example of a texture created in Photoshop is shown in Figure 1.7.

FIGURE 1.6   Photoshop CS 2.

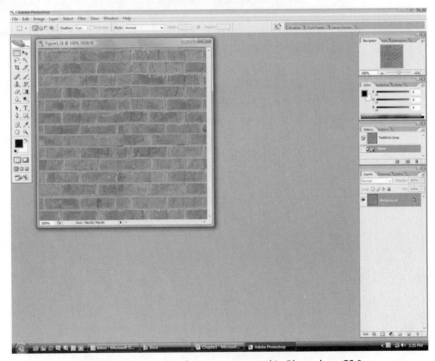

FIGURE 1.7   Example of a texture created in Photoshop CS 2.

ON THE CD

As mentioned earlier, I do not consider myself an artist, at least not a professional artist, but with the tools I have available to me I've been able to create some pretty impressive content for this book. If you are not artistically inclined, you can always work with artists or find plenty of free content available on the Internet. Since this is a programming-oriented book, you do not have to worry about finding content to use to test your code because the accompanying CD-ROM has a few good resources that you can play with for your own personal use. Different resources can be found in the various folders for each chapter sample on the CD-ROM. You can also download plenty of free tools such as Blender (3D modeling and animation), NVIDIA's FX Composer (shader development), World Craft (3D environment creation), and many more. Check out Appendix C for a list of recommended resources and tools.

SUMMARY

In this chapter we introduced what you can expect out of this book, what you need to know before attempting to tackle this book, and what tools you need to have to follow along with the chapter samples. After reading through this chapter you should have a good understanding of what is to come and how beneficial it will be to you and your learning about computer graphics in video games.

The following elements were discussed in this chapter:

- General uses of computer graphics in the entertainment industry
- Brief overview of 2D computer graphics
- Brief overview of 3D computer graphics
- Brief overview of ray tracing
- Brief overview of rasterization
- Brief overview of OpenGL, Direct3D, and XNA
- Common tools used in computer graphics
- The specific tools used throughout this book for the textures, models, shaders, and all other resources used for each of the chapter samples
- Knowledge you need to have to complete this book

In the next chapter we take a closer look at the common mathematics that are used in video game graphics as well as other topics such as geometry, primitives, transformation spaces, colors, pixels, and more.

CHAPTER QUESTIONS

Answers to the following chapter review questions can be found in Appendix A, "Answers to Chapter Questions."

1. What is a preprocessed effect?
   A. An effect often created offline
   B. An effect created during a rendered frame
   C. An effect created after the rendering of a scene
   D. None of the above
2. What is a postprocessed effect?
   A. An effect often created offline
   B. An effect created during a rendered frame
   C. An effect created after the rendering of a scene
   D. None of the above
3. What is a real-time effect?
4. What is the rasterization technique and what role does it play in game development today?
5. What is the ray tracing technique and what major role does it play in the computer graphics field?
6. True or false: OpenGL and Direct3D are software rendering APIs.
7. True or false: XNA is a cross-platform rendering API.
8. True or false: Ray tracing is a rendering technique that is more expensive to process on modern hardware than rasterization techniques.
9. True or false: Polygons are clipped to the screen bounds in ray tracing.
10. True or false: XNA is based on DirectX 10–only technology.

2D AND 3D GRAPHICS

In This Chapter

- Bits and Bytes
- Color Ranges
- 2D Graphics
- 3D Graphics
- Geometry and Primitives
- Mathematics Used in Computer Graphics

Games are either in 2D, 3D, or a combination of both. 2D and 3D graphics have some areas in common and areas that are unique to each. The core knowledge that makes up both 2D and 3D graphics is mathematics and computer architecture. Everything in computer graphics is mathematical. This includes colors, virtual objects, and interactions with game objects, lighting, shadows, and so forth. One of the main requirements to being able to work in the computer graphics field is to have a solid understanding of different mathematics because without this knowledge, computer graphics are very difficult to master.

In this chapter we look at and discuss the fundamental topics that make up 2D and 3D graphics. The information covered in this chapter will be expanded upon and built on in later chapters. The first section examines how computers represent information, which is important to being able to work with computer graphics and understanding what is going on inside the machine.

BITS AND BYTES

The smallest unit of memory that users work with in a computer is the bit, and the next smallest unit of memory is a byte. Eight bits make a byte, four bytes make an integer, and so forth. Bits and bytes are very important in computer graphics, where the higher the number of bits, the higher the precision we can represent. What this means is that the more bits there are in a variable, the higher the range of values that can be represented. Table 2.1 lists a few common C++ data type names and the total number of bits that make them up.

Table 2.1 Common 32-bit Data Types

Name	Size
Byte (char)	8 bits (1 byte)
Integers	32 bits (4 bytes)
Short	16 bits (2 bytes)
Floating-point values	32 bits (4 bytes)

In this section we examine memory bits and bytes a little more closely to gain a deeper understanding of them. This deeper level of understanding can be used in learning about various rendering topics that we will be discussing throughout this book. We also discuss general game mathematics that can be found in computer graphics and geometry and primitives in 2D and 3D.

Memory Bits

In computers, a bit is a value that is either a 0 or a 1 and is also known as a binary digit. The 1 or 0 value of a bit can be thought of as being either true or false, or it can be thought of as being on or being off. The bit is the smallest memory unit that is used for storing data.

The more bits that are used, the more data can be stored. A single bit is one of two values. Add another bit and, with the use of some binary mathematics, higher values can be stored. For example, in our base-10 number system we have a ones position, a tens position, a hundreds position, a thousands position, and so forth. The number in each of these positions tells us something about the value it represents. If we see a 7 in the ones position, that is a value of 7. If the ones position has a value of 5 and the tens position has a value of 7, the number is 75. It is natural for us to deduce this because this is the numbering system we've used throughout our lives.

Base-10 mathematics is trivial. Binary mathematics follows the same rules with the exception that instead of using base-10 we are using base-2. That means each position can be one of two values instead of one of 10 values as seen with base-10. In the first position in base-2 a value is either 0 or 1. The second position represents how many objects are in the "twos" position, the third position represents how many "fours" objects there are, and so forth. A visual example of 8 bits (i.e., eight total base-2 positions) is shown in Figure 2.1.

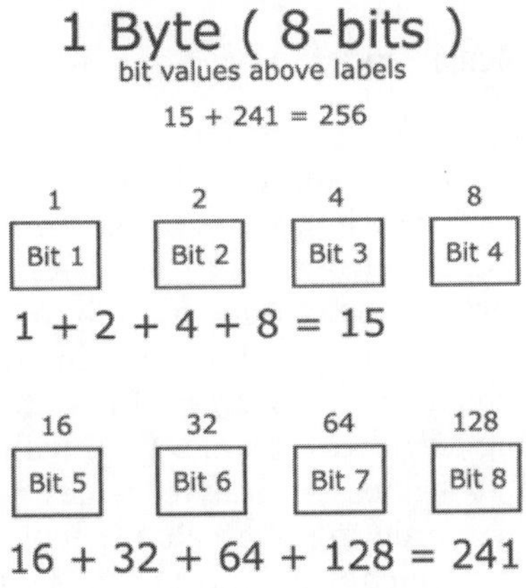

1 Byte (8-bits)
bit values above labels

15 + 241 = 256

1	2	4	8
Bit 1	Bit 2	Bit 3	Bit 4

1 + 2 + 4 + 8 = 15

16	32	64	128
Bit 5	Bit 6	Bit 7	Bit 8

16 + 32 + 64 + 128 = 241

FIGURE 2.1   A visual of 8 bits.

Looking at Figure 2.1, we can see that 1 bit can store up to two values (0 through 1), 2 bits can store up to four values, 3 bits can store up to eight values, 4 bits can store up to 16 values, 5 bits can store up to 32 values, 6 bits can store up to 64 values, 7 bits can store up to 128 values, and

8 bits can store up to 256 values, or 0 through 255 in some programming languages. A char data type in the computer programming languages C and C++ is made up of 8 bits. This means a char can store values between 0 and 255. Keep this in mind because we will revisit it when we talk about colors, which are often represented as three chars with one for the red, one for the green, and one for the blue component in a 24-bit (i.e., 3-byte) color.

 If one needs to store a certain range of values, the necessary number of bits must be available. Going past a range a set of bits can store leads to overflowing.

Memory storage is typically labeled based on the total number of bits. For example, a byte is 8 bits. A kilobit is 1,000 bits, a megabit is 1 million bits, a gigabit is 1 billion bits, a terabit is 1 trillion bits, a petabit is 1 quadrillion bits, and so forth. In the computer market we usually discuss memory in terms of bytes, with a kilobyte being 1,000 bytes (8,000 bits), a megabyte being 1 million bytes, and so forth.

 Actually, a megabyte is 1,024 kilobytes, and so on, but values are commonly rounded down to the nearest 100 or 1,000 in some discussions. Because we are dealing with base-2, each position is raised to the second power, so the number 2^{10} is equal to 1,024, which is often rounded down to 1,000.

Memory Bytes

Bytes are the second-smallest memory unit we commonly use in computer programming. The ASCII characters we use can be represented in a byte, also known as a char in programming languages such as C, C++, and C#. String objects are made up of an array of bytes, with one byte for each character (which can be a letter, symbol, number, etc.) in the string.

Multibyte values are common in computer programming, most of which can be seen in Table 2.1. Multibyte values allow us to store a higher range of values than with a single byte, which only has a range of 256 values. Multibyte values have byte-ordering, or "endianess." The byte-ordering of a value specifies which byte is the least significant byte and which is the most significant byte. If the first byte is the least significant byte, then the last byte is the most significant byte and vice versa. The most significant byte is stored at the memory location with the lowest or highest address in the range of addresses that make up the variable. Little-endian order, which is a type of byte-ordering, has its most significant byte at the lowest address, while big-endian order has its most significant byte opposite that of the little endian order. A visual of this is shown in Figure 2.2.

value = 0xAABB

Little Endian   Big Endian
43707   *48042*

FIGURE 2.2   A visual of byte-ordering.

 Little- and big-endian order are the most common byte orders. There is also middle-endian order.

In computer hardware the byte-ordering is very important when storing and transmitting data between two or more machines that operate using different byte-ordering. For example, Intel Pentium processors use little-endian order, and PowerPC processors (common in Mac computers) use big-endian order. To have hardware systems that use different byte-ordering be able to communicate with one another, the data must have their bytes swapped so that the destination machine is able to interpret correctly any data it receives. This solution is simple and can be done by casting a variable to a character pointer and perform the swapping in a loop, but programmers who are unaware of byte-ordering can encounter what appear to be mysterious critical errors when trying to share and transmit data between different platforms. No action needs to be taken regarding endianess when working with machines that use the same byte-ordering, but be aware of it otherwise.

Hexadecimal Values

Another common type of value is called hexadecimal value. These values operate in base-16, whereas binary values operate in base-2 and our decimal system numbers operate in base-10. In hexadecimal values each position is a value between 0 and F. This means one hexadecimal position can be either 0, 1, 2, 3, 4, 5, 6, 7, 8, 9, A, B, C, D, E, or F. The hexadecimal value "BA," for example, has the base-10 value of 186. The math to determine this is as follows:

$$BA = 186$$
$$BA = (B = 11) * (16 = \text{value of this position}) + (A = 10) * (1 = \text{value of this position})$$
$$BA = (11 * 16) + (10 * 1)$$
$$BA = (176) + 10$$
$$BA = 186$$

Hexadecimal values can come in a triplet known as the hex triplet. This is commonly used in different technologies such as HTML and cascading style sheets as a means to specify color values. In a three-component 24-bit color specified in HTML there are two values for each component. For example, pure white is #FFFFFF, where # is a symbol used to mark the start of a hexadecimal value; the first FF is the red component (with a value of 255 or 240 [15 * 16] for the first F plus 15 for the second F), the second FF is the green component, and the third FF is the blue component. As another example, the color #68A3F8 can be translated as

Color = #68A3F8
Red = 68 = (6 * 16) + (8 * 1) which = 96 + 8 or 104
Green = A3 = (10 * 16) + (3 * 1) which = 160 + 3 or 163
Blue = F8 = (15 * 16) + (8 * 1) which = 240 + 8 or 248
Final Color = Red(104), Green(163), Blue(248)

Many tools allow colors to be chosen and displayed in hexadecimal form. Adobe Photoshop is one of these tools that allow a color to be specified by choosing it from a color picker, specifying the value of each component's byte, or by specifying a hexadecimal triplet. A visual of this in Photoshop is shown in Figure 2.3.

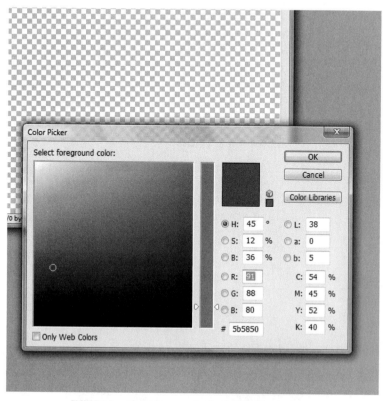

FIGURE 2.3   Choosing a color in Adobe Photoshop.

COLOR RANGES

The human eye can see a lot of detail in a wide range of luminous values. When people look at something artificial like computer graphics it is at times very easy for the human eye to pick out things that are not true to nature. The closer we can get to creating scenes that are believable to the human eye, the more realistic our scenes will look to us and those around us.

In computer graphics, the representation of color values and how they are translated to the computer monitor (or TV screen) is very important to being able to create the types of imagery you are looking to create, especially if realism is the goal. As color information moves throughout the rendering pipeline, it is operated on to build the final color. The information that makes up this data can become lost due to inadequate precision in the color's memory. Colors in computer graphics are generally in a low dynamic range of values or a high dynamic range.

Low-Dynamic-Range Colors

Low-dynamic-range, or LDR rendering, is what is commonly referred to as rendering in the traditional manner or, in other words, basically not using a high dynamic range of values during the rendering pipeline. Commonly, although not necessarily, we use a maximum of 8 bits per component for the color values in a rendered scene. The range of colors that can be displayed is very limited—hence the "low" in LDR. When rendering in LDR, the detail, precision, and quality of the colors of the rendered scene can be lost throughout the rendering pipeline. When this happens, the final results often have various artifacts visible to the screen. Also, saturated colors can dominate the rendered scene if colors that are brighter than the display attempt to be drawn.

Using a maximum of 8 bits per component is not necessarily a bad thing. Throughout most of this book we'll use the traditional range of values to create rendering results that are more than acceptable, but for some techniques a higher range and precision of values are more beneficial, such as when performing a bloom filter, than using 8 bits. Also, for lighting, a higher range of values is very beneficial to not only decrease rendering artifacts but also to retain as much quality throughout the pipeline as possible. This can be seen in many of today's modern games and is becoming quite common in the industry.

High-Dynamic-Range Colors

When working with 8-bit color components, or less, there is a low limited range of values that can be used for a color that can have a negative impact on the final rendered scene. As we already know, 8 bits can store

256 values. For lighting, colors, and what the human eye can see this is not a lot of detail, even for a color that is made up of four 8-bit components (32-bit RGBA). Also, the limited, and in this case fixed, range of values does not allow for high dynamic contrast. If colors are too bright, they are saturated, and eventually the detail can't be seen. In reality the human eye can see detail in a very large range of luminance colors, and we can adapt to different levels of brightness.

Modern video games, and other graphical products, make use of high-dynamic-range rendering, also known as HDR rendering. The idea behind HDR rendering is to use more bits per color component so that not only a higher precision of values can be stored, but also a higher range. Using HDR for rendering allows us to retain quality and to decrease rendering artifacts such as banding (see Figure 2.4). Once rendered, this HDR data has various algorithms applied to it to map those high ranges of values to a range that can be rendered to modern TV screens and monitors. This adjustment, which happens after adding various special effects such as blooms, streaks, and so on (covered in Chapter 11, "Special Effects: High Dynamic Range"), is known as exposure adjustment and is something the human eye does naturally when moving from a dark environment to a light one and vice versa (e.g., getting up in the middle of the night and turning on the light after spending hours in the dark).

 Exposure adjustment is also known as tone mapping.

FIGURE 2.4   Banding artifacts.

The purpose of HDR rendering is to preserve lighting and color detail throughout the rendering pipeline and to display that information to the screen. Before displaying the results to the screen, a process commonly referred to as tone mapping is performed to transform that HDR information into a range that can be displayed on a monitor. This tone mapping process attempts to mimic the human eye's ability to adjust to the information it is viewing by adapting to the visual information. This can be seen in many games, such as Ubisoft's *Splinter Cell Double Agent* for the Xbox 360.

 Using a higher precision for colors can allow you to retain more data during renderings.

HDR rendering is discussed in great detail in Chapter 11. HDR is definitely important to research when learning and trying to implement computer graphics because the final results of a rendered scene can be affected by the quality and detail of the image that is generated. In games, graphics are very important, and this quality, as well as the ability to add various and natural special effects, can help improve the look of the overall rendered scene. HDR has become standard in modern 3D video games.

Additional Color Information

We discuss colors and the rendering of colors in more detail in Chapter 3, "Ray Tracing," and in Chapter 4, "Rasterization." We discuss colors in more detail in Chapter 6, "Mapping Surfaces," and in Chapter 7, "Additional Surface Mapping," when we move the discussion to texture images. Lighting and shadows, which are huge topics in video games, are discussed in Chapter 8, "Lighting and Materials," Chapter 9, "Advanced Lighting and Shadows," and Chapter 10, "Global Illumination Techniques," in detail, including information related to both direct lighting and indirect (global) illumination.

2D Graphics

2D graphics have been around since the very beginning of gaming. The way 2D images are generated and displayed to the screen has evolved quite a bit since the first video games and remains a very popular way to make and play games.

Before the Nintendo 64 and PlayStation era of home gaming consoles, most of the console video games were created in 2D. The Nintendo 64/PlayStation/Sega Saturn generation (among other consoles that were not as successful) helped to further popularize 3D video games, which were already used on the PC and in some arcade machines, and over time 2D games on the home consoles slowly started to become rare and took second place to 3D video games.

Although 3D games are still the dominant force in the games industry, today more 2D video games are being produced for the PC and home consoles. Microsoft's XNA has provided new opportunities for individuals to get into making games. Because of this new opportunity, many independent 2D XNA games are appearing on the Internet. Also, a surge of new casual gamers have lately been buying and playing simple and fun games, many of which are 2D based.

 XNA can be used for 3D games as well. XNA allows development on a major home console, whereas in the past such support did not exist to the extent that it does now. Sony allowed hobby game development on each of the PlayStation consoles. This came at a price and with very limited access, tools, documentation, and support.

Sprites

2D games use what are known as sprites for the virtual objects and elements that can be found in a video game. A sprite is a 2D rectangular image that is drawn to the screen. In 3D games, sprites are normally used for things such as particle effects, where the 2D representation of such small entities is reasonable for the simulation. In 2D games, sprites are used for everything that is visible.

There are generally two types of sprites: static and dynamic. A static sprite is a single sprite image that consists of a nonanimating character, object, or element. An example of a static sprite is shown in Figure 2.5.

FIGURE 2.5 A static sprite.

A dynamic sprite is made up of a collection of images that, when viewed one after the other, form an animation. This animation is similar to a flip-book in the sense that each frame, which is a single image of the animation, is a different snap-shot of the animation being performed. An example of a dynamic sprite is shown in Figure 2.6.

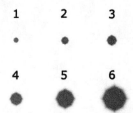

FIGURE 2.6   A dynamic sprite.

Tiled Images and Backgrounds

In 2D game graphics, sprites are used together to create the environments and backgrounds. Often, one or more sprite images act as the environment's background (e.g., sky, clouds, underwater, etc.). This background often scrolls with the player to give the effect of the player moving through the environment.

In addition to the background environment, there is often also a foreground environment. Often, this foreground environment is made up of tiles. A tile is an image, in this case a sprite image, that is composed of a repeatable pattern. By placing a tile-able image next to other tile-able images of the same set, an artist can create complex environments out of a small and simple image-set.

3D GRAPHICS

3D graphics are at the front of game development in modern times. 3D games can be found everywhere from PCs, home consoles, handheld consoles, and even mobile devices, such as cell phones. One of the main focuses of 3D game development is computer graphics. Often, the goal is to achieve realistic real-time graphics in games, as is *Alan Wake* (see Figure 2.7), but graphics can also be nonrealistic, as in Nintendo's *The Legend of Zelda: The Wind Waker*.

FIGURE 2.7 Realistic graphics from *Alan Wake*.

3D games started to play a major role in console game development in the mid 1990s, whereas on the PC they took hold slightly earlier. With the advancements of computers and the adoption of graphics hardware by consumers and console makers, game developers where able to push the envelope of what was considered next-generation farther than what was seen in the early days of video games.

The Z Buffer

In modern 3D games, one of the important pieces of information used during the rendering process is depth information. Depth information, which is stored in the Z buffer, is a value that informs the rendering API about the calculated depth of each pixel of the screen. This information is used mainly to determine what objects are in front of others. An example is shown in Figure 2.8, and this is a process that is commonly known as depth testing.

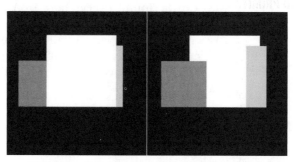

FIGURE 2.8 Depth testing off (left) and on (right).

In 2D games, the sprites are simple enough that they can be given a draw order, and the objects are drawn in the order specified. Since the objects are flat, one value can be used for each sprite. In 3D games this is not as simple, as surfaces are not 2D and can have varying positions and orientations. Neighboring pixels can have different depths across even a single surface. When it comes to lighting and other common rendering techniques that are done in 3D, it is not possible to use one value for an entire surface as you can with 2D. This assumes that the surface isn't perfectly flat and facing the camera.

 Although the Z buffer can do a good job ensuring that objects are drawn correctly, other algorithms and techniques can be used to speed up the process of avoiding calculations on information that is not visible. We cover this more later in the book.

Shading Surfaces

One of the main advantages 3D games have over 2D games is the ability to dynamically calculate surface information in the scene. By being able to shade the surfaces that compose the scene of a video game, developers are able to perform many calculations that can affect the final result dynamically. One of the best examples of this is real-time lighting. By using the information in the scene we are able to take a surface in 3D and shade each point that makes up the geometry, or even each fragment that makes up the surface, and give it a realistic appearance and interactions.

The shading of surfaces is the entire point of 3D computer graphics. Many algorithms and techniques can be used, which we'll be discussing throughout this book. The goal of this book is to learn how to do advance techniques in complex scenes that can be used in modern video games. We discuss 2D and 3D graphics and the steps used to render to a screen throughout this book in more detail.

GEOMETRY AND PRIMITIVES

The heart of 3D lies in using various geometric entities to represent the objects and environments of a virtual scene. In 3D video games this information is usually processed by a dedicated piece of hardware: the graphics card. This information moves through the rendering pipeline, which can be thought of as a series of algorithmic steps that operate on the data that make up the scene to be rendered. Once processed, the final image is displayed to the monitor and the next rendering pass can start. In this section we talk generally about some of the geometric primitives that are seen throughout this book before moving onto the topic of general game and graphics mathematics.

Lines

A line is a simple primitive that has a starting location and an ending location that are connected as shown in Figure 2.9. With two points, a line segment can be represented in 2D or 3D space and can take on the following form using two dimensions, for example:

```
struct Point
{
   int x;
   int y;
}

struct Line
{
   Point start;
   Point end;
}
```

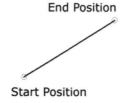

End Position

Start Position

FIGURE 2.9   A line segment.

Lines can be used to form mathematical rays where the starting point of a line is the ray's origin and the ending point of the line can be used to determine the ray's direction. Rays are discussed in more detail later on in this chapter and are used heavily in computer graphics and in game programming.

 Lines are not used as often as polygons for rendering in video games. It is rare to come across a situation where a line is needed for rendering in a modern video game.

Polygons

Polygons form many, if not all, of the geometric shapes seen in today's 3D games. A polygon is a geometric shape that is made up of three or more points, where the lines that connect the outer area of the shape are called edges. The area that makes up the surface within this shape is often filled in using various algorithms (e.g., lighting, texturing mapping, etc.) by the hardware that is assigned the rendering task. The more points that are used, the more complex a shape can look. An example of a polygon is shown in Figure 2.10 and can be represented in pseudo-code as follows:

```
struct Polygon
{
    int total_points;
    array<Point> points;
}
```

FIGURE 2.10   A simple polygon (left) and a complex polygon (right).

The edges of a polygon are the lines that connect one point of the polygon to another point. With a line there are no real edges since the primitive does not enclose an area. Polygons, on the other hand, do enclose an area, and the edges that surround it can be easily identified.

Triangles

Triangles are the most common type of primitive used in 3D video games. Triangles are three-point polygons whose three edges are used to connect each of the points that make up the shape of the primitive. This is shown in Figure 2.11 with a single triangle object.

FIGURE 2.11   A triangle polygon.

Graphics hardware is very efficient at processing triangle primitives. Because of this, triangles are the focus of this book. Although the specific algorithms that are discussed are not specific to triangles, the applications that demonstrate them use triangles for the geometry.

Games often use three types of triangles. Triangle lists are individual triangles specified in an array that is sometimes referred to as a buffer (Figure 2.12). In a triangle list each triangle is individually specified. Points of a triangle can be shared by using indices to reduce the amount of data that must be passed to the graphics hardware. An index, which is the singular form of indices, is an array index into a list of points. An example of using indices is shown in Figure 2.13, where four points are used to specify two distinct triangles.

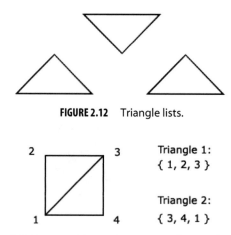

FIGURE 2.12   Triangle lists.

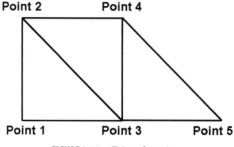

Triangle 1:
{ 1, 2, 3 }

Triangle 2:
{ 3, 4, 1 }

FIGURE 2.13   Using indices to specify triangles.

There are also triangle strips, which are defined by specifying the first three points of the first triangle and then one point for each additional triangle that branches off the first. Using a triangle strip is a way to reduce the amount of data that must be passed to the graphics hardware. By using six points we can form four separate triangles, as shown in Figure 2.14. Triangle strips are commonly used for terrain geometry, where a terrain is normally a rectangular grid with varying Y-axis (height) values for each of its polygons. An example of a terrain is shown in Figure 2.15.

Point 2   Point 4

Point 1   Point 3   Point 5

FIGURE 2.14   Triangle strips.

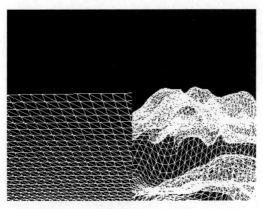

FIGURE 2.15   Flat terrain (left) and the same terrain with varying height values (right).

The last type of triangle is triangle fans, which are triangles that all connect to the same common point on the mesh (Figure 2.16). By specifying a common point that all triangles connect to, you can create various shapes that would require more information to create with triangle lists.

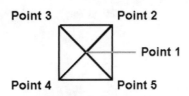

FIGURE 2.16   Triangle fans.

Convex and Concave Polygons

Polygons and shapes in computer graphics can be either convex or concave. A convex polygon, or shape, has a convex set for its surface, which means that if a line segment is created between any two points that make up the object, it cannot penetrate any edge of said object. If a line segment does penetrate one of the object's edges, it is considered concave.

A strict convex polygon or shape is one that has at most a 180-degree angle between each edge that makes up the object.

Using convex geometry is a better choice for things such as collision detection because convex shapes and polygons are more efficient to calculate and work with mathematically on a processor. Although physics and collision detection are not the focus of this text, some principles that are used for the calculation of light maps and shadows are discussed later throughout this book.

Triangles, because of the number of points that make them up, are always convex. This is because no line connecting any of a triangle's points can possibly cross an edge of the triangle.

Spheres and Boxes

Spheres and boxes are commonly used in video games, not just for rendering but also for physics and collision calculations. A sphere is a mathematical object with a position and a radius, which specifies the circular region that surrounds the position (see Figure 2.17). Spheres can take on the following form in pseudo-code:

```
struct Sphere
{
    int radius;
    Point position;
}
```

FIGURE 2.17 A sphere.

Spheres and boxes are used to surround complex objects in virtual scenes. If a complex object such as a character model is surrounded with a sphere or box primitive, which are much simpler shapes, they can be used in the collision and physics tests as a fast way to determine what action needs to be taken. For example, the test between two spheres colliding in a virtual scene is much faster than testing two triangles, let alone two sets of thousands of triangles, which are common in today's character models. By testing two simple spheres you can quickly determine if a collision is even possible between two complex character models. This is shown in Figure 2.18.

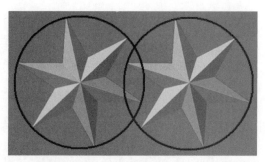

FIGURE 2.18   Testing two simple spheres enables you to determine if a collision is possible between two complex character models.

 Simplified shapes such as sphere or box objects can be used to test if they potentially collide with one another. The term potentially is used because most simplified objects have some wasted space, which means some collision checks might return true when there is no collision.

When it comes to collision detection against spheres, spheres are much faster than other basic primitives such as triangles, boxes, and so forth. This speed comes at a cost of accuracy because the region that surrounds most objects tends to have a lot of wasted space, as shown in Figure 2.19.

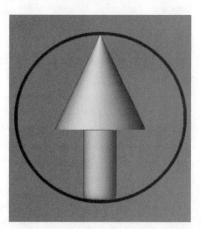

FIGURE 2.19   A bounding sphere with a lot of empty space.

Without simplifying these tests and by using models with hundreds or thousands of polygons the CPU power required to calculate the average game physics using triangle-to-triangle tests would be so vast that games like *Halo 3*, *Assassins Creed*, *Metal Gear Solid 4*, and even *Super Mario 64* (during its time) would be impossible. The triangle-to-triangle collision test is so expensive that game developers avoid them altogether and instead perform collisions on groups of very simple shapes. An example of this is shown in Figure 2.20, where a hierarchy of simple shapes can be used to represent a more complex model with acceptable accuracy. In video games, performance and accuracy/realism are often balanced based on the target hardware's abilities.

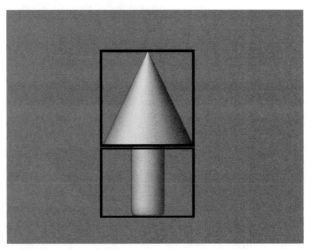

FIGURE 2.20   Bounding hierarchies around complex objects.

The use of simplified geometry for collisions falls under the topic of scene management, which is discussed in more detail in Chapter 15 "Optimization." Modern video games must have various scene management techniques like this to be able to render the vast amount of data at an acceptable rate, and in some games to be able to render at all.

Boxes and cubes are used a lot in video games. They offer a more accurate bounding volume than a sphere, but, although fast, they are not as fast to process as spheres (see Figure 2.21). They are also used in many game editors for building game worlds. You can combine a box and other primitives to create entire game worlds using simple shapes. In *Half-Life 2*, Valve used their *Hammer* editor, which comes with the game to create the game levels. By building a game world essentially out of boxes and other primitives, the creators of the game were able to create every level you see in the game. Terrain, on the other hand, is often modeled differently than the rest of the geometry, but for interiors, buildings, and so forth using boxes can be very powerful.

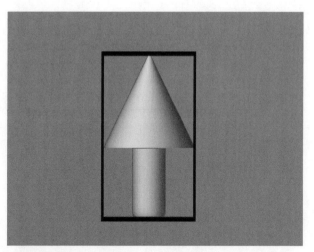

FIGURE 2.21   A bounding box with less empty space.

The difference between a box and a cube is that a box can have different values for its width, height, and depth (length), whereas a cube has the same value for all three of its properties, thus creating a shape that is even on all sides. A box and a cube in general could take on the following form, where position is the center of the object:

```
struct Box
{
    int width, height, depth;
    Point position;
}

struct Cube
{
    int size;
    Point position;
}
```

Groups of convex polygons in most game editors are called brushes. The term brush *is often used as the name of these groups of polygons, which form a convex shape.*

Additional Geometric Objects

A vast number of additional geometric objects exist mathematically. Some of these objects can be found in video games, but if they are, they are often created using triangles rather than some mathematical equation. In ray tracing, representing some objects using mathematical formulas is quite common, which is covered in Chapter 3. Some of these additional objects include but are not limited to the following:

* Cones
* Pyramids
* Cylinders
* Toruses
* Torus knots
* Disks
* Ellipsoids
* Bezier curves
* Bezier patches
* Nurbs

Loading Geometry

In video games, geometry is usually loaded into an application during runtime from an external file. Games use many types of files. These files can include but are not limited to the following:

* Static models
* Animation files
* Terrains
* Environment files
* Collision meshes

ON THE CD

Throughout this book many of the samples on the CD-ROM load geometry from a very simple file format called the Wavefront OBJ file. This format is optional and is only used to store and load complex models that would not be efficient or practical to hand-code in the source files. An extensive overview and C++ loader for the file format can be found in Appendix D, "The OBJ File Format." The Wavefront OBJ file format is used by many modeling applications such as Milkshape3D, 3D Studio Max, and ZBrush. If you are not familiar with the OBJ file format and have no experience with it, it is recommended that you read through Appendix D so that you are able to load this generally simple file format into your own applications to test your code with complex models. If you prefer to use another geometry file format, then by all means use that.

Mathematics Used in Computer Graphics

Games, especially game graphics, are made up of a lot of mathematics. The mathematics used in game graphics, physics, and so forth can become quite complex and advanced. Having a firm understanding of the different types of mathematics that are used in game development can allow you to have an easier time understanding and implementing the information.

In this section we review briefly the different types of mathematics that are common in game development. One could write an entire book on game math, so this section will serve as a quick review of the topics you should be familiar with coming into this book. Appendix C, "Recommended Resources," lists recommended math-related resources that can help you if you have no experience with the common areas of game math.

Vectors, Vertices, and Points

Vectors are the fundamental mathematical objects that are used in every 3D game and game engine. Vectors define a direction in virtual space, but they can also be used to define points called vertices (plural of vertex), orientations, or even surface normals, which are the directions surfaces face. For example, a triangle is made up of three of these points. In game-related books the terms *vertex* and *vector* are often used synonymously to refer to a virtual point.

Technically, vectors and vertices are different, but they are used the same way most of the time in games. Vectors are spatial directions, and vertices are points of a primitive.

Vectors come in many types, with the most common ones being 2D, 3D, and 4D. A vector is made up of n number of dimensions that describe the total number of axes it uses. For example, a 2D vector only has an X and Y axis, a 3D vector has an X, Y, and Z axis, and a 4D vector has the same axes as a 3D vector in addition to a W axis. A vector can generally be written as shown in Equation 2.1.

$$V = (V^1, V^2, ..., V^n) \quad (2.1)$$

In a language such as C or C++ a 3D vector can have the following structures:

```
struct Vector3D
{
    float x, y, z;
};
```

```
struct Vector3D
{
   float pos[3];
}
```

Vectors can be operated on by scalars, which are floating-point values. For example, you can add, subtract, multiply, and divide a vector with another vector or a scalar. Equation 2.2 shows an example of adding vectors. Adding a vector to a scalar, A, can be written as shown in Equation 2.3.

$$V.x = V1.x + V2.x \quad (2.2)$$
$$V.y = V1.y + V2.y$$
$$V.z = V1.z + V2.z$$
$$V.x = V1.x + A \quad (2.3)$$
$$V.y = V1.y + A$$
$$V.z = V1.z + A$$

Equation 2.2 and 2.3 show that vectors are operated on by their components. The same goes for subtraction, multiplication, and division of vectors with other vectors or scalars.

The length of a vector, also known as the vector's magnitude, is very common in computer graphics. A vector with a magnitude of 1 is called a unit-length vector or just unit vector, and it refers to a vector that is perpendicular to a point on a surface. The magnitude can be calculated as shown in Equation 2.4.

$$\text{Magnitude} = \text{Square\_Root}(\ V.x^2 + V.y^2 + V.z^2\ ) \quad (2.4)$$

To create a unit vector from a non–unit vector, all that needs to occur is dividing the vector's magnitude by the vector itself. This is shown in Equation 2.5, where the square root of the square of each added component is divided by the vector.

$$V = V\ /\ \text{Square\_Root}(\ V.x^2 + V.y^2 + V.z^2\ ) \quad (2.5)$$

 A normal refers to a unit-length vector.

Turning a vector into a unit vector is known as normalization and is a highly common operation in computer graphics. Other very common operations are the dot product and cross product vector operations. The dot product of two vectors, also known as the scalar product, calculates the difference between the directions the two vectors are pointing. The dot product is used to calculate the cosine angle between vectors without using the cosine mathematical formula, which can be more CPU expensive, and the result is not another vector, but a scalar value. This calculation is used to perform lighting in Chapter 8. To calculate the dot product, multiply each component of the two vectors then add them together. This is shown in Equation 2.6.

$$d = (V1.x * V2.x + V1.y * V2.y + V1.z * V2.z) \quad (2.6)$$

 The equations used in this chapter follow the order of operations when calculating values. For example, multiplication occurs before addition and subtraction.

Being able to find the angle of difference between two vectors is useful in lighting, which we look at later. If the dot product between two vectors is 0, the two vectors are perpendicular to one another and are orthogonal. Another thing to note is that the sign of the dot product tells us what side one vector is to another. If the sign is negative, the second vector is behind the first; if it is positive, then it is in front. If it is 0, they are perpendicular.

The cross product of two vectors, also known as the vector product, is used to find a new vector that is perpendicular to two tangent vectors. This is commonly used to find the direction a polygon is facing by normalizing the cross product of the edge vectors of a triangle. The cross product is calculated by multiplying the cross components together and then adding them all together component by component. This is shown in Figure 2.22.

$$\begin{bmatrix} 2 \\ 4 \\ 7 \end{bmatrix} \times \begin{bmatrix} 5 \\ 1 \\ 4 \end{bmatrix} \quad \begin{matrix} 2 \\ 16 \\ 35 \end{matrix}$$

$$[x] = 2x1$$
$$[y] = 4x4$$
$$[z] = 7x5$$

FIGURE 2.22   A visual of calculating the cross product.

To find a triangle's normal, for example, we first find two edge vectors. This is done by calculating a vector between the first and second point of a triangle and normalizing the result (edge 1) and by doing the same things with the first and third points of the same triangle. The next step is to find the cross product of these two vectors and normalize the results to find the surface's normal. The direction of the normal depends on the order in which the vertices were defined. If the vertices are clockwise, the direction will point in the opposite direction that it would point if they were counterclockwise, even though it is the same information. Equation 2.7 shows how to find a polygon's normal.

$$e1 = normalize(\ V1\ -\ V2\ )\quad(2.7)$$
$$e2 = normalize(\ V1\ -\ V3\ )$$
$$normal = normalize(\ cross\_product(\ e1, e2\ )\ )$$

 To find a normal of a polygon you only need three points, which form a perpendicular triangle to the surface. Even if the polygon has more than three points, you only need three to find the normal. This assumes that all points fall perpendicular to the polygon's plane.

Transformations

When data are submitted data in a 3D game, the information is passed to the graphics hardware as 3D data. This data must be processed in a way so that it can be displayed onto a 2D view, which is the screen. During the rendering process of the rendering pipeline, various coordinate spaces are used together to perform this task.

3D computer graphics incorporate the idea of many different coordinate spaces. A coordinate space represents an object's relationship to the rest of the scene. For example, the vertices of a 3D model are often stored in object-space, which is a space local to the model itself. To render out an object that is in object-space, it must be transformed to the world-space position at which you want to render it. World-space is the virtual position and orientation (rotation) of 3D models in the scene.

It is efficient to specify geometry in one space and then convert it whenever necessary during the rendering process. Say you have two boxes that you want to draw in a 3D scene. If these boxes are 100% identical, it would not be efficient to have two (or more) boxes loaded into memory with different vertex positions if you can just load one box and position it throughout the scene as many times as necessary.

As another example, imagine that you have a complex scene that you've created, and you want to change the positions of objects throughout the scene. Being able to position these object-space models is more efficient than trying to alter the individual points of every model that was specified in world-space.

When rendering objects in a 3D scene, we use positions and orientations to represent how an object is located. This information is used to create a mathematical matrix that can be used to transform the vertex data of rendered geometry from one space to another. The positions and orientation, which we'll call orientation for short, are specified in world-space, which is also known as model-space.

Once an object in object-space is transformed to world-space, it is transformed to screen-space, which corresponds to the X and Y axes that are aligned to the screen. Since the 3D information has depth and distance with objects that are farther from the camera, a projection is applied to the geometry to add perspective to the data. The projection matrices that are used on geometry are called homogeneous clip space matrices, which clip the geometry to the boundaries of the screen to which they are being rendered. Two types of projection are generally used in video games: orthogonal projection and perspective projection.

 By altering the projection matrix you can alter the field-of-view and other properties of the view to create different visual effects, such as a fish-eye lens, for example.

 You can also apply a view to the world matrix to account for a virtual camera's position and orientation. This is known as the world-view (or model-view) matrix.

Orthogonal projection maps a 3D object to a 2D view, but objects remain the same size regardless of their distance from the camera. In perspective projection perspective is added to the rendered scene, which makes objects smaller as they move farther from the camera. A comparison of orthogonal and perspective projection is shown in Figure 2.23, where both scenes use the exact same information but different projections. Perspective projection uses a horizon, which represents the vanishing point of the view. Artists reading this book will most likely know all about perspective and vanishing points, as it is an important topic when drawing and painting pictures.

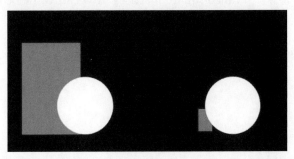

FIGURE 2.23   Orthogonal projection (left) versus perspective projection (right).

These coordinate spaces are represented by matrices, which we discuss in the next section. Matrices have the ability to be concatenated together into one matrix. For example, if the world-space matrix is combined with the eye-space matrix, it is the model-view matrix and can be used to transform geometric object-space models directly into eye-space. Combining the world, view (camera), and projection together gives you the model-view projection matrix, which is used to transform a vertex into screen space.

Other spaces such as texture space (tangent space) and light space, for example, are normally used when performing a number of special effects such as bump mapping, shadow mapping, and so on.

In the next section we discuss matrices in more detail. In 3D games, matrices have a lot of uses and are very important. Vectors and matrices are among the most important topics to understand in video games and game graphics.

Matrices

A matrix is a mathematical structure that is used in computer graphics to store information about a space. In computer graphics matrices are often used for storing orientations, translations, scaling, coordinate spaces, and more. In game development we usually work with 3×3 and 4×4 matrices. A matrix is essentially a table, for example,

```
float matrix3x3[3][3];
matrix3x3[0] = 1;   matrix3x3[1] = 0;   matrix3x3[2] = 0;
matrix3x3[3] = 0;   matrix3x3[4] = 1;   matrix3x3[5] = 0;
matrix3x3[6] = 0;   matrix3x3[7] = 0;   matrix3x3[8] = 1;
```

A matrix is a table that can be represented in code as a 2D array or as a set of vectors. Matrices with the same number of rows as columns are called square matrices. A vector can be considered a 1D array, whereas a matrix can be considered an array of vectors that together represent a space. For example, a 3×3 matrix can be created out of three 3D vectors, as follows:

```
struct Matrix
{
    Vector3D col1;
    Vector3D col2;
    Vector3D col3;
}

struct Matrix
{
    Vector3D mat[3];
}
```

When it comes to orientations in video games, a matrix is used to store rotational and positional information along with scaling. Mathematically, matrices can be added and subtracted by other matrices of the same size by performing each operation on their equivalent table elements. This can be seen as follows:

```
M[0] = M1[0] + M2[0], M[1] = M1[1] + M[2], …
```

Multiplying matrices is not as straightforward as adding or subtracting. To multiply each matrix, start by multiplying the first element in the first row in matrix A by the first element in the first column in matrix B. The result of this operation is stored in the first column's first element in a new matrix; let's call it N. This continues until every element has been processed in the matrices. Travel along the first matrix's rows and along the second matrix's columns. To be multiplied, matrices must have the same number of rows and columns, which is not referring to square matrices specifically. When it comes to multiplication, it is not commutative with matrices, and they preserve the determinant, which we discuss later in this section. Multiplying matrices works as follows:

```
new_mat[0] = m1[r1_c1] * m2[r1_c1] *
             m1[r2_c1] * m2[r1_c2] *
             m1[r3_c1] * m2[r1_c3];
new_mat[1] = m1[r1_c2] * m2[r1_c1] *
             m1[r2_c2] * m2[r1_c2] *
             m1[r3_c2] * m2[r1_c3];
new_mat[2] = m1[r1_c3] * m2[r1_c1] *
             m1[r2_c3] * m2[r1_c2] *
             m1[r3_c3] * m2[r1_c3];
new_mat[3] = 0;
new_mat[4] = m1[r1_c1] * m2[r2_c1] *
             m1[r2_c1] * m2[r2_c2] *
             m1[r3_c1] * m2[r2_c3];
new_mat[5] = m1[r1_c2] * m2[r2_c1] *
             m1[r2_c2] * m2[r2_c2] *
             m1[r3_c2] * m2[r2_c3];
new_mat[6] = m1[r1_c3] * m2[r2_c1] *
             m1[r2_c3] * m2[r2_c2] *
             m1[r3_c3] * m2[r2_c3];
new_mat[7] = 0;

new_mat[8] = m1[r1_c1] * m2[r3_c1] *
             m1[r2_c1] * m2[r3_c2] *
             m1[r3_c1] * m2[r3_c3];
```

```
new_mat[9]  = m1[r1_c2] * m2[r3_c1] *
              m1[r2_c2] * m2[r3_c2] *
              m1[r3_c2] * m2[r3_c3];
new_mat[10] = m1[r1_c3] * m2[r3_c1] *
              m1[r2_c3] * m2[r3_c2] *
              m1[r3_c3] * m2[r3_c3];
new_mat[11] = 0;

new_mat[12] = m1[r1_c1] * m2[r4_c1] *
              m1[r2_c1] * m2[r4_c2] *
              m1[r3_c1] * m2[r4_c3];
new_mat[13] = m1[r1_c2] * m2[r4_c1] *
              m1[r2_c2] * m2[r4_c2] *
              m1[r3_c2] * m2[r4_c3];
new_mat[14] = m1[r1_c3] * m2[r4_c1] *
              m1[r2_c3] * m2[r4_c2] *
              m1[r3_c3] * m2[r4_c3];
new_mat[15] = 1;
```

A matrix is considered an identity matrix if the elements starting from the first element going downward in a diagonal direction are set to 1. As we will discuss later, if we transform a vector against an identity matrix, then nothing will change since we will be literally multiplying the components of a vector by 1, which does not change the value. An example of an identity matrix is as follows:

```
matrix[0]  = 1;   matrix[1]  = 0;   matrix[2]  = 0;   matrix[3]  = 0;
matrix[4]  = 0;   matrix[5]  = 1;   matrix[6]  = 0;   matrix[7]  = 0;
matrix[8]  = 0;   matrix[9]  = 0;   matrix[10] = 1;   matrix[11] = 0;
matrix[12] = 0;   matrix[13] = 0;   matrix[14] = 0;   matrix[15] = 1;
```

 You can calculate the transpose of a matrix by swapping its rows and columns.

The determinant of a matrix is like the length of a vector. You can only find the determinant of a square matrix, which has the same number of rows and columns. Matrices that have a nonzero determinant can be inverted. For a matrix to be inverted, not only does it have to be a square matrix, but it cannot contain a row with all zeros.

A vector can be transformed by a matrix by multiplying the vector against the matrix. This is used in the rendering pipeline to convert vectors from one space to another. When you multiply a vector by a matrix you are applying the matrix's information to the vector. This occurs as follows.

```
Vector3D out;
out.x = (v.x * matrix[0]) + (v.y * matrix[4]) +
        (v.z * matrix[8]) + matrix[12];
out.y = (v.x * matrix[1]) + (v.y * matrix[5]) +
        (v.z * matrix[9]) + matrix[13];
out.z = (v.x * matrix[2]) + (v.y * matrix[6]) +
        (v.z * matrix[10]) + matrix[14];
```

A matrix can be used to store a translation (position). In computer graphics, 3×3 matrices are used to store the scaling and rotational information, but if another row is added, for example, if we create a 3×4 or have a 4×4 matrix, the last row can literally store the X, Y, and Z positional information. To translate a matrix set the last row to the position you want. This is shown in the following pseudo-code (assuming M is an array that represents the matrix):

```
M[12] = X, M[13] = Y, M[14] = Z, M[15] = 1;
```

A vector can be scaled by a matrix. Take, for example, the 3×3 matrix in Equation 2.1. By multiplying a vector against the matrix, we would have effectively multiplied each component of the vector with the three values in the matrix that represent the X, Y, and Z axes. If each of these elements in the matrix is equal to 1, that is the same as multiplying a vector by 1, which does not change its value. However, a value other than 1 scales the vector, with values less than 1 making it smaller and values greater than 1 making it larger. If you are working with matrices in video games, these three elements of a matrix are used to store the scaling information. An example of a scaling matrix (the 3×3 part of a 4×4 matrix) is as follows:

```
mat[0]  = scale_val;   mat[1]  = 0;            mat[2]  = 0;
mat[4]  = 0;           mat[5]  = scale_val;    mat[6]  = 0;
mat[8]  = 0;           mat[9]  = 0;            mat[10] = scale_val;
```

You can also use matrices for rotations. To perform rotations in 3D you need at least a 3×3 matrix. Rotations can be performed around an axis or arbitrary axes. When you multiply a vector by a matrix that stores rotation values, it rotates the vector based on that information. This can be seen as follows, where you can rotate along the X, Y, and Z axes by creating a rotation matrix:

```
void Rotate(float *matrix, double angle, float x, float y, float z)
{
    float sine = (float)sin(angle);
    float cosine = (float)cos(angle);
    float sinAngle = (float)sin(3.14 * angle / 180);
    float cosAngle = (float)cos(3.14 * angle / 180);
    float oneSubCos = 1.0f - cosAngle;
    matrix[0] = (x * x) * oneSubCos + cosAngle;
    matrix[4] = (x * y) * oneSubCos - (z * sinAngle);
    matrix[8] = (x * z) * oneSubCos + (y * sinAngle);
    matrix[1] = (y * x) * oneSubCos + (sinAngle * z);
    matrix[5] = (y * y) * oneSubCos + cosAngle;
    matrix[9] = (y * z) * oneSubCos - (x * sinAngle);

    matrix[2] = (z * x) * oneSubCos - (y * sinAngle);
    matrix[6] = (z * y) * oneSubCos + (x * sinAngle);
    matrix[10] = (z * z) * oneSubCos + cosAngle;
}
```

Note that $\cos2(a) + \sin2(a) = 1$, which means the vector is not scaled by the matrices that are strictly rotation matrices. If a scale is added, that information is added to the rotational information, which applies both operations on a vector. Rotations and translations are among the most common uses for matrices in computer graphics, along with representing coordinate spaces.

Rays

Rays are used a lot in computer graphics. A ray is a mathematical object that has an origin (starting position) and a direction. The direction specifies where the ray is going, and it is considered infinite. Scalar values can be used to limit the distance of a ray, but traditional rays are infinite. You can think of a ray as an infinite line.

Rays can be used for many different things. Ray casting, which is a technique used to test objects against a ray, can be used to test if one object can see another, collision detection, rendering, user interactions, and so forth. When testing if one object can see another, which is also known as line-of-sight, for example, the test can create a ray that originates from object A and points toward object B and test that ray against all nearby objects in a scene to see if the ray passes through any of them. If the ray passes through any object, not counting object B, then there would be no line-of-sight. This could be used in artificial intelligence to test if a wall or some other obstacle is between a player and an enemy. If there is a line-of-sight between the two characters, the AI character can attack the player or perform some other action.

Another use of rays is user selection of virtual objects. Selection, also known as picking, is very common in games such as real-time strategy games where the user must select virtual objects to manipulate them in some fashion. Editors such as level editors also use selection in this manner. Selection works by creating a ray that goes from the point on the screen that the user clicked straight into the scene.

To be able to perform selection you need access to the mouse location. With that information you project the 2D screen position into a 3D position. The direction of the ray can be the normalized camera's position minus the projected 3D position. Once you have the ray, you can test it against the objects in your scene and determine which object the ray passes through. If there is more than one object that the ray passes through, the one closest to the viewer is the one chosen. Projecting a 2D point into a 3D position is the opposite of transforming a 3D point to 2D and can be done using the following pseudo-code algorithm:

```
function Project2DTo3D(pos2D, viewDir, upDir, fov, height)
{
    // height is the window's height
    // fov is the field-of-view
    // upDir is a direction vector that points up
    rightPos = CrossProduct(upDir, viewDir);
    distance = height / tan(fov);
    return viewDir * distance -
           upDi2r * pos2D.y +
           rightPos * pos2D.x;

}
```

Rays can also be used for rendering a scene image. In ray tracing the idea is to create and cast multiple rays from all light sources into a scene going in different directions. If a ray hits an object in the scene and if that object is in the camera's view, then that point of intersection is recorded. That 3D point of intersection can be projected to screen space where the corresponding pixel takes on the color of the object that was intersected. Of course, in ray tracing you only record the information of the closet intersection. An example of a ray traced image is shown in Figure 2.24.

FIGURE 2.24 Ray tracing.

We discuss ray tracing in more detail in the following chapter. Using the brief explanation above, or an optimization from the next chapter, we can create a simple ray tracer. Add features such as lighting, textures, shadows, and so forth along with useful optimizations, and you can create your own ray tracing rendering engine. In the next chapter we talk about both CPU ray tracing and real-time ray tracing, which is starting to gain some momentum thanks in part to the advances in computer CPU and GPU technology.

Rays are simple to represent in code. A ray is made up of a point of origin (position) and a direction. An example pseudo-code of defining a ray structure follows:

```
struct Ray
{
    Vector3D origin;
    Vector3D direction;
};
```

Planes

A plane is an infinitely flat surface that expands indefinitely across two axes. Planes can be thought of as flat walls that have a height and width that do not end with an indefinitely flat depth. Planes have many uses in game development such as collision detection and culling (the process of determining what information can be omitted from the rendering process), which is done for objects that are not in the camera's sight. The equation used to represent a plane commonly looks like the following:

$$Ax + By + Cz + D = 0$$

where A, B, and C are the X, Y, and Z axes of the plane's normal, and D is equal to the dot product of $-N$ (the normal) and a point on the plane. Planes can be represented in a number of ways, for example, by using a point and a direction. The direction specifies the direction the plane is facing, and the point specifies some point that lies on the infinite plane. The point on the plane in this example can be used to determine how far the plane is from the origin based on their relationship.

Any point of the surface can be used. Since a plane is infinite, the number of points that happen to lie on that plane is also infinite. The pseudo-code representing a plane in this manner can appear as the following:

```
struct Plane
{
    Vector3D point;
    Vector3D direction;
    float d;
};
```

Planes are useful when you want to classify a point or test for plane intersection. Classifying for planes means that you determine which side of the plane the point is on. A point can be in front of the plane, behind the plane, or on the plane. An intersection against a plane is a test that determines if a primitive crosses a plane at any point. To determine which side of a plane a point is on you can use the plane equation $Ax + By + Cz + D = 0$. If the result is positive, the point is in front of the plane; if it is negative, is it behind the plane; if it is 0, it is on the plane. The pseudo-code to classify a point is as follows:

```
function ClassifyPoint(float x, float y, float z,
                       float a, float b, float c, float d)
{
    var distance = a * x + b * y + c * z + d;
    if(distance > 0.001)
        return FRONT_OF_PLANE;
```

```
    if(distance < -0.001)
        return BEHIND_PLANE;
    return ON_PLANE;
}
```

When classifying a point in the above pseudo-code, note that it does not test for 0 but tests for 0.001. Floating-point errors can occur, and testing a value that is close to 0 instead of 0 can help adjust for this.

Line and Triangle Intersection

Testing for intersections against a plane is different for each primitive. A line is made up of two points that represent the start position and the end position. To test if a line intersects a plane you can test if the classification of both points is different. For example, if the start point is on the front side of the plane and the end point is on the other side of the plane, it can be determined that the line intersects the plane. A visual example is shown in Figure 2.25.

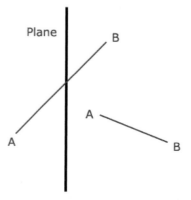

FIGURE 2.25   A line intersecting a plane (left) and a line not intersecting a plane (right).

We can take this a step further and test a triangle for intersection. One method is to take the three points of a triangle and create three different lines out of it. The first and second point makes the first line, the second and third point makes the second line, and the first and third point makes the third line. You can loop through these three lines, and the first line intersection to pass the test (i.e., the first line to intersect the plane) means the triangle intersects the plane. A visual of a triangle–plane intersection is shown in Figure 2.26.

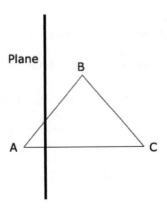

FIGURE 2.26   A triangle intersecting a plane at the first and
second points as well as the first and third points.

Rather than creating and testing three lines for triangle intersection,
there is a faster way to perform the test. Since there are three points, you
can simply classify each point and test if their classifications all equal one
another. If they do, they are all on the same side and cannot intersect the
plane. If any points appear on a different side than the others, then there
is intersection. If a point is on a plane, it does not intersect, so checking to
see if some points are on the front while others are on the back of the
plane is all that is needed. A simple pseudo-code example for a triangle
intersection is as follows:

```
function Triangle_Intersection(Plane plane, Vector3D v1,
                               Vector3D v2, Vector3D v3)
{
    var v1_result = Classify(plane, v1);
    var v2_result = Classify(plane, v2);
    var v3_result = Classify(plane, v3);
    if(v1_result == v2_result == v3_result)
    {
        return false;
    }
    return true;
}
```

Additional Primitive Intersections

Any primitive can intersect a plane. To test a sphere against a plane you
can get the distance between the center of the sphere and the plane using
the plane equation $Ax + By + Cz + D$. If the result is less than the radius of

the sphere, the sphere intersects the plane. The pseudo-code for a sphere–plane intersection is as follows (see Figure 2.27):

```
function Sphere_Intersection(Plane plane, Vector3D center, float r)
{
   var d = plane.x * center.x +
           plane.y * center.y +
           plane.z * center.z + plane.d;
   if(d <= r)
   {
      return true;
   }
   return false;
}
```

FIGURE 2.27   No intersection (left) and a sphere–plane intersection (right).

Another shape that is common to test is boxes. To test if a box intersects a plane each of the four corners that make up the box can be tested using line intersections. A faster way is to use the normal of the plane to determine what the minimum and maximum points of the box should be. That way a single line intersection is all that is needed, rather than the much larger number of unique lines that need to be tested using the first method. The pseudo-code for a box (defined by a minimum and maximum position) is as follows:

```
bool Box_Intersect(Plane plane, Vector3D bbMin, Vector3D bbMax)
{
   Vector3D min, max;
   Vector3D normal(plane.a, plane.b, plane.c);

   if(normal.x >= 0.0)
      {
         min.x = bbMin.x;
         max.x = bbMax.x;
      }
   else
      {
         min.x = bbMax.x;
```

```
            max.x = bbMin.x;
        }

    if(normal.y >= 0.0)
        {
            min.y = bbMin.y;
            max.y = bbMax.y;
        }
    else
        {
            min.y = bbMax.y;
            max.y = bbMin.y;
        }

    if(normal.z >= 0.0)
        {
            min.z = bbMin.z;
            max.z = bbMax.z;
        }
    else
        {
            min.z = bbMax.z;
            max.z = bbMin.z;
        }

    if((normal.Dot3(min) + d) > 0.0f)
        return false;
    if((normal.Dot3(max) + d) >= 0.0f)
        return true;

    return false;
}
```

Frustums

A frustum is a series of planes that are used to define a volume. With this volume we can test if objects are inside of, outside of, or penetrating the frustum. One common use of a frustum is to create a view frustum. A view frustum is a volume that encloses what the viewer can see by defining bottom and top planes, near and far planes, and left and right planes. A visual example of a frustum is shown in Figure 2.28.

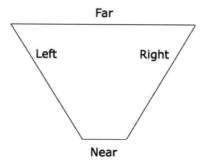

FIGURE 2.28 A frustum.

By enclosing the view volume we can determine if an object is visible or not. Objects that are not visible are not sent down the rendering pipeline, whereas those that are visible are drawn. This can be a huge optimization if we are able to use a frustum to cull a large number of polygons from the rendering process. If enough polygons are quickly culled out, the performance benefits can become apparent early on in the development of a game environment. This is commonly called frustum culling and is a very effective technique used to speed up the rendering of a complex scene.

We revisit the topic of frustums in Chapter 15. To represent a frustum in code we need to store an array of planes that define the frustum. An example of this is as follows in pseudo-code:

```
struct Frustum
{
    array<Plane> plane_list;
    int total_planes;
};
```

When testing if an object is within a frustum, simply loop through each of the planes of the frustum and perform classification tests against each of the objects in the scene. Any object that appears on the back side of any one plane is not visible. This holds true even if the object is on the front side of every other plane. An object is culled out if at least one plane classifies it as being behind it, as shown in Figure 2.29.

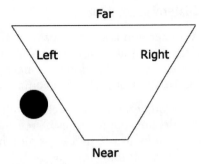

FIGURE 2.29   It takes one frustum plane to cull the object.

Occlusions

An occluder is an object that blocks the sight of another object or objects. When performing occlusion culling, the idea is to determine which objects in the visible view frustum are blocked by other objects. By performing this test quickly on key objects we can avoid rendering objects that we cannot see. A visual of this is shown in Figure 2.30, where a large object blocks the view of two smaller objects.

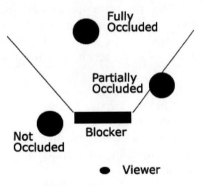

FIGURE 2.30   Occlusion culling.

The topic of occlusion culling is revisited in Chapter 15. Occlusion culling, like frustum culling, is a technique that can be used to increase the rendering speed of a game. Care must be taken when performing occlusion culling because if too many occlusion fields exist in the view, the potential for the occlusion process taking longer to execute than simply rendering out all objects can arise.

Quaternion Rotations

A quaternion is a mathematical object that can be used to represent rotations. The quaternion is often thought of as a substitute for matrix rotations in game development because it has numerous advantages over matrix rotations. These advantages include the following:

- A quaternion is a special kind of 4D vector, which means it takes four floating-point values to represent it, whereas a 3×3 rotation matrix would use 9 floating-point numbers (4×4 would use 16, which makes it four times bigger).
- Concatenating quaternions is faster than concatenating matrices.
- Quaternions can produce smooth interpolated rotations that do not suffer from rotation errors like gimble-lock, whereas matrices can have such errors occur by nature.

A quaternion is an object made up of a w, x, y, and z set of values. Quaternions are a natural extension to complex numbers. The quaternion element has the following form mathematically, where q is the quaternion, and i, j, and k are imaginary numbers:

$$q = w + xi + yj + zk$$

The conjugate of a quaternion can be found by negating the x, y, and z values of the element, which would also negate a 3D vector. This is represented by the following; note that the w component is not negated along with the rest in a quaternion:

$$q = w + -xi + -yj + -zk$$

Quaternions can have arithmetic operations applied to them in a straightforward manner just like 4D vectors, but when it comes to multiplication, quaternions, like matrices, are not commutative. This means that to multiply two quaternions together you would use the following equation:

$$q1 * q2 = w1 * w2 + v1 \char`\^ v2 + w1 * v2 + w2 * v1 + v1 \times v2$$

where ^ is the dot product, x is the cross product, w is the w component of the quaternion, and v is the x, y, z component of the quaternion.

Rotations with Quaternions

Quaternions are good at calculating rotations. The total number of calculations needed to rotate a quaternion is lower than that of a matrix, so there is a performance benefit to using them. Also, quaternions can be stored using less memory, which is another improvement. If a lot of quaternions are being operated on in a game environment, these benefits can add up, especially with complex character animations using a skeleton system. The equation to rotate a quaternion around an axis *a* can use the following, where *cos* is the cosine, *sin* is the sine, and *angle* is the rotation angle:

$$q = \cos(\text{angle} / 2) + \sin(\text{angle} / 2)a$$

Interpolation with Quaternions

Quaternions can be interpolated like other mathematical elements we've seen in this chapter. In video game and engine programming it is very likely that you will come across linear and spherical interpolation. Linear interpolation is the easiest type of interpolation and takes the following form:

$$q(t) = (1 - t)q1 + tq2$$

which states that the interpolated quaternion *q(t)* is equal to $1 - t$, where *t* represents a scalar value between 0 and 1, multiplied by the first quaternion plus *t* multiplied by the second quaternion. In the early days of game development linear interpolation was used heavily in 3D animations. In the past, character models were animated by using linear interpolation against the vertices in two meshes, where one mesh had a pose that represented the current animation and the other represented the next animation in the sequence. The more poses a model had, the smoother the animation was. Because these required game developers to essentially create and load many of the same models but with slightly different poses for the animations they wanted to represent, a lot of memory was consumed by just one animated model. Today, character models use skeleton animation, which does not suffer from the same memory drawbacks. It is also easier to work with in animation editors and allows for the possibility of character models sharing the same animations (or even have animations applied to them that were not originally created with the model).

The second type of interpolation is spherical interpolation. Spherical interpolation can trace an arc at a constant rate between two elements that are being interpolated between. The equation used to perform spherical interpolation is

$$qt = q1(\sin(1 - t)a / \sin(a)) + q2(\sin(t)a / \sin(a))$$

When performing spherical interpolation, it is assumed that the quaternions are unit-length (normalized), which are done in the same manner as vectors. The length throughout the spherical interpolation remains 1, so the animation is smooth and constant between the two arcs. Spherical interpolation is often used in skeleton animation when interpolating smoothly between two frames of animation.

 A quaternion can be used as a substitute for a matrix's rotational part. To position objects you still need a vector for the position.

SUMMARY

This chapter covered a lot of information and served as a quick review of the things that are important for you to know before coming into this book. Each topic discussed in this chapter could have filled its own book. Appendix C provides additional resources you can explore if you are interested in furthering your knowledge in areas in which you feel are lacking.

The following elements were discussed in this chapter:

- Colors in computer graphics
- Bits and bytes
- Hex colors
- 2D computer graphics
- 3D computer graphics
- Primitives
- Geometry
- Vectors
- Matrices
- Rays
- Planes
- Interpolations
- Quaternions

CHAPTER QUESTIONS

Answers to the following chapter review questions can be found in Appendix A, "Answers to Chapter Questions."

1. How many bits are in a byte?
   A. 1
   B. 4
   C. 8
   D. None of the above

2. How many bits are in a binary digit?
    A. 1
    B. 2
    C. 4
    D. 8
3. How many bits are in an integer?
    A. 8
    B. 16
    C. 24
    D. 32
4. How many bytes are in an integer?
    A. 1
    B. 4
    C. 8
    D. 16
5. How many kilobytes are in a megabyte?
    A. 10
    B. 100
    C. 1,024
    D. 1 million
6. How many components are in a 24-bit color?
    A. 3
    B. 4
    C. 24
    D. None of the above
7. What are base-2 values?
8. What are base-10 values?
9. What are hexadecimal values, and what base do they use?
10. What value is BA in hexadecimal?
    A. 124
    B. 238
    C. 180
    D. 186
11. What is a polygon?
12. What is the difference between a concave and a convex mesh? Describe both.
13. A triangle has how many edges?
    A. 2
    B. 3
    C. 4
14. Which kind of intersection test is faster: a sphere to sphere or a box to box? Why?
15. What is a vector?
16. What is a vector that has a length of 1 called?

17. What is a dot product?
18. What is a cross product?
19. What is a matrix?
20. What is the length of a matrix called?
21. What is a ray?
22. What is a plane?
23. What is the definition of a scalar?
24. Which of the following is true for matrix and quaternion multiplication?
    A. Associative
    B. Commutative
    C. Cannot be performed
    D. None of the above
25. What is rasterization?
26. What is ray tracing?
27. What are quaternions?
28. List three reasons why a quaternion is a better option than a matrix.
29. Describe linear interpolation.
30. Describe spherical interpolation.

CHAPTER EXERCISES

Exercise 1: Implement code to convert a hex triplet into an RGB color. Create a structure to hold this color information and create a demo application that uses the color to shade a sphere.

Exercise 2: Create a demo application that defines a sphere at (0, 25, 0) located above a plane. This plane should be located somewhere under the origin and point up the positive Y axis (0, 1, 0). Move the sphere down a little each frame until it intersects the plane. When the intersection occurs, move the sphere to the last known position it had before the intersection took place. Draw a large square to represent the plane.

Exercise 3: Expand upon the last demo and create another plane that is above the sphere. Place the sphere at the origin, and place the original plane below the sphere. Move the sphere down until it hits a plane. When it hits a plane, reverse the direction the sphere is moving. Allow this to continue to give the impression of the sphere bouncing off of both planes.

Exercise 4: Implement linear interpolation between vectors based on the formula presented earlier in this chapter. Create a demo application using the rendering API of your choice to move a box from one location to another using this type of interpolation.

Exercise 5: Implement spherical interpolation based on the formula presented earlier in this chapter. Create a demo application using the rendering API of your choice to move a box from one location to another using this type of interpolation.

3

RAY TRACING

In This Chapter

- Ray Tracing in Computer Graphics
- Tracing Primitives
- Implementing Ray Tracing
- Real-Time Ray Tracing

In this chapter we discuss the topic of ray tracing in computer graphics. Ray tracing has a very important role in computer graphics, even in video games to some extent, which we discuss throughout this chapter and book. The purpose of this chapter is to not only talk about ray tracing but to implement a simple CPU ray tracer using C++. Having an understanding of game mathematical topics such as vectors, rays, primitives, and geometry makes it possible to create a simple ray tracer with relatively little code.

This chapter discusses the various types of ray tracing algorithms as well as real-time ray tracing efforts that are taking place today. A few years ago real-time ray tracing was not a commercially reasonable possibility, but today it is a reality, although it still has a ways to go before the industry can use it for the entire rendering solution of a game.

The purpose of this chapter is to provide experience with a hands-on simple CPU ray tracer. Later in this book we will use the underlying ideas behind ray tracing to implement advanced effects that are seen in modern video games such as precomputed lighting and shadowing effects.

RAY TRACING IN COMPUTER GRAPHICS

One of the oldest techniques used for generating rendered images on the CPU is ray tracing. Ray tracing is used in many different entertainment industries and has been for a number of decades now. One of the most well-known uses of ray tracing–based algorithms is in animated movies such as *Teenage Mutant Ninja Turtles*.

Ray tracing is based on the idea that you can perform ray intersection tests on all objects within a scene to generate an image. Every time a ray hits an object the point of intersection is determined. If that point of intersection falls within the view volume of the virtual observer, then the pixels on the screen image that is being rendered are colored based on the object's material information (e.g., color, texture, etc.) and the scene's properties (e.g., fog, lighting, etc.). An example of this is shown in Figure 3.1.

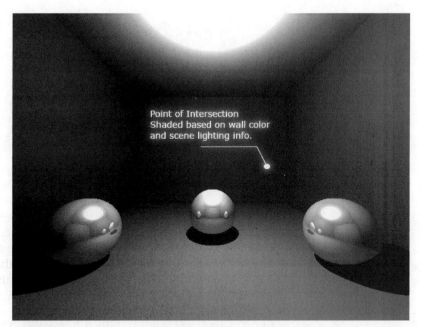

Point of Intersection
Shaded based on wall color
and scene lighting info.

FIGURE 3.1   A point of intersection matching a pixel on the rendering image.

Forward Ray Tracing

Different types of ray tracing are used in computer graphics. In the first type of ray tracing that will be discussed, known as forward ray tracing, mathematical rays are traced from a light source into a 3D scene. When a ray intersects an object that falls within the viewing volume, the pixel that corresponds to that point of intersection is colored appropriately. This method of ray tracing is a simple attempt at simulating light rays that strike surfaces in nature, although far more simplistic and general than anything seen in the real world.

Tracing rays in this sense means starting rays at some origin, which in the case of forward ray tracing would be the light position, and pointing those rays outward into a scene in different directions. The more rays that are used, the better are the chances of them hitting objects that fall within the viewing volume. A simplistic example of this is shown in Figure 3.2.

FIGURE 3.2   A few rays being traced from a light source into a scene (left). Many rays being traced from a light source (right).

To create a simple forward ray tracer, for example, one that traces spheres, one generally requires the following steps:

1. Define the scene's spheres and light sources.
2. For every light source send a finite number of rays into the scene, where more rays equal a better potential for quality but at a cost of performance.
3. For every intersection, test if the intersection has occurred within the viewing volume.
4. For every intersection, test that it does fall within the viewing volume and shade the image pixel for that ray based on the sphere's and light's (also scene's) properties.
5. Save the image to a file, display it to the screen, or use it in some meaningful way to your application.

This quick overview of forward ray tracing does not appear complex at first glance, and a ray tracer that did only what was just described would be pretty bare-bones. We've already discussed ray–object intersections in Chapter 2, "2D and 3D Graphics," and the preceding steps seem pretty straightforward. The pseudo-code used to perform the following list of steps could look something like the following:

```
function Forward_RayTracing(scene)
{
   foreach(light in scene)
   {
      foreach(ray in light)
      {
         closestObject = null;
         minDist = "Some Large Value";
```

```
        foreach(object in scene)
        {
            if(ray->Intersects(object) && object->distance <
minDist)

            {
                minDist = object->distance;
                point_of_intersect = ray->Get_Intersection();
                closestObject = object;
            }
        }

        if(Is_In_View(point_of_intersect) && closestObject !=
NULL)
        {
            Shade_Pixel(point_of_intersect, light,
closestObject);
        }
        }
    }

    Save_Render("output.jpg");
}
```

Assuming that you have a scene object that holds a list of lights and geometric objects, a ray structure, a function to test if a point of intersection falls on a pixel of the rendered image, and a function to shade that pixel based on the scene's information, then you can create a complete, yet simple, ray traced image using the pseudo-code above. The pseudo-code is just an example and does not take into account textures and other material properties, shadows, reflections, refractions, and other common effects that are used in ray tracing rendering engines.

If you were to code an application that uses forward ray tracing, you would quickly realize that many problems are associated with the technique. For one, there is no guarantee that the rays sent from a light source would eventually strike an object that falls within the viewing volume. Also, there is no guarantee that every pixel that should be shaded will be shaded, which would only happen if one of the rays that were traced from the light sources happened to strike it. This is shown in Figure 3.2, where sending too few rays does not produce enough information to cover the entire scene and "wasted" rays were traced. In nature, light rays bounce around the environment many times while moving at the speed of light. There are so many light rays in nature that, eventually, every surface is hit. In the virtual world we need to send more and more distributed rays throughout a scene to shade an entire environment. The processing of each of these rays is not done at the speed of light, and the processing of one ray could be costly on its own. When using forward ray tracing, we have to find some way to ensure that all screen pixels that should be shaded have at least one ray strike them so that the point of intersection is shaded and is visible in the final render.

The biggest problem with forward ray tracing is that the more rays we use, the slower the performance is, and to have the potential for an increase in quality, a lot of rays need to be used. In the pseudo-code we have to trace every object in the scene against every ray for every light. If there were 100 lights, each sending 10,000 rays into the scene, a program would need millions of intersection tests for every object in the scene, and this would only be for one rendered frame that does not use any techniques that cause additional rays to be generated. The number of rays can increase exponentially if reflections are also included, which cause rays to bounce off of objects back into the scene. Global illumination techniques that use light bounces in the calculation of lights and shadows also dramatically increase the number of rays and information used to complete the scene. Other techniques including anti-aliasing, refractions, volumetric effects, and so forth increase this effort exponentially. With the required number of operations needed for even a simple scene, it should be no wonder why ray tracing has traditionally been a technique that was only used for non–real-time applications.

Forward ray tracing can be improved. We can try to limit the number of rays that are used; we can use spatial data structures to cull out geometry from a scene for each ray test and other such improvements, but the application will still be performing many tests that end up being a waste of CPU processing time, and it would be very difficult to determine which rays would be wasted and which ones would not. Optimizing a forward ray tracer is also not a trivial task and could become quite tricky and complex. Even with optimizations, the processing time is still quite high compared to the next type of ray tracing we will discuss. The downsides to using forward ray tracing include the following:

- CPU costs are far beyond other methods used to perform ray tracing on the same information (discussed later in this chapter).
- The quality of the rendered result depends highly on the number of rays that are traced in the scene, many of which could end up not affecting the rendered scene.
- If not enough rays are used or if they are not distributed effectively, some pixels might not be shaded, even though they should be.
- It cannot be reasonably done in real time.
- It is generally obsolete for computer and game graphics.
- It can be harder to optimize.

The major problem with forward ray tracing is that regardless of how many rays we generate for each light, only a very small percentage will affect the view (i.e., will hit an object we can see). This means we can perform millions or billions of useless intersection tests on the scenes. Since a scene can extend beyond the view volume and since factors such as reflections can cause rays to bounce off surfaces outside the view and then back into it (or vice versa), developing algorithms to minimize the number of wasted light rays can be very difficult. Plus, some rays might start off striking geometry that is outside the view volume and eventually bounce around and strike something that is in the view volume, which is common for global illumination.

The best way to avoid the downsides of forward ray tracing is to use backward ray tracing. In the next section we look into backward ray tracing and implement a simple ray tracer that supports spheres, triangles, and planes. Later in this book we will add features to the ray tracer such as lighting, reflections, and refractions.

Backward Ray Tracing

Backward ray tracing takes a different approach than that discussed so far in this chapter. With backward ray tracing the rays are not traced from the light sources into the scene, but instead they are traced from the camera into the scene. In backward ray tracing every ray that is sent is traced toward each pixel of the rendered scene, whereas in forward ray tracing an application sends thousands of rays from multiple light sources. By sending the rays from the camera into the scene, where each ray points toward a different pixel on an imaginary image plane, they are guaranteed to be shaded if the ray intersects any objects. A visual of backward ray tracing is shown in Figure 3.3.

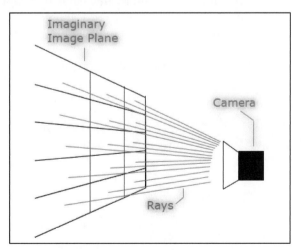

FIGURE 3.3 Backward ray tracing.

Assuming that one ray is used for every screen pixel, the number of minimum rays depends on the image's resolution. By sending a ray for each pixel the ray tracer can ensure that all pixels are shaded if that pixel's ray intersects anything. In forward ray tracing the traced rays do not necessarily fall within the view volume all the time. By sending rays from the viewer in the direction the viewer is looking, the rays originate and point within the view volume. If there are any objects along that path, the pixel for that ray will be shaded appropriately.

The algorithm to take the simple forward ray tracer from earlier in this chapter and convert it to a backward ray tracer can follow these general steps:

- For each pixel create a ray that points in the direction of the pixel's location on the imaginary image plane.
- For each object in the scene test if the ray intersects it.
- If there is intersection, record the object only if it is the closest object intersected.
- Once all objects have been tested, shade the image pixel based on the point of intersection with the closest object and the scene's information (e.g., object material, light information, etc.).
- Once complete, save the results or use the image in some other meaningful way.

The algorithm discussed so far for both types of ray tracers does not take into account optimizations or factors such as anti-aliasing, texture mapping, reflections, refractions, shadows, depth-of-field, fog, or global illumination, all of which are discussed throughout this book in terms of how they are used in video game development.

The steps outlined for a simple backward ray tracer can be turned into pseudo-code that may generally look like the following:

```
function Backward_RayTracing(scene)
{
    foreach(pixel in image)
    {
        ray = Calculate_Ray(pixel);
        closestObject = null;
        minDist = "Some Large Value";

        foreach(object in scene)
        {
            if(ray->Intersects(object) && object->distance <
minDist)
            {
                minDist = object->distance;
```

```
                point_of_intersect = ray->Get_Intersection();
                closestObject = object;
            }
        }

        if(closestObject != null)
        {
            foreach(light in scene)
            {
                Shade_Pixel(point_of_intersect, light,
closestObject);
            }
        }
    }

    Save_Render("output.jpg");
}
```

 Backward ray tracing is also known as ray casting.

In the pseudo-code above the simple backward ray tracing algorithm is similar to the one for forward ray tracing but with a number of key differences. The major difference between the two can be seen with the start of the algorithm. In a forward ray tracer we trace X amount of rays from each light source. In the backward ray tracer a ray traveling toward each screen pixel is traced, which greatly reduces the number of rays used in a scene compared to forward ray tracing without sacrificing the final quality at all, assuming the same conditions exist in both scenes. The breakdown of the lines of code in the pseudo-code sample for the backward ray tracer is as follows:

- For each pixel that makes up the rendered image create a direction that points from the viewer's position toward the current pixel, which is a vector built from the pixel's X and Y index and a constant value used for the depth.
- Normalize this direction and create a ray out of it based on the viewer's position.
- For each object in the scene test if the ray intersects any of the objects and record the object closet to the viewer.
- If an object was found to have intersected the ray, color the pixel that corresponds to the ray by adding the contributions of all lights that affect this object.
- Once complete, save the image to a file, present it to the screen, or use it in some meaningful manner.

The pseudo-code samples do not describe complex ray tracers or ray tracing–related algorithms. Although simple in design, the pseudo-code ray tracers do provide an impressive look into what it takes to create a ray tracer, and they should give you an idea of the amount of work, CPU-wise, done by the processor even for simple ray tracing. The key idea is to use ray intersections to gradually build the rendered image. Most ray intersections are CPU expensive, and doing hundreds of thousands or even millions of these tests can take a lot of processing power and time. The number of objects that need to be tested for can also greatly affect the number of intersection tests that must be performed.

When you create a ray based on a screen pixel, the origin of the ray can be based on the viewer's position, for example, and the direction can be based on the pixel's width and height location on the imaginary image plane. A pixel value of 0 for the width and 0 for the height would be the first pixel, normally located at the upper-left corner of the screen. A pixel with the width that matches the image's width resolution and a height that matches the height resolution would be the lower-right corner of the image. All values in between would fall within the image's canvas.

By using the pixel's width, height, and some constant for the depth (let's use 255 for example), a vector can be built and normalized. This vector needs to be unit-length to ensure accurate intersection tests. Assuming a variable x is used for the pixel's width location and a variable y is used for the height, the pseudo-code to build a ray based on the pixel's location may look like the following, which could take place before object intersection tests:

```
ray.direction = Normalize(Vector3D(x - (width / 2),
                                   y - (height / 2),
                                   255));
```

Note that the above sample adjusts x and y so that the origin marks the center of the image and the middle of the screen, which marks the middle of the camera, is pointing straight forward. Once you have this ray, you can loop through each of the objects in the scene and determine which object is closest. The object's information and the point of intersection are used to color the pixel at the current location.

Tracing Primitives

The heart of ray tracing is using ray intersection tests on various objects in the scene. Performing a ray intersection test with a ray and the objects in the scene is known as tracing. This term is used throughout this book to describe intersecting a primitive with a ray. When you trace a ray, you start at some specified origin and move toward a specified direction. This origin does not have to be the eye position, which was assumed earlier in the discussion of the forward and backward ray tracers. Later in this book we will use ray tracing techniques to precompute, also known as baking, lighting and shadowing information of a virtual scene into texture images known as light maps.

In this section we discuss the intersection tests that can be performed on a few different objects. Each of these objects is used in the chapter's sample application to render a ray traced scene. These objects include spheres, triangle polygons, and planes.

Tracing Spheres

Spheres are a very common shape that can be found in many ray tracing rendering engines. A sphere is generally a very fast primitive used to calculate tests against; it is simplistic to represent and has detail and an interesting geometric shape. In video games spheres are often used as stand-in representations of objects when quickly trying to determine collisions between other objects and the environment, which is discussed in more detail in Chapter 15 "Optimizations." The intersection test between a sphere and a ray can have the following steps:

- Get the vector between the sphere's location and the ray's location.
- The cosine angle between the ray-to-sphere vector and the ray's direction tells us if the ray passes through some of the area of the sphere (anything less than 0 for this angle means the ray does not hit the sphere).
- If the previous test proves true, the next step is to use the square of the sphere's radius, the ray-to-sphere vector length, and the square of the angle between the two vectors to test if the ray passes through the radius of the sphere.
- If the previous test proves true, there is definitely an intersection, and the intersection distance is the angle between the ray-to-sphere vector and the ray's direction minus the square root of the radius test

These steps can be broken down into testing if the ray passes through the general area of the sphere, which is done in the first test, and then, if the first test does not fail, we can test if the ray penetrates the radius area of the sphere. A visual example is shown in Figure 3.4.

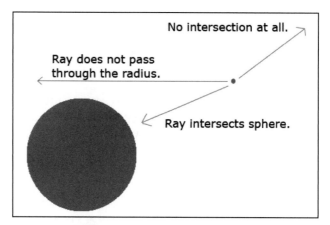

FIGURE 3.4 Ray-to-sphere intersection.

The pseudo-code for the previous steps can be straightforward. By having a structure for the vector, a sphere made up of a position and a radius value and a ray made up of a position and a direction could look like the following, where two tests are used to determine if a ray intersects a sphere and the distance along the infinite ray where the intersection has occurred:

```
function Intersect(Sphere sphere, Ray ray, float *dist)
{
    Vector3D rsVec = sphere.center - ray.origin;

    float testA = rsVec.Dot3(ray.direction);

    if(testA < 0)
        return false;

    float rsLength = rsVec.Dot3(rsVec);

    float testB = (sphere.radius * sphere.radius) - rsLength +
                  (testA * testA);

    if(testB < 0)
        return false;

    if(dist != null)
        *dist = testA - square_root(testB);

    return true;
}
```

By returning the distance for the intersection we can calculate the point of intersection on an object if we need it. This point of intersection is calculated by starting at the ray's origin and moving in the direction of the ray by the distance amount.

 If you wanted to limit your ray's reach, that is, instead of having it infinite, you can specify a value for the ray's maximum length. During the intersection test, at the end, you would simply test if the ray-to-object intersection distance is smaller than the ray's maximum length. If so, there is an intersection; otherwise, there is not.

Tracing Planes

Planes are often used not for visual rendering but for culling, collision detection, and so forth in video games, although many ray tracing engines offer the option to render a plane if desired. Planes are infinite, but since a finite number of pixels make up the rendered scene, planes visually have a cutoff point. Planes are great to use for surfaces that must extend as far as the view can see, an example of which is shown in Figure 3.5.

FIGURE 3.5   A box on a plane in a ray traced image.

The intersection of a plane can be more straightforward than that of the sphere we discussed earlier in this section. The steps to test if a ray intersects a plane can take on the following form, where a plane is defined by a normal and a distance *d*:

- Get the angle between the plane's normal and the ray's direction.
- Test if the absolute value of the angle is less than 0, where less than 0 means there is no intersection because the ray is parallel to the plane.
- If the previous test passes, we get the ray's distance from the plane using the ray's position with that of the plane.
- By dividing the cosine angle between the plane's normal and the ray's direction with the ray's origin distance from the plane, we can determine if the ray is pointing at or away from the plane, where a negative value means it points away from the plane.
- If the ray does not point away from the plane and if it is not parallel to the plane, then it must intersect it.

In the steps above the ray-to-plane intersection test starts by quickly testing if the ray is parallel to the plane. If so, there is no way the ray can intersect the plane, which is shown in Figure 3.6.

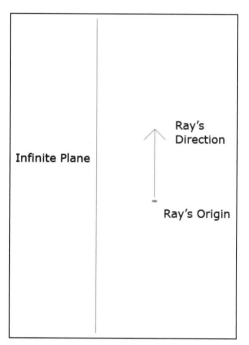

FIGURE 3.6 A ray is parallel to a plane.

If the ray is not parallel to the plane, the next step is to determine if the ray points at the plane. Since the plane is infinite, the ray is guaranteed to intersect the plane as long as it is not parallel to the plane and as long as it does not point away from the plane. The origin's distance from the plane divided by the cosine angle between the ray's direction and plane's normal gives you the distance that can be used to calculate the point of intersection. The pseudo-code to perform the ray-to-plane intersection test can take on the following form:

```
function Intersect(Plane plane, Ray ray, float *dist)
{
    float rayPlaneAngle = plane.normal.Dot3(ray.direction);

    if(fabs(rayPlaneAngle) < 0.00001f)
        return false;

    float originD = -(plane.normal.Dot3(ray.origin) + plane.d);

    float intersectDist = originD / rayPlaneAngle;

    if(intersectDist < 0.0f)
        return false;

    if(dist != NULL)
        *dist = intersectDist;

    return true;
}
```

Tracing Triangles

The ray-to-triangle intersection test is generally pretty expensive compared to most primitives that can be found in most ray tracers such as spheres, planes, and boxes. Triangle-to-ray or triangle-to-triangle tests are so expensive that they are often avoided whenever possible in video games by substituting them for much more simple and efficient tests. In video games this can be seen in collision detection, for example, where bounding volumes such as spheres or boxes are used to do the calculations rather than the individual triangles of the geometry models. This is discussed in more detail in Chapter 15 along with other topics. The triangle-to-ray intersection test can take the following steps:

- Get two edges from the triangle (points 1 to 2 and points 1 to 3, for example).
- Get the vector product (cross) between the first edge and the ray's direction.
- If the cosine angle between the vector product of the previous test result and the first edge is less than 0, then the ray passes outside of the edge (i.e., does not pass through the surface and thus the test fails).

- If the previous test passes, we can test if the ray is pointing away from the triangle's plane.
- If that test passes, we then test if the ray passes through the surface of the triangle by testing if the ray is within the remaining edges and penetrates the surface.

Performing each of these steps is not trivial and is not as cheap as the other two tests we've seen in this chapter. When performing triangle-to-ray intersection using the steps above, most of the mathematics is performed using vectors. To get an edge of a triangle you get the vector between two points that make up the triangle. The plane of a triangle can be calculated since a triangle is completely flat and a plane that parallels a triangle can be used as a quick rejection test. The pseudo-code to implement the triangle intersection based on the steps above can be seen as follows:

```
function Intersect(Triangle triangle, Ray &ray, float *dist)
{
   Vector3D vecAB = triangle.p2 - triangle.p1;
   Vector3D vecAC = triangle.p3 - triangle.p1;

   Vector3D origin = ray.origin;
   Vector3D direction = ray.direction;
   Vector3D cross = direction.CrossProduct(vecAC);

   float det = vecAB.Dot3(cross);

   if(det < 0.0001f)
      return false;

   Vector3D rayPointVec = origin - triangle.p1;

   float test1 = rayPointVec.Dot3(cross);

   if(test1 < 0.0f || test1 > det)
      return false;

   Vector3D cross2;
   cross2 = rayPointVec.CrossProduct(vecAB);
   float test2 = direction.Dot3(cross2);

   if(test2 < 0.0f || test1 + test2 > det)
      return false;

   float inverseDet = 1.0f / det;
```

```
    if(dist != NULL)
      {
          *dist = vecAC.Dot3(cross2);
          *dist *= inverseDet;
      }

    return true;
  }
```

Tracing Additional Primitives

By writing ray intersection testing code you can use any shape, object, or primitive in a ray tracer. For more advanced features such as lighting, shadows, and texture mapping, it is important to be able to get the normal at the point of intersection, which is the normal on the object for that specific intersection point. Using a triangle model, for example, the normal could be the triangle's normal since the entire surface of the triangle is facing in the same direction. Additional types of objects that are commonly found in many 3D modeling applications that use ray tracing, for example, 3D Studio Max, include but are not limited to the following:

- Boxes and cubes
- Torus rings
- Cones
- Pyramids
- Disks
- Cylinders
- Patches

IMPLEMENTING RAY TRACING

There has been a bit of discussion of the basics of ray tracing in computer graphics. In ray tracing, backward ray tracing is the more favorable path, as opposed to forward ray tracing. This section implements a CPU backward ray tracer using the C++ programming language. The demo application for this section has the following features:

- Can trace spheres
- Can trace planes
- Can trace triangles
- Can output to a TGA file at any resolution

On the accompanying CD-ROM is a demo application called Ray Tracing in the Chapter 3 folder. In this section we examine the code for the demo. The code can be compiled and executed on any hardware as long as you have a C++ compiler.

Mathematics for Ray Tracing

Ray tracing, and computer graphics in general, are heavy in mathematics. To create a ray tracer with the features mentioned in the previous section we need a few mathematical objects. These objects include the following:

- Vectors
- Rays
- Planes
- Colors

The vector is a class that stores a 3D vector object. This vector will be used for both vertices and vector directions since the components of the two and their operations are represented identically. The vector class needs the ability to perform arithmetic on vectors (e.g., addition, subtraction, multiplication, and division), needs to be able to find the dot product of two vectors and the length of a vector, and needs to normalize a vector as well as finding the cross product between two vectors. These operations are needed for the various intersection algorithms discussed earlier in this chapter. Each of these operations were first discussed in Chapter 2. Vector mathematics is fairly straightforward; the class declaration for the 3D vector is shown in Listing 3.1.

LISTING 3.1 THE VECTOR3D CLASS

```
class Vector3D
{
   public:
      Vector3D();
      Vector3D(float X, float Y, float Z);
      Vector3D(const Vector3D &v);


      void Add(const Vector3D &v1, const Vector3D &v2);
      void Subtract(const Vector3D &v1, const Vector3D &v2);
      void Multiply(const Vector3D &v1, const Vector3D &v2);
      void Divide(const Vector3D &v1, const Vector3D &v2);
```

```
void Add(const Vector3D &v1, float f);
void Subtract(const Vector3D &v1, float f);
void Multiply(const Vector3D &v1, float f);
void Divide(const Vector3D &v1, float f);


void operator=(const Vector3D &v);
void operator+=(const Vector3D &v);
void operator-=(const Vector3D &v);
void operator/=(const Vector3D &v);
void operator*=(const Vector3D &v);


Vector3D operator+(const Vector3D &v2);
Vector3D operator-(const Vector3D &v2);
Vector3D operator/(const Vector3D &v2);
Vector3D operator*(const Vector3D &v2);


Vector3D operator+(float f);
Vector3D operator-(float f);
Vector3D operator/(float f);
Vector3D operator*(float f);


void Negate();
float Dot3(const Vector3D &v);
float Magnitude();


void Normalize();
void Normalize(Vector3D p1, Vector3D p2,
               Vector3D p3);


Vector3D CrossProduct(const Vector3D &v);


float x, y, z;
};
```

The ray is the heart of ray tracing. A ray is made up of at least two properties: the ray's position, known as the origin, and the ray's direction. For the sample ray tracer developed here each primitive implements an intersection function that tests if a ray intersects the object. Because of this, the ray class itself is fairly small; it is shown in Listing 3.2. The 3D vector makes passing information between ray objects much easier.

LISTING 3.2 THE RAY CLASS

```
class Ray
{
   public:
      Ray()
      {

      }

      Ray(Vector3D &pos, Vector3D &dir) :
         origin(pos), direction(dir)
      {

      }

      ~Ray()
      {

      }

      void operator=(const Ray &r)
      {
         origin = r.origin;
         direction = r.direction;
      }

      Vector3D origin, direction;
};
```

The plane class for the sample ray tracer in this chapter is treated as a primitive that can be rendered to the scene. All primitives in the ray tracer derive from a common base class called shape. The shape class is examined in an upcoming section and is an abstract class. The plane class itself stores the plane's normal in a 3D vector and the plane's distance in a floating-point variable, and it specifies a function that is used for testing for intersection against a ray. The class for the plane is shown in Listing 3.3. Notice that the constructor defaults the normal to point up the positive Y axis. Since the normal has to have a length that equals 1, this can at least ensure that the default plane has a normal that is unit-length.

LISTING 3.3 THE PLANE CLASS

```
class Plane : public Shape
{
    public:
        Plane() : d(0)
        {
            // Default the normal to point up.
            normal.y = 1;
        }

        Plane(Vector3D &n, Vector3D &p, Color3 col)
        {
            normal = n;
            normal.Normalize();
            d = -(p.Dot3(normal));
            color = col;
        }

        ~Plane()
        {

        }

        bool Intersect(const Ray &ray, float *dist);


    private:
        Vector3D normal;
        float d;
};
```

The plane's intersection function takes as parameters a ray and an address to a variable that stores the intersection distance, which can be used, in conjunction with the ray, to calculate the point of intersection. The implementation of the plane's intersection function is based on the pseudo-code from Chapter 2 and is a Boolean function that returns true upon intersection and false upon a miss. The plane's intersection function is shown in Listing 3.4. Keep in mind that since both rays and planes are infinite, the main tests performed are whether or not the ray is parallel to the plane and whether it is pointing away from the plane. If both cases are not true, we find the distance along the ray that corresponds to the point of intersection.

 Distance tracking is optional. If you are using these intersection functions to test if an intersection occurs but do not care about where it occurs, you don't need to know the distance, and the point-of-intersection does not need to be calculated.

LISTING 3.4 THE PLANE CLASS'S INTERSECTION FUNCTION

```
bool Plane::Intersect(const Ray &ray, float *dist)
{
    float rayPlaneAngle = normal.Dot3(ray.direction);

    // No intersection if the ray is parallel to the plane.
    if(fabs(rayPlaneAngle) < 0.00001f)
        return false;

    float originD = -(normal.Dot3(ray.origin) + d);

    float intersectDist = originD / rayPlaneAngle;

    // Ray is behind the plane, no intersection.
    if(intersectDist < 0.0f)
        return false;

    // Else we have a hit.
    if(dist != NULL)
        *dist = intersectDist;

    return true;
}
```

The last class we look at in this section is a color class. This class stores a 24-bit RGB color where 8-bits are used for each color component. Since the output of the rendering will be stored in a TGA image file this will allow the color array that stores the rendered scene to be directly written to the file. The color class is kept simple and can be seen in Listing 3.5.

LISTING 3.5 THE COLOR3 CLASS

```
class Color3
{
    public:
        Color3() : r(0), g(0), b(0)
        {

        }

        Color3(char R, char G, char B) : r(R), g(G), b(B)
        {

        }

        ~Color3()
        {

        }

        void operator=(Color3 &c)
        {
            r = c.r;
            g = c.g;
            b = c.b;
        }


        char r, g, b;
};
```

Data Structures for Ray Tracing

The data structures that are used by the ray tracing demo application include a shape base class, a sphere class, a plane class, and a triangle class.
The shape class is the base class to all objects that the ray can intersect
with within the ray tracer. The class itself has a global color for the entire
object for simplicity, a function to retrieve this color, and a virtual intersection function. As seen with the plane class earlier in this chapter, each
shape must implement its own intersection function since each primitive
is different. The shape's base class can be seen in Listing 3.6.

Virtual functions can be slower than using non-virtual functions. In the case of the simple ray tracer, and since this is going to be an offline tool, any additional cost in using the convenience factor of virtual functions and inheritance is minimal.

LISTING 3.6 THE SHAPE CLASS

```
#include"Color.h"

class Shape
{
    public:
        Shape()
        {

        }

        virtual ~Shape()
        {

        }

        virtual bool Intersect(const Ray &ray, float *dist) = 0;

        virtual Color3 GetColor()
        {
            return color;
        }

    protected:
        Color3 color;
};
```

The first shape that will be implemented is the sphere. A sphere, as described in Chapter 2, is defined by a position, which is its center represented by a 3D vector, and a radius represented by a floating-point variable. The class for the sphere shape will also implement the intersection function and use the algorithm that was discussed earlier in this chapter. The sphere class declaration can be seen in Listing 3.7. The sphere's ray intersection testing function can be seen in Listing 3.8

LISTING 3.7 THE SPHERE CLASS

```cpp
#include"Ray.h"
#include"Shapes.h"
#include"Vector3D.h"


class Sphere : public Shape
{
   public:
      Sphere() : radius(0)
      {

      }

      Sphere(Vector3D pos, float r, Color3 col) :
            center(pos), radius(r), color(col)
      {

      }

      ~Sphere()
      {

      }

      bool Intersect(const Ray &ray, float *dist);


   private:
      Vector3D center;
      float radius;
};
```

LISTING 3.8 THE SPHERE CLASS'S INTERSECTION FUNCTION

```cpp
bool Sphere::Intersect(const Ray &ray, float *dist)
{
   // Get the ray to sphere vec and it's length.
   Vector3D rsVec = center - ray.origin;
   float rsLength = rsVec.Dot3(rsVec);
```

```
// Does the ray pass through the sphere?
float intersectDistA = rsVec.Dot3(ray.direction);


// If not then no intersection with the ray.
if(intersectDistA < 0 )
    return false;


// Does the ray fall within the sphere's radius?
float intersectDistB = (radius * radius) - rsLength +
                            (intersectDistA * intersectDistA);


// If not then no intersection with the ray.
if(intersectDistB < 0)
    return false;


// There is a hit so we record the results.
if(dist != NULL)
    *dist = intersectDistA - (float)sqrt(intersectDistB);


    return true;
}
```

The last class we'll look at in this section is the triangle class. The triangle is made up of three vertex points, each of which is represented by 3D vector objects. These points are declared as three separate variables for clarity but they can also be defined as an array or any other valid method. The triangle's class can be seen in Listing 3.9 and is based on the discussion on triangles from Chapter 2.

LISTING 3.9 THE TRIANGLE CLASS

```
class Triangle : public Shape
{
    public:
        Triangle(Vector3D &P1, Vector3D &P2,
                Vector3D &P3, Color3 col) :
                p1(P1), p2(P2), p3(P3), color(col)
        {
```

```
    }

    bool Intersect(const Ray &ray, float *dist);



    Vector3D p1, p2, p3;
};
```

The triangle's ray intersection function is based on the algorithm discussed earlier in this chapter. The implementation is more complex than the other shapes seen so far and makes heavy use of vector mathematics. The C++ triangle/ray intersection function's implementation that is based on the pseudo-code from earlier in this chapter can be seen in Listing 3.10.

LISTING 3.10 THE TRIANGLE CLASS'S INTERSECTION FUNCTION

```
bool Triangle::Intersect(const Ray &ray, float *dist)
{
   // Edges of the triangle.
   Vector3D vecAB = p2 - p1;
   Vector3D vecAC = p3 - p1;

   Vector3D origin = ray.origin;
   Vector3D direction = ray.direction;

   // Vector between the ray's direction and edge 2.
   Vector3D cross = direction.CrossProduct(vecAC);


   // Calculate the determinate.
   float det = vecAB.Dot3(cross);

   // Anything less than 0 and the ray does not hit.
   if(det < 0.0001f)
      return false;


   Vector3D rayPointVec = origin - p1;

   // Test if the ray is behind the plane of the triangle.
   float test1 = rayPointVec.Dot3(cross);

   if(test1 < 0.0f || test1 > det)
```

```
        return false;


    Vector3D cross2;

    cross2 = rayPointVec.CrossProduct(vecAB);
    float test2 = direction.Dot3(cross2);

    // If true then there is not intersection.
    if(test2 < 0.0f || test1 + test2 > det)
        return false;


    // If we get here then the ray hits the triangle.
    float inverseDet = 1.0f / det;

    if(dist != NULL)
    {
        *dist = vecAC.Dot3(cross2);
        *dist *= inverseDet;
    }

    return true;
}
```

The Ray Tracer

The last class that is part of the ray tracing demo application is the ray tracer itself. For the sample demo application in this chapter the ray tracer will have several member variables and functions. For member variables it will have a canvas used for rendering, which will be an array of color objects that were defined earlier in this chapter. It will also have a default color that the buffer will be cleared to, which will be black, and it will also have a resolution and depth. The depth is the distance used for the calculation of the imaginary image plane.

The functions of the ray tracer include a function to render the objects of a scene to the canvas, a trace function that is used by the rendering function to trace an individual ray in the scene for intersection, and functions to save the rendered image to a file and to release any memory used by the ray tracer. Each of these functions will be examined in the following sections. The ray tracer class can be seen in Listing 3.11.

LISTING 3.11 THE RAYTRACER CLASS

```cpp
class RayTracer
{
    public:
        RayTracer(int w, int h, float d) :
                    width(w), height(h), depth(d)
        {
            // Allocate rendering buffer.
            primaryBuffer = new Color3[width * height];
        }

        ~RayTracer()
        {
            Release();
        }

        bool Render(vector<Shape*> &objList);

        bool SaveImage(char *fileName);
        void Release();


    private:
        Color3 Trace(Ray &primaryRay, vector<Shape*> &objList);


    private:
        int width, height;
        float depth;
        Color3 *primaryBuffer;

        // Default to (0, 0, 0) black.
        Color3 defaultColor;
};
```

The first function that will be looked at is the Release() function. It is the smallest function in the entire class and is called by the destructor when the class object is being destroyed. Users can call this function outside of the application as well and it, as far as this demo is concerned, deletes the color buffer for the rendering canvas. The Release() function can be seen in Listing 3.12.

LISTING 3.12 CLEANING UP AFTER THE RAY TRACER

```
void RayTracer::Release()
{
   if(primaryBuffer != NULL)
      {
         delete[] primaryBuffer;
         primaryBuffer = NULL;
      }
}
```

The next function that will be discussed is the rendering function `Render()`. The rendering function takes a list of shapes that makes up the scene and generates an entire scene from it. The function works by using two loops where the outer loop is used to move down the height of the canvas and the inner loop moves across the width. During each pass of the inner loop a ray is calculated based on the pixel being processed and the image depth that was specified for the ray tracer. Once the ray is created the tracing function is called, which will return a color of the closest intersected object. If no objects were intersected, then the default color is returned. The rendering function is fairly straightforward and can be seen in Listing 3.13.

LISTING 3.13 THE CREATION OF PIXEL RAYS

```
bool RayTracer::Render(vector<Shape*> &objList)
{
   // Error checking...
   if(primaryBuffer == NULL)
      return false;


   // The primary ray and the current image pixel.
   Ray primaryRay;
   int index = 0;

   // Starting point for the ray.
   primaryRay.origin = Vector3D(0, 0, -600);


   // Generate image based on ray / object intersections.
   for(int y = 0; y < height; y++)
   {
```

```
for(int x = 0; x < width; x++)
{
    // Get the direction from the view to the pixel.
    primaryRay.direction = Vector3D(x - (float)(width >> 1),
                                    y - (float)(height >> 1),
                                    depth);

    primaryRay.direction.Normalize();

    primaryBuffer[index++] = Trace(primaryRay, objList);
}
}

return true;
}
```

Tracing Rays

The heart of the ray tracer is the tracing of individual rays. In the tracing function of the ray tracer it takes as parameters the ray to be traced and a list of objects. The function loops through every object and performs an intersection test against them and the ray. If an object passes the intersection test then the distance for the point of intersection is examined along with the current minimum distance. If the distance of the intersected object is the smallest distance encountered, then that object is marked as the closest intersected object. Once all objects have been tested the function returns either the color of the closest intersected object or it will return the default color, which would happen if the ray did not intersect any objects. The tracing function for this simple ray tracer boils down to an un-optimized search for the closest intersected object within the loop of the function. General optimizations are the focus of Chapter 15 so here we will focus on getting a simple introduction to ray tracing. The Trace() function can be seen listed in Listing 3.14.

 There are ways to optimize the search for the closest intersected object using topics like spatial partitioning, which will be discussed in Chapter 15.

LISTING 3.14 TRACING INDIVIDUAL RAYS IN THE RAY TRACER

```
Color3 RayTracer::Trace(Ray &ray, vector<Shape*> &objList)
{
   // Closest intersected object and distance.
   float closestDist = 1000000;
   int closestObj = -1;


   // Loop through and find the closest intersection.
   for(int i = 0; i < (int)objList.size(); i++)
   {
      if(objList[i] == NULL)
         continue;

      // Intersection test.
      float dist = 0;

      // If the ray hits this object...
      if(objList[i]->Intersect(ray, &dist) == true)
      {
         // Record if this is the closest object.
         if(dist < closestDist)
         {
            closestDist = dist;
            closestObj = i;
         }
      }
   }


   // Return intersected object (if any).
   if(closestObj != -1)
      return objList[closestObj]->GetColor();

   // Return default color;
   return defaultColor;
}
```

Storing Rendering Results to External Files

At this point the code necessary to perform backward ray tracing has been discussed and seen. The remaining code deals with saving the rendered image to a file and the demo's main.cpp source file. The ray tracer itself has a function called SaveImage(), which takes the location to where the rendered image will be saved to. The function itself calls another function called WriteTGA(), which will create the actual TGA image. Once saved the rendered image can be opened and viewed in any image editor that supports the reading of uncompressed TGA images. The ray tracer's SaveImage() function can be seen listed in Listing 3.15.

LISTING 3.15 SAVING IMAGES FROM THE RAY TRACER

```
bool RayTracer::SaveImage(char *fileName)
{
    return WriteTGA(fileName, width, height,
                    (unsigned char*)primaryBuffer);
}
```

The TGA and DDS image formats will be discussed in detail in Chapter 6, "Mapping Surfaces." For now the function used to write a TGA file takes the file's name, resolution, and the image data. The function saves each part that makes up a standard uncompressed TGA image starting with the file header followed by the image header, which has information such as width, height, image type (i.e., RGB, RGBA, luminance, etc.), and a few other properties, and the function ends by writing out the image data before closing the file and exiting the function. TGA 24-bit images are not in the form of RGB but instead are in the form of BGR. This means that the blue component is written first, then the green, and last the red. This is a property of the image's file format and if we want our image editors to be able to open the file and display the correct colors, the blue and red components must be swapped before the data is saved to the file. That is the purpose of the for-loop that appears near the end of the function. The WriteTGA() function can be seen in Listing 3.16. The TGA file format will be discussed in detail for both reading and writing in Chapter 6.

LISTING 3.16 THE TGA WRITING FUNCTION

```
bool WriteTGA(char *file, int width, int height,
              unsigned char *outImage)
{
   // Uncompressed file header (tgaHeader) and image header.
   unsigned char tgaHeader[12] = {0, 0, 2, 0, 0, 0, 0,
                                  0, 0, 0, 0, 0};
   unsigned char header[6];

   // Open the file and make sure it actually opened.
   FILE *pFile = fopen(file, "wb");

   if(pFile == NULL)
      return false;

   // Number of components and total bits (3 * 8 = 24)
   int colorMode = 3;
   unsigned char bits = 24;

   // Tga header.  Set image width.
   header[0] = width % 256;
   header[1] = width / 256;

   // Set image height.
   header[2] = height % 256;
   header[3] = height / 256;

   // Component bits (RGB).
   header[4] = bits;
   header[5] = 0;

   // Write out TGA file headers.
   fwrite(tgaHeader, sizeof(tgaHeader), 1, pFile);
   fwrite(header, sizeof(header), 1, pFile);

   // Used for color swapping below.
   unsigned char tempColors = 0;

   // Now switch image from RGB to BGR for the TGA file.
   for(int i = 0; i < width * height * colorMode; i +=
   colorMode)
   {
      tempColors = outImage[i];
```

```
        outImage[i] = outImage[i + 2];
        outImage[i + 2] = tempColors;
    }

    // Finally write the image.
    fwrite(outImage, width * height * colorMode, 1, pFile);

    // close the file.
    fclose(pFile);

    return true;
}
```

The Ray Tracer's Main Source File

The last and final part of the ray tracing demo application for this chapter is the main source file. The main source file is also straightforward and it uses an STL vector for the list of objects. Everything that occurs in the main source file occurs in the `main()` function.

The `main()` function starts by defining a vector to store the list of objects and it defines the ray tracer. The function moves on to define two spheres, a triangle, and a plane that will be rendered to the canvas. Once the objects are defined the main function calls the ray tracer's `Render()` function to generate the image, `SaveImage()` function to save the data, and `Release()` to free the ray tracer's used memory. Between each of these calls output text is displayed as a simple form of feedback for when the application is executed. Since ray tracing can take quite a bit of time for some scenes, this allows the user to have an idea of which step the ray tracer is at. Feel free as an exercise to add more feedback information as the image is being rendered to make feedback more useful and frequent. The main.cpp source file from the ray tracing demo application can be seen in Listing 3.17. A screenshot of the rendered results from the demo application can be seen in Figure 3.7.

LISTING 3.17 THE MAIN.CPP SOURCE FILE FOR THE RAY TRACING DEMO

```
#include<iostream>
#include<vector>
#include<algorithm>
#include"Sphere.h"
#include"Plane.h"
#include"Triangle.h"
```

```
#include"RayTracer.h"

using namespace std;


// Used to delete objects in a STL container.
struct DeleteMemObj
{
   template<typename T>
   void operator()(const T* ptr) const
   {
      if(ptr != NULL)
         delete ptr;

      ptr = NULL;
   }
};


int main()
{
   cout << "C++ Ray Tracing..." << endl;
   cout << "Created by Allen Sherrod..." << endl << endl;

   vector<Shape*> objList;
   RayTracer rayTracer(600, 480, 255);


   // Create the green sphere at (-120, 0, 50).
   objList.push_back(new Sphere(Vector3D(-120, 0, 50),
                     100, Color3(0, 255, 0)));

   // Create the blue sphere at (120, 0, 50).
   objList.push_back(new Sphere(Vector3D(120, 0, 50),
                     100, Color3(0, 0, 255)));

   // Create a white plane below the origin.
   objList.push_back(new Plane(Vector3D(0, 1, 0),
                        Vector3D(0, -150, 0),
                        Color3(255, 255, 255)));

   // Create a red triangle behind the spheres.
   objList.push_back(new Triangle(Vector3D(300, -100, 200),
                           Vector3D(-300, -100, 200),
```

```
                                      Vector3D(0, 300, 200),
                                      Color3(255, 0, 0)));

        // Render the scene.
        cout << "Starting trace." << endl;
        rayTracer.Render(objList);
        cout << "Trace over.  Saving Image..." << endl;

        // Take our ray traced scene and save it as a .tga image file.
        rayTracer.SaveImage("RayTracedScene.tga");
        cout << "Traced scene saved...shut down starting..."
            << endl << endl;


        // Release all resources and data we used.
        rayTracer.Release();

        for_each(objList.begin(), objList.end(), DeleteMemObj());


        return 1;
}
```

FIGURE 3.7   A screenshot from the Ray Tracing demo application.

The structure DeleteMemObj is used as a way to delete the dynamic memory from the STL vector using the STL algorithmic function for_each(). Using STL algorithms can give code a performance boost and can be more efficient than using loops. Although such a performance gain is not evident in this demo of three objects, the use of the STL algorithm was chosen to demonstrate how it can be done.

The `for_each()` function takes a starting iterator and ending iterator that specifies the range of elements that are to be operated on and a structure that will be applied on each element. The structure overloads the `operator ()`, which is called for each object specified within the range. We can use this to call delete on the allocated memory elements and to nullify the pointers all in one function call. Since memory was allocated onto the STL vector, it must be destroyed. STL does not do this automatically and it is up to the programmer to figure out how and when the memory is to be freed. In this demo we use the `for_each()` STL algorithm to apply the deletion on each of the allocated objects in the list.

 Unless there is a good reason otherwise, you should always try to use STL algorithms with STL containers, or arrays whenever possible, instead of doing things manually. STL is optimized and efficient and can be used with containers and arrays.

REAL-TIME RAY TRACING

Typically, in ray tracing we are tracing one or more rays for each pixel into the scene and testing intersection against all objects that exist. This process is remarkably straightforward and, as seen in this chapter, requires little code to get a simple ray tracer running on the CPU.

Until now the discussion has been focused on ray tracing for non–real-time applications. Because of the CPU cost of the processing, expensive calculations and operations used in ray tracing, along with the vast number of times these operations are performed, ray tracing has traditionally been considered something that would not be possible in real time for at least the foreseeable future. But because of the advancements in computer hardware and architecture we have reached a point where real time ray tracing is not only possible but it is now an area of research that many find worth exploring. Compared to rasterization, ray tracing still has a ways to go before it can be used in complex scenes for real-time applications such as video games, but progress is being made. Thanks to the increased power of computers the possibility of using real-time ray tracing in a commercial application is approaching a lot more rapidly than many would have assumed a decade or two ago.

Ray Tracing on Multi-Core Processors

The ray tracing algorithm is one that can be run in parallel. This means that the rays that are traced in the scene are independent of one another. During a single rendering frame the information about a scene would be accessed but not manipulated, which would have already been done (e.g., performing physics on the objects in the scene before rendering them). Because the scene information would be read but not written to and since rays are independent of one another it is possible to increase the performance of ray tracing using multi-core processors.

Multi-core processors are being used heavily in today's computers. Most modern computers are equipped with multiple cores. This could mean that a computer has a dual-core (2 processors), triple-core (3 processors, used in the Xbox 360, for example), quad-core (4 processors), oct-core (8 processors), or more inside of it. Each processor in a multi-core chip can run its own instructions in parallel to one another.

In ray tracing it is possible to use a multi-core processor to increase the performance of a rendered scene. For example, using a quad-core processor, such as Intel's Q6600, it is possible to have each processor generating a different section of the image to be rendered. Since a quad-core has four processors the rendering canvas can be divided in quarters.

Multi-core processors are a huge topic in modern game development. By having multiple processors available developers can perform more work in parallel more efficiently than what was done in the past using single-core processors. In ray tracing it can be used to allow for the scene to be rendered much faster. Also, if the processor supports instructions that can be executed on multiple pieces of data in parallel on a single CPU (known as SIMD (Single Instruction Multiple Data) instructions, which are discussed in Chapter 16), then even more performance can be gained from a processor with many of these operations. Vector and matrix mathematics are ideal candidates for SIMD instructions because of their structure and many of their operations.

Rendering Farms

The idea behind using multi-core processors presented in the previous section was that the work needed to generate a scene can be split up and performed in parallel. This works not only for multi-core CPUs but also with multiple computers connected over a network. This is known as a rendering farm and has been used as a way to speed up the rendering of computer-generated scenes for years, most noticeably in the movie and television entertainment industries.

In 2006, Stanford University has brought its Folding@Home distributed computer solution to Sony's Playstation 3. The general idea behind Folding@Home is that individual computer PC, and currently PS3, users can connect their machines to the Folding@Home network using specialized software created by the university. Each machine connected to the network calculates a small piece of a much larger puzzle. For example, some calculations that are being performed involved studying diseases such as Alzheimer's and Huntington's disease, various cancers and other diseases. Although not a rendering farm, Folding@Home is a great example of how many individual computers can work together as a whole on a common goal. In ray tracing this same idea is used in rendering farms where each computer works on a small piece of a larger puzzle. In the case of the movie industry this large puzzle can be an animated film such as Pixar's *Finding Nemo*.

Ray Tracing on the GPU

Previously, it has been mentioned that newer graphics hardware has become more general purpose than their predecessors of the past. Today, graphics hardware such as NVIDIA's GeForce 8800 is capable of calculating physics, raster-based graphics, and, with some cleaver programming, ray tracing. Ray tracing on the GPU are done using programmable graphics shaders such as OpenGL's GLSL and Direct3D's HLSL.

If you want to create a GPU ray tracer, using triangles for example, you could write a shader program that calculates a ray for the current fragment of the screen and performs intersection tests against all objects in view. This shader would be executed on a full-screen-sized quad, which is just a trick you can do to have the graphics hardware process the shader program for each pixel. During the pixel shader you would build a ray out of that pixel's information, you would then take a list of objects that makes up the scene, and you will find the closest intersected object for that pixel. Once found you would shade the pixel however you decide is appropriate.

The main question is how to you get a large list of primitives to the GPU. One easy way to pass this information along is in a texture. Let's assume your GPU ray tracer is only tracing triangles. One option you have is to store each piece of information about the triangle that you will need in a different pixel of a texture image. For example, if you needed to supply three vertices and a normal for every triangle, then the first three pixels could store the three vertices and the fourth can store the normal. That means that every four pixels of a texture image specify a different triangle.

There are still limitations to this. First, it would be important to use floating-point textures for precision with the triangle's information. Secondly, you will need a shader profile that allows you to access the pixels of a texture image freely in a loop. Another major limitation is texturing the surfaces of triangles or using multiple materials. Most GPU ray tracers that you can see across the Internet do not worry about texturing their primitives unless it is a procedural (dynamically generated) texture since it would be extremely difficult, assuming if even possible or efficient, to allow each primitive to have its own separate texture image applied to it.

With some clever thinking and programming it is more than possible to create a ray tracer on today's graphics hardware and even the last few generations of hardware. There are many individuals across the Internet performing GPU ray tracing on off-the-shelf hardware and it could make for a fun and interesting programming project.

Ray Tracing Hardware

Ray tracing hardware is also being researched and developed by various companies and universities. Saarland University has developed and published two designs they call the SaarCor and the RPU (ray tracing processing unit). Saarland University presented its ray tracing hardware at the 2004 and 2005 Siggraph. Although there are no commercially available real-time ray tracers to date, there are people working on developing such technology. These dedicated ray tracing hardware devices show a lot of promise and can be an indication of what's to come in the future for gaming and computer graphics as a whole.

Additional Ray Tracing Topics

There are other ways to improve the performance of ray tracing. A few of these methods include but are not limited to the following:

- Spatial partitioning
- Down-sampling (also known as subsampling)
- Precomputed scene information such as light maps, ambient occlusion maps, and so forth
- Limiting ray maximums
- Limiting recursion depths for topics such as reflections, refractions, and so forth
- Using lookup tables such as cube maps to perform reflections and refractions, which can otherwise dramatically increase the ray count
- Using varying levels-of-detail with polygonal objects based on their positional relationship with the camera

Each of these topics will be discussed in Chapter 15. For example, spatial partitioning is the process of dividing a scene into multiple sections where these sections are used to quickly determine if specific calculations need to be operated on them or not. An example of this can be seen in rendering where each whole section can be tested to see if it lies within the camera's view in order to determine if that geometry should be rendered or not.

SUMMARY

Ray tracing is a fascinating topic in computer graphics. The purpose of this chapter was not to create a ray tracer as much as it was to serve as a simple exercise for those unfamiliar with ray tracing concepts. In later chapters we'll use some of these concepts to create various effects that have become standard in the gaming industry. One of these effects is to precompute the lighting and shadowing information of a scene in a special texture known as a light map. By using ray tracing principles we can create a tool that can generate these images offline and can be mapped using straightforward and standard texture mapping at run-time.

In this chapter we discussed the following information related to ray tracing:

- What ray tracing is
- What forward ray tracing is
- What backward ray tracing is
- How to implement a simple CPU ray tracer
- Real-time ray tracing

CHAPTER QUESTIONS

Answers to the following chapter review questions can be found in Appendix A, "Answers to Chapter Questions," at the end of this book.

1. What is ray tracing?
2. What is forward ray tracing?
3. What is backward ray tracing?
4. List at least three benefits to using backward ray tracing over forward ray tracing.
5. What is another name for a backward ray tracer?
    A. Forward ray tracer
    B. CPU ray tracer
    C. GPU ray tracer
    D. Ray caster
6. List the first three steps needed to test a sphere for intersection using the algorithm presented in this chapter.
7. List the first three steps needed to test a plane for intersection using the algorithm presented in this chapter.
8. List the first three steps needed to test a triangle for intersection using the algorithm presented in this chapter.
9. List three disadvantages to using forward ray tracing.
10. List three advantages to using backward ray tracing.

11. If you have the distance of an intersection, how do you calculate the point of intersection using that and a ray?
12. Which of these would NOT increase the number of rays that are traced in a scene?
    A. Reflections
    B. Refractions
    C. Anti-aliasing
    D. Depth-of-Field
    E. None of the above
13. Describe how the multi-core CPUs can help the performance of a CPU ray traced scene.
14. What is a server farm?
    A. Another term for a computer with multiple processors.
    B. A collection of machines working on a problem.
    C. Another term for a super computer.
    D. None of the above
15. True or false: Forward ray tracing is generally more efficient than backward ray tracing.
16. True or false: Another term for a forward ray tracer is ray castering.
17. True or false: Line-of-sight uses some properties of ray tracing.
18. True or false: Backward ray tracing traces rays from the light to the camera instead of the camera to the light.
19. True or false: There exists ray tracing hardware along with graphics rendering hardware and physics processing hardware.
20. True or false: It is not possible to perform ray tracing on modern graphics hardware.
21. True or false: The point of intersection can be found by moving a ray's origin it the ray's direction for a specified distance.
22. True or false: Spheres are faster to intersect with a ray than boxes but not as fast as triangles.
23. True or false: Computer animated movies use real-time ray tracing.
24. True or false: Real-time ray tracing can be done today.
25. True or false: Ray tracing can be done on modern graphics cards.

CHAPTER EXERCISES

Exercise 1: Create your own ray traced scene with 4 spheres of varying sizes inside a box made of polygons.

Exercise 2: Extend the CPU ray tracer to include the ability to intersect boxes. Add two small boxes to the scene you've created in Exercise 1.

Exercise 3: Extend the application you've created in Exercise 2 and add the ability to load shapes from a file. Create a simple text file format that reads each shapes, information line by line. Give each shape type a unique ID so that your application can read that ID first, which will allow it to know what information to read afterward. For example, giving a sphere shape an ID of "SPHERE" would allow you to specify a line of text that looks like the following example:

```
SPHERE 0 0 0 100 255 255 0
```

Where "SPHERE" is the ID, the next three values are the center position X, Y, and Z axis, the 100 is the radius, and the last three values are the sphere's color.

4

RASTERIZATION

In This Chapter

- Software Rendering
- Rasterizing Primitives
- Rendering Buffers
- Additional Rasterization Topics
- OpenGL
- Hardware Rendering with Direct3D 9 and 10

Modern video games use rasterization techniques to generate computer images that are displayed to the screen. In computer graphics there are usually two general types of computer-generated imagery: software generated, which means the application does its processing internally on the CPU, and hardware-generated by a dedicated device such as a graphics cards that is used for the generation of each rendered frame. Rasterization techniques are generally more complex to implement than most equivalent ray tracing techniques but can be performed fast enough on modern hardware to be done in real time. Because of its speed and efficiency, rasterization is the technique of choice for the video games industry. This speed does come at a cost since many effects are often trickier or harder to realistically implement using rasterization than with other techniques such as ray tracing, and often developers must sacrifice quality for performance when rendering scenes. A simple example of this can be seen with performing reflections on surfaces, where in ray tracing the primary ray being traced is reflected using a simple vector equation against the ray's direction and the intersection point's normal. In rasterization it is not that simple and can require methods such as texture mapping, dynamic cube mapping, and multiple rendering targets (MRT).

ON THE CD

In this chapter we discuss and implement examples of software and hardware rendering. The software rendering discussion is used to provide a hands-on look at rasterization beyond API function calls that are used in technologies such as OpenGL and Direct3D. This discussion is limited to the basics since a complete rasterization rendering system would be complex and can span one or more books on its own. In the games industry, and for the remainder of this book, we focus on hardware rendering and, when appropriate, ray tracing algorithms. Hardware rendering in this book is done using both Direct3D 9 and 10, which are part of Microsoft's DirectX technology framework, and OpenGL 2.0. Experimenting with software rendering yourself can allow you to gain a different perspective and appreciation for rendering graphics than having only experienced making calls to OpenGL or Direct3D. Since many Windows-based PC users have Direct3D 9 compatible hardware over Direct3D 10, both Direct3D 9 and 10 samples are provided on the CD-ROM, so no user is left out. OpenGL is used for Windows, Mac, and Linux users. In the book the focus is on shaders, and the rendering of objects is straightforward enough that it is assumed that you already know how to perform it using the API of your choice.

This book assumes that you are familiar with either Direct3D or OpenGL. You do not need to be an expert in either of these technologies, but because this is an intermediate-level book, it is assumed that you've used at least one of these.

SOFTWARE RENDERING

Software rendering is slow compared to hardware rendering. In software rendering everything that is displayed is calculated on the computer's CPU. In hardware rendering the CPU offloads the task of creating a rendered image to another processor known as the GPU (graphics processing unit). Freeing up the graphical responsibility from the CPU and giving it to the GPU allows the CPU to focus on other video game tasks such as artificial intelligence, decompression, physics, memory management, networking, and so forth, which can take place in parallel to the GPU.

Because of the recent advancements of GPU devices, the "G" in GPU is sometimes referred to as general *instead of* graphics. *This is because modern GPUs, such as NVIDIA's GeForce 8800, are capable of more than graphics processing. A few examples of such abilities of newer GPUs include the ability to calculate physics, complex mathematical equations (check out NVIDIA's CUBA for more information), and animations, to name a few.*

Graphics hardware is faster than the CPU at rendering graphics because graphical devices are optimized for the various algorithms and requirements that are used in rasterization, whereas the CPU is a general-purpose processor. Being able to tailor a device to process a specific set of algorithms in an optimized manner can often allow the device to perform said tasks much more efficiently than their general processing counterparts. Ageia's physics processing device, Physx, specializes in the algorithms and requirements of real-time physics, collision detections, and responses. Although its use is not as profound as graphics hardware and is often optional in games that support it, it serves the same purpose by allowing the CPU to offload some of its work to another processor so it can focus on other tasks in parallel.

Ageia's Physx API is capable of running on the CPU or, if the framework detects it, the Physx processor.

In today's marketplace there is little need to use software rendering in a video game because of the benefits and accessibility of GPU devices. Cell phones and PDAs are also starting to take advantage of graphics hardware. In the early days of video games, software rendering took on a larger role because of the early rise and availability of commercial graphics hardware. Today, to create a cutting-edge video game, the use of graphics hardware is a necessity for 3D applications.

In this section, and in this book, the goal is not to create a complete commercial software rendering system. Instead we discuss the software rendering topics in this chapter to give you hands-on experience with rasterization by creating a few simple software rendering demo applications. With the information in this chapter, along with the information in the remainder of this book, if you choose to, you will be able to expand upon the software rendering code developed throughout this chapter (and preferably redesign it) to create something more sophisticated. Having created your own software rendering system might look good on a resume, but in the games industry the primary focus is on hardware rendering, which is discussed later in this chapter and throughout the remainder of this book.

Software rendering still exists today, although it is rarely used in a commercial 3D product. Direct3D, which is part of Microsoft's DirectX framework, offers the option to place Direct3D in software rendering mode. This can be useful for programmers looking to test features of Direct3D that their hardware does not support. However, outside of testing, software rendering in Direct3D has little use since the rendering of even a relatively small number of triangles in Direct3D 10 can bring down the frame rate considerably.

CPU Software Rendering

Software rendering involves processes that allow the application to create CG images using the CPU processor. In video games the CPU has the added responsibility to process other data such as artificial intelligence and so forth as mentioned earlier in this chapter. Having to handle the graphics can burden the CPU with work that it is not optimized to handle efficiently. In 3D games the impact of software rendering can be more profound than in most 2D games mostly because the detail and the amount of data and processing in modern 3D games far exceed what is commonly seen in 2D games.

Hardware rendering exists in the form of dedicated devices used for the creation of a rendered scene, although they are starting to take on other roles. These devices often have special optimizations and features that make them more efficient than the CPU at graphics rendering. Although CPU processors are very fast, devices that are designed for specific tasks are often more efficient than general-purpose processors since assumptions can be made during the algorithms and short cuts can be taken. One such device is NVIDIA's DirectX 10 compatible GeForce 8800 PCI-Express graphics board.

In Chapter 3, "Ray Tracing," a scene was rendered on the CPU. In the following sections we create similar demo applications but using different algorithms on the CPU. In the ray tracing chapter we only rendered a single frame, but in this chapter we attempt to render multiple frames in succession, as is a requirement of a real-time video game.

A frame is what is referred to as a single rendering of a scene. The number of times your application is able to render frames in a second is known as the frames per second, or FPS.

RASTERIZING PRIMITIVES

Rasterization is the process of transforming data, which in video games are often three-point polygons known as triangles, into a 2D representation. This 2D representation is clipped to the screen's viewport and is drawn using scan-line conversion. When discussing 3D geometry, the geometry is transformed, as mentioned in Chapter 2, "2D and 3D Graphics," by a series of matrices that, when combined, form a virtual representation of how to convert data from one space to another space. Once a primitive is transformed to screen space, which is the space where data is specified in screen pixel locations, it is clipped to the screen bounds, and the region of the screen that corresponds to the primitive is processed. During this processing all pixels that make up the primitive being drawn are shaded appropriately.

In backward ray tracing we process all objects for each pixel that makes up the screen in order to determine how the pixel is to be shaded. In rasterization we find the range of pixels that corresponds to an individual primitive and we shade those pixels appropriately. Although these methods sound similar, they are different in their operation. In rasterization you look at a single primitive at a time, while in ray tracing you look at all objects at the same time when trying to shade a pixel, especially when factors like reflections and refractions are involved.

 In this section we discuss each of these steps and implement various demo applications that perform them on the CPU. The full implementation for each of the chapter demo applications can be found on the book's accompanying CD-ROM in the Chapter 4 folder.

ON THE CD

Clipping

Clipping in rasterization means to literally clip the data that need to be rendered to the area that makes up a screen. This has two main purposes. The first purpose is to handle the case when data outside of the viewport are out of range. When using an array to render the canvas, you can receive an "out-of-bounds" logic error if the out-of-range data aren't taken care of and you try to set elements beyond the array's range. The second, and main, purpose is to avoid processing data that are not within the viewport of the screen. Modern video games use various techniques that require a number of operations to be performed on each pixel that is shaded. One example is normal mapping, which has become a common technique that is discussed in Chapter 8, "Lighting and Materials." Clipping primitive data early can avoid the processing of data that are not within view, which is essential for large polygons that would take up a considerable region. Figure 4.1 shows a visual example of this.

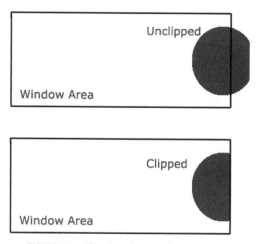

FIGURE 4.1   Clipping data to the viewport.

Various clipping algorithms exist for various primitives in rasterization. In this chapter we look at drawing lines and triangles, along with points, and discuss clipping in their respective sections.

Scan-Line Conversion

In the ray tracing demos in Chapter 3 each object was tested against each ray that made up the scene. No attempts at optimizations were made in these demos, but, optimizations aside, some rays that were tested against some objects could have had no way of intersecting. In rasterization one of the processes is to define a bounding rectangle that encloses the pixel area range where a polygon is to be drawn. That way the only pixels processed are the ones that can, most likely, fall within the area of the primitive. This is shown in Figure 4.2.

FIGURE 4.2   Defining a bounding rectangle around a primitive.

Every row of pixels that are processed is known as a scan-line. As each line is scanned, the pixels that make up the line are shaded as necessary. When all of the rows of lines that make up the rectangular area have been processed, the primitive is considered drawn to the screen's canvas.

In the ray tracing demos in Chapter 3 the closest intersected primitive is found before a pixel is shaded. In rasterization, by default using no other techniques, there is no way to determine if a primitive has already been drawn in a location or if the existing primitive is closer or further than the primitive currently being rendered. This leads to what is known as pixel overdraw and can be a serious performance bottleneck problem in video games. Id Software had pixel overdraw problems during the development of *Quake* in the mid-1990s, which they solved using very cleaver data structures and algorithms. This method has had an impact on the gaming industry to this day. *Quake* relied on data structures such as binary space partitioning trees and potential visibility sets.

These issues are not without solutions, as seen in the advancements the original *Quake* game made when it was released. Another solution to solving the problem of drawing objects in the correct order is to use the Z buffer algorithm. This is a very common technique used in video games and is currently a standard feature in major graphical APIs, which we discuss in more detail later in this chapter. Other solutions to drawing primitives in the correct order, or to attempting to minimize or eliminate pixel overdraw, include binary space partitioning trees, potential visibility sets, and other data structures and algorithms that have become commonplace in the video games industry, each of which is discussed in Chapter 15, "Optimization." In the following sections we discuss the implementation of the following rasterization topics:

- Creating, clearing, and displaying a rendering canvas
- Drawing pixels
- Drawing lines
- Drawing triangles
- Secondary buffers
- Transformations and spaces

We also discuss other important rendering topics such as depth (Z) buffers, stencil buffers, back-face culling, and triple buffering. This chapter gives you introductory hands-on experience with raster-based rendering but does not aim to create a complete or commercial rendering system.

Creating, Clearing, and Displaying the Canvas

ON THE CD

In this section we discuss how to implement the creation, clearing, and display of a rendering canvas. The accompanying CD-ROM includes a demo application in the Chapter 4 folder called Blank Window, which performs each of these implementation goals.

The design of these demos is simple, so as to make them easier to understand and follow. This demo uses a class called SoftwareCanvas to represent the software rendering system. This class stores the width and height resolution of the rendering surface that is drawn along with an array of red, green, and blue color values that make up the rendering surface. The color array is of type Color3, which was first discussed in Chapter 2 and is displayed to the screen after each frame has been processed.

The SoftwareCanvas class has a member function used to clear the rendering surface as well as access functions for its private members. Clearing a rendering canvas means setting each color that makes up the canvas to a specified color. In OpenGL this is done with the glClear() function, which can be used to clear various OpenGL buffers in addition to the color buffer (canvas), after calling glClearColor() to specify what color glClear() will use on the color buffer. In Direct3D this can be done using the Direct3D device's member function Clear(). In the SoftwareCanvas class the function Clear() takes a color value as a parameter and sets the entire buffer to that value. The SoftwareCanvas class is shown in Listing 4.1.

LISTING 4.1 THE SOFTWARE RENDERING CLASS SoftwareCanvas

```
class SoftwareCanvas
{
   public:
      SoftwareCanvas(int width, int height) : resWidth(width),
                                              resHeight(height)
      {
         primaryBuffer = new Color3[width * height];
      }
```

```cpp
        ~SoftwareCanvas()
        {
           if(primaryBuffer != NULL)
           {
              delete[] primaryBuffer;
              primaryBuffer = NULL;
           }
        }


        void Clear(Color3 &col)
        {
           if(primaryBuffer == NULL)
              return;

           for(int i = 0; i < resWidth * resHeight; i++)
           {
              primaryBuffer[i] = col;
           }
        }


        char *GetRender()
        {
           return (char*)primaryBuffer;
        }


        int GetWidth()
        {
           return resWidth;
        }


        int GetHeight()
        {
           return resHeight;
        }


    private:
        Color3 *primaryBuffer;
        int resWidth, resHeight;
};
```

The code in Listing 4.1 is all that is required to create a blank window application using software rendering. The only remaining obstacle is how to display the results to the window. In this book there are demo applications for Windows, Mac, and Linux-based PCs, none of which use a cross-platform standard for application creation. Since this is an intermediate-level book, it is assumed you are familiar with creating and working with windows and applications for your operating system of choice. In this section we take a look at the Windows-based code for a quick example. You can find the Blank Window demo implementation for Windows, Mac, and Linux on the book's accompanying CD-ROM.

ON THE CD

The main functions for the Blank Window demo application are the Initialize() and RenderScene() functions. For now, each of these functions are empty with the exception of the RenderScene() function, and serve as a placeholder for upcoming demos. In the RenderScene() function the Clear() function of the rendering canvas is used. Since the method of displaying image information in OS-based applications varies from OS to OS, the rendering function of this demo is only responsible for generating the image and storing the results internally in the rendering canvas class. The main demo application functions for the Blank Window demo are shown in Listing 4.2.

LISTING 4.2 THE MAIN BLANK WINDOW DEMO APPLICATION FUNCTIONS (WIN32 VERSION)

```
#include<windows.h>
#include"../Canvas.h"

#define WINDOW_NAME     "Software Rendering Blank Window"
#define WINDOW_WIDTH    640
#define WINDOW_HEIGHT   480


SoftwareCanvas canvas(WINDOW_WIDTH, WINDOW_HEIGHT);


bool Initialize()
{
   return true;
}
```

```
void RenderScene()
{
    canvas.Clear(Color3(255, 0, 0));
}
```

Color3 *was first discussed in Chapter 2 and is a simple class that stores three bytes, with one byte for a color's red, one for the green, and one for the blue component.*

As mentioned previously, we look at the Win32 Windows-based implementation as an example of displaying the contents of a rendering to the screen. Win32 applications consist generally of two functions: one for the application entry, called WinMain(), and one for the message callback. The message callback function is called by the application whenever it receives a message from the operating system. A message that the application can receive from the operating system that is of interest to us is a message informing the application that it must redraw its window. In response to this message we can use various Windows-based functions to take the rendering of the scene and display it across the surface of the window. During the application loop, which we look at next, we can force paint messages to be passed to the application. The Windows callback function is shown in Listing 4.3 with the paint message handler along with a handler for when the user attempts to quit or close the application and when a key press is detected, which in this case looks for the escape key to quit the program.

LISTING 4.3 WINDOWS PROCEDURE CALLBACK FUNCTION

```
LRESULT CALLBACK WndProc(HWND hwnd, UINT m, WPARAM wp, LPARAM lp)
{
    HDC hdc, canvasHdc;
    PAINTSTRUCT paintStruct;
    HBITMAP canvasBitmap;

    switch(m)
    {
        case WM_PAINT:

            hdc = BeginPaint(hwnd, &paintStruct);

            canvasBitmap = CreateCompatibleBitmap(hdc,
                canvas.GetWidth(), canvas.GetHeight());
```

```
BITMAPINFO bm;
memset(&bm.bmiHeader, 0, sizeof(BITMAPINFOHEADER));
bm.bmiHeader.biBitCount = 24;
bm.bmiHeader.biCompression = BI_RGB;
bm.bmiHeader.biHeight = canvas.GetHeight();
bm.bmiHeader.biPlanes = 1;
bm.bmiHeader.biSize = sizeof(BITMAPINFOHEADER);
bm.bmiHeader.biWidth = canvas.GetWidth();


SetDIBits(hdc, canvasBitmap, 0, canvas.GetHeight(),
        (void*)canvas.GetRender(), &bm,
              DIB_RGB_COLORS);

canvasHdc = CreateCompatibleDC(hdc);
SelectObject(canvasHdc, canvasBitmap);

BitBlt(hdc, 0, 0, canvas.GetWidth(),
                  canvas.GetHeight(),
       canvasHdc, 0, 0, SRCCOPY);


DeleteDC(canvasHdc);
DeleteObject(canvasBitmap);

EndPaint(hwnd, &paintStruct);

break;


case WM_CLOSE:
case WM_DESTROY:

  PostQuitMessage(0);
  return 0;

  break;


case WM_KEYDOWN:
  switch(wp)
  {
  case VK_ESCAPE:
```

```
              PostQuitMessage(0);

              break;

          default:
              break;
      }
      break;


    default:
        break;
  }

  // Pass remaining messages to default handler.
  return (DefWindowProc(hwnd, m, wp, lp));
}
```

For the Win32 implementation of the Blank Window demo the only remaining code is the application's main entry point, the `WinMain()` function. This function calls each of the demo functions from Listing 4.2. After each time the scene is rendered, a call to the Win32 function `InvalidateRect()` is issued to force the window to update itself, which means a `WM_PAINT` message is triggered and is handled in the callback function from Listing 4.3. The Blank Window demo application's main entry point function is shown in Listing 4.4.

LISTING 4.4 THE BLANK WINDOW APPLICATION'S ENTRY POINT

```
int WINAPI WinMain(HINSTANCE hInstance, HINSTANCE prev,
        LPSTR cmd, int show)
{
  MSG msg;

  // Describes a window.
  WNDCLASSEX windowClass;
  memset(&windowClass, 0, sizeof(WNDCLASSEX));
  windowClass.cbSize = sizeof(WNDCLASSEX);
  windowClass.style = CS_OWNDC | CS_HREDRAW | CS_VREDRAW;
  windowClass.lpfnWndProc = WndProc;
  windowClass.hInstance = hInstance;
  windowClass.hIcon = LoadIcon(NULL, IDI_APPLICATION);
  windowClass.hCursor = LoadCursor(NULL, IDC_ARROW);
```

```
        windowClass.hbrBackground =
                (HBRUSH)GetStockObject(BLACK_BRUSH);
        windowClass.lpszClassName = "APPCLASS";
        windowClass.hIconSm = LoadIcon(NULL, IDI_APPLICATION);


        if(!RegisterClassEx(&windowClass))
           return 0;



        // Create the window.
        HWND hwnd = CreateWindowEx(WS_EX_OVERLAPPEDWINDOW,
                                  "APPCLASS",
                                  WINDOW_NAME,
                                  WS_OVERLAPPEDWINDOW |
                                  WS_VISIBLE | WS_SYSMENU |
                                  WS_CLIPCHILDREN |
                                  WS_CLIPSIBLINGS,
                                  100, 100, WINDOW_WIDTH,
                                  WINDOW_HEIGHT, 0, 0,
                                  hInstance,
                                  NULL);

        if(!hwnd)
           return 0;



        ShowWindow(hwnd, SW_SHOW);
        UpdateWindow(hwnd);



        // If initialize fail, then we don't want the program to run.
        if(!Initialize())
        {
           MessageBox(NULL, "Error in initialize!", "Error", MB_OK);
        }
        else
        {
           // This is the messsage loop.
           while(1)
           {
              if(PeekMessage(&msg, 0, 0, 0, PM_REMOVE))
              {
                 // If a quit message then break;
```

```
            if(msg.message == WM_QUIT)
                break;

            TranslateMessage(&msg);
            DispatchMessage(&msg);
        }
        else
        {
            RenderScene();
            InvalidateRect(hwnd, NULL, false);
        }
    }
}

// Unregister the class.
UnregisterClass("APPCLASS", windowClass.hInstance);

return (int)msg.wParam;
}
```

Compiling, building, and executing the Blank Window demo application displays a window that is bright red, which is the color specified during the call to `Clear()` in the `RenderScene()` function. By changing the clear color you can change what is displayed to the window. Although the rendering results are static, that is, the results do not change from frame to frame, the application still renders multiple frames per second, which is a major requirement for all types of video games. A screenshot of the Blank Window demo application is shown in Figure 4.3.

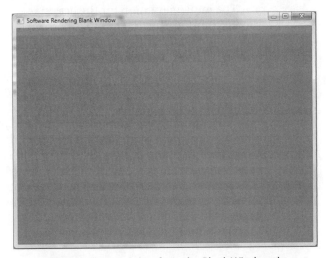

FIGURE 4.3   A screenshot from the Blank Window demo.

Drawing Pixels

The first operation to be added to the software rendering system is the ability to plot individual pixels. The plotting of a pixel can go a long way to generating any type of computer-generated image. Since drawing individual pixels is trivial, we discuss it here first.

The plotting of a pixel requires a color to be set for the pixel at the pixel's location. In the software rendering system for this chapter we can perform this using a function called DrawPixel(), which takes the X and Y position for the pixel's location along with the desired color. The added function prototypes for drawing individual pixels to the software rendering class are shown in Listing 4.5.

LISTING 4.5 THE FUNCTION ADDED TO THE SoftwareCanvas CLASS FOR DRAWING PIXELS

```
class SoftwareCanvas
{
    public:
        void DrawPixel(Point2D &pos, const Color3 &col);
        void DrawPixel(int width, int height, const Color3 &col);
};
```

 Point2D *is a simple class that stores two integer variables for the X and Y position of a point. Along with* Color3 *it was first discussed in Chapter 2.*

The implementation for the DrawPixel() function starts by calculating the location for the pixel that is being colored. Since the canvas is a 1D array, the location can be found by multiplying the pixel's height by the total width of the canvas, which will give you the starting row for the pixel, plus the width location of the pixel, which when added to the starting row gives you the pixel's column and final position. Before the color for the pixel is set, a conditional test is used to make sure that (a) memory is allocated for the canvas and (b) the pixel's location is not out of bounds. The implementation for the pixel-drawing functions is shown in Listing 4.6. Clipping is the processes of truncating a primitive to the window. Since a pixel is either in or out of the window, clipping cannot occur on an individual pixel because moving the pixel point by forcing it along the edge of the window does not give the desired effect. Instead, testing if the pixel is in bounds is enough.

LISTING 4.6 IMPLEMENTATION FOR THE PIXEL-DRAWING FUNCTIONS

```cpp
void SoftwareCanvas::DrawPixel(Point2D &pos, const Color3 &col)
{
   DrawPixel(pos.x, pos.y, col);
}



void SoftwareCanvas::DrawPixel(int width, int height,
                               const Color3 &col)
{
   if(primaryBuffer == NULL)
      return;

   int location = height * resWidth + width;

   if(location < 0 || location >= (resWidth * resHeight))
      return;

   primaryBuffer[location] = col;
}
```

Drawing Lines

In this section we look at drawing lines in the software rendering system. A line is defined by two end points. When drawing a line to the canvas, the idea is to shade each pixel that corresponds to each end point of the line and to shade any pixels that fall along the line's slope between those two points. The drawing of a line can fall within one of three situations: the line is completely outside of the canvas, the line is completely inside of the canvas, or the line is partially inside and outside the canvas. Lines that span the bounds of the canvas must be clipped.

ON THE CD

The software rendering class adds two functions for the drawing of a line and the clipping of a line, which would only need to be called internally by the drawing function. The added functions are shown in Listing 4.7. The book's accompanying CD-ROM contains a demo called Lines in the Chapter 4 folder that demonstrates the drawing of a line using the algorithm that will be discussed in the upcoming section.

LISTING 4.7 FUNCTIONS ADDED TO THE SoftwareCanvas CLASS FOR LINES

```
class SoftwareCanvas
{
   public:
      void DrawLine(const Point2D &start, const Point2D &end,
                    const Color3 &col);


   private:
      bool ClipLine(Point2D &start, Point2D &end);
};
```

To draw a line the demo uses Bresenham's algorithm. The algorithm clips lines that span the boundaries of the canvas by determining which area each point falls on. A point can be to the left, top, right, bottom, and between each corner of the canvas.

To draw a line the points are first clipped to the canvas. Once the points are clipped, the slope of the line is determined and the pixels from the starting position to the ending position are shaded along the slope. Using the slope of a line allows the line to be rendered smoothly between the points.

To draw the line we can use the DrawPixel() function from earlier in this chapter and a loop that travels along the slope until it reaches the end. The implementation for the DrawLine() function is shown in Listing 4.8.

LISTING 4.8 IMPLEMENTATION OF THE FUNCTIONS USED FOR DRAWING LINES

```
void SoftwareCanvas::DrawLine(const Point2D &start,
                const Point2D &end,
                const Color3 &col)
{
   if(primaryBuffer == NULL)
      return;

   // We don't want to alter the original data.
   Point2D newStart = start;
   Point2D newEnd = end;
```

```
// Clip the line to fall within the screen.
if(ClipLine(newStart, newEnd) == false)
return;


// Get the line of the slope.
double slope = (double)(newEnd.y - newStart.y) /
               (double)(newEnd.x - newStart.x);

// Just so we can use double when adding slope.
double y = newStart.y;


// Loop through the pixel that makes up the line and draw.
for(int x = newStart.x; x <= newEnd.x; x++)
{
    DrawPixel(Point2D(x, (int)(y + 0.5)), col);
    y = y + slope;
}
}
```

The code for the clipping of a line looks long, but the idea is fairly straightforward and is composed of a lot of similar operations that are performed on both points of the line. The function starts by determining which area of the canvas the line falls on. If the line is determined to be either completely outside or within the canvas, there is nothing the clip function can do to the geometry, so the function is free to return. If the line is not completely on one side, each of the line points that exist outside of the canvas is moved based on the area it is on. For points that lie on multiple sides (corners) a loop is used to ensure that the function doesn't return until each point is completely clipped to the canvas. Although the code is long, it is composed of nested conditional statements. This means only a few operations of the whole function are actually executed. Since the operations are not expensive, this clipping algorithm is not slow. The implementation for the ClipLine() function is shown in Listing 4.9.

LISTING 4.9 FUNCTION USED TO CLIP A LINE TO THE VIEWPORT

```
bool SoftwareCanvas::ClipLine(Point2D &start, Point2D &end)
{
    double slope = (double)(end.y - start.y) /
                   (double)(end.x - start.x);
```

```
int clipS = 0, clipE = 0;

// Loop while at least one point is outside the canvas.
do
{
   // Location tests for the start point.
   clipS = ((start.x < 0) << 3) | ((start.x >= resWidth) << 2) |
            ((start.y < 0) << 1) | (start.y >= resHeight);

   // Location tests for the end point.
   clipE = ((end.x < 0) << 3) | ((end.x >= resWidth) << 2) |
            ((end.y < 0) << 1) | (end.y >= resHeight);


   // The line is completely outside of the canvas.
   if(clipS & clipE)
      return false;


   // If the start is outside then clip it based on location.
   if(clipS)
   {
      // Left side.
      if(clipS & 8)
      {
         start.y -= (int)((double)start.x * slope);
         start.x = 0;
      }
      else
      {
         // Right side.
         if(clipS & 4)
         {
            start.y += (int)((double)(resWidth - start.x) *
                        slope);

            start.x = resWidth - 1;
         }
         else
         {
            // Top side.
            if(clipS & 2)
            {
               start.x -= (int)((double)start.y / slope);
```

```
            start.y = 0;
        }
        else
        {
            // Bottom side.
            if(clipS & 1)
            {
                start.x += (int)((double)(resHeight -
                        start.y) / slope);

                start.y = resHeight - 1;
            }
        }
    }
}


// Clip end point if it is anywhere outside of the canvas.
if(clipE)
{
    // Left side.
    if(clipE & 8)
    {
        end.y += (int)((double)(0 - end.x) * slope);

        end.x = 0;
    }
    else
    {
        // Right side.
        if(clipE & 4)
        {
            end.y += (int)((double)(resWidth - end.x) * slope);

            end.x = resWidth - 1;
        }
        else
        {
            // Top side.
            if(clipE & 2)
            {
                end.x += (int)((double)(0 - end.y) / slope);
```

```
                end.y = 0;
            }
            else
            {
                // Bottom side.
                if(clipE & 1)
                {
                    end.x += (int)((double)(resHeight - end.y) /
                            slope);

                    end.y = resHeight - 1;
                }
            }
        }
    }
} while(clipS | clipE);

return true;
}
```

The last code that needs to be examined from the Lines demo application is the RenderScene() function. The rendering function purposely draws a line that is not completely outside of or within the rendering canvas. The RenderScene() function from the Lines demo application is shown in Listing 4.10. A screenshot of the Lines demo application in action is shown in Figure 4.4.

LISTING 4.10 RenderScene() FUNCTION FROM THE LINES DEMO APPLICATION

```
void RenderScene()
{
    canvas.Clear(Color3(0, 0, 0));

    canvas.DrawLine(Point2D(-100, 310), Point2D(150, 100),
            Color3(255, 255, 255));
}
```

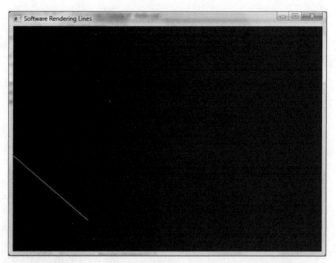

FIGURE 4.4   A screenshot of the Lines demo application.

Drawing Polygons

Drawing polygons, triangles in this section, can be a little more involved with some algorithms than drawing a line. On the book's accompanying CD-ROM is a demo application called Triangles in the Chapter 4 folder that demonstrates the rendering of a triangle using the CPU software rendering system. The functions added to the software rendering system appear in Listing 4.11.

LISTING 4.11 NEW FUNCTIONS ADDED FOR THE RENDERING OF TRIANGLES

```
inline int FindMin(int a, int b, int c)
{
   return ((a < b) ? ((a < c) ? a : c) : ((b < c) ? b : c));
}


inline int FindMax(int a, int b, int c)
{
   return ((a > b) ? ((a > c) ? a : c) : ((b > c) ? b : c));
}
```

```
class SoftwareCanvas
{
   public:
      void DrawPixelTriangle(const Point2D &p1, const Point2D &p2,
                             const Point2D &p3, const Color3 &col);
};
```

The algorithm used to draw the triangle has a few steps. The first step is to define a bounding rectangle that surrounds the triangle primitive. This rectangle tells us what area we need to focus the algorithm on, and the rest of the canvas can be ignored. Because we are dealing with a bounding rectangle, it is easy to clip the rectangle to the bounds of the canvas by ensuring that the maximum X and Y axis is not greater than the width and height, respectively, of the canvas and by ensuring that the minimum X and Y axes are not less than 0.

For the Triangles demo we define a triangle in screen space. In a game situation you would project the triangle's vertices by the model-view projection matrix and use the projected data with the code developed in the following section. Transforming a vector against a matrix is a very common and straightforward operation in video games. For now we focus on the difficult task of rasterizing a triangle's projected geometry data.

Once the bounding rectangle is found and once it is clipped to the bounds of the screen, the last step is to loop through each pixel of the bounding rectangle and shade each pixel appropriately. Pixels that do not fall within the triangle's area are unaffected, whereas pixels that do fall within the region are shaded. The implementation of the triangle rendering function is shown in Listing 4.12, and the discussion of its implementation follows in the next section.

LISTING 4.12 DRAWING A TRIANGLE

```
void SoftwareCanvas::DrawPixelTriangle(const Point2D &p1,
                                       const Point2D &p2,
                                       const Point2D &p3,
                                       const Color3 &col)
{
   if(primaryBuffer == NULL)
      return;

   // Used to calculated the rectangle that makes
   // up the area surrounding the triangle.
   int minX = FindMin(p1.x, p2.x, p3.x);
   int maxX = FindMax(p1.x, p2.x, p3.x);
```

```
int minY = FindMin(p1.y, p2.y, p3.y);
int maxY = FindMax(p1.y, p2.y, p3.y);


// If the rectangle is completely outside of
// the canvas then we can quickly reject it here.
if(((minX >= resWidth) || (maxX < 0)) ||
   ((minY < 0) || (maxY >= resHeight)))
   return;


// Cap bounding rectangle for easy triangle clip.
// This will clip the rectangle, which auto clips the tri.
if(minX < 0)         minX = 0;
if(maxX > resWidth) maxX = resWidth;

if(minY < 0)          minY = 0;
if(maxY > resHeight) maxY = resHeight;


// Pre-computed constants for the upcoming loop.
int p1p2X = p1.x - p2.x,
    p2p3X = p2.x - p3.x,
    p3p1X = p3.x - p1.x;

// Pre-computed constants for the upcoming loop.
int p1p2Y = p1.y - p2.y,
    p2p3Y = p2.y - p3.y,
    p3p1Y = p3.y - p1.y;

// Pre-computed during each iteration over the Y.
int yp1Y = 0, yp2Y = 0, yp3Y = 0;


// Move to the start of the triangle's area.
Color3 *ptr = primaryBuffer + (minY * resWidth);


// Loop over the rectangle that makes up this triangle
// and fill in only the pixels that fall within the tri.
for(int y = minY; y < maxY; y++)
{
   yp1Y = y - p1.y;
   yp2Y = y - p2.y;
```

```
        yp3Y = y - p3.y;

        // Process entire line.
        for(int x = minX; x < maxX; x++)
        {
           if(p1p2X * yp1Y - p1p2Y * (x - p1.x) > 0 &&
              p2p3X * yp2Y - p2p3Y * (x - p2.x) > 0 &&
              p3p1X * yp3Y - p3p1Y * (x - p3.x) > 0)
           {
              ptr[x] = col;
           }
        }

        // Move to the next line.
        ptr += resWidth;
     }
  }
```

The code in Listing 4.12 finds the bounding rectangle of the triangle by finding the minimum and maximum axes that define the triangle. Once the rectangle is found, a few simple conditional statements are used to quickly clip the bounding rectangle to the region of the canvas. After that step a few deltas are precomputed so they do not have to be calculated many times throughout the execution of this function. With the precomputed deltas and starting at the first row and column of the bounding rectangle, we loop through each pixel that makes up the rectangle, row by row, and we shade all pixels that fall within the triangle to the specified color. This is done by using the deltas to test if the current pixel is outside or within the triangle's area. If the current pixel is within the triangle, then the color is set, or else it is left alone. Once each row and column of the bounding rectangle has been processed, the function can return and the primitive is rendered onto the canvas. The Triangles demo application renders a single white triangle to the screen, as shown in Figure 4.5. The RenderScene() function for the demo application is shown in Listing 4.13.

LISTING 4.13 THE RenderScene() FUNCTION OF THE TRIANGLES DEMO

```
void RenderScene()
{
   canvas.Clear(Color3(0, 0, 0));
```

```
canvas.DrawPixelTriangle(Point2D(100, 200),
                         Point2D(-100, 200),
                         Point2D(0, 300),
                         Color3(255, 255, 255));
}
```

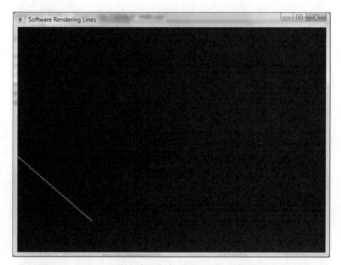

FIGURE 4.5   A screenshot from the Triangle 1 demo application.

RENDERING BUFFERS

Rendering buffers are used throughout the generation of a rendered scene in all modern rasterization-based video games. A rendering buffer is an array of memory that is written to and/or read from. We have already discussed one such common buffer, known as the primary color rendering buffer. A primary color buffer is the main buffer that has color values written to it. In the case of the software rendering system we've created up to this point, this is the rendering canvas that has values written to it during the rendering of a scene and has its contents read from it during the displaying of a scene.

Other types of rendering buffers exist in computer graphics. Some of these buffers involve rendering colors, whereas others can be used for rendering other pieces of information that can be useful for calculating various effects in a scene. In the upcoming sections we discuss a few of the common types of buffers that you will most likely encounter in game graphics. These buffers include but are not limited to the following:

- Secondary rendering buffers
- Tertiary rendering buffers
- Depth (Z) buffers
- Stencil buffers

Secondary Buffers

A secondary buffer is used along with the primary color buffer to allow for smooth renderings of multiple frames of animation. Up to this point we've used only one buffer for the output of color. If the screen needed to be displayed before a rendering was complete, artifacts could appear on the screen. In the previous Windows-based examples this could potentially happen quite often. Since paint messages are not instant, there is no guarantee when the paint message would be handled. This can be solved by taking the display code out of the message handler and placing it in the application loop, but other situations that can also cause the artifacts to appear, which would occur anytime the screen (like a monitor) needs a refresh that coincides with a render update.

Another scenario is if we were rendering and/or displaying in parallel to the rest of the application. If the window needs to be displayed before the rendering of the next frame is complete, you can have a partial scene update, which would cause choppy artifacts. These artifacts include flickering effects, tearing effects, and shearing effects. If the application is set to run at 60 frames per second, probably the window region of the screen will need to be redrawn, even if it is during the rendering of the next frame.

Secondary buffers are used to solve this problem. By using another buffer one could be displayed (current frame) whenever necessary while the other is being rendered (next frame). When the rendering is done on the secondary buffer, the contents can be copied to the primary buffer, which is known as double buffering. Another technique that can be used instead of copying the contents is to display the buffer that is not the current one being rendered to directly instead of using one buffer specifically for the primary and one for the secondary. Using the second method, and in the case of having two rendering buffers, you would switch between them each frame. This method is known as page flipping.

The major graphics APIs, which include OpenGL and Direct3D, include support for multiple color rendering buffers. The plus side to using multiple buffers is that it solves the updating artifacts that exist when using just one buffer. The downside, which is not really an issue in today's video games and graphics hardware outside of some mobile and other resource-limited devices, is that the addition of another buffer consumes more video memory. This means that if you add another buffer, you use up twice as much video memory than you did with just the one buffer as far as color rendering buffers are concerned.

ON THE CD

Today's hardware memory is cheap, and graphics devices have enough memory that the consumption from a secondary buffer is not considered an issue on PCs and home consoles. The implementation of secondary buffers is relatively straightforward and is something we can implement into the software rendering system as a quick exercise. On the accompanying CD-ROM is a demo application called Double Buffering that implements a secondary buffer. We discuss the implementation in the following paragraphs.

 Sometimes the terms page flipping *and* double buffering *are used synonymously. The demo we implement does not bother with copying data from one buffer to another since a faster and more simple alternative exists, which you'll see soon by performing page flipping.*

To implement a secondary buffer we first need to create another buffer in the software rendering system that is the same size as the primary buffer. To avoid expensive memory copies every frame we also use another pointer, called the `currentBuffer`, in the `SoftwareCanvas` class, which is used to point to the current rendering buffer to which we are drawing. When the application requests the rendered scene, the current buffer's pointer returns the buffer that is not being rendered to. The updated `SoftwareCanvas` class is shown in Listing 4.14.

LISTING 4.14 THE UPDATED SoftwareCanvas CLASS TO INCLUDE A SECONDARY BUFFER

```
class SoftwareCanvas
{
   public:
      SoftwareCanvas(int width, int height) : resWidth(width),
         resHeight(height), bufferFlag(0)
      {
         primaryBuffer = new Color3[width * height];
         secondaryBuffer = new Color3[width * height];
         currentBuffer = primaryBuffer;
      }

      ~SoftwareCanvas()
      {
         currentBuffer = NULL;

         if(primaryBuffer != NULL)
         {
            delete[] primaryBuffer;
            primaryBuffer = NULL;
         }

         if(secondaryBuffer != NULL)
```

```
         {
             delete[] secondaryBuffer;
             secondaryBuffer = NULL;
         }
     }


     void SwapBuffers();


     char *GetRender()
     {
         if(currentBuffer == primaryBuffer)
             return (char*)secondaryBuffer;
         else
             return (char*)primaryBuffer;
     }


  private:
     Color3 *primaryBuffer,
             *secondaryBuffer,
             *currentBuffer;

     char bufferFlag;
};
```

Switching between the rendering buffers is done in a function called `SwapBuffers()`, which checks the buffer flag value. If the value is 0, the secondary buffer is set as the current buffer, or else the primary buffer is set. The flag's value is swapped using the bit operator ^=, which flips the bits of a variable. In the case of a 0 or a 1, flipping bits using this operator switch between these two values happens very quickly. The implementation for the `SwapBuffers()` function is shown in Listing 4.15.

 Bit operators are fast operators.

LISTING 4.15 `SwapBuffers()` FUNCTION IMPLEMENTATION

```
void SoftwareCanvas::SwapBuffers()
{
   if(bufferFlag ^= 1)
      currentBuffer = primaryBuffer;
   else
      currentBuffer = secondaryBuffer;
}
```

Once a secondary buffer has been added, the last step is to update each of the functions that previously directly accessed the primary buffer to now reference the current buffer pointer. This is as straightforward as using `currentBuffer` instead of `primaryBuffer` in the remaining functions of the software rendering class. For those coding along with this chapter the functions affected include the following (the altered code is shown in Listing 4.16):

- `Clear()`
- `DrawPixelTriangle()`
- `DrawPixel()`
- `DrawPixelLine()`

LISTING 4.16 UPDATING EACH FUNCTION THAT RENDERS

```
void SoftwareCanvas::Clear(Color3 &col)
{
   if(currentBuffer == NULL)
      return;


   for(int i = 0; i < resWidth * resHeight; i++)
   {
      currentBuffer[i] = col;
   }
}



void SoftwareCanvas::DrawPixelTriangle(Point2D &p1, Point2D &p2,
                                       Point2D &p3,
                                       const Color3 &col)
{
   if(currentBuffer == NULL)
      return;
```

```
        ...

        // Move to the start of the triangle's area.
        Color3 *ptr = currentBuffer + (minY * resWidth);

        ...
    }


void SoftwareCanvas::DrawPixel(int width, int height,
                               const Color3 &col)
{
    if(currentBuffer == NULL)
        return;


    currentBuffer[height * resWidth + width] = col;
}


void SoftwareCanvas::DrawPixelLine(Point2D &start, Point2D &end,
                                   const Color3 &col)
{
    if(currentBuffer == NULL)
        return;

    ...
}
```

 You can avoid the conditional statement to test if the current buffer's pointer is null by assuming that it will be valid. You can alternatively use an assertion to catch times when it does show up as being null during development and debugging sessions.

The last piece of code dealing with the Double Buffering demo application is the rendering function for the demo. This function adds a quick and easy implementation of an animated triangle by moving the X axis position of each vertex point of the primitive a little each frame. When the middle of the triangle makes it to one side of the screen or the other, it switches direction. The RenderScene() function for the Double Buffering demo is shown in Listing 4.17. A screenshot of the demo application in action is shown in Figure 4.6.

LISTING 4.17 THE RENDERING CODE FROM THE DOUBLE BUFFERING DEMO

```
int xPos = 0, step = 5;


void RenderScene()
{
   canvas.Clear(Color3(0, 0, 0));

   xPos += step;

   if(xPos < 0 || xPos > WINDOW_WIDTH)
      step *= -1;

   canvas.DrawPixelTriangle(Point2D(xPos + 100, 200),
                            Point2D(xPos - 100, 200),
                            Point2D(xPos, 300),
                            Color3(255, 255, 255));

   canvas.SwapBuffers();
}
```

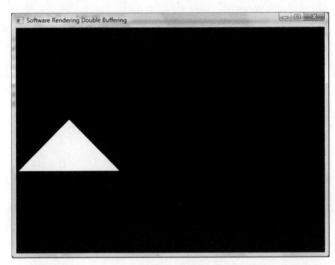

FIGURE 4.6   A screenshot from the Double Buffering demo.

The Depth Buffer

The depth buffer, also known as the Z buffer, is one of the most useful areas of rasterization during the rendering of a scene. During rendering, 3D geometry objects are presorted and rendered in a specified order or tests are used to determine which object is the closest to the viewer. In Chapter 3, each ray for each pixel has to perform intersection tests against all objects to determine which is the closest. Not being able to determine which objects are closer to the viewer makes it very hard to draw objects in the correct order without presorting them each frame.

The depth buffer is a simple idea that is a very powerful and efficient solution to handling depth orders. The depth buffer is a buffer of memory normally the same size as the rendering canvas. When objects are drawn to the screen, their projected depths from the viewer are saved for each pixel that makes up the object being rendered in the depth buffer. Every time an object is drawn the depth buffer is first checked to see if the pixel's depth value is greater than the pixel of the object that is being rendered. If the object that is being rendered is closer to the viewer than what was rendered in the past, the current color buffer's pixel is overridden (pixel overdraw) and the depth buffer's pixel is updated. This process is similar to ray tracing, where the closest intersected object is found before the rendering image is set. The difference with the depth buffer is that an entire buffer is stored and kept during the rendering of a frame. With the depth buffer, only the current object's depths are examined, rather than the depths it so far has marked as being closest.

When a scan-line of a polygon's surface is being rendered, the projected depth of each of pixel that makes up the surface is calculated. The only time the color buffer is updated is for the pixels that pass the depth test, known as depth testing. This allows a graphics application to draw geometry in any order it likes, and the results are always correct because the depth buffer is an extremely accurate way of drawing geometry in the sorted order on a pixel level using a conditional check.

If the geometry of a scene can be efficiently sorted and used during run-time with very little overhead, then that can also be used. This was done in the original Quake *by Id Software. Some algorithms, such as potential visibility sets and binary space partitioning trees, can sort geometry and be used with depth testing to give even greater performance. This is used in games such as Valve's* Half-Life 2.

Implementing a depth buffer is fairly trivial in a software rendering system. The key is to check the depth buffer to see if the projected depth of the pixel that is being rendered is less than the value stored in the depth buffer, that is, closer to the viewer. If it is, the pixel location in the depth buffer is updated, and the color buffer's location for that pixel is also updated. Before each frame of rendering, it is important to clear the depth buffer to some constant value. Often, this value is the value for the maximum depth, also known as the far plane. The side effect of this is that any geometry that happens to be further than the value of the far plane is not drawn. The far plane can be thought of as a wall that once passed culls geometry out of the scene.

When it comes to depth testing, since the geometry is not sorted, it is possible to get a worst-case scenario when using the depth buffer if all objects are rendered from furthest to closest but need to be drawn from closet to furthest. Even if the worst-case scenario does not happen, doing a lot of pixel overdraw, which is the process of rendering to pixel locations more than once, in a single frame can have an impact on performance. Id Software had this problem with the first *Quake* game, which had costly rendering bottlenecks in some levels that were caused by excessive pixel overdraw. John Carmack, one of the cofounders of Id Software and the company's technical director, created a technique that is commonly known as potential visibility sets, which is used to help eliminate overdraw. The result was that certain level areas in *Quake* that suffered from performance problems no longer exhibited them. Potential visibility sets are commonly used together with various spatial data structures such as binary space partitioning trees (BSP trees). In Chapter 15, we discuss potential visibility sets and other popular algorithms that are used in the games industry.

Tertiary Buffers

Triple buffering is similar to double buffering. In double buffering rendering calls alternate between a primary and secondary buffer to prevent the rendering of the next frame from showing up over the currently displayed frame, which can cause unsightly rendering artifacts. In triple buffering the same concept is used to add a tertiary rendering buffer. The major drawback to using more than two buffers for rendering is that with each buffer that is added, more video memory is used for, in most if not all cases, no gain in animation quality. Graphics hardware has a finite amount of memory that is used for many things such as buffers and textures. The addition of a tertiary buffer along with primary, secondary, depth, and so on can be an unnecessary cost in memory. There should rarely, perhaps never, be a situation when more than two buffers are needed for rendering in a video game.

Stencil Buffers

A stencil buffer is used in the same manner as real-life stencils. In a stencil buffer each pixel is a flag, whereas in color buffers each pixel is a multicomponent color, and the depth buffer's pixels are floating-point elements. Normally, a stencil buffer uses a multipass approach. For example, let's say you want to render anywhere on the screen except for a specific region in the center. Using a stencil buffer, you can render a rectangle only to that buffer so that the pixels that makes up that region have their flags set to, let's say, 1 for true. In the second pass you can render the scene normally but before each pixel is set in the current color buffer, you test if the stencil buffer flag for that area is set. If it is, you do not update the color buffer; otherwise, you do. An example of this is shown in Figure 4.7.

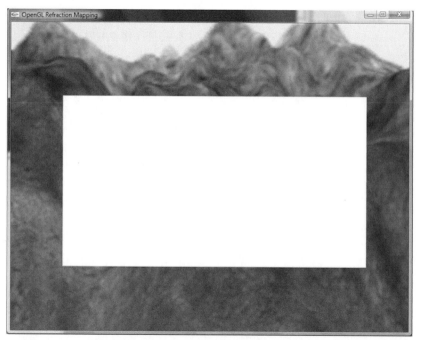

FIGURE 4.7   Drawing to all areas of a screen except to a rectangular area in the center.

The stencil buffer can be thought of as a mask, and it can be used in any manner you can think of. For example, you can use this stencil mask to say that you only want to render to the areas of a screen where the stencil flag is set.

When implementing a stencil buffer, you can use 1-byte character variables for each pixel of the screen. This would work if the stencil flags were to be set to either true or false (1 or 0) or if each flag can be incremented up to 255, which can be done in rendering APIs such as OpenGL. An example of this is shown in the following pseudo-code using the example from Figure 4.7. Note that using the code sample from earlier in this chapter, you could add the conditional check for the stencil before any pixel is drawn to the current color buffer.

```
function Render_Scene()
{
   Enable_Stencil_Buffer();
   Disable_Color_Buffer();

   Render_To_Stencil(rectangle);

   Enable_Color_Buffer();

   Render_To_Color_On_False_Stencil_Flags(scene);

   Disable_Stencil_Buffer();
   Swap_Buffers();
}


function Render_To_Stencil(scene)
{
   for_each(obj in scene)
   {
      raster_area = Rasterize(obj);

      for_each(pixel that falls within raster_area)
      {
         Render_Stencil(pixel);
      }
   }
}


function Render_To_Color_On_False_Stencil_Flags(scene)
{
   for_each(obj in scene)
   {
      raster_area = Rasterize(obj);

      for_each(pixel that falls within raster_area)
      {
         if(Stencil_Buffer(pixel) == false)
         {
            Render_Pixel(pixel);
         }
      }
   }
}
```

```
function Stencil_Buffer(pixel)
{
    return (boolean)stencil_buffer[pixel.location];
}


function Render_Stencil(pixel)
{
    stencil_buffer[pixel.location] = true;
}


function Render_Pixel(pixel)
{
    color_buffer[pixel.location] = pixel.color;
}
```

You can also implement the stencil buffer using single bytes, where eight pixels are used for each byte. This would work if each stencil flag was only to be set to either true or false. This trick, which requires knowledge of bit manipulation operators, can allow you to reduce the memory footprint of the stencil buffer eight to one if your buffer was originally using a byte per pixel—more if you were using integers and so on. This means the stencil buffer can be about eight times smaller since each byte of the stencil buffer can be used for eight screen pixels. If you need to increment the elements in the stencil buffer beyond 0 or 1 and if you need values higher than 255, you'll have to use multibyte elements for the stencil buffer. The approach taken for the stencil buffer depends on how it is used.

ADDITIONAL RASTERIZATION TOPICS

Additional topics are important for those looking to create a 3D rasterization rendering system. In this chapter we've touched upon a few topics to allow you to get a feel of what it would be like to attempt creating your own rendering system. Before we end the discussion of rasterization, a few other topics should be mentioned. These topics include transformations, spaces, and back-face culling.

Transformation and Spaces

In this chapter we've specified the data in each demo application in 2D screen space. In modern video games we specify data in 3D, which means we need a way to transform the 3D data to 2D. Chapter 2 included a discussion of transformations, spaces, and matrices and how they are used in computer graphics. Transformations allows you to render any 3D geometry created from any package and are something you need to add support for if you plan on extending the software rending system.

Back-Face Culling

Polygons can have a directional property that is defined by a normal that specifies the direction the surface is facing. For most objects that have a volume, it is not necessary to render geometry that is not facing the camera. Since the geometry facing the camera blocks the view of polygons that face away from the camera, it is more beneficial to avoid rendering that geometry. This is known as back-face culling, and it can be used as a performance boost to complex 3D scenes. This can be done by simply checking the plane of the polygon and determining on which side the viewer is. If the viewer is behind the plane, the polygon can be culled out.

There is also front-face culling, which is the culling of geometry that faces the camera versus ones that face away.

OpenGL

Throughout the remainder of this book we focus on hardware-based rendering using OpenGL and Direct3D as well as programmable shaders. Both OpenGL and Direct3D use rasterization algorithms on graphics devices. For OpenGL there are code samples for Windows-, Mac-, and Linux-based operating systems. Each OpenGL demo has at least two files: a header file and the main source file. The header file includes the various OpenGL header files that are needed for each OS. In OpenGL some operating systems need some files that others don't, and they reference different folders. For example, for a Mac the OpenGL headers can be found in the OpenGL framework, whereas on Windows they can, if you have Visual Studio, be found in the Platform SDK VC folder. Each OpenGL demo in this book uses a header file that looks like the one in Listing 4.18.

LISTING 4.18 THE GENERAL OPENGL HEADER FILE FOR THE BOOK'S DEMOS

```
#ifdef _WIN32
    // Windows.
    #include<gl/glee.h>
    #include<gl/glut.h>
    #pragma comment(lib, "glee.lib")
#else
#ifdef _MAC_OSX
    // Mac.
    #include<glut/glut.h>
    #include<stdlib.h>
#else
    // Linux.
    #include<GL/glee.h>
    #include<GL/glut.h>
    #include<stdlib.h>
#endif
#endif
```

Loading OpenGL extensions is necessary on Windows and Linux operating systems. The way extensions are loaded is operating system dependent. To avoid having to worry about the details of extension loading, this book uses the OpenGL Easy Extension library (GLee). Each demo application uses the OpenGL utility toolkit (GLUT) to avoid operating system–dependent code when working with OpenGL. If you prefer, you can create your own OS-based windows (such as Win32 on Windows), and you can load the extensions yourself. To speed things along the sample code in this book uses GLUT and GLee to allow the focus to remain on the topics and techniques that are being discussed. You can find links to download the latest versions of both these tools in Appendix B, "Compiling Sample Code," and Appendix C, "Recommended Resources." You can also find information on compiling with these tools in Appendix B.

ON THE CD

On the CD-ROM is a demo application in the Chapter 4 folder called OpenGL. The main source file for this demo can be used as a starting point for the OpenGL demos for those who want to follow along with the code samples without having to rewrite redundant code. The main source file for the OpenGL template is shown in Listing 4.19.

LISTING 4.19 OPENGL TEMPLATE

```c
#include"OpenGL.h"
#include<stdio.h>


void RenderScene();
void KeyDown(unsigned char key, int x, int y);
void Resize(int width, int height);
bool InitializeApp();
void ShutdownApp();


int main(int arg, char **argc)
{
   glutInitWindowSize(800, 600);
   glutInitWindowPosition(100, 100);
   glutInitDisplayMode(GLUT_RGB | GLUT_DOUBLE | GLUT_DEPTH);
   glutInit(&arg, argc);

   glutCreateWindow("OpenGL using GLUT");

   glutDisplayFunc(RenderScene);
   glutReshapeFunc(Resize);
   glutKeyboardFunc(KeyDown);

   if(InitializeApp() == true)
      glutMainLoop();
   else
      printf("Error in InitializeApp()!\n\n");

   ShutdownApp();

   return 1;
}


void Resize(int width, int height)
{
   glViewport(0, 0, width, height);
   glMatrixMode(GL_PROJECTION);

   gluPerspective(60, width/height, 0.1, 200.0);
   glMatrixMode(GL_MODELVIEW);
}
```

```
void KeyDown(unsigned char key, int x, int y)
{
   switch(key)
   {
      case 27:
         exit(0);
         break;
   }
}


bool InitializeApp()
{
   glClearColor(0.0f, 0.0f, 0.0f, 1.0f);
   glShadeModel(GL_SMOOTH);
   glEnable(GL_DEPTH_TEST);

   return true;
}


void ShutdownApp()
{

}


void RenderScene()
{
   glClear(GL_COLOR_BUFFER_BIT | GL_DEPTH_BUFFER_BIT);
   glLoadIdentity();

   glTranslatef(0.0f, 0.0f, -5.0f);

   glBegin(GL_TRIANGLES);
      glColor3f(1, 0, 0);  glVertex3f(-1, 0, 0);
      glColor3f(0, 1, 0);  glVertex3f( 1, 0, 0);
      glColor3f(0, 0, 1);  glVertex3f( 0, 1, 0);
   glEnd();

   glutSwapBuffers();
   glutPostRedisplay();
}
```

One important fact to realize about OpenGL is that it is not efficient to render geometry by manually calling glBegin(), glEnd(), and glVer-tex*f(). Instead, you should always try to use vertex arrays since the performance is better and using vertex arrays is not only easy but is straightforward. The example in Listing 4.19 did not use a vertex array. Often, people avoid using vertex arrays without fully understanding that not using them is not efficient or effective, especially for video games. The OpenGL template demo application does use vertex arrays and so do all the demos throughout this book. In Listing 4.20 we take the Render-Scene() function from Listing 4.19 and use vertex arrays.

LISTING 4.20 USING VERTEX ARRAYS IN OPENGL

```
void RenderScene()
{
   glClear(GL_COLOR_BUFFER_BIT | GL_DEPTH_BUFFER_BIT);
   glLoadIdentity();

   glTranslatef(0.0f, 0.0f, -5.0f);

   float vertices[] = { -1, 0, 0,  1, 0, 0,  0, 1, 0 };
   float colors[]   = {  1, 0, 0,  0, 1, 0,  0, 0, 1 };

   glEnableClientState(GL_VERTEX_ARRAY);
   glVertexPointer(3, GL_FLOAT, 0, vertices);

   glEnableClientState(GL_COLOR_ARRAY);
   glColorPointer(3, GL_FLOAT, 0, colors);

   glDrawArrays(GL_TRIANGLES, 0, 3);

   glDisableClientState(GL_VERTEX_ARRAY);
   glDisableClientState(GL_COLOR_ARRAY);

   glutSwapBuffers();
   glutPostRedisplay();
}
```

DIRECT3D 9 AND 10

Direct3D is Microsoft's 3D graphics API that is used for their Windows-based operating systems as well as their Xbox line of video game consoles. Direct3D (actually DirectX as a whole) has played a major part in multimedia programming since the launch of Windows 95 in the mid-1990s. Since its first version, DirectX has become one of the top tools used by developers to create a host of different types of applications across the years. Today DirectX is a strong piece of technology that shows no sign of slowing down.

ON THE CD

In this book we focus only on the graphics rendering services DirectX offers through Direct3D. Both Direct3D 9 and 10 are used throughout this book. Although these APIs are extremely similar, Direct3D 10 was built from the ground up and is not compatible with past versions. To use Direct3D 10 you have to have Windows Vista. Vista users can still use Direct3D 9 since Microsoft includes a version of it with the DirectX SDK. This is good because it is not DirectX 10 or nothing for Vista users. The CD-ROM includes demo applications called Direct3D9 and Direct3D10 in the Chapter 4 folder. Like the OpenGL demo we saw in the previous section, these demos are template demos that can be used when following along with the code samples throughout this book. They are starting files that can be edited to keep you from rewriting redundant code. These demo applications simply draw single triangles to the window.

Direct3D9 Demo

First, we briefly discuss the template demo for Direct3D 9, called Direct3D9. This demo is similar to the OpenGL template demo with the exception of Direct3D-specific calls. In the first section of the demo's main source file are a few global variables, a resizing function, and a device initialization function. In the global section are the Direct3D object and device objects that are needed to initialize and use Direct3D as well as a vertex structure and buffer. A vertex structure is a structure that represents an individual vertex with all of its attributes and properties. A vertex buffer is similar to OpenGL vertex arrays in the sense that they allow you to send geometry to the hardware in one efficient call. There is the option to not use vertex buffers, but, like using `glBegin()`, `glVertex*f()`, `glEnd()`, and so on in OpenGL, this is strongly discouraged, and vertex buffers should always be used, especially in commercial gaming applications. It is far more efficient and effective to use vertex buffers when it comes to performance, and that is the option taken throughout this book.

ON THE CD

The first section of the Direct3D9 demo's main source file is shown in Listing 4.21. The initialization function of the device sets up Direct3D and prepares if for use by the application. In this function it attempts to set up in hardware rendering mode if it is available or software mode if hardware is not detected. The function that is called during the window's resizing is essentially called whenever the window changes its dimensions. This is captured in the windows callback procedure, which can also be seen on the main source file for this demo in the CD-ROM.

LISTING 4.21 THE FIRST SECTION OF THE DIRECT3D9 MAIN SOURCE FILE

```
#include<windows.h>
#include<d3d9.h>
#include<d3dx9.h>

#pragma comment(lib, "d3d9.lib")
#pragma comment(lib, "d3dx9.lib")

#define WINDOW_NAME      "Direct3D 9 Example"
#define WINDOW_CLASS     "UPGCLASS"
#define WINDOW_WIDTH     800
#define WINDOW_HEIGHT    600

HWND g_hwnd;


// Direct3D objects.
LPDIRECT3D9 g_d3dObject = NULL;
LPDIRECT3DDEVICE9 g_d3dDevice = NULL;


// Vertex specified by position and color.
struct Vertex
{
   FLOAT x, y, z;
   DWORD color;
};

#define D3DFVF_D3DVertex (D3DFVF_XYZ | D3DFVF_DIFFUSE)

LPDIRECT3DVERTEXBUFFER9 g_vertexBuffer = NULL;


void ResizeD3D9Window(int width, int height)
{
```

```
    if(g_d3dDevice == NULL)
       return;

    D3DVIEWPORT9 viewport;
    viewport.X = 0;
    viewport.Y = 0;
    viewport.Width = width;
    viewport.Height = height;
    viewport.MinZ = 0.0f;
    viewport.MaxZ = 1.0f;

    g_d3dDevice->SetViewport(&viewport);

    D3DXMATRIX projMat;
    D3DXMatrixPerspectiveFovLH(&projMat, D3DXToRadian(60.0f),
                               (float)width / (float)height,
                               0.1f, 1000.0f);

    g_d3dDevice->SetTransform(D3DTS_PROJECTION, &projMat);
}


bool InitializeD3D9()
{
    D3DDISPLAYMODE displayMode;
    D3DPRESENT_PARAMETERS params;
    D3DCAPS9 caps;

    ZeroMemory(&params, sizeof(params));

    g_d3dObject = Direct3DCreate9(D3D_SDK_VERSION);

    if(g_d3dObject == NULL)
       return false;

    HRESULT hr;

    hr = g_d3dObject-
>GetAdapterDisplayMode(D3DADAPTER_DEFAULT,
                                           &displayMode);
    if(FAILED(hr))
       return false;

    hr = g_d3dObject->GetDeviceCaps(D3DADAPTER_DEFAULT,
                                    D3DDEVTYPE_HAL, &caps);
```

```
    if(FAILED(hr))
      return false;

    // Use hardware if it was found, else software.
    DWORD flags = 0;

    if(caps.VertexProcessingCaps != 0)
        flags |= D3DCREATE_HARDWARE_VERTEXPROCESSING;
    else
        flags |= D3DCREATE_SOFTWARE_VERTEXPROCESSING;

    params.Windowed = TRUE;
    params.SwapEffect = D3DSWAPEFFECT_DISCARD;
    params.BackBufferFormat = displayMode.Format;
    params.BackBufferCount = 1;
    params.EnableAutoDepthStencil = TRUE;
    params.AutoDepthStencilFormat = D3DFMT_D16;

    hr = g_d3dObject->CreateDevice(D3DADAPTER_DEFAULT,
        D3DDEVTYPE_HAL, g_hwnd, flags, &params, &g_d3dDevice);

    if(FAILED(hr) || g_d3dDevice == NULL)
        return false;

    ResizeD3D9Window(WINDOW_WIDTH, WINDOW_HEIGHT);

    return true;
}
```

The last section of the Direct3D9 demo's main source file has demo initialize, render, update, and shutdown functions. This demo does not use the update this time, but later demos do, so an empty one is placed here to indicate that. An update function is useful for things that are not specific to rendering actual geometry, such as updating animations and physics. The shutdown function is used to release anything used by the application, which in this case is the allocated Direct3D objects that were created. It is important to release these objects to avoid memory leaks.

The function for the demo-specific initialization is used for tasks such as creating and loading geometry and effects. In this demo the vertex buffer is created and filled with the geometry of a single triangle as an example. The rendering function of the demo renders out this single triangle to a black canvas so that there is some type of output. The second half of the Direct3D9 demo's main source file is shown in Listing 4.22.

LISTING 4.22 THE SECOND SECTION OF THE DIRECT3D9 DEMO'S MAIN SOURCE FILE

```
bool InitializeDemo()
{
    g_d3dDevice->SetRenderState(D3DRS_LIGHTING, FALSE);
    g_d3dDevice->SetRenderState(D3DRS_CULLMODE, D3DCULL_NONE);

    Vertex obj[] =
    {
        {-0.5f, -0.5f, 1.0f, D3DCOLOR_XRGB(255,   0,   0)},
        { 0.5f, -0.5f, 1.0f, D3DCOLOR_XRGB(  0, 255,   0)},
        { 0.0f,  0.3f, 1.0f, D3DCOLOR_XRGB(  0,   0, 255)}
    };


    // Create the vertex buffer.

    int numVerts = sizeof(obj) / sizeof(obj[0]);
    int size = numVerts * sizeof(Vertex);

    HRESULT hr = g_d3dDevice->CreateVertexBuffer(size, 0,
        D3DFVF_D3DVertex, D3DPOOL_DEFAULT, &g_vertexBuffer, NULL);

    if(FAILED(hr))
        return false;


    // Load data into vertex buffer.

    Vertex *ptr = NULL;

    hr = g_vertexBuffer->Lock(0, sizeof(obj), (void**)&ptr, 0);

    if(FAILED(hr))
        return false;

    memcpy(ptr, obj, sizeof(obj));
    g_vertexBuffer->Unlock();

    return true;
}
```

```
void Update()
{
    // Nothing to update.
}


void RenderScene()
{
    g_d3dDevice->Clear(0, NULL, D3DCLEAR_TARGET |
                        D3DCLEAR_ZBUFFER,
                        D3DCOLOR_XRGB(0,0,0), 1.0f, 0);

    g_d3dDevice->BeginScene();

        // Setup geometry to render.
        g_d3dDevice->SetStreamSource(0, g_vertexBuffer,
                                    0, sizeof(Vertex));

        g_d3dDevice->SetFVF(D3DFVF_D3DVertex);

        // This will draw everything in the buffer.
        g_d3dDevice->DrawPrimitive(D3DPT_TRIANGLELIST, 0, 1);

    g_d3dDevice->EndScene();

    g_d3dDevice->Present(NULL, NULL, NULL, NULL);
}


void Shutdown()
{
    // Here we release the Direct3D objects.
    if(g_d3dDevice != NULL) g_d3dDevice->Release();
    g_d3dDevice = NULL;

    if(g_d3dObject != NULL) g_d3dObject->Release();
    g_d3dObject = NULL;

    if(g_vertexBuffer != NULL) g_vertexBuffer->Release();
    g_vertexBuffer = NULL;
}
```

Direct3D 10

ON THE CD

There are a few similarities between Direct3D 9 and Direct3D 10. On the CD-ROM is a demo application called Direct3D 10 in the Chapter 4 folder. This demo's main source file starts off in the same manner as the Direct3D9 demo, with the major exception being the number of Direct3D objects that need to be created in addition to the specific headers and libraries needed for Direct3D 10. In Direct3D 10 it is necessary to create your own rendering buffers (rendering targets) to be able to render anything at all. Direc3D 9 doesn't require this, but Direct3D 10 does, which gives it a feeling of giving you more control over the lower-level details compared to Direct3D 9. Also, Direct3D 10 is shader-only, so at least one shader effect must be created if you plan on rendering any geometry to the screen. (In Chapter 5, "Programmable Shaders," we discuss shaders in more detail.) The first half of the Direct3D10 demo application's main source file is shown in Listing 4.23. The code in Listing 4.23 is almost the same as the Direct3D 9 code, with Direct3D 10 specifics implemented instead of Direct3D 9.

Because this is not a beginners' OpenGL and Direct3D 9/10 book, it is assumed that you have at least some experience with one or more of these technologies. The sections in this chapter on these APIs are meant as an introduction to the template source files, not the APIs themselves.

LISTING 4.23 THE FIRST HALF OF THE DIRECT3D10 DEMO'S MAIN SOURCE FILE

```
#include<windows.h>
#include<d3d10.h>
#include<d3dx10.h>

#pragma comment(lib, "d3d10.lib")
#pragma comment(lib, "d3dx10.lib")

#define WINDOW_NAME      "Direct3D 10 Example"
#define WINDOW_CLASS     "UPGCLASS"
#define WINDOW_WIDTH     800
#define WINDOW_HEIGHT    600


// Global window handles.
HINSTANCE g_hInst = NULL;
HWND g_hwnd = NULL;
```

```
// Direct3D 10 objects.
ID3D10Device *g_d3dDevice = NULL;
IDXGISwapChain *g_swapChain = NULL;
ID3D10RenderTargetView *g_renderTargetView = NULL;

ID3D10Effect *g_shader = NULL;
ID3D10EffectTechnique *g_technique = NULL;
ID3D10InputLayout *g_layout = NULL;
ID3D10Buffer *g_vertexBuffer = NULL;


void ResizeD3D10Window(int width, int height)
{
   if(g_d3dDevice == NULL)
      return;

   D3D10_VIEWPORT vp;
   vp.Width = width;
   vp.Height = height;
   vp.MinDepth = 0.0f;
   vp.MaxDepth = 1.0f;
   vp.TopLeftX = 0;
   vp.TopLeftY = 0;

   g_d3dDevice->RSSetViewports(1, &vp);
}


bool InitializeD3D10()
{
   DXGI_SWAP_CHAIN_DESC swapDesc;
   ZeroMemory(&swapDesc, sizeof(swapDesc));

   swapDesc.BufferCount = 2;
   swapDesc.BufferDesc.Width = WINDOW_WIDTH;
   swapDesc.BufferDesc.Height = WINDOW_HEIGHT;
   swapDesc.BufferDesc.Format = DXGI_FORMAT_R8G8B8A8_UNORM;
   swapDesc.BufferDesc.RefreshRate.Numerator = 60;
   swapDesc.BufferDesc.RefreshRate.Denominator = 1;
   swapDesc.BufferUsage = DXGI_USAGE_RENDER_TARGET_OUTPUT;
   swapDesc.OutputWindow = g_hwnd;
   swapDesc.SampleDesc.Count = 1;
   swapDesc.SampleDesc.Quality = 0;
   swapDesc.Windowed = TRUE;
```

```
    HRESULT hr = S_OK;
    unsigned int flags = 0;

#ifdef _DEBUG
    flags |= D3D10_CREATE_DEVICE_DEBUG;
#endif

    D3D10_DRIVER_TYPE driverType = D3D10_DRIVER_TYPE_NULL;

    D3D10_DRIVER_TYPE driverTypes[] =
    {
        D3D10_DRIVER_TYPE_HARDWARE,
        D3D10_DRIVER_TYPE_REFERENCE,
    };

    unsigned int numDriverTypes = sizeof(driverTypes) /
                                  sizeof(driverTypes[0]);

    for(unsigned int i = 0; i < numDriverTypes; i++)
    {
        driverType = driverTypes[i];

        hr = D3D10CreateDeviceAndSwapChain(NULL, driverType, NULL,
                                           flags, D3D10_SDK_VERSION,
                                           &swapDesc, &g_swapChain,
                                           &g_d3dDevice);
        if(SUCCEEDED(hr))
            break;
    }

    if(FAILED(hr))
        return false;

    ID3D10Texture2D *buffer = NULL;
    hr = g_swapChain->GetBuffer(0, __uuidof(ID3D10Texture2D),
                                (LPVOID*)&buffer);

    if(FAILED(hr))
        return false;

    hr = g_d3dDevice->CreateRenderTargetView(buffer, NULL,
                                             &g_renderTargetView);
    buffer->Release();
```

```
        if(FAILED(hr))
            return false;

        g_d3dDevice->OMSetRenderTargets
                (1, &g_renderTargetView, NULL);

        ResizeD3D10Window(WINDOW_WIDTH, WINDOW_HEIGHT);

        return true;
    }
```

The last half of the demo's main source file deals with the demo-specific initialize, render, update, and shutdown functions. The initialize function has to load the shader effect that is used for the rendering, which is a simple effect that renders colored geometry, which is discussed in more detail in the next chapter. The update function is empty for the time being since this simple template demo application does not have a use for it. The rendering function does the same thing as the Direct3D9 demo's rendering function, with the addition of using a shader. Since Direct3D 10 is slightly more involved than Direct3D 9, there is more setup code for rendering in Direct3D 10. This includes having to set the destination rendering buffer, effect, geometry input layout and buffers, and having to render out the geometry for each pass of the effect. Since the effect uses only one rendering pass, this is not entirely necessary, but doing it this way does not incur any negative consequences and it allows us to see what would be necessary for shaders with more than one pass. The second half of the Direct3D10 demo's main source file is shown in Listing 4.24.

LISTING 4.24 THE REST OF THE DIRECT3D10 DEMO'S MAIN SOURCE FILE

```
    bool InitializeDemo()
    {
        // Load the shader.

        DWORD shaderFlags = D3D10_SHADER_ENABLE_STRICTNESS;

    #if defined( DEBUG ) || defined( _DEBUG )
        shaderFlags |= D3D10_SHADER_DEBUG;
    #endif

        HRESULT hr = D3DX10CreateEffectFromFile("shader.fx",
                    NULL, NULL,
```

```
                                        "fx_4_0", shaderFlags,0,
                                        g_d3dDevice, NULL, NULL,
                                        &g_shader, NULL, NULL);
            if(FAILED(hr))
               return false;


            g_technique = g_shader->GetTechniqueByName("PassThrough");


            // Create the geometry.

            D3D10_INPUT_ELEMENT_DESC layout[] =
            {
               { "POSITION", 0, DXGI_FORMAT_R32G32B32_FLOAT, 0, 0,
                 D3D10_INPUT_PER_VERTEX_DATA, 0 },
            };

            unsigned int numElements = sizeof(layout) /
                            sizeof(layout[0]);
            D3D10_PASS_DESC passDesc;

            g_technique->GetPassByIndex(0)->GetDesc(&passDesc);

            hr = g_d3dDevice->CreateInputLayout(layout, numElements,

passDesc.pIAInputSignature,

passDesc.IAInputSignatureSize,
                                        &g_layout);
            if(FAILED(hr))
               return false;

            D3DXVECTOR3 vertices[] =
            {
               D3DXVECTOR3( 0.0f,  0.5f, 0.5f),
               D3DXVECTOR3( 0.5f, -0.5f, 0.5f),
               D3DXVECTOR3(-0.5f, -0.5f, 0.5f),
            };


            // Create the vertex buffer.

            D3D10_BUFFER_DESC buffDesc;
            buffDesc.Usage = D3D10_USAGE_DEFAULT;
```

```
    buffDesc.ByteWidth = sizeof(D3DXVECTOR3) * 3;
    buffDesc.BindFlags = D3D10_BIND_VERTEX_BUFFER;
    buffDesc.CPUAccessFlags = 0;
    buffDesc.MiscFlags = 0;

    D3D10_SUBRESOURCE_DATA resData;
    resData.pSysMem = vertices;

    hr = g_d3dDevice->CreateBuffer(&buffDesc, &resData,
                                   &g_vertexBuffer);

    if(FAILED(hr))
        return false;

    return true;
}


void Update()
{
    // Nothing to update.
}


void RenderScene()
{
    float col[4] = { 0, 0, 0, 1 };

    g_d3dDevice->ClearRenderTargetView(g_renderTargetView, col);

    unsigned int stride = sizeof(D3DXVECTOR3);
    unsigned int offset = 0;

    g_d3dDevice->IASetInputLayout(g_layout);

    g_d3dDevice->IASetVertexBuffers(0, 1, &g_vertexBuffer,
                                    &stride, &offset);
    g_d3dDevice->IASetPrimitiveTopology(
        D3D10_PRIMITIVE_TOPOLOGY_TRIANGLELIST);

    D3D10_TECHNIQUE_DESC techDesc;
    g_technique->GetDesc(&techDesc);

    for(unsigned int i = 0; i < techDesc.Passes; i++)
```

```
      {
          g_technique->GetPassByIndex(i)->Apply(0);
          g_d3dDevice->Draw(3, 0);
      }

      g_swapChain->Present(0, 0);
  }


  void Shutdown()
  {
     if(g_d3dDevice) g_d3dDevice->ClearState();
     if(g_swapChain) g_swapChain->Release();
     if(g_renderTargetView) g_renderTargetView->Release();

     if(g_shader) g_shader->Release();
     if(g_layout) g_layout->Release();
     if(g_vertexBuffer) g_vertexBuffer->Release();

     if(g_d3dDevice) g_d3dDevice->Release();
  }
```

SUMMARY

Graphics hardware uses rasterization to render the video games we play today. Although rasterization is fast, it is not the easiest technique to implement, as we've seen in this chapter. Throughout the remainder of this book the focus is on using Direct3D and OpenGL for rendering graphics. By having a brief, hands-on experience with software rendering you now have an idea of what it takes to render without the use of common graphics APIs.

The following elements were discussed in this chapter:

- Software versus hardware rendering
- Rasterization
- Rendering pixels
- Rendering lines
- Rendering polygons
- Double buffering using a secondary rendering buffer
- Triple buffering
- Depth (Z) buffering
- Stencil buffers

- Clipping primitives
- Transformation and spaces
- OpenGL quick recap
- Direct3D 9 and 10 quick recap

CHAPTER QUESTIONS

Answers to the following chapter review questions can be found in Appendix A, "Answers to Chapter Questions," at the end of this book.

1. What is the name for the technique of choice in the video games industry for rendering computer-generated graphics?
    - A. Software rendering
    - B. Hardware rendering
    - C. Rasterization
    - D. Ray tracing
    - E. None of the above
2. Define rasterization.
3. What is the purpose of using a separate hardware processing unit for the generation of computer images in video games?
4. What do a graphics processing unit and a physics processing unit have in common?
5. Define clipping and how it is used in rasterization.
6. Projected geometry is in what dimension?
    - A. 2D
    - B. 3D
7. What does FPS stand for in terms of rendering scenes? What is the easiest way to calculate the FPS of an application?
8. Define double buffering.
9. Define page flipping.
10. What is the benefit to using either double buffering or page flipping?
11. What do you think is more efficient: double buffering or page flipping? Please describe why you chose your answer.
12. What is the purpose of depth testing? How is depth testing generally performed in rasterization?
13. What is the purpose of a stencil buffer? If stencil elements could only be a 0 or 1, what is one way that you could optimize the stencil buffer?
14. What is it called when you render over pixels that have already been set?
    - A. Depth testing
    - B. Stencil testing
    - C. Pixel overdraw
    - D. None of the above

15. What is back-face culling? How is back-face culling used to speed up the rendering of a scene?
16. What are tertiary buffers?
17. Describe the general steps needed to render a line as described earlier in this chapter.
18. Describe the general steps needed to render a triangle as described earlier in this chapter.
19. How many combined matrices make up the model-view projection matrix? What does each matrix represent?
20. True or false: Direct3D supports both software and hardware rendering in the graphics API.
21. True or false: Page flipping and double buffering are the exact same thing in code.
22. True or false: Pixel overdraws are eliminated using the depth buffer.
23. True or false: The stencil buffer is a rendering mask.
24. True or false: 3D graphics hardware is more efficient at rendering 3D graphics than 2D graphics.
25. True or false: There is no need to use depth testing when using back-face culling.

CHAPTER EXERCISES

Exercise 1: Implement a stencil buffer using the algorithm mentioned earlier in this chapter and apply it to the software rendering system developed throughout this text. Use single bytes for each stencil flag that represent either an on (1) or an off (0) state.

Exercise 2: Implement back-face culling to the software rendering system developed throughout this chapter for triangles. If a triangle that is being rendered to the screen is facing away from the viewer, discard it from the rendering pipeline. This can be done by testing the plane of the triangle and at which side of the plane the viewer is located. For projected polygonal data the origin can be assumed to be (0, 0, 0).

Exercise 3: Implement depth buffering using a floating point buffer. Allow depth testing to be used for the rendering of pixels, lines, and triangles.

PROGRAMMABLE SHADERS

In This Chapter

- Shaders in Computer Graphics
- Low-Level Shaders
- High-Level Shaders
- OpenGL's GLSL
- Direct3D's HLSL
- Additional Shader Technologies and Tools

Modern 3D video games are often rich sources of graphical effects and technology. Throughout the years the primary focus in game development has traditionally been the graphics. Although today graphics are not as important as they once were when compared to other areas of a game, they are still very important and are still a focus that many hard-core gamers have come to expect from their blockbuster triple-A titles. By programming directly onto the graphical hardware, game developers are able to tap into the potential the hardware has to offer to create very visually appealing scenes using custom-written effects. This power and flexibility allows game developers to create styles all their own, which wasn't possible before the time of shaders in common video games.

In this chapter we briefly discuss and review programmable graphics shaders in terms of their history, types, and how to generally set them up in OpenGL and Direct3D. In this chapter we also discuss various high-level shading languages that are available today. The purpose of this chapter is to serve as a quick review to ensure that everyone reading this book is ready for the remainder of the text.

SHADERS IN COMPUTER GRAPHICS

Graphical application programming interfaces are used to talk directly to the graphics hardware attached to a computer or gaming console. The most popular two graphics APIs are Direct3D and OpenGL. In the past graphical APIs offered a set of algorithms and rendering states that a programmer could enable or disable any time in an application. This set of algorithms and rendering states is known as the fixed-function pipeline, and it provides developers a high-level point of access to the underlying hardware and features that are common in 3D video games.

Although the fixed-function pipeline does offer some convenience when it comes to running specific algorithms that a particular API supports, its major downside is that it is restrictive in the number of features and the way developers talk to the hardware, and it lacks the customization of allowing developers to write their own algorithms and execute them in the graphics hardware. Programmable shaders are the solution to the limitations and restrictions of a graphical API's fixed-function pipeline. Since the introduction of programmable hardware, the visuals seen in the games industry have grown in quality and complexity, among other things, by leaps and bounds.

A shader is executable code that can be run on the graphics hardware. A programmable shader is a way for developers to write custom algorithms that can operate on the data that compose their virtual scenes.

Shaders can be used to create just about any effect you can think of, which gives developers a high level of freedom and flexibility regardless of the API being utilized.

Types of Shaders

Today there are three different types of shaders that can be used to operate on the various pieces of information that compose a virtual scene. These shaders are vertex shaders, geometry shaders, and pixel shaders. When combined into one effect, a set of shaders is collectively called a shader program. Only one shader type can be active at a time. This means, for example, that it is not possible to enable two vertex shaders at the same time to operate on the same data.

Vertex shaders are code that is executed on each vertex that is passed to the rendering hardware. The input of a vertex shader comes from the application itself, whereas the other types of shaders receive their input from the shader that comes before it, excluding uniform and constant variables, which we discuss in more detail later in this chapter. Vertex shaders are often used to transform vertex positions using various matrices such as the model-view project matrix, and they are used to perform calculations that need to be performed once per vertex. Examples of operations that are often done on a per-vertex level include:

- Per-vertex level lighting
- GPU animations
- Vertex displacements
- Calculating values that can be interpolated across the surface in the pixel shader (e.g., texture coordinates, vertex colors, vertex normals)

Geometry shaders sit between the vertex shader and the pixel shader. Once data have been operated on by the vertex shader, they are passed to the geometry shader, if one exists. Geometry shaders can be used to create new geometry and can operate on entire primitives. Geometry shaders can emit zero or more primitives, where emitting more than the incoming primitive generates new geometry and emitting zero primitives discards the original primitive that was passed to the geometry shader. Geometry shaders are a new type of shader that is available in Shader Model 4.0, which is currently supported by the Direct3D 10 and OpenGL 3.0 graphical APIs.

The third type of shader is the pixel shader, also known as the fragment shader. A pixel shader operates on each rasterized pixel that is displayed on the screen. In Chapter 4, "Rasterization," we saw that once a primitive has been transformed and clipped, the area that makes up the primitive is filled in (shaded). If you are using a pixel shader, each pixel that is shaded and that falls within the area of the primitive is operated on by the algorithm defined in the pixel shader. The input for the pixel shader can be either the output from the vertex shader or, if one exists, the output from the geometry shader.

LOW-LEVEL SHADERS

In the early days of programmable shaders, developers had to use a RISC-oriented assembly language to code the effects they wanted to use in games. RISC, short for reduced instruction set compiler, is a CPU design that favors using an instruction set that is reduced in size and complexity. Most programmers familiar with assembly language will agree that, although you can get a lot of control over the instructions on a lower level, it is harder to develop and maintain assembly-based code than a high-level language such as C or C++. Before high-level shader languages became commonplace, it was low-level shaders that developers had to work with. In addition, the two main graphics APIs, OpenGL and Direct3D, had slightly different assembly-based languages, so a shader written for one would not work in the other. This means developers often had to create effects not only for the different shader versions they wanted to support but for both APIs.

In the early days of shaders only vertex and pixel shaders were available. In the very beginning some hardware didn't even have efficient pixel shaders. A vertex shader is program code for the vertex processor. In shaders all data were stored in four 128-bit floating-point variables that resembled 4D vectors. An example of this is shown in Figure 5.1.

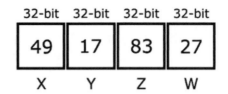

FIGURE 5.1 A four-paired 128-bit shader variable.

The variables in programmable shaders are floating-point values. When it came to working with individual values instead of four-pair values, this was often simulated using the individual 32-bit element of one of these values. In early shaders placing values in temporary registers was very common because instructions only operated on registers, not on hard-coded constant values such as 10.5 or 1.

Graphics hardware uses single instruction multiple data (SIMD) processors, which allows for a single instruction to be used on multiple elements. When performing an operation on a single instruction, for example, an add instruction, you would use it on one of these shader variables and it would effect all elements of it.

In the early days of vertex shaders there was also no support for loops, conditional statements, or any instruction that would break the linear nature of code execution. Support for such instructions did come later in limited fashion in Shader Model 2.0 and fully in Shader Model 3.0 and higher. The lack of support for such instructions in the beginning limited what could be done in shaders and made performing operations that could benefit from them tricky. For loops this also meant that anything that had to be executed a specific number of times had to be rolled out. Even in Shader Model 2.0 loops could not have variable conditions that could change but had to use constants, so there were still some limitations.

Early vertex shaders also had very limited instruction count sizes. For example, a vertex shader in DirectX 8 was limited to 128 instructions. Effects that required computations that would exceed this limit were impossible on early shader models. Some effects where made possible by finding as many shortcuts and workarounds as possible to reduce the instruction count and incurred performance hits (e.g., using lookup textures instead of using multiple instructions to compute a value), but this was still quite tricky at times.

Assembly is all about registers, and working with low-level shaders is no exception. Early vertex shaders used up to 16 input registers (v0 through v15), 13 or so output registers depending on the specific hardware board you had, 12 temporary registers (r0 through r11), and varying numbers of constant registers that depended on the specific hardware board you had. For example, some graphics cards such as the GeForce TI (GeForce 4) had 96 constant registers, whereas some ATI cards such as the Radeon 8500 had 192. All registers used 128-bit four-element variables as well. Input registers are registers that store input information from the application. Output registers stored outgoing information from the current shader to the next process (e.g., going from the vertex to the pixel shader).

Temporary registers are used to store temporary information in memory, and constant registers are used to bind data that do not vary from vertex to vertex or pixel to pixel. An example of something that would be stored in a constant register is the model-view projection matrix, which would not change for each vertex or pixel. Constant registers could only be read by a shader but not written to from inside the shader's code, which is what makes those registers constant.

The difference in register counts made it a challenge to create shaders for different hardware boards. Typically, developers would target the lowest hardware specs and use shaders built specifically for those specs.

 There is also a single address register starting with shader profile 1.1, with more address registers available in later shader versions. The address register can be used to offset the constant memory starting location.

Pixel shaders are operated on each raster pixel that is shaded. Pixel shaders are fed information from the vertex shader or from a geometry shader in Shader Model 4.0. In the early days of shaders pixel shaders were much more limited than they are now. This was especially true in performance, where a lot of floating-point operations were calculated, and more complex effects such as bump mapping were not practical at one point in real time on some hardware. When situations like this occurred, developers often found tricks and shortcuts to get around the limitations of the hardware. For example, per-pixel lighting normalization cube maps, which are cube maps that store normal values instead of colors, were used to approximate the normalization of a vector by using the vector as a 3D texture coordinate. In the early days of programmable graphics, hardware operations such as normalizations and other operations that used things such as square roots, powers, and so forth were so slow that developers needed tricks like this that often gave a needed boost in performance for some effects.

Another of the major downfalls to using early pixel shaders was that they didn't allow developers to sample the same texture more than once. This eventually changed, but the limitation presented by early pixel shaders, and shaders in general, sometimes made it very difficult to create a lot of different and complex effects. This can be seen in older graphics programming books based on low-level shaders, where even some simple effects were tricky to perform using shaders or were tricky to perform efficiently. Per-pixel lighting is a great example since in general it is a pretty straightforward effect to implement today. Textures were also used in per-pixel lighting for some effects such as attenuation lookup textures for representing point lights.

The register count wasn't as high with pixel shaders as it was in vertex shaders in the early days. Using Shader Model 1.0 as an example, the number of constant registers for pixel shader versions 1.1 through 1.4 were eight, whereas vertex shaders on some hardware devices had 96 registers and higher. Temporary registers in version 1.1 through 1.3 in pixel shaders only had two, whereas version 1.4 had six.

Working with Low-Level Shaders

Working with low-level shaders requires you to be familiar with how assembly language works and operates. Shaders can be compiled into binary form and loaded as-is or can be loaded in ASCII format and compiled at run-time, which is an option commonly available in both OpenGL and Direct3D. Loading and rendering with a low-level shader in a graphical API such as OpenGL or Direct3D requires the following general steps to be taken at some point in the application:

- Load the vertex and pixel shaders (precompiled or compiled at run-time).
- Bind the vertex and pixel shaders.
- Bind any constant variables (registers) that the shader needs.
- Bind any textures and set any necessary render states needed for the effect.
- Render the geometry.

ON THE CD

In this section we briefly look at the implementation of a low-level shader in Direct3D. The goal of this book is not to learn low-level shader programming, so we focus on a single demo as a quick example. On the CD-ROM you can find the Low-Level Shader demo application and source code in the Chapter 5 folder. The demo application uses a simple set of shaders where the vertex shader transforms the incoming vertex by the model-view projection matrix and passes along the vertex color to the pixel shader, which is interpolated across the surface (Figure 5.2). The example's vertex shader source code is shown in Listing 5.1 for Direct3D.

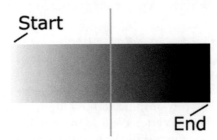

FIGURE 5.2   Interpolating values across a surface from a vertex shader.

LISTING 5.1 A LOW-LEVEL VERTEX SHADER

```
vs.2.0

dcl_position v0              // Vertex postion (x, y, z).
dcl_color    v1             // Vertex color.


m4x4 r0, v0, c0             // Transform the position.
                            // r0 is a temp register
                            // to hold transformed position.

mov oPos, r0               // Move to output (oPos).
mov oD0, v1                // Move color to output color.
```

The vertex shader defines two input registers: v0 and v1. The v0 register is used for the incoming vertex position, which is defined by the dcl_position keyword, whereas the color uses register v1, which is defined by the dcl_color keyword. Earlier it was mentioned that constant registers are c0 through whatever maximum your hardware used, which in some cases can be c95 or higher. Later we discuss how the Direct3D application sets the model-view project matrix to be in c0 through c3. Since each register is essentially a 4D vector, it takes four of these to hold a 4×4 matrix. The fourth line of the example vertex shader performs a matrix–vector transformation using the m4x4 keyword with the vertex position in v0 and the model-view matrix in c0-c3 and stores the results in the temporary register r0. Moving values is done with the mov instructions.

 Remember that for vertex shaders r* are temporary registers, c* are constant registers, and v* are input registers. Registers starting with an o are used for output registers.

The last two lines of the example vertex shader pass the transformed vertex position to the output register's output position oPos and pass the input vertex color to the output register oD0. Without comments it would be more difficult to determine at first glance what each line of the code does. Since there are not too many instructions in the example vertex shader, it is easier to read over its contents and figure out what it is doing, but if the shader was far more complex, its readability would decrease as more lines were added to the source.

 Placing descriptive comments on each line of assembly source code is highly recommended.

The pixel shader for the example demo is much smaller than its vertex shader counterpart. The major difference in the pixel shader compared to the vertex shader is that pixel shaders output color. This is done primarily through the r0 register, which, in a pixel shader, is not a temporary register but is an output color register. The pixel shader for the demo application, shown in Listing 5.2, simply passes the incoming interpolated vertex color, v0, to the output color register, r0.

LISTING 5.2 A LOW-LEVEL PIXEL SHADER

```
ps.1.1

mov r0, v0                    // Move input color to output color.
```

 All low-level shaders have a version number that must be displayed at the top of the file. This allows shader compilers to know what shader model and version the shader source uses.

Low-level shaders in Direct3D 9 can be loaded into LPDIRECT3DVERTEXSHADER9 and LPDIRECT3DPIXELSHADER9 for vertex and pixel shaders, respectively. For the Low-Level Shader demo application the global variables used to define these shaders are shown in Listing 5.3. When loading shaders, it is common to check to make sure the hardware supports the shader types you want to load before loading in the shader source. In Direct3D the capabilities of the hardware can be gathered and examined using the device's GetDeviceCaps() function. The loading of low-level shaders in Direct3D 9 is done with D3DXAssembleShaderFromFile(), assuming you are loading an ASCII file that needs compiling, CreateVertexShader(), and CreatePixelShader() of the device class. To load a vertex shader from an ASCII text file refer to Listing 5.4, which is taken out of the Low-Level Shader demo application.

 In Direct3D 10 the only option is to use the high-level shading language.

LISTING 5.3 LOW-LEVEL SHADER DEMO GLOBAL VARIABLES

```
// Low level shaders.
LPDIRECT3DVERTEXSHADER9 g_vertexShader = NULL;
LPDIRECT3DPIXELSHADER9 g_pixelShader = NULL;
```

LISTING 5.4 CODE CLIP USED TO CHECK FOR SHADER SUPPORT AND TO LOAD THE SHADERS

```
D3DCAPS9 caps;

g_d3dObject->GetDeviceCaps(D3DADAPTER_DEFAULT,
                           D3DDEVTYPE_HAL, &caps);


if(caps.VertexShaderVersion < D3DVS_VERSION(2, 0))
   return false;

if(caps.PixelShaderVersion < D3DPS_VERSION(1, 1))
   return false;

ID3DXBuffer *source = NULL;


// Vertex shader.
hr = D3DXAssembleShaderFromFile("vs.vsh", NULL, NULL,
                                NULL, &source, NULL);

if(hr != D3D_OK) return false;

hr = g_d3dDevice->CreateVertexShader(
        (DWORD*)source->GetBufferPointer(), &g_vertexShader);

if(hr != D3D_OK) return false;
if(source != NULL) source->Release();


 // Pixel shader.
 hr = D3DXAssembleShaderFromFile("ps.psh", NULL, NULL,
                                 NULL, &source, NULL);

 if(hr != D3D_OK) return false;

 hr = g_d3dDevice->CreatePixelShader(
         (DWORD*)source->GetBufferPointer(), &g_pixelShader);

 if(hr != D3D_OK) return false;
 if(source != NULL) source->Release();
```

If you are loading an already-compiled shader from a file or from another resource, you have to use the appropriate function rather than D3DXAssembleShaderFrom-File(), *which loads and compiles a shader for you at run-time.*

According to the vertex shader for the demo application (shown in Listing 5.1), one constant register is set by the application. This constant variable in the demo stores the model-view projection matrix and, based on what is defined in the vertex shader, uses registers c0 through c3. To set a constant register in Direct3D 9 you use the device's function SetVertexShaderConstantF(). To set the shaders you use SetVertexShader() and SetPixelShader(), respectively. The rendering code from the Low-Level Shader demo application is shown in Listing 5.5. Figure 5.3 shows a screenshot of the demo application in action.

LISTING 5.5 THE RENDERING FUNCTION FROM THE LOW-LEVEL SHADER DEMO

```
void RenderScene()
{
   g_d3dDevice->Clear(0, NULL, D3DCLEAR_TARGET |
                      D3DCLEAR_ZBUFFER,
                      D3DCOLOR_XRGB(0,0,0), 1.0f, 0);

   g_d3dDevice->BeginScene();

   // Setup geometry to render.
   g_d3dDevice->SetStreamSource(0, g_vertexBuffer,
                                0, sizeof(Vertex));


   // Adding the world and view matrices is not technically
   // necessary since nothing is set (they are identity
                         matrices).
   // Since the MVP is used by the shader this makes the
                         example
   // clear as to what it being passed.

   D3DXMATRIX worldMat, viewMat;
   D3DXMatrixIdentity(&worldMat);
   D3DXMatrixIdentity(&viewMat);

   D3DXMATRIX mvp = worldMat * viewMat * g_projMat;
   D3DXMatrixTranspose(&mvp, &mvp);
```

```
      // The only variable the vertex shader needs is the mvp.
      g_d3dDevice->SetVertexShaderConstantF(0, (float*)mvp, 4);

      // Set vertex format.
      g_d3dDevice->SetFVF(D3DFVF_D3DVertex);

      // Set the shaders.
      g_d3dDevice->SetVertexShader(g_vertexShader);
      g_d3dDevice->SetPixelShader(g_pixelShader);


      // This will draw everything in the buffer.
      g_d3dDevice->DrawPrimitive(D3DPT_TRIANGLELIST, 0, 1);

      g_d3dDevice->EndScene();

      g_d3dDevice->Present(NULL, NULL, NULL, NULL);
   }


   void Shutdown()
   {
      // Here we release the Direct3D objects.

      if(g_d3dDevice != NULL) g_d3dDevice->Release();
      g_d3dDevice = NULL;

      if(g_d3dObject != NULL) g_d3dObject->Release();
      g_d3dObject = NULL;

      if(g_vertexBuffer != NULL) g_vertexBuffer->Release();
      g_vertexBuffer = NULL;

      if(g_pixelShader != NULL) g_pixelShader->Release();
      g_pixelShader = NULL;

      if(g_vertexShader != NULL) g_vertexShader->Release();
      g_vertexShader = NULL;
   }
```

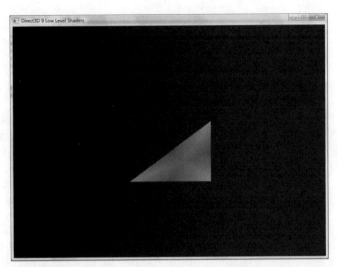

FIGURE 5.3 Screenshot from the Low-Level Shader demo.

HIGH-LEVEL SHADERS

High-level shading languages offer a flexible alternative to the low-level shading languages that developers had to use in the early days of programmable graphics hardware. A high-level shading language based on a very popular language, such as C, allows developers already working with that language to more easily write, read, and maintain shader code because they are already familiar with the syntax being used. High-level languages have always traditionally had the following benefits over low-level languages:

- Easier to read
- Easier to modify
- Easier to track errors
- Easier to write
- Faster to develop for since low-level shaders take more time in general than their high-level counterparts

The main benefit to low-level languages is that the developers have ultimate control over how the machine's registers are used, while in a high-level language a compiler has the job of generating the low-level code. Some compilers are really good at optimizations and are very efficient, but that does not always lead to the fastest and most efficient code possible. Although this can or cannot be much of an issue when discussing some topics, especially with the sophistication most modern compilers have, it is still true that the convenience of a high-level language is often at the cost of low-level control. The large majority of developers around the world are satisfied with this, although sometimes low-level code needs to be revisited from time to time.

It was quickly realized that high-level shading languages would need to be developed for programmable hardware in the early days of shaders. NVIDIA took the initiative and created Cg, while Microsoft, which had a hand in the creation of Cg, developed HLSL, and OpenGL had GLSL. Each of these high-level shading languages is based on C, and they are very similar to one another.

Variables in high-level shading languages are defined using integer or floating-point data types built into the language. Integers are a feature of the language rather than being a register type used by the graphics hardware. Variables in a high-level shading language are translated into the appropriate input, output, constant, and temporary registers of the GPU. Variables in the high-level shading languages we look at in this chapter have variable scopes, which can define a scope to be a program, shader, or function level. Function scope is the same as it is in a language like C, where a variable is visible to only that function. Shader scope is a global variable that can be seen by any block of code or function in the current shader. Program scopes are higher level global variables that can be seen by each of the shaders that make up the shader program (i.e., can be seen by the vertex, pixel, and geometry shaders).

Functions in high-level shading languages operate in a similar manner as they do in languages like C++. You can define functions with return types, parameters, and so forth. In the high-level shading languages the rules of the scope of variables and objects exist in the same way they do in C++, where a function can declare variables local to that function and outside the scope of other functions, unless originally declared global. Although none of the high-level shading languages we discuss support de-referencing operators such as C and C++, special keywords allow for reference functionality, which we discuss later in this chapter.

 Scope can also be defined using single or nested curly braces within a function in a high-level language.

OpenGL's GLSL

The OpenGL Shading Language (GLSL) is the standard high-level shading language for the OpenGL graphics API. GLSL, like Direct3D's HLSL and NVIDIA's Cg, is based on the C programming language with a bit of C++ in some aspects, but although the languages of GLSL and C are similar, there are also many differences that we will see throughout this section.

Like some C applications, you use a main() function to mark the shader's entry point in GLSL. This function does not return anything, that is, not using a keyword like return, and encompasses the execution of the shader's algorithm. An example simple vertex shader is shown here:

```
varying vec4 color;

unifor vec4 scale;


void main()
{
    gl_Position = gl_ModelViewProjectionMatrix * gl_Vertex;

    color = gl_Color * scale;
}
```

Note the keywords varying and uniform. The keyword varying is used for output variables that are passed along, in the case of this vertex shader, to the pixel shader. The keyword uniform is used to declare variables that are set by the application (i.e., constant registers). You should also notice variables of the type vec4. A vec4 variable is a four-component 128-bit structure, which is what shaders use naturally, as mentioned earlier in this chapter. There are also vec2 and vec3 along with many other types that compile down to declaring and writing to 128-bit structures. The high-level language allows us to represent and work with these data on a higher level, so the low-level details are not visible.

 Comments are performed using // or /* */ like in the C++ programming language.

Overview to GLSL

OpenGL's GLSL uses the extensions ARB_shading_language_100, ARB_vertex_shader, ARB_fragment_shader, and ARB_shader_objects. GLSL was first promoted to the OpenGL core in version 2.0 of the graphics API and has been a major addition to it.

Variables in GLSL are type safe and can be declared anywhere in a function just like they can in C++. There is no implicit type casting in GLSL, which means data types must match when variables are assigned (e.g., unlike in C++, where you can set an integer to a floating-point variable). Although there is no implicit casting, there is explicit casting from different types. The variable types that GLSL supports are shown in Table 5.1.

Table 5.1 Variable Types Supported by GLSL

Name	Description
float	Floating-point scalar
int	Integer
bool	Boolean variable
vec2	Floating-point two-component vector
vec3	Floating-point three-component vector
vec4	Floating-point four-component vector
vec2i	Integer two-component vector
vec3i	Integer three-component vector
vec4i	Integer four-component vector
vec2b	Boolean two-component vector
vec3b	Boolean three-component vector
vec4b	Boolean four-component vector
mat2	2x2 matrix
ma3	3x3 matrix
mat4	4x4 matrix
sampler1D	1D texture
sampler2D	2D texture
sampler3D	3D texture
samplerCube	Cube map texture
sampler1DShadow	1D shadow map
sampler2DShadow	2D shadow map
void	Used by functions to tell the compiler that it doesn't return a value or, if used in the parameter list, takes any parameters

Integers can be used in GLSL to specify things such as loop counters, array sizes, and things that typically are not expressed using floating-point variables. Integers are a feature of the language, and they can have their uses when declaring non-floating-point variables. Vectors in high-level shading languages are the most used types, and they can be used for everything from vertex positions to texture coordinates to vertex colors and so forth. Vectors also allow you to define which components you are accessing using access swizzling. For example:

```
vec4 new_color = old_color.bgra;
```

Matrices are self-explanatory and allow you to define a 2×2, 3×3, or 4×4 matrix of floating-point values. Samplers are special types used to specify a texture in GLSL. When using textures in a vertex shader or a pixel shader, you must use the type based on what kind of texture it is. For example, a 2D texture uses `sampler2D` and so forth. Obtaining a color from a texture in GLSL can look like the following, where `texture2D()` is a built-in GLSL function for accessing 2D texture image data using 2D coordinates.

```
sampler2D decal;
vec2 tex_coord = vec2(0.5, 0.5);

vec4 color = texture2D(decal, tex_coord);
```

As with the C programming language, you can also define structures in GLSL. For example:

```
struct material
{
   vec4 diffuse;
   vec4 specular;
};
```

You can also define arrays of variables or structures just like you can in the C/C++ programming languages. You cannot dynamically allocate arrays, but you can statically allocate them like the following.

```
material mat_list[10];
```

Type qualifiers are types that you can prefix with any variable in a shader. For GLSL there are the following type qualifiers.

- default
- uniform
- varying
- const
- in
- out
- inout

The `default` type qualifier is the default for all declared variables. A variable that has a default type qualifier can be both read and written. You do not have to specify `default` for variables in GLSL.

The `uniform` type qualifier is used by variables that are set by the application that do not change often. This change can occur usually per object(s), per frame, or per set of frames. Uniform variables are constant registers when you look at shaders from a low-level standpoint. An example of a common variable that has a uniform type is the model-view projection matrix, which changes each object, assuming each object has its own local (model) transformation.

The varying type qualifier is used by variables that are passed to the next process (e.g., from the vertex shader to the pixel shader). These variables are used for values that are often interpolated, such as texture coordinates, vertex colors, and normal vectors.

The const type qualifier in terms of GLSL is used to create constant variables. These are variables that can only be read and not written. The term *const* is not related to constant registers and is used in the high-level language to allow you to specify variables you don't want accidentally written, such as const in C or C++.

The in type qualifier can only be used for function parameters and is used to specify a variable that can only be read but not written. The out type qualifier is the opposite of the in qualifier and specifies that a variable can only be written and not read. The inout type qualifier specifies that a variable can be read or written to, which works a lot like references in C and C++, which are de-referenced using the & symbol before the variable. The in, out, and inout type qualifiers are basically references in GLSL, and they should be used with care just like C and C++ references.

GLSL allows for flow control and conditional statements in the same manner as C and C++. In the early shader versions and models shaders did not support flow controls or conditional statements. In Shader Model 3.0 and up they were added and are now fully supported. Flow controls in GLSL include the following.

- For loops
- While loops
- Do-while loops
- If and if-else statements
- Breaks
- Continues
- Functions

 High-level shading languages such as Cg, GLSL, and HLSL also support preprocessor directives, many of which can be found in C and C++.

Close to 100 built-in variables and functions are part of GLSL. For a complete listing of these built-in functions consult the documentation. Throughout this book we discuss various built-in functions as they are used.

Setting up and Using GLSL

A vertex and pixel shader written in GLSL are compiled and linked together into one shader program that represents the coded graphical effect. To do this, various OpenGL function calls are used to create the shader program, which we discuss briefly in this section.

A GLSL shader is represented by a `GLhandleARB` variable. Like textures, frame-buffer objects, and other resources in OpenGL, handles are used to represent the object(s) being created. The two common types of objects when working with GLSL are program objects and shaders. Shaders are the individual shader code, while program objects represent the linked compiled code. In other words, a shader program is a set of vertex, pixel, and/or geometry combined into one effect. To create a shader program you would use the OpenGL function `glCreateProgramObjectARB()`, which returns a handle to the program object and takes no parameters. The function prototype for `glCreateProgramObjectARB()` takes the following form.

```
GLhandleARB glCreateProgramObjectARB(void)
```

The second type of object, the individual shader itself, is created by calling the OpenGL function `glCreateShaderObjectARB()`. This function takes one parameter, which can have a value of either `GL_VERTEX_SHADER_ARB` or `GL_FRAGMENT_SHADER_ARB`. The function prototype for `glCreateShaderObjectARB()` takes the following form.

```
GLhandleARB glCreateShaderObjectARB(GLenum shaderType)
```

With a handle to the shader resource, you can now attach source code to it. This is done with a call to `glShaderSourceARB()`, and it takes a handle, the size of the array that stores the shader's source strings, the shader source as an array of strings, and an array that stores an array of lengths, which is the lengths of each string. If the shader's code is stored in one large character buffer, you can pass `NULL` for the lengths and use a size of 1 for the number of strings. The function prototype for the `glShaderSourceARB()` function is as follows.

```
void glShaderSourceARB(GLhandleARB shader,
                       GLsizei nstrings,
                       const GLcharARB **strings,
                       const GLint *lengths)
```

To compile a shader you would call the OpenGL function `glCompileShaderARB()`, which takes the shader's hander as a parameter. This function should be called after the `glShaderSourceARB()` function has been called so the source is ready for compilation. The function prototype is as follows.

```
void glCompileShaderARB(GLhandleARB shader)
```

At any time you can get a parameter value from GLSL in OpenGL. For example, if you want to get the result of a compilation process, this function can be called to get the value. The function parameters for this function include the shader's, or program, handle, the parameter you are querying for, and the address where the value will be stored. Check the GLSL documentation for a full list of possible parameters that can be used. The function prototype for glGetObjectParameterARB*v() is as follows.

```
void glGetObjectParameterARBfv(GLhandleARB object,
                               GLenum pname,
                               GLfloat *params)

void glGetObjectParameterARBiv(GLhandleARB object,
                               GLenum pname,
                               GLint *params)
```

The next function we look at is used to get the information log of an OpenGL object. This is done by calling glGetInfoLogARB(), which can be used to get the information log of a shader object after a compilation or a linking operation. The function takes the shader's handle, the maximum length of the buffer used for the information log, the address of a variable that will store the length of the returned information log, and the character data for the information log. The function prototype for the glGet-InfoLogARB() function is as follows.

```
void glGetInfoLogARB(GLhandleARB object,
                     GLsizei maxLength,
                     GLsizei *length,
                     GLcharARB *infoLog)
```

The last functions we look at are glAttachObjectARB(), glDeleteObjec-tARB(), and glUseProgramObjectARB(). The glAttachObjectARB() function is used to attach a shader to a program. The glDeleteObjectARB() function is used to delete a GLSL program or shader, much like glDeleteTextures() is used to delete OpenGL textures. The last function, glUseProgramObjec-tARB(), is used to bind a shader program, which applies the shader to the rendering API. Sending 0 to this function disables shaders and returns to the fixed-function pipeline. The function prototype for these three functions is as follows.

```
void glAttachObjectARB(GLhandleARB program,
                       GLhandleARB shader)

void glDeleteObjectARB(GLhandleARB object)

void glUseProgramObjectARB(GLhandleARB program)
```

GLSL Example Shader

ON THE CD

On the book's accompanying CD-ROM there is a demo application called GLSL in the Chapter 5 folder. This demo application demonstrates the simple use of GLSL using the functions mentioned earlier in this section. The OpenGL demo applications found throughout this book use GLUT and GLee. Refer to Appendix B, "Compiling the Sample Source Code," for more detailed information on compiling and using these tools.

The GLSL demo application starts with the shaders, which consist of vertex and pixel shaders that are used to transform incoming geometry and output vertex colors for each primitive. The vertex shader transforms the incoming vertex by the model-view projection matrix, which OpenGL internally makes available using the built-in variables gl_Vertex and gl_ModelViewProjectionMatrix. The vertex shader also passes along the vertex color to be interpolated by the pixel shader using a varying variable. The vertex shader's full source is show in Listing 5.6. The pixel shader, shown in Listing 5.7, takes the incoming interpolated vertex color and sets it to the output color, which is done using the built-in variable gl_FragColor.

LISTING 5.6 THE GLSL DEMO'S VERTEX SHADER

```
// color will be passed to the pixel shader.
varying vec4 color;


void main()
{
    // Transform vertex.
    gl_Position = gl_ModelViewProjectionMatrix * gl_Vertex;

    // Pass along the color.
    color = gl_Color;
}
```

LISTING 5.7 THE GLSL DEMO'S PIXEL SHADER

```
varying vec4 color;


void main()
{
   // Pass along incoming color to the output.
   gl_FragColor = color;
}
```

The demo is made up of a single source file called main.cpp. The source file has one global that is the handle to the GLSL shader program that makes up the effect we are going to model. This is shown in Listing 5.8, which creates a single GLhandleARB object.

LISTING 5.8 GLSL DEMO'S SINGLE GLOBAL

```
GLhandleARB g_shader;
```

The next code we look at from the demo application is the code used to load the shader into memory. We have to load the shader's source code ourselves, which will be passed to OpenGL for compilation. This function is called LoadText(), and it takes a file name of the ASCII text file to load and returns the characters from the file. The function ends by cutting off any garbage characters that happened to exist in the file, depending on the text editor, so that only valid GLSL code is parsed by the GLSL compiler. The LoadText() function is shown in Listing 5.9.

LISTING 5.9 LOADING A TEXT FILE INTO MEMORY

```
char* LoadText(char *file)
{
   FILE *fp = fopen(file, "r");

   if(fp == NULL)
      return NULL;

   fseek(fp, 0, SEEK_END);
   int size = ftell(fp);
   fseek(fp, 0, SEEK_SET);
```

```
   if(size == 0)
      return NULL;


   char *source = new char[size + 1];

   fread(source, 1, size, fp);

   // Trim exceess characters that might exist.  Some text
   // editors do not save text after the last character in
   // the text file, which can force errors.  Replace EOF
   // with a string delim.
   while(size-- > 0)
   {
      if(source[size] == (char)10)
      {
         source[size] = '\0';
         break;
      }
   }


   return source;
}
```

The next function we examine is used to load a GLSL shader file. This function is called LoadShader(), and it takes the file name for the shader, the type of shader (e.g., vertex or pixel shader), and a handle for the shader program that the loaded shader file will be linked to. If any errors are found in the compilation of the shader, they are displayed to the console window, and the function will return false. The LoadShader() function is shown in Listing 5.10.

LISTING 5.10 FUNCTION USED TO LOAD A SHADER FILE INTO OPENGL

```
bool LoadShader(char *file, GLenum type, GLhandleARB context)
{
   // GLSL shader.
   GLhandleARB shader;

   // Load shader's source text.
   char *code = LoadText(file);
```

```
            if(code == NULL)
               return false;

            // Create the shader from a text file.
            shader = glCreateShaderObjectARB(type);
            glShaderSourceARB(shader, 1, (const char**)&code, NULL);
            glCompileShaderARB(shader);

            int result;
            char error[1024];

            // Returns the results of the shader compilation.
            glGetObjectParameterivARB(shader,
GL_OBJECT_COMPILE_STATUS_ARB,
                                      &result);
            delete[] code;

            // Display shader errors if any.
            if(!result)
            {
               // Get the error message and display it.
               glGetInfoLogARB(shader, sizeof(error), NULL, error);
               printf("Error in shader...\n%s\n", error);

               return false;
            }

            // Attach to the effect's context.
            glAttachObjectARB(context, shader);

            glDeleteObjectARB(shader);

            return true;
         }
```

The next function is used to load an entire shader program. This function uses the shader loading function from Listing 5.10 and takes as parameters a vertex shader file name, a pixel shader file name, and a shader program handle. If the compilation and linkage are successful, the function returns true and the shader program is stored in the reference handle parameter. The shader program loading function is shown in Listing 5.11.

LISTING 5.11 A FUNCTION TO LOAD A SHADER PROGRAM INTO OPENGL

```
bool CreateGLSLShader(char *vsFile, char *psFile,
                      GLhandleARB &shader)
{
    bool ret = false;

    // Create the shader.
    shader = glCreateProgramObjectARB();

    // Load the vertex shader.
    if(LoadShader(vsFile, GL_VERTEX_SHADER_ARB, shader) ==
false)
        return false;

    // Load the pixel shader.
    if(LoadShader(psFile, GL_FRAGMENT_SHADER_ARB, shader) ==
false)
        return false;

    // Link together the vertex and pixel shaders.
    glLinkProgramARB(shader);

    int link = 0;
    char error[1024];

    glGetObjectParameterivARB(shader,
GL_OBJECT_LINK_STATUS_ARB,
                              &link);

    if(!link)
    {
        // Get the error message and display it.
        glGetInfoLogARB(shader, sizeof(error), NULL, error);
        printf("Error linking shader...\n%s\n", error);

        return false;
    }

    return true;
}
```

The last three functions of the demo application are a function called during the initialization, a function called during the closing of the application, and the rendering function. The initialization function sets a few common OpenGL rendering states and loads a shader program by calling the function from Listing 5.11, `CreateGLSLShader()`. The shutdown function calls `glDeleteObjectARB()` to delete the loaded shader handle from OpenGL. The rendering function renders a single colored triangle to the screen using the loaded shader. The last three functions from the GLSL demo application are shown in Listing 5.12. Figure 5.4 shows the screenshot of the GLSL demo application in action.

LISTING 5.12 THE REMAINING FUNCTIONS OF INTEREST FROM THE GLSL DEMO

```
bool InitializeApp()
{
    glClearColor(0.0f, 0.0f, 0.0f, 1.0f);
    glShadeModel(GL_SMOOTH);
    glEnable(GL_DEPTH_TEST);

    if(!CreateGLSLShader("../vs.glsl", "../ps.glsl",
g_shader))
        return false;

    return true;
}


void ShutdownApp()
{
    glDeleteObjectARB(g_shader);
}


void RenderScene()
{
    glClear(GL_COLOR_BUFFER_BIT | GL_DEPTH_BUFFER_BIT);
    glLoadIdentity();

    glTranslatef(0.0f, 0.0f, -5.0f);

    glUseProgramObjectARB(g_shader);
```

```
float vertices[] = { -1, 0, 0,  1, 0, 0,  0, 1, 0 };
float colors[]   = {  1, 0, 0,  0, 1, 0,  0, 0, 1 };

glEnableClientState(GL_VERTEX_ARRAY);
glVertexPointer(3, GL_FLOAT, 0, vertices);

glEnableClientState(GL_COLOR_ARRAY);
glColorPointer(3, GL_FLOAT, 0, colors);

glDrawArrays(GL_TRIANGLES, 0, 3);

glDisableClientState(GL_VERTEX_ARRAY);
glDisableClientState(GL_COLOR_ARRAY);

glUseProgramObjectARB(0);

glutSwapBuffers();
glutPostRedisplay();
}
```

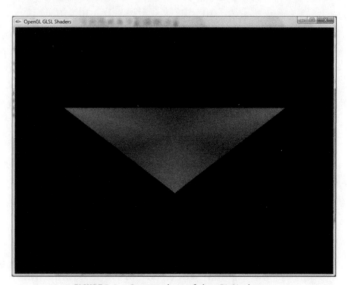

FIGURE 5.4   Screenshot of the GLSL demo.

Direct3D's HLSL

The High-Level Shading Language (HLSL) is the standard shading language created by Microsoft for their Direct3D graphics API, which is also now being used on Microsoft's XNA. Microsoft also worked to create the high-level shading language Cg, which is why the two shading languages are extremely similar. In the beginning, Cg and HLSL were the same language that was being developed by Microsoft and NVIDIA, but the two went in separate directions, which eventually gave us two separate but similar languages.

 XNA and Direct3D 10 do not offer a fixed-function pipeline, and you can only use HLSL for all rendering.

HLSL and GLSL, and thus also Cg, are all based on the C programming language. Like GLSL, HLSL supports the following.

- Preprocessor directives
- Flow control (e.g., functions, conditional statements, etc.)
- Standard set of built-in functions
- Type qualifiers such as in and out
- Various data types

GLSL shares some of the same data types but a few of them have different keywords. For example, in GLSL a four-component vector is vec4, which in HLSL is called float4. Another example can be seen with matrices, where a 4×4 matrix in GLSL uses the keyword mat4, while in HLSL it is float4x4. In GLSL there is also what are known as storage class modifiers, which are similar to GLSL type qualifiers. These storage class modifiers include

- extern
- shared
- static
- uniform
- volatile

The extern keyword is used for variables in the shader program that have global scope, which is the default for variables defined in the global section of shaders. The variables typed with the shared keyword that can be shared between multiple effect files that have been loaded into the graphics API.

The static keywords, which can't be used for globals, are variables that have values that persist even after the function has returned, which operate like C and C++ static variables. The uniform type is for variables that can be set outside by the application, just like with GLSL, and the `volatile` keyword simply tells the HLSL compiler that the variable changes frequently.

Semantics

HLSL has semantics that are used to link the input and output of values from the graphics pipeline. In GLSL built-in variables are used to get input or set output values. For example, in GLSL gl_Vertex stores the incoming vertex from the application. In HLSL a semantic is a keyword used to bind your variables to the inputs and outputs of a shader, and it tells the HLSL how the variable is used. An example is shown as follows, where the semantic comes after the variable name and a colon.

```
float4x4 worldViewProj : WorldViewProjection;


// Incoming vertex structure.
struct Vs_Input
{
   float3 vertexPos  : POSITION;
   float4 color      : COLOR0;
};


// Output vertex information to the pixel shader.
struct Vs_Output
{
   float4 vertexPos  : POSITION;
   float4 color      : COLOR0;
};


// Output from pixel shader.
struct Ps_Output
{
      float4 color   : COLOR;
};
```

Like GLSL, close to a hundred built-in functions are part of HLSL. We discuss various semantics and functions as we use them throughout the book.

Shaders, Techniques, and Passes

Shaders do not have reserved names for their entry points in HLSL. In GLSL you could use the main() function as the entry point. In HLSL you would create the function, name it whatever you wanted, and tell the HLSL compiler its name. This is done in the shader's technique.

A technique is basically an effect that is specified by a set of vertex, pixel, and geometry shaders. You can have as many techniques in one shader file as you want. You can also have as many different vertex and pixel shaders as you want in one file. When creating a technique, you can only use one vertex, pixel, or geometry shader for each rendering pass. In a technique you can specify more than one rendering pass for effects that require them. You can also set rendering states for each pass. An example of a technique is shown as follows.

```
technique SimpleEffect
{
   pass Pass0
   {
      // No lighting in this effect is used.
      Lighting = FALSE;


      // Compile and set the vertex and pixel shader.
      VertexShader = compile vs_3_0 VertexShaderMain();
      PixelShader  = compile ps_3_0 PixelShaderMain();
   }
}
```

To specify a technique you give it a name, which comes after the technique keyword, and you specify one or more passes. In a pass you can optionally set rendering states, which in the example set hardware lighting to false, and specify the various shaders the pass uses. For the shader compilation you can specify the shader model you want to use as well.

Setting Up and Using HLSL

Using HLSL in a Direct3D application is fairly straightforward. Effects are stored in a LPD3DXEFFECT object, an example of which is as follows.

```
LPD3DXEFFECT effect = NULL;
```

To load an HLSL shader from a file you can use the DirectX Utility function D3DXCreateEffectFromFile(). The function takes as parameters the Direct3D device, a file name for the effect file, an optional array of

preprocessor macros, an optional interface pointer used to handle #include
directives that is found in the file, loading flags, a list of shared parameters
from other already-loaded effects, the address to the effect that will be created by the function's call, and a buffer to save any compilation errors that
might arise. If all succeeds, this function will return S_OK. An example of
using this function is as follows.

```
LPD3DXBUFFER errors = NULL;

D3DXCreateEffectFromFile(g_d3dDevice, "effect.fx", NULL,
                         NULL, 0, NULL, &effect, &errors);
```

The function prototype for D3DXCreateEffectFromFile() is shown as
follows.

```
HRESULT D3DXCreateEffectFromFile(
    LPDIRECT3DDEVICE9 pDevice,
    LPCTSTR pSrcFile,
    CONST D3DXMACRO * pDefines,
    LPD3DXINCLUDE pInclude,
    DWORD Flags,
    LPD3DXEFFECTPOOL pPool,
    LPD3DXEFFECT * ppEffect,
    LPD3DXBUFFER * ppCompilationErrors
);
```

When loading shader effects into Direct3D, you can load the effect
from a file or from a resource. The following four Direct3D functions
allow you to do this.

- D3DXCreateEffectFromFile()
- D3DXCreateEffectFromFileEx()
- D3DXCreateEffectFromResource()
- D3DXCreateEffectFromResourceEx()

When a shader is loaded, it is ready for use in Direct3D. An HLSL
shader can have more than one effect defined inside it. Because of this, it
is necessary to set the technique you want to use before rendering with a
shader applied. Once the technique is set, any uniform variables can be set
with calls to functions such as SetMatrix() (to set a matrix), SetFloat(),
and so forth.

When all uniform variables are set and the geometry is ready to be
rendered, we render each pass of the effect, typically in a loop, one at a
time. During each pass we draw the geometry by using Begin() and End()

functions to mark the start and end of a technique along with Begin-Pass() and EndPass(), which mark the start and end of each pass declared within the technique. A simple rendering with an effect shader can look like the following.

```
g_effect->SetTechnique("SimpleEffect");
g_effect->SetMatrix("worldViewProj", &mvp);


UINT totalPasses;

g_effect->Begin(&totalPasses, 0);


// Loop through each pass of the effect and draw.
for(UINT pass = 0; pass < totalPasses; pass++)
{
    g_effect->BeginPass(pass);

    g_d3dDevice->DrawPrimitive(D3DPT_TRIANGLELIST, 0, 1);

    g_effect->EndPass();
}


g_effect->End();
```

The function to set the technique, SetTechnique(), takes the name of the technique that is to be set. The two functions we mentioned that could be used to set uniform values, SetFloat() and SetMatrix(), take the name of the variable and the value that is to be set. The Begin() function used to mark the start of a technique takes the address of a variable that will store the total number of passes of the technique and optional flags, while BeginPass() takes the index of the pass, from 0 to the total number of passes minus 1, that is to be rendered with. The function prototypes for each of these functions are as follows.

```
HRESULT SetTechnique(
    D3DXHANDLE hTechnique
);
```

```
HRESULT SetFloat(
    D3DXHANDLE hParameter,
    FLOAT f
);


HRESULT SetMatrix(
    D3DXHANDLE hParameter,
    CONST D3DXMATRIX* pMatrix
);


HRESULT Begin(
    UINT* pPasses,
    DWORD Flags
);


HRESULT BeginPass(
    UINT Pass
);


HRESULT EndPass();
```

Other uniform binding functions can be used in addition to `SetFloat()` *and* `Set-Matrix()`. *Consult the DirectX documentation for more. We discuss other functions as we use them throughout this book.*

HLSL Example Shader

On the book's accompanying CD-ROM is a demo application called HLSL 9 for Direct3D 9 that demonstrates the use of a simple HLSL shader. The demo application renders a colored triangle using HLSL, similar to the GLSL demo application from earlier in this chapter. The HLSL shader defines an incoming and outgoing vertex for the vertex shader that is defined by a position and a color. It also defines the output from the pixel shader to be a single color. The only uniform variable is for the model-view project matrix, which is defined in the global scope.

Since Direct3D 10 requires shaders, we've already implemented a Direct3D 10 version of this demo in Chapter 4. Refer to that demo, called Direct3D10, if you are using Direct3D 10.

The shader is made up of two functions. One function acts as the entry point to the vertex shader, and the other acts as an entry point to the pixel shader. A technique is created at the end of the file that uses both functions as one shader program effect that uses a single rendering pass. The HLSL shader from the HLSL 9 demo application is shown in Listing 5.13.

LISTING 5.13 THE HLSL 9 DEMO'S SHADER

```
/*
    Direct3D 9 HLSL
    Game Graphics Programming (2007)
    Created by Allen Sherrod
*/


// The only variable needed to be set by the application.
float4x4 worldViewProj : WorldViewProjection;


// Incoming vertex structure.
struct Vs_Input
{
    float3 vertexPos  : POSITION;
    float4 color      : COLOR0;
};


// Output vertex information to the pixel shader.
struct Vs_Output
{
    float4 vertexPos  : POSITION;
    float4 color      : COLOR0;
};


// Output from pixel shader.
struct Ps_Output
{
```

```
   float4 color        : COLOR;
};


Vs_Output VertexShaderEffect(Vs_Input IN)
{
   Vs_Output vs_out;

   // Transform the original vertex.
   vs_out.vertexPos = mul(worldViewProj,
                          float4(IN.vertexPos, 1));

   // Pass along the incoming color.
   vs_out.color = IN.color;

   return vs_out;
}


Ps_Output PixelShaderEffect(Vs_Output IN)
{
   Ps_Output ps_out;

   // Pass the incoming color on to the output.
   ps_out.color = IN.color;

   return ps_out;
}


technique SimpleEffect
{
   pass Pass0
   {
      // No lighting in this effect is used.
      Lighting = FALSE;

      // Compile and set the vertex and pixel shader.
      VertexShader = compile vs_2_0 VertexShaderEffect();
      PixelShader  = compile ps_2_0 PixelShaderEffect();
   }
}
```

Next we look at the main source file's global section. Here we define a vertex structure to be a position and a color, which is what the shader expects. We also have an object to store the effect, the projection matrix, and the vertex buffer. Since this demo does not use any view or local model transformations, the projection matrix can be passed to the shader as the model-view projection since the model and view would be identity matrices, which would have no impact on the projection matrix. The global section from the HLSL 9 demo application is shown in Listing 5.14.

LISTING 5.14 THE GLOBAL SECTION OF THE HLSL 9 DEMO APPLICATION

```
#include<windows.h>
#include<d3d9.h>
#include<d3dx9.h>

#pragma comment(lib, "d3d9.lib")
#pragma comment(lib, "d3dx9.lib")

#define WINDOW_NAME      "Direct3D 9 HLSL"
#define WINDOW_CLASS     "UPGCLASS"
#define WINDOW_WIDTH     800
#define WINDOW_HEIGHT    600

HWND g_hwnd;


// Direct3D objects.
LPDIRECT3D9 g_d3dObject = NULL;
LPDIRECT3DDEVICE9 g_d3dDevice = NULL;


// Vertex specified by position and color.
struct Vertex
{
   FLOAT x, y, z;
   DWORD color;
};

#define D3DFVF_D3DVertex (D3DFVF_XYZ | D3DFVF_DIFFUSE)

LPDIRECT3DVERTEXBUFFER9 g_vertexBuffer = NULL;
```

```
// High level shaders.
LPD3DXEFFECT g_effect = NULL;



// Matrices.
D3DXMATRIX g_projMat;
```

The next function we look at from the demo application is the demo's initialize function. In this function we set the rendering states for Direct3D, create the vertex buffer, and load the HLSL shader. If any errors are encountered during the compilation of the shader, the error is displayed to the window using a message box. This is very useful if syntax errors are found in the shader, as this error would give us the source of the problem and what line it is on. The initialization function from the HLSL 9 demo is shown in Listing 5.15.

LISTING 5.15 THE INITIALIZATION OF THE HLSL 9 DEMO

```
bool InitializeDemo()
{
    g_d3dDevice->SetRenderState(D3DRS_LIGHTING, FALSE);
    g_d3dDevice->SetRenderState(D3DRS_CULLMODE, D3DCULL_NONE);

    Vertex obj[] =
    {
        {-0.2f, -0.2f, 1.0f, D3DCOLOR_XRGB(255,   0,   0)},
        { 0.2f, -0.2f, 1.0f, D3DCOLOR_XRGB(  0, 255,   0)},
        { 0.0f,  0.1f, 1.0f, D3DCOLOR_XRGB(  0,   0, 255)}
    };


    // Create the vertex buffer.

    int numVerts = sizeof(obj) / sizeof(obj[0]);
    int size = numVerts * sizeof(Vertex);

    HRESULT hr = g_d3dDevice->CreateVertexBuffer(size, 0,
        D3DFVF_D3DVertex, D3DPOOL_DEFAULT, &g_vertexBuffer, NULL);

    if(FAILED(hr))
        return false;
```

```
// Load data into vertex buffer.

Vertex *ptr = NULL;

hr = g_vertexBuffer->Lock(0, sizeof(obj), (void**)&ptr, 0);

if(FAILED(hr))
   return false;

memcpy(ptr, obj, sizeof(obj));
g_vertexBuffer->Unlock();


// Load shaders.

LPD3DXBUFFER errors = NULL;

hr = D3DXCreateEffectFromFile(g_d3dDevice, "effect.fx", NULL,
                             NULL, 0, NULL, &g_effect,
                             &errors);

if(FAILED(hr))
{
   LPVOID compileErrors = errors->GetBufferPointer();

   // Show the errors to the user.
   MessageBox(NULL, (const char*)compileErrors,
              "Shader Errors...", MB_OK |
MB_ICONEXCLAMATION);

   return false;
}

return true;
}
```

The last two functions of interest are the rendering and shutting down functions. During the rendering function we loop through each pass of our technique and draw the geometry. This is not necessary since we know there is only one pass, but doing this each time can be good practice since adding passes does not affect the rendering code in terms of handling the additional passes. Before rendering occurs, the model-view projection is set, which is essential to correctly rendering with the shader since the shader expects the data to need to be transformed in the vertex shader. The transformation can be avoided if the data were specified already in their transformed position, although that wouldn't be practical in a real game. The rendering and shutdown functions are shown in Listing 5.16. For the shutdown function it is important to release all resources, even the shader, to avoid memory leaks. A screenshot of the HLSL 9 demo in action is shown in Figure 5.5.

LISTING 5.16 THE RENDERING AND SHUTDOWN FUNCTIONS FROM THE HLSL 9 DEMO

```
        void RenderScene()
    {
        g_d3dDevice->Clear(0, NULL, D3DCLEAR_TARGET |
D3DCLEAR_ZBUFFER,
                            D3DCOLOR_XRGB(0,0,0), 1.0f, 0);


        g_d3dDevice->BeginScene();

        // Setup geometry to render.
        g_d3dDevice->SetStreamSource(0, g_vertexBuffer,
                                0, sizeof(Vertex));


        g_d3dDevice->SetFVF(D3DFVF_D3DVertex);



        // Not technically necessary since nothing is set.
        D3DXMATRIX worldMat, viewMat;
        D3DXMatrixIdentity(&worldMat);
        D3DXMatrixIdentity(&viewMat);


        D3DXMATRIX mvp = worldMat * viewMat * g_projMat;
        D3DXMatrixTranspose(&mvp, &mvp);



        // Set the shader technique and set its only variable.
        g_effect->SetTechnique("SimpleEffect");
        g_effect->SetMatrix("worldViewProj", &mvp);


        UINT totalPasses;
        g_effect->Begin(&totalPasses, 0);

        // Loop through each pass of the effect and draw.
        for(UINT pass = 0; pass < totalPasses; pass++)
```

```
      {
         g_effect->BeginPass(pass);

            g_d3dDevice->DrawPrimitive(D3DPT_TRIANGLELIST, 0, 1);

         g_effect->EndPass();
      }

      g_effect->End();

      g_d3dDevice->EndScene();

      g_d3dDevice->Present(NULL, NULL, NULL, NULL);
   }


   void Shutdown()
   {
      // Here we release the Direct3D objects.
      if(g_d3dDevice != NULL) g_d3dDevice->Release();
      g_d3dDevice = NULL;

      if(g_d3dObject != NULL) g_d3dObject->Release();
      g_d3dObject = NULL;

      if(g_vertexBuffer != NULL) g_vertexBuffer->Release();
      g_vertexBuffer = NULL;

      if(g_effect != NULL) g_effect->Release();
      g_effect = NULL;
   }
```

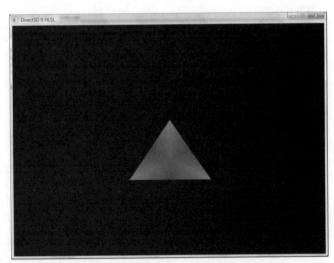

FIGURE 5.5   Screenshot from the HLSL 9 demo.

ADDITIONAL SHADER TECHNOLOGIES AND TOOLS

A number of tools and technologies can be used to create programmable shaders and use them in 3D virtual scenes. In this section we briefly discuss NVIDIA's Cg and Pixar's RenderMan.

NVIDIA's Cg

NVIDIA's Cg is a high-level shading language developed by NVIDIA when shaders were becoming more commonplace in the industry. Cg was welcomed by the game development scene at a time where shaders were mostly written in assembly language. The great thing about Cg is that it is cross-platform across a large number of machines and graphical APIs. NVIDIA's Cg is currently supported on:

- Windows (32- and 64-bit)
- Mac (PowerPC and i386)
- Linux (32- and 64-bit)
- Solaris
- OpenGL
- Direct3D
- PlayStation 3

    Cg stands for "C for graphics."

For developers comfortable with HLSL, Cg will seem like a very familiar technology. The benefit to using Cg is that it allows developers to write one set of high-level shaders that can be used across multiple platforms. This can be seen when using shaders on OpenGL and Direct3D, where using Cg allows developers to write just one shader instead of multiple shaders.

Pixar's RenderMan

RenderMan is a collection of highly customizable tools created by Pixar, which is one of the leading animation and digital effects companies in the world. These tools include RenderMan for Maya, RenderMan Studio, and RenderMan Pro Server. RenderMan gives artists the following tools.

- Network rendering with support for render farms
- Rendering system
- High-level shading language creation and management
- Powerful image tool

Pixar's RenderMan can also be integrated into Maya Pro. RenderMan is often used in high-production animated films such as Disney/Pixar's *The Incredibles*.

SUMMARY

Programmable shaders have allowed game developers to push the envelope of computer graphics in ways that nothing else has. The fixed-function pipeline was far too restrictive in what graphics APIs exposed to developers, thus making it very difficult to perform various graphical effects without often coding many different tricks, workarounds, and hacks, assuming the effect could even be done. Also, the limitation of the fixed-function pipeline limited the creative freedom of game developers during the time before programmable hardware.

It is clear that programmable shaders and the hardware they run on are the future of graphical APIs such as OpenGL and Direct3D. In the beginning, working with shaders (low-level) was often harder than it had to be. Assembly language has traditionally been a difficult language to code and modify due to its syntax. Higher-level languages make programming graphical effects easier to manage, code, and modify. This results in faster development time.

The following elements were discussed throughout this chapter:

- Low-level shading languages
- High-level shading languages
- The OpenGL Shading Language (GLSL)

- The High-Level Shading Language (HLSL)
- NVIDIA's Cg
- NVIDIA's FX Composer
- RenderMan

CHAPTER QUESTIONS

Answers to the following chapter review questions can be found in Appendix A, "Answers to Chapter Questions."

1. What is the fixed-function pipeline?
2. What is the difference between low- and high-level shading languages?
3. List at least three benefits to using high-level shading languages versus low-level languages.
4. What is GLSL short for?
5. What is HLSL short for?
6. What is Cg short for?
7. Describe what semantics and techniques are and how they are used in HLSL.
8. List five types of registers in low-level shaders.
9. What are type qualifiers? List three GLSL type qualifiers and describe what they are.
10. True or false: NVIDIA's Cg is only supported on NVIDIA hardware.
11. True or false: Low-level shaders are generally faster to develop than high-level shaders.
12. True or false: Direct3D 10 only supports a high-level shading language.
13. True or false: There currently exist only two types of shaders, which are vertex and pixel shaders.
14. True or false: Programmable shaders can be used as a replacement for the fixed-function pipeline.
15. True or false: RenderMan is just another high-level shading language.
16. True or false: Cg, GLSL, and HLSL are all shading languages based on C.
17. True or false: Shaders are interpreted on the fly and are not compiled.
18. True or false: Low-level shading languages have been around since the beginning of 3D graphics hardware.
19. True or false: High-level shading languages are object-oriented languages.
20. True or false: Programmable shaders are also known as materials.

SHADING AND SURFACES

MAPPING SURFACES

In This Chapter

Graphical details in modern video games, for the most part, start at the texture mapping level of surfaces when it comes to adding detail to scenes. Texture mapping has traditionally been a technique that game developers used to add detail to surfaces without the high cost of adding additional polygons. A classic example of this can be seen with a brick wall. Using a brick wall image on a surface and sending that to the hardware can be more quickly processed than creating thousands or millions of small colored polygons to represent the same level of detail. Not only does using textures save processing time, but it also gives artists a more practical way to create the detail we see in virtual environments.

In this chapter we discuss the various topics that are associated with texture mapping of surfaces. Texture mapping has become the foundation of most graphical effects seen in modern video games. This includes but is not limited to the following common effects.

- Bump and normal mapping
- Displacement mapping
- Reflection mapping
- Light mapping
- Shadow mapping
- Particle systems

TEXTURE MAPPING IN GAMES

Various types of texture maps exist in video games. Traditionally, texture maps were used to describe color images that can be created with image editors such as Microsoft Paint, Adobe Photoshop, and so forth. The purpose of a texture map is to add pixel-level details to surfaces specified on the vertex level. Taking the aforementioned brick wall example (shown in Figure 6.1), the number of individual colored polygons necessary to create such detail would easily span into the millions. For one surface, that is clearly far more geometry than modern graphics hardware can handle. If an entire scene had to be represented in that manner, the scenes we enjoy in modern video games wouldn't be practical with the hardware available.

FIGURE 6.1   A brick wall texture.

Even if the hardware was able to handle such extreme geometric data, it would still be inefficient in terms of hardware processing and artistically to create extremely detailed surfaces with polygons that can be dramatically reduced by using an imposter. Textures are in essence a form of imposter that can be used to represent high levels of color detail without using a lot of geometry. Another benefit to using textures to reduce the geometry data of a scene is that resources can then be directed to other areas of a game such as artificial intelligence and physics.

Every extension to texture mapping has the same purpose. Bump mapping, which is the process of lighting a surface with fine detail without the detail being present, uses the same idea. Although texture mapping is not the cheapest operation in video games, the expense it saves is far worth its weight. To see how much detail texture mapping adds to a scene, compare the first *Virtual Fighter* game with the second. Although these games are separated by more than just textures, the use of textures compared to the lack of them is evident and drastic.

Color Formats

A color format tells us what information is used to describe the colors of individual pixels in an image and how it is represented. In video games, many color component formats can be used in the common graphical APIs available. One format is the RGB8, which represents three color components that are 8 bits each. The RGB8 is a 24-bit color because 8 bits per component multiplied by the total components that make up a single pixel, which is 3, equals 24. The number of bits can dictate how much precision can be used for a single component. If a component is stored in 8 bits, then each component is essentially a byte. A byte can store up to 256 different values, which is normally in the 0 to 255 range. This range of values tells us how bright or dark a color component is, where the lower the value, the darker the color. In an RGB image three colors are combined to make up the individual pixel in question. By mixing red, green, and blue intensity values we are able to represent a large range of colors that can be seen using a television or monitor.

Some of the other common formats include but are not limited to the following.

- R5G6B5, which uses 5 bits for red and blue while using 6 for green
- RGBA8, which has four components of 8 bits each, with the fourth being an alpha value
- RGBA16, which has four components of 16 bits each
- RGBE8, which has four components of 8 bits each, with the last being an exponent that is applied to the other components

Alpha, which is represented using the A component in many color formats, is very common in video games. Alpha commonly controls the opacity of a color, where 0 represents invisible and 1 (using a 0 to 1 scale) represents 100% visible. An example of alpha is shown in Figure 6.2, where the image on the left is fully visible, the image in the middle is partially visible at 50%, and the image on the right is almost invisible at 10%.

 You can use the alpha channel to represent anything you want that can be stored in a single component.

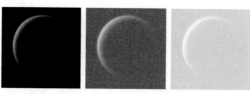

FIGURE 6.2   Alpha at 100% (left), alpha at 50% (middle), and the alpha at 10% (right).

In this book we focus on the color formats RGB8 and RGBA8 or, in other words, 24- and 32-bit images. We also focus on loading and using TGA and DDS images, both of which will be discussed later in this chapter.

IMAGES

Textures are often images loaded from a file. In OpenGL and Direct3D you can load any image file you want into memory as long as you load it in or can convert its internal format to one that OpenGL or Direct3D supports. In Direct3D you can use utility functions to load textures from files. These image formats include the following:

- TGA
- BMP
- JPG
- DDS
- DIB
- HDR
- PFM
- PNG
- PPM

In this chapter we look at loading TGA and DDS images into both OpenGL and Direct3D. Since Direct3D loads both of these for us, when the time comes, we'll use various DirectX functions to do that job. The file formats will still be covered for convenience, but manually loading them in code only needs to be done by OpenGL users since OpenGL does not offer utility functions to load these files and create textures from them for us.

Image Compression

Compression has always been an important topic in computer science. *Compression* is the term for an algorithm that converts data into a smaller representation. In the days of the Internet compression has become quite commonplace across many different storage media. On the Internet, JPG images, one of the most popular image file formats there are, use a type of compression known as lossy compression. Lossy compression means that quality is sacrificed for file size. On the other end of the spectrum, lossless compression retains original quality by sacrificing potential reduction in file size. With lossy compression the original quality is lost. Because of this, it is not recommended to recompress data because since quality is lost during lossy compression, further compressing something that is already at a lower quality will further degrade all compressed versions afterward. If necessary, you should try to compress the original versions of textures rather than recompressing already-compressed data. The same can be said for audio, video, and so forth.

Compression is important to the game industry as well. A lot of information is compressed in a video game, some of which includes the following:

- Images
- Audio
- Geometry
- Video
- Transmitted network data

This chapter deals with textures, so it is appropriate to also deal with texture compression. Textures compression is very useful in game development, and it allows developers to get more out of the storage and memory available to them. In modern video games large amount of textures can exist in a single environment. The amount of space consumed by textures alone is large, and high-definition resolution textures are becoming more commonplace. Because of this, we discuss the important topic of texture compression.

Working with TGA Images

Targa images have the extension .TGA and are a supported image format in many image editors. In this section we look at the TGA file format and how we can load the file's data into memory so that it can be used as a texture. Direct3D, as mentioned earlier, has a texture loading utility function that supports this file format, so Direct3D users do not need to understand the file format if using this function. Because OpenGL does not have any TGA loading functions, or any texture loading functions, we must manually open and load the file's contents and create a texture out of it ourselves.

The TGA file format is broken up into two sections that make up the image's file header and the image's color data. The header of the TGA file stores information about the image's data and how it is represented and stored. This information includes the data type, compression flags, image resolution, and other properties. The data section consists of the color information for the image. TGA files support the following file types:

- Uncompressed and compressed RGB images
- Uncompressed and compressed RGBA images
- Uncompressed and compressed luminance images

TGA files support compression using run-length encoding. Run-length encoding works by recording consecutive pixels using a single value rather than writing each of them out repeatedly. For example, take the following pixels.

(255, 128, 128), (255, 128, 128), (255, 128, 128), (124, 18, 228), (124, 18, 228)

Using run-length encoding we can specify a run length, which means how many times a pixel is repeated for each color, followed by the color value. Taking the previous example, using run-length encoding would look more like:

3 (255, 128, 128), 2 (124, 18, 228)

If each value is a byte, the original set of pixels is composed of 15 bytes. The run length encoding (RLE) compressed version would then be composed of 8 bytes including the run counts, which is almost half just for those five pixels in the original set. If there are many repeated pixels throughout an image, the savings can be drastic. This is especially true for images with large areas of solid colors, which, when compressed, would greatly reduce its representation without sacrificing quality. RLE compression is a lossless type of compression.

In this chapter we do not focus on RLE compression since the graphics hardware does not support it. This means that if images are RLE encoded, the information will need to be decoded at run-time and used in an application. Other compression formats that we will look into later in this chapter are directly supported by graphics hardware.

Loading a TGA image is done by loading the header and then using that information to load the data. For the TGA loading code used by the OpenGL demos of this book the code starts off by loading the entire file into a buffer. Once loaded, the header information is extracted and examined. Because in this book we are only concerned about RGB and RGBA color images, we make sure that any files being loaded are one of these uncompressed formats. This is done by checking if the third byte in the header is a 2, which stands for uncompressed, and if the bit count is either 24 or 32, which can be found in the 18th byte. The byte breakdown for the TGA header is as follows, where most fields can be ignored:

1st byte	Image identification length
2nd byte	The type of color map; this field is always 0
3rd byte	File format code, where 2 is uncompressed, 3 is luminance, 10 is compressed RGB, and 11 is compressed luminance
4th and 5th bytes	Color map origin; always 0
6th and 7th bytes	Length of the color map; always 0
8th and 9th bytes	Entry size of the color map; always 0
10th and 11th bytes	X coordinate of the lower-left of the image; always 0
12th and 13th bytes	Y coordinate of the lower-left of the image; always 0

14th and 15th bytes	Image's width in pixels
16th and 17th bytes	Image's height in pixels
18th byte	Number of color components; 16, 24, or 32
19th byte	Image descriptor; 0x00 for 24-bit images; 0x08 for 32-bit images

Once the TGA header information is loaded, the image information starts the byte that immediately follows. For uncompressed color information we can just load in the color data as an array. For compressed data you have to uncompress it first to use in OpenGL.

Another thing to note is that TGA images store data in the BGR format instead of the RGB format. To change between the two we can simply use a loop to swap between the red and blue components, which can be done if you want the data stored in RGB format. The TGA loading function code is shown in Listing 6.1. Because of how TGA images store the width and height, they must be calculated by adding the two bytes that make up the property and multiplying that by 256. This allows the resolution to be stored in 2 bytes for the width and height instead of 4 bytes.

LISTING 6.1 A FUNCTION THAT CAN LOAD A TGA IMAGE INTO MEMORY

```
cnsigned char* LoadTGA(char* file, int &width, int &height,
                       int &components)
{
   FILE *pfile;
   int length = 0;
   unsigned char *image = NULL;

   if(!file) return NULL;
   pfile = fopen(file, "rb");
   if(!pfile) return NULL;

   fseek(pfile, 0, SEEK_END);
   length = ftell(pfile);
   fseek(pfile, 0, SEEK_SET);


   // Read in all data from the file.
   char *data = new char[(length + 1) * sizeof(char)];
   if(!data) return NULL;

   fread(data, 1, length, pfile);
```

```
data[length] = '\0';


fclose(pfile);


unsigned char tempColor;
unsigned char unCompressHeader[12] = {0, 0, 2, 0, 0, 0,
                                      0, 0, 0, 0, 0, 0};
char *ptr = data;
long tgaSize = 0;
unsigned char *image = NULL;

// We only want to read uncompressed tga's at this time.
if(memcmp(unCompressHeader, ptr, sizeof(unCompressHeader)) != 0)
{
   return NULL;
}


ptr += sizeof(unCompressHeader);


// Calculate image stats.
width = ptr[0] + ptr[1] * 256;
height = ptr[2] + ptr[3] * 256;
components = ptr[4] / 8;
tgaSize = width * height * components;

ptr += 6;

// We only care for RGB and RGBA images.
if(components != 3 && components != 4)
   return NULL;


// Allocate data for the image and load it.
image = new unsigned char[sizeof(unsigned char) * tgaSize];
memcpy(image, ptr, sizeof(char) * tgaSize);

// Convert from BGR(A) to RGB(A) format.
for(long index = 0; index < tgaSize; index += components)
{
```

```
            tempColor = image[index];
            image[index] = image[index + 2];
            image[index + 2] = tempColor;
      }

      delete[] data;

      return image;
   }
```

Writing a TGA image is as straightforward as reading it. When writing, we literally can reverse the read calls with write calls in the code in Listing 6.1. Writing TGA images was first discussed and examined in Chapter 3 "Ray Tracing." After this discussion on the TGA file format, the code discussed in Chapter 3 should be clarified as to what it is doing and why the values that were being written were being written. The code for writing a TGA file in Chapter 3 writes uncompressed RGB rendered images.

Working with DDS Images

The next type of image we look at is the DDS image. DDS stands for DirectDraw Surface and is a format that got its start with DirectX. To load and use DDS images you do not need Direct3D, so it is possible to load them into OpenGL on Windows, Mac, Linux, and so forth.

DDS images each have an ID associated with them that tells us what internal format they use. DDS images use the DXTC version 1 through 5 formats, which deal with image compression. We discuss the details of DXTC and other texture compression formats later in this chapter. Listing 6.2 lists a few defined macros that are used by each of the demos that load DDS images to create a flag that can be tested to see what type of image the DDS file being loaded is.

LISTING 6.2 DEFINE MACROS TO BUILD A FLAG THAT CAN BE TESTED WITH A DDS FILE

```
#ifndef MAKE4CC
    #define MAKE4CC(ch0, ch1, ch2, ch3) \
                ((unsigned long)(unsigned char)(ch0) | \
                ((unsigned long)(unsigned char)(ch1) << 8) | \
                ((unsigned long)(unsigned char)(ch2) << 16) | \
                ((unsigned long)(unsigned char)(ch3) << 24 ))
#endif
```

```
#define DS_FOURCC_DXT1    (MAKE4CC('D','X','T','1'))
#define DS_FOURCC_DXT2    (MAKE4CC('D','X','T','2'))
#define DS_FOURCC_DXT3    (MAKE4CC('D','X','T','3'))
#define DS_FOURCC_DXT4    (MAKE4CC('D','X','T','4'))
#define DS_FOURCC_DXT5    (MAKE4CC('D','X','T','5'))
```

The DDS images we are loading will be loaded across different types of hardware. Because of this we have to be aware of file endianess, which is the byte ordering of multibyte variables such as floating-point and integer values. There are three main types of endian order; two of these are common, and we need to consider them when working on the PC. These include little, big, and middle endian order. The byte ordering of a variable specifies which byte that makes up the variable is the least significant and which is the most. What this means, in plain terms, is that byte ordering defines which byte comes first and which comes last. In little endian order of an integer the bytes are read from left to right when looking at the data as an array like the following.

[Byte 1], [Byte 2], [Byte 3], [Byte 4]

In big endian order the data are read in the opposite direction from little endian, which using the example above would make the fourth byte the first and the first byte the last. It is important to be aware of the byte ordering for many reasons. The first reason is that if you read in a value that is in a different byte ordering than what is expected, you can end up reading in incorrect values, which can cause bugs and other errors that are hard to trace. When reading and writing variables to and from a file, the byte ordering is very important to programmers and the applications they develop. The same can be said about transmitted information across a network between machines that operate using different byte ordering.

Examples of hardware that uses different byte ordering are Intel-based processors such as the Pentium 4 (little endian) and PowerPC processors (big endian), which are very common in Mac computers. The Xbox 360 also uses big endian order.

There is no way to know what byte order data is in when it is read. It is the responsibility of the programmer to know how his data are being represented or how data are being read from external sources. Many file formats state in their documentation what byte ordering they use so that developers reading or writing to the file format can do so correctly. When machines are connected to a network, it is up to the programmer to decide what byte ordering the application will use and to stick with it. Of course, if machines use the same endian order, such as an Xbox talking only to other Xbox systems, then endian order is not an issue.

To determine what byte ordering a machine uses a simple test can be performed in code at run-time. This test is as simple as creating a multi-byte variable, casting it to a character array, and testing the individual bytes that make up the variable. For example, if you create a variable and initialize it to the value 0×12,345,678, then you can test if the first byte is 0×12, the second byte is 0×34, and so forth. If the tests pass, the byte order of the machine is little endian; otherwise, it is big endian. If the machine the application is running on uses a different byte ordering than a file that is being loaded or information being passed across a network, the most straightforward solution is to swap the bytes by casting the variable to a character pointer and using a simple loop. This is shown in Listing 6.3, which is used by the DDS loading code to ensure that users using processors that are not little endian based are able to load the images safely.

LISTING 6.3 DETECTING THE BYTE ORDERING AND SWAPPING BYTES

```
enum ENDIAN { ENDIAN_UNKNOWN = 0, ENDIAN_LITTLE, ENDIAN_BIG };


ENDIAN GetEndian()
{
   unsigned long data = 0x12345678;
   unsigned char *ptr = (unsigned char*)&data;

   if(*ptr == 0x12 && *(ptr+1) == 0x34 &&
      *(ptr+2) == 0x56 && *(ptr+3) == 0x78)
   {
      return ENDIAN_BIG;
   }
   else if(*ptr == 0x78 && *(ptr + 1) == 0x56 &&
        *(ptr + 2) == 0x34 && *(ptr + 3) == 0x12)
   {
      return ENDIAN_LITTLE;
   }

   return ENDIAN_UNKNOWN;
}


void SwapBytes(char *data, int size)
```

```
{
    assert((size & 1) == 0);

    char *ptr = data;
    char temp = 0;

    for(int i = 0, j = size - 1; i < size / 2; i++, j--)
    {
        temp = ptr[i];
        ptr[i] = ptr[j];
        ptr[j] = temp;
    }
}
```

 With TGA images you do not have to worry about byte ordering because everything is specified in bytes, not multibyte variables such as integers. A single byte has no order because there is just 1 byte, while something like an integer has 4 bytes.

The DDS loading code in this book can load images using DXTC 1, 3, and 5 compressions. To be able to load a DDS image file, the steps to reading the information from a file are as follows.

- Read the file ID, which is the first four bytes, and test for the characters "DDS " with the last character being a space.
- Move the file pointer to the image resolution, which appears 12 bytes from the start of the file and read it.
- Read the size of the data.
- Read the number of mipmaps.
- Read the compression type.
- Read the compressed image data.

The code that loads a DDS image is performed in a function called LoadDDS(). The LoadDDS() function starts by determining the byte ordering of the machine running the application code. If the byte ordering is not little endian order, the code will swap the bytes of any multibyte variable it reads. After the endian order has been determined, the function opens the file, reads the first four bytes, and tests to see if it matches the file ID DDS.

Once the code has determined that a valid DDS image is being read based on finding the DDS ID, the next step in the function is to read the width and height resolutions. After the resolution has been read, the function will read the size of the image data, the number of mipmaps, and the type of compression the image uses. This information is followed by the compressed image data itself. The function used to load DDS images is shown in Listing 6.4, which performs each of the loading steps mentioned in this section.

LISTING 6.4 THE FUNCTION USED TO LOAD A DDS IMAGE

```
unsigned char *LoadDDS(char *file, ImageInfoDDS &info)
{
   const int ddsHeightOffset = 12;
   const int ddsWidthOffset = 16;
   const int ddsLinearSizeOffset = 20;
   const int ddsMipMapNumOffset = 28;
   const int ddsFourCCOffset = 84;
   const int ddsImageDataOffset = 128;


   ENDIAN e = GetEndian();
   bool byteSwap = false;

   if(e == ENDIAN_BIG)
      byteSwap = true;


   FILE *fp = fopen(file, "rb");

   if(fp == NULL)
      return NULL;


   char imageID[4];
   fread(imageID, 1, 4, fp);

   if(strncmp(imageID, "DDS ", 4) != 0)
   {
      fclose(fp);
      return false;
   }


   unsigned int dwHeight = 0, dwWidth = 0,
                dwLinearSize, dwMipMaps = 0,
                dwFourCC = 0;

   fseek(fp, ddsHeightOffset, SEEK_SET);
```

```
fread(&dwHeight, sizeof(unsigned int), 1, fp);

if(byteSwap == true)
   SwapBytes((char*)&dwHeight, sizeof(unsigned int));

fseek(fp, ddsWidthOffset, SEEK_SET);
fread(&dwWidth, sizeof(unsigned int), 1, fp);

if(byteSwap == true)
   SwapBytes((char*)&dwWidth, sizeof(unsigned int));

fseek(fp, ddsLinearSizeOffset, SEEK_SET);
fread(&dwLinearSize, sizeof(unsigned int), 1, fp);

if(byteSwap == true)
   SwapBytes((char*)&dwLinearSize, sizeof(unsigned int));

fseek(fp, ddsMipMapNumOffset, SEEK_SET);
fread(&dwMipMaps, sizeof(unsigned int), 1, fp);

if(byteSwap == true)
   SwapBytes((char*)&dwMipMaps, sizeof(unsigned int));

fseek(fp, ddsFourCCOffset, SEEK_SET);
fread(&dwFourCC, sizeof(unsigned int), 1, fp);

if(byteSwap == true)
   SwapBytes((char*)&dwFourCC, sizeof(unsigned int));

if(dwLinearSize == 0)
   dwLinearSize = dwHeight * dwWidth;

if(dwLinearSize <= 0)
{
   fclose(fp);
   return NULL;
}


info.m_numMipMaps = dwMipMaps;
info.m_width = dwWidth;
info.m_height = dwHeight;


int mipFactor = 0;
```

```
switch(dwFourCC)
{
   case DS_FOURCC_DXT1:
      mipFactor = 2;
      info.m_components = 3;
      info.m_type = DDS_DXT1;
      break;

   case DS_FOURCC_DXT3:
      mipFactor = 4;
      info.m_components = 4;
      info.m_type = DDS_DXT3;
      break;

   case DS_FOURCC_DXT5:
      mipFactor = 4;
      info.m_components = 4;
      info.m_type = DDS_DXT5;
      break;

   default:
      fclose(fp);
      return NULL;
      break;
}


int totalSize = 0;

// Take into account multiple mipmaps.
if(dwMipMaps > 1)
   totalSize = dwLinearSize * mipFactor;
else
   totalSize = dwLinearSize;

unsigned char *image = NULL;

image = new unsigned char[totalSize * sizeof(unsigned char)];

if(image != NULL)
{
   fseek(fp, ddsImageDataOffset, SEEK_SET);
```

```
        fread(image, 1, totalSize, fp);
    }


    fclose(fp);

    return image;
}
```

DDS images can store multiple mipmap resolutions of the image.

TEXTURE MAPPING IN GRAPHICS APIS

Texture mapping in Direct3D and OpenGL generally consists of either loading the image data from some external source or generating it in code. Once the image information is loaded, it can be applied to any surface as long as the texture is bound to a specific texture unit. Binding a texture to a surface is known as applying a texture. A texture unit is like an index for an array of textures that can be applied. Since you can have more than one texture applied at the same time, a process known as multi-texturing, you can specify which texture unit (index) you apply each texture. We discuss multi-texturing in more detail later in this chapter.

In this section we discuss texture mapping in a bit more detail and implement it using Direct3D and OpenGL. We also look at topics such as texture compression and texture filtering effects later in this chapter.

Texture Coordinates

Texture coordinates are a property of a vertex that is used to texture-map a surface. A texture coordinate is a percentage that tells the graphics hardware the starting pixel of the image that is to be mapped at the surface. The remaining vertex points and their texture coordinates determine how a texture is mapped to the surface. This is shown in Figure 6.3 with a 2D texture image.

2D textures, although not the only ones, are the most common types of textures used in modern video games. A 2D texture requires a two-set pair of texture coordinates, where the first value, called the U or S texture coordinate, represents the width starting percentage and the second value, called the V or T texture coordinate, represents the height starting percentage. Taking Figure 6.3 as an example, the bottom left vertex has a texture coordinate of (0, 0). This marks its starting texture pixel at the start of the texture. This start depends on the coordinate system being used, which differs for OpenGL and Direct3D. In OpenGL the starting location is the lower left of the texture image, while in Direct3D it is the upper left. This difference is important because, like in geometry, the differences in coordinate systems can play a role in how you load and use data across APIs that use different coordinate systems.

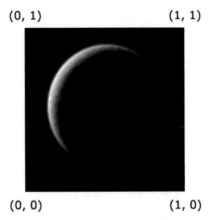

(0, 1)   **(1, 1)**

(0, 0)   **(1, 0)**

FIGURE 6.3   Texture coordinates of a surface.

Some texture coordinates, such as OpenGL texture rectangles, can be specified in indexes instead of percentages.

As mentioned earlier, texture coordinates are a property of a vertex. In Chapter 4, "Rasterization," the only properties used were a vertex position and color. Adding texture coordinates adds two floating-point variables, 8 bytes in total, to each vertex. To map a surface you need to apply a texture to the hardware and supply texture coordinates. Throughout this book we look at other vertex properties such as tangents and bi-normals, which are important to bump and normal mapping.

Texture Filtering and Mipmaps

Texture coordinates are specified on the vertex level. When a surface is being rendered, the texture coordinates for each vertex are interpolated across the surface. If linear interpolation is used and if the surface is viewed at an angle, discontinuities across multiple triangles can be visible. This is shown in Figure 6.4, where a surface is seen head-on (left), and the same surface is seen at an angle (right). Linear interpolating a texture image's data using interpolated texture coordinates across a surface is known as affine texture mapping.

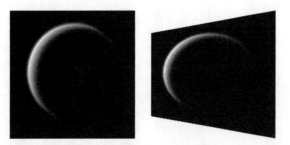

FIGURE 6.4   Flat view of a surface (left). Angled view of a surface (right).

Texture filters are used by graphics APIs and hardware to reduce artifacts and discontinuities that can be seen in texture mapping. The main types of texture filtering are

- Point
- Linear
- Anisotropic

Point texture filtering refers to rendering surfaces that have no filtering applied and are just rendered using affine texture mapping. Linear filtering includes bilinear and trilinear filtering, which sample neighboring pixels when determining an individual pixel's final color. Anisotropic filtering is the most expensive of the group and is used to change a surface's appearance as its orientation changes to avoid blurry fall offs that can be seen for surfaces at sharp angles at far distances. An example of anisotropic compared to nonanisotropic filtering is shown in Figure 6.5. Bilinear and trilinear filtering do not take into account the angle of the surface, which can lead to blurry results for distant surfaces.

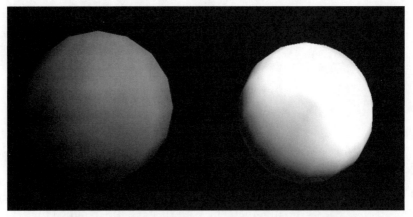

FIGURE 6.5   Nonanisotropic (left) and anisotropic (right) filtering.

Bilinear filtering is used to display a texture across a surface smoothly when that texture is being rendered at a different size than its original pixel resolution. In video games we commonly texture-map surfaces of different sizes and orientations throughout the scene. It is rare to display a texture exactly how it is stored in its file. Because the textures are rendered at different sizes from how they are stored and at different angles, textures can appear distorted and blurry when viewing them from some angles. Texture filtering is used to reduce this blurriness and to sharpen the rendering results. With bilinear filtering the four points closest to the point being processed are combined to represent the final output color.

Trilinear filtering is an extension of bilinear filtering, but it filters between what are known as mipmaps. A mipmap is a scaled-down version of the original texture. When textures are filtered, their effectiveness is often limited to half their resolution whether it is up-scaled or down-scaled. Using mipmaps means using smaller resolutions of a texture as a textured surface gets farther away from the viewer. With trilinear filtering the filtering takes place between mipmap levels. An example of mipmaps is shown in Figure 6.6.

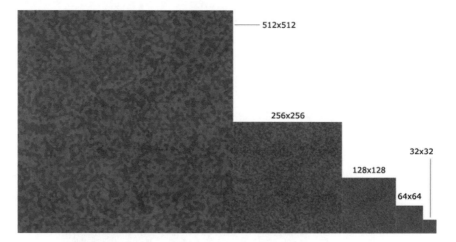

FIGURE 6.6   Five levels of mipmaps starting with the original at 512×512.

OpenGL Texture Mapping in Shaders

ON THE CD

On the CD-ROM is a demo application called GL Textures in the Chapter 6 folder. This demo shows how to load a TGA texture into memory and display it on a surface. The demo uses a texture-mapping GLSL shader for the effect. In this section we briefly look at the demo application as a review to texture mapping with shaders. It is assumed that you are familiar with texture mapping in OpenGL or Direct3D. This section briefly describes the demos since they are simple and do not need much explanation.

On the application side the demo uses three main global variables, with one for the texture, one for the shader effect, and one for the shader's texture variable. In OpenGL objects are often represented as unsigned integers, which has a type definition of GLuint. The global section from the GL Textures demo is shown in Listing 6.5.

LISTING 6.5 GLOBALS FROM THE GL TEXTURES DEMO

```
// OpenGL Texture.
GLuint g_texture;

// GLSlang objects.
GLhandleARB g_shader;

// Shader variables we will bind to.
GLuint g_glslDecal;
```

The initialization of the GL Textures demo sets the initial rendering states for the scene at the start. As mentioned previously, OpenGL uses a fixed-function pipeline, which means states can be enabled and disabled at any time. For this demo the back buffer clear color is set to black, smooth shading is turned on, depth testing is enabled (but is not necessary for this demo), and texture mapping is enabled.

The function then loads the shaders used by the demo, followed by the loading and creation of the texture that will be displayed. During the texture creation the texture data are loaded, the OpenGL texture resource is created, and texture filtering and mipmaps are set up. One thing to note with the shader is that the variable within the GLSL shader is bound so that the shader can have access to it. The initialization function from the GL Textures demo is shown in Listing 6.6. Along with the initialization code is the demo's shutdown code, which releases the resources used by the OpenGL shaders and textures. Most resource release functions are optional. For example, textures are released from OpenGL automatically at the end of the application, but glDeleteTextures() can be used to delete texture resources manually, which is useful for textures that must be released during an application and not at the end.

LISTING 6.6 THE GL TEXTURES INITIALIZATION FUNCTION

```
bool InitializeApp()
{
   glClearColor(0.0f, 0.0f, 0.0f, 1.0f);
   glShadeModel(GL_SMOOTH);
   glEnable(GL_DEPTH_TEST);
   glEnable(GL_TEXTURE_2D);

   if(!CreateGLSLShader("../vs.glsl", "../ps.glsl", g_shader))
   {
      if(!CreateGLSLShader("../../vs.glsl", "../../ps.glsl",
         g_shader))
         return false;
   }

   // Bind our shader variables.
   g_glslDecal = glGetUniformLocationARB(g_shader, "decal");


   // Load TGA image.
   int width = 0, height = 0, comp = 0;
   unsigned char *image;

   image = LoadTGA("../image.tga", width, height, comp);

   if(image == NULL)
   {
      image = LoadTGA("../../image.tga", width, height, comp);

      if(image == NULL)
         return false;
   }

   glGenTextures(1, &g_texture);
   glBindTexture(GL_TEXTURE_2D, g_texture);

   glTexParameteri(GL_TEXTURE_2D, GL_TEXTURE_MIN_FILTER,
               GL_LINEAR);
   glTexParameteri(GL_TEXTURE_2D, GL_TEXTURE_MAG_FILTER,
               GL_LINEAR);

   // Copy image data into OpenGL texture that is bound.
   int type = comp == 3 ? GL_RGB : GL_RGBA;
```

```
        gluBuild2DMipmaps(GL_TEXTURE_2D, type, width, height, type,
                          GL_UNSIGNED_BYTE, image);

    delete[] image;

    return true;
}


void ShutdownApp()
{
    glDeleteTextures(1, &g_texture);
    glDeleteObjectARB(g_shader);
}
```

The rendering code for the GL Textures demo is kept relatively simple for this application by rendering a single textured surface. The surface is made up of two polygons, where each point is specified by a vertex texture coordinate in addition to position. The code for the rendering function is shown in Listing 6.7.

LISTING 6.7 THE GL TEXTURES RENDERING CODE

```
    void RenderScene()
    {
      glClear(GL_COLOR_BUFFER_BIT | GL_DEPTH_BUFFER_BIT);
      glLoadIdentity();

      float vertices[]  = { -0.8f, -1, -6, 0.8f, -1, -6, 0.8f, 1, -6,
                            0.8f, 1, -6, -0.8f, 1, -6, -0.8f, -1, -6 };
      float texCoords[] = { 0, 0, 1, 0, 1, 1, 1, 1, 0, 1, 0, 0 };

      glEnableClientState(GL_VERTEX_ARRAY);
      glVertexPointer(3, GL_FLOAT, 0, vertices);

      glEnableClientState(GL_TEXTURE_COORD_ARRAY);
      glTexCoordPointer(2, GL_FLOAT, 0, texCoords);

      glUseProgramObjectARB(g_shader);
      glUniform1iARB(g_glslDecal, 0);

      glBindTexture(GL_TEXTURE_2D, g_texture);
      glDrawArrays(GL_TRIANGLES, 0, 6);
```

```
        glDisableClientState(GL_VERTEX_ARRAY);
        glDisableClientState(GL_TEXTURE_COORD_ARRAY);

        glutSwapBuffers();
        glutPostRedisplay();
    }
```

The vertex shader for the GL Textures demo is also straightforward. The properties that are given to the shader are the vertex position, the vertex texture coordinates, and the model-view projection (MVP) matrix. Because the pixel shader is the shader that needs to sample colors from a texture, the texture coordinates and transformed vertex position can be passed along. The vertex shader for the GL Textures demo application is shown in Listing 6.8. The pixel shader itself is shown in Listing 6.9, where the texture coordinates that were received interpolated from the vertex shader are used to sample a texture color. This is done by using the GLSL function texture2D(), which takes the texture object, of type sampler2D, and the texture coordinates. A screenshot from the GL Textures demo is shown in Figure 6.7.

LISTING 6.8 THE GL TEXTURES VERTEX SHADER

```
varying vec2 texCoords;


void main()
{
    // Transform vertex.
    gl_Position = gl_ModelViewProjectionMatrix * gl_Vertex;

    // Pass the tex coords to the pixel shader.
    texCoords = gl_MultiTexCoord0.xy;
}
```

LISTING 6.9 THE GL TEXTURES PIXEL SHADER

```
varying vec2 texCoords;

uniform sampler2D decal;
```

```
void main()
{
    gl_FragColor = texture2D(decal, texCoords);
}
```

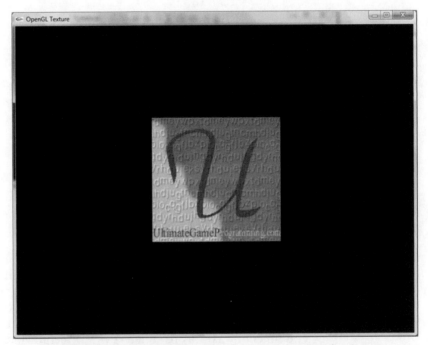

FIGURE 6.7   A screenshot from the GL Texture demo application.

Direct3D 9 Texture Mapping in Shaders

ON THE CD

On the CD-ROM is a demo application called D3D9 Textures that demonstrates the same application as the GL Textures demo but using Direct3D 9. Texture mapping in Direct3D 9, and 10 for that matter, makes loading texture images into the API easy through the use of various utility functions. In this demo the application renders a simple textured square. The global section from the D3D 9 Textures demo is shown in Listing 6.10.

LISTING 6.10 THE GLOBAL SECTION OF THE D3D9 TEXTURES DEMO

```
// Direct3D objects.
LPDIRECT3D9 g_d3dObject = NULL;
LPDIRECT3DDEVICE9 g_d3dDevice = NULL;
```

```
// Vertex specified by position and color.
struct Vertex
{
   FLOAT x, y, z;
   FLOAT tu, tv;
};


#define D3DFVF_D3DVertex (D3DFVF_XYZ | D3DFVF_TEX1)

LPDIRECT3DVERTEXBUFFER9 g_vertexBuffer = NULL;
LPDIRECT3DTEXTURE9 g_decal = NULL;



// High-level shaders.
LPD3DXEFFECT g_effect = NULL;



// Matrices.
D3DXMATRIX g_projMat;
```

The initialization of the demo is straightforward as it was with the GL Textures demo. In the initialization, after the rendering states are set, the texture is loaded with a call to D3DXCreateTextureFromFile(). This file, along with D3DXCreateTextureFromFileEx(), places everything you need for loading and creating a texture resource in one easy-to-use function. The function takes as parameters the Direct3D device, the file name of the resource, and the address of the object that will store the Direct3D texture resource. The initialization from the D3D9 Textures demo is shown in Listing 6.11.

LISTING 6.11 THE D3D9 TEXTURES DEMO'S INITIALIZATION SECTION

```
bool InitializeDemo()
{
   g_d3dDevice->SetRenderState(D3DRS_LIGHTING, FALSE);
   g_d3dDevice->SetRenderState(D3DRS_CULLMODE, D3DCULL_NONE);


   // Load the texture.

   HRESULT hr = D3DXCreateTextureFromFile(g_d3dDevice,
                                          "decal.tga",
                                          &g_decal);
```

```
if(FAILED(hr))
   return false;


// Create the vertex buffer and load the geometry.


Vertex obj[] =
{
   {-0.2f, -0.2f, 1.0f,  0.0f, 1.0f},
   { 0.2f, -0.2f, 1.0f,  1.0f, 1.0f},
   { 0.2f,  0.2f, 1.0f,  1.0f, 0.0f},
   { 0.2f,  0.2f, 1.0f,  1.0f, 0.0f},
   {-0.2f,  0.2f, 1.0f,  0.0f, 0.0f},
   {-0.2f, -0.2f, 1.0f,  0.0f, 1.0f}
};

int numVerts = sizeof(obj) / sizeof(obj[0]);
int size = numVerts * sizeof(Vertex);

hr = g_d3dDevice->CreateVertexBuffer(size, 0,
D3DFVF_D3DVertex,
        D3DPOOL_DEFAULT, &g_vertexBuffer, NULL);

if(FAILED(hr))
   return false;


// Load data into vertex buffer.

Vertex *ptr = NULL;

hr = g_vertexBuffer->Lock(0, sizeof(obj), (void**)&ptr, 0);

if(FAILED(hr))
   return false;

memcpy(ptr, obj, sizeof(obj));
g_vertexBuffer->Unlock();


// Load shaders.

LPD3DXBUFFER errors = NULL;
```

```
        hr = D3DXCreateEffectFromFile(g_d3dDevice, "effect.fx", NULL,
                                      NULL, 0, NULL, &g_effect,
                                      &errors);

    if(FAILED(hr))
    {
        LPVOID compileErrors = errors->GetBufferPointer();

        // Show the errors to the user.
        MessageBox(NULL, (const char*)compileErrors,
                   "Shader Errors...", MB_OK |
MB_ICONEXCLAMATION);

        return false;
    }

    return true;
}
```

The rendering function from the D3D9 Textures demo starts by setting up the vertex buffer stream of the object that will be drawn. The shaders for the demo application require the model-view projection matrix and the texture resource to be sent to the effect. In Direct3D HLSL shaders we must manually provide the model-view projection and other matrices, which is unlike GLSL, where the information is provided by the API without further work by the programmer. To set the texture we use SetTexture() of the effect object similarly to how we use SetMatrix() to set a matrix, SetFloat() to set a floating-point value, and so on. The rendering function for the D3D9 Textures demo is shown in Listing 6.12.

LISTING 6.12 THE D3D9 TEXTURES RENDERING FUNCTION

```
    void RenderScene()
    {
        g_d3dDevice->Clear(0, NULL, D3DCLEAR_TARGET |
D3DCLEAR_ZBUFFER,
                           D3DCOLOR_XRGB(0,0,0), 1.0f, 0);

        g_d3dDevice->BeginScene();

        // Setup geometry to render.
        g_d3dDevice->SetStreamSource(0, g_vertexBuffer,
                                     0, sizeof(Vertex));
```

```
g_d3dDevice->SetFVF(D3DFVF_D3DVertex);


// Calculate MVP.
D3DXMATRIX mvp = g_projMat;
D3DXMatrixTranspose(&mvp, &mvp);


// Set the shader technique and set its variables.
g_effect->SetTechnique("SimpleEffect");
g_effect->SetMatrix("worldViewProj", &mvp);
g_effect->SetTexture("decal", g_decal);

UINT totalPasses;
g_effect->Begin(&totalPasses, 0);

// Loop through each pass of the effect and draw.
for(UINT pass = 0; pass < totalPasses; pass++)
{
    g_effect->BeginPass(pass);

        g_d3dDevice->DrawPrimitive(D3DPT_TRIANGLELIST, 0, 2);

    g_effect->EndPass();
}

g_effect->End();

g_d3dDevice->EndScene();

g_d3dDevice->Present(NULL, NULL, NULL, NULL);
}
```

The last code to look at for the D3D9 Textures demo is the effect for texture mapping. This effect has two uniform variables that include the model-view projection matrix and the decal texture that will be sampled by the pixel shader, which uses linear filtering for the mip, mag, and min filters. Since the vertex shader does not sample the texture, it needs to pass along the incoming vertex texture coordinate to the pixel shader. This value will be interpolated across the surface for each pixel with no additional work on the part of the programmer. In the pixel shader the tex2D() function is used to sample a color from the texture, and the function takes as parameters the texture sampler, which in the case of a 2D texture is sampler2D, and a pair of texture coordinates of the type float2 (structure with two floating-point members). The texture mapping effect for the D3D9 Textures demo is shown in Listing 6.13. When you are sampling a texture, the texture sampler that is defined is used. The texture sampler couples the texture data along with all of its states and flags (e.g., filters, etc.) that are to be used. You can have more than one sampler if you choose for a texture. A screenshot of the output from the D3D9 Textures demo is shown in Figure 6.8.

LISTING 6.13 THE D3D9 TEXTURES TEXTURE MAPPING EFFECT

```
// The only variable needed to be set by the application.
float4x4 worldViewProj : WorldViewProjection;

// Texture that will be mapped and its sampler.
texture decal;

sampler DecalSampler = sampler_state
{
   Texture = (decal);
   MipFilter = LINEAR;
   MagFilter = LINEAR;
   MinFilter = LINEAR;
};


// Incoming vertex structure.
struct Vs_Input
{
   float3 vertexPos  : POSITION;
   float2 tex0       : TEXCOORD0;
};

// Output vertex information to the pixel shader.
struct Vs_Output
{
   float4 vertexPos  : POSITION;
   float2 tex0       : TEXCOORD0;
};

// Output from pixel shader.
struct Ps_Output
{
   float4 color      : COLOR;
};
```

```
Vs_Output VertexShaderEffect(Vs_Input IN)
{
    Vs_Output vs_out;

    // Transform the original vertex.
    vs_out.vertexPos = mul(worldViewProj,
float4(IN.vertexPos, 1));

    // Pass along the incoming tex coordinate.
    vs_out.tex0 = IN.tex0;

    return vs_out;
}


Ps_Output PixelShaderEffect(Vs_Output IN)
{
    Ps_Output ps_out;

    // Grab color from texture.
    ps_out.color = tex2D(DecalSampler, IN.tex0);

    return ps_out;
}


technique SimpleEffect
{
    pass Pass0
    {
        // No lighting in this effect is used.
        Lighting = FALSE;

        // Compile and set the vertex and pixel shader.
        VertexShader = compile vs_2_0 VertexShaderEffect();
        PixelShader  = compile ps_2_0 PixelShaderEffect();
    }
}
```

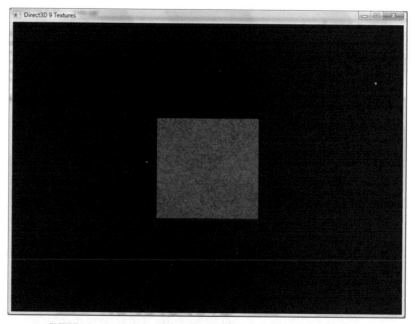

FIGURE 6.8   Screenshot from the D3D9 Texture demo application.

Direct3D 10 Texture Mapping in Shaders

ON THE CD

In this section we discuss the D3D10 Textures demo application, which can be found on the CD-ROM in the Chapter 6 folder. As previously mentioned, Direct3D 10 has many differences from its Direct3D 9 predecessor. In Direct3D shader variables are obtained and set in the application by using an ID3D10Effect*Variable, where the * can be a matrix if the variable is indeed a matrix type, shader resource, and so forth. The name of the effect variable reflects the name of the type of variable you are binding to (e.g., ID3D10EffectShaderResourceVariable, ID3D10Effect-MatrixVariable, and so forth).

The global section of the D3D10 Textures demo is shown in Listing 6.14. Along with the usual global variables from past demos, there are also the effect variables for a texture and the various matrices that make up the model-view projection matrix. Technically, the model-view projection matrix, as a single matrix, is all the shader needs. This demo will show how to send multiple matrices as well as how to use each separately in a shader. Inside the shader that will be seen later in this section we use different constant buffers for the different matrices. Constant buffers are discussed in more detail later in this section along with the effect file. In Listing 6.14 we also look at how to create the projection matrix in Direct3D 10 in the altered ResizeWindow() function, which uses the same utility function that is used in Direct3D 9, called D3DXMatrixPerspectiveFOVLH().

LISTING 6.14 THE GLOBAL SECTION OF THE D3D10 TEXTURES DEMO

```
// Direct3D 10 objects.
ID3D10Device *g_d3dDevice = NULL;
IDXGISwapChain *g_swapChain = NULL;
ID3D10RenderTargetView *g_renderTargetView = NULL;

struct DX10Vertex
{
   D3DXVECTOR3 pos;
   D3DXVECTOR2 tex0;
};

ID3D10InputLayout *g_layout = NULL;
ID3D10Buffer *g_vertexBuffer = NULL;
ID3D10ShaderResourceView *g_decalView = NULL;

ID3D10Effect *g_shader = NULL;
ID3D10EffectTechnique *g_technique = NULL;
ID3D10EffectShaderResourceVariable *g_decalEffectVar = NULL;
ID3D10EffectMatrixVariable *g_worldEffectVar = NULL;
ID3D10EffectMatrixVariable *g_viewEffectVar = NULL;
ID3D10EffectMatrixVariable *g_projEffectVar = NULL;

D3DXMATRIX g_worldMat, g_viewMat, g_projMat;


void ResizeD3D10Window(int width, int height)
{
   if(g_d3dDevice == NULL)
      return;

   D3D10_VIEWPORT vp;
   vp.Width = width;
   vp.Height = height;
   vp.MinDepth = 0.0f;
   vp.MaxDepth = 1.0f;
   vp.TopLeftX = 0;
   vp.TopLeftY = 0;

   g_d3dDevice->RSSetViewports(1, &vp);

   D3DXMatrixPerspectiveFovLH(&g_projMat, (float)D3DX_PI * 0.25f,
                             width/(FLOAT)height, 0.1f, 1000.0f);
}
```

The initialization for the D3D10 Textures function binds to each shader variable after the effect file and technique have been loaded and set up. When binding to a variable, we use the shader's member function `GetVariableByName()`, which takes as a parameter a string that matches the name of a global variable in the effect file. When receiving this variable, we must get the variable as the right type. What this means, for example, is that something like a matrix would need to call the variables' member function `AsMatrix()` to correctly gain access to the shader's variable. This is shown in Listing 6.15, where, in addition to the effect variables, the other new code specifies an additional triangle to the scene that uses texture coordinates.

LISTING 6.15 THE D3D10 TEXTURES INITIALIZE FUNCTION

```
bool InitializeDemo()
{
  // Load the shader.

  DWORD shaderFlags = D3D10_SHADER_ENABLE_STRICTNESS;

#if defined( DEBUG ) || defined( _DEBUG )
  shaderFlags |= D3D10_SHADER_DEBUG;
#endif

  HRESULT hr = D3DX10CreateEffectFromFile("shader.fx", NULL, NULL,
                                          "fx_4_0", shaderFlags,
                                          0, g_d3dDevice, NULL,
                                          NULL, &g_shader, NULL,
                                          NULL);

  if(FAILED(hr))
    return false;

  g_technique = g_shader->GetTechniqueByName("TextureMapping");

  g_worldEffectVar = g_shader->GetVariableByName(
    "World")->AsMatrix();

  g_viewEffectVar = g_shader->GetVariableByName(
    "View")->AsMatrix();

  g_projEffectVar = g_shader->GetVariableByName(
    "Projection")->AsMatrix();
```

```
g_decalEffectVar = g_shader->GetVariableByName(
   "decal")->AsShaderResource();


// Load the Texture
hr = D3DX10CreateShaderResourceViewFromFile(g_d3dDevice,
   "seafloor.dds", NULL, NULL, &g_decalView, NULL);

if(FAILED(hr))
   return false;


// Create the geometry.

D3D10_INPUT_ELEMENT_DESC layout[] =
{
   { "POSITION", 0, DXGI_FORMAT_R32G32B32_FLOAT, 0, 0,
     D3D10_INPUT_PER_VERTEX_DATA, 0 },
   { "TEXCOORD", 0, DXGI_FORMAT_R32G32_FLOAT, 0, 12,
     D3D10_INPUT_PER_VERTEX_DATA, 0 },
};

unsigned int numElements = sizeof(layout) / sizeof(layout[0]);
D3D10_PASS_DESC passDesc;

g_technique->GetPassByIndex(0)->GetDesc(&passDesc);

hr = g_d3dDevice->CreateInputLayout(layout, numElements,
                                    passDesc.pIAInputSignature,
                                    passDesc.IAInputSignatureSize,
                                    &g_layout);

if(FAILED(hr))
   return false;

DX10Vertex vertices[] =
{
   { D3DXVECTOR3( 0.5f,  0.5f, 1.5f), D3DXVECTOR2(1.0f, 1.0f) },
   { D3DXVECTOR3( 0.5f, -0.5f, 1.5f), D3DXVECTOR2(1.0f, 0.0f) },
   { D3DXVECTOR3(-0.5f, -0.5f, 1.5f), D3DXVECTOR2(0.0f, 0.0f) },
    { D3DXVECTOR3(-0.5f, -0.5f, 1.5f), D3DXVECTOR2(0.0f, 0.0f)
},

   { D3DXVECTOR3(-0.5f,  0.5f, 1.5f), D3DXVECTOR2(0.0f, 1.0f) },
   { D3DXVECTOR3( 0.5f,  0.5f, 1.5f), D3DXVECTOR2(1.0f, 1.0f) }
};
```

```
// Create the vertex buffer.

D3D10_BUFFER_DESC buffDesc;
buffDesc.Usage = D3D10_USAGE_DEFAULT;
buffDesc.ByteWidth = sizeof(DX10Vertex) * 6;
buffDesc.BindFlags = D3D10_BIND_VERTEX_BUFFER;
buffDesc.CPUAccessFlags = 0;
buffDesc.MiscFlags = 0;

D3D10_SUBRESOURCE_DATA resData;
resData.pSysMem = vertices;

hr = g_d3dDevice->CreateBuffer(&buffDesc, &resData,
                               &g_vertexBuffer);

if(FAILED(hr))
   return false;


// Set the shader matrix variables that won't change once here.
D3DXMatrixIdentity(&g_worldMat);
D3DXMatrixIdentity(&g_viewMat);

g_viewEffectVar->SetMatrix((float*)&g_viewMat);
g_projEffectVar->SetMatrix((float*)&g_projMat);

return true;
}
```

One thing to note about Listing 6.15 is that at the end the shader variables that do not change during the application's execution are set. In the shader file the constant buffers, which we discuss later in this section, are set up to anticipate these variables not changing often. Since the view matrix is here as a demonstration, it is also set in a constant buffer that does not have frequent change. In a game situation chances are that the view changes rapidly along with the model matrix. The projection matrix does not change often, or even at all in some cases.

The last function to see from the D3D10 Textures demo application is the rendering function. This function sets the model matrix every frame. In this demo this isn't necessary, but it is done as an example since the example constant buffer in the shader specifies that it changes often. Also set in the rendering function is the decal texture resource variable that the effect file will need to properly texture-map the surface of the scene. The rendering function is shown in Listing 6.16 for the D3D10 Textures demo application. Also in Listing 6.16 is the Shutdown() function, which demonstrates how to release a Direct3D 10 texture from memory. Unlike previous versions of Direct3D, we must get and release the resource as well as the Direct3D resource view (Direct3D texture object).

LISTING 6.16 THE RENDERING FUNCTION FROM THE D3D10 TEXTURES DEMO

```
void RenderScene()
{
   float col[4] = { 0, 0, 0, 1 };

   g_d3dDevice->ClearRenderTargetView(g_renderTargetView, col);

   g_worldEffectVar->SetMatrix((float*)&g_worldMat);
   g_decalEffectVar->SetResource(g_decalView);

   unsigned int stride = sizeof(DX10Vertex);
   unsigned int offset = 0;

   g_d3dDevice->IASetInputLayout(g_layout);

   g_d3dDevice->IASetVertexBuffers(0, 1, &g_vertexBuffer,
                                   &stride, &offset);

   g_d3dDevice->IASetPrimitiveTopology(
      D3D10_PRIMITIVE_TOPOLOGY_TRIANGLELIST);

   D3D10_TECHNIQUE_DESC techDesc;
   g_technique->GetDesc(&techDesc);

   for(unsigned int i = 0; i < techDesc.Passes; i++)
   {
      g_technique->GetPassByIndex(i)->Apply(0);
      g_d3dDevice->Draw(6, 0);
   }

   g_swapChain->Present(0, 0);
}


void Shutdown()
{
```

```
        if(g_d3dDevice) g_d3dDevice->ClearState();
        if(g_swapChain) g_swapChain->Release();
        if(g_renderTargetView) g_renderTargetView->Release();

        if(g_shader) g_shader->Release();
        if(g_layout) g_layout->Release();
        if(g_vertexBuffer) g_vertexBuffer->Release();

        if(g_decalView)
        {
           ID3D10Resource *pRes;
           g_decalView->GetResource(&pRes);

           pRes->Release();
           g_decalView->Release();
        }

        if(g_d3dDevice) g_d3dDevice->Release();
    }
```

The D3D10 Textures demo's effect file starts by defining the global variables that are set by the application. This is done by creating a Texture2D object for the 2D texture and by creating each of the three matrices the application sets. All textures have a sampler state that is used by the pixel shader to sample pixels from the texture image. For the sampler in this effect, DecalSampler, the min, mag, and mip filters are all set to linear and the texture coordinate addresses are set to wrap. This is no different from what is done in Direct3D 9, except that Shader Model 4.0 HLSL files use a slightly different syntax.

The matrices are each specified in a constant buffer. A constant buffer, which is new to Shader Model 4.0, is used to specify to the application how frequently a shader variable (also known as shader constant) is updated. Three types of constant buffers can be declared: cbChanges-EveryFrame, cbChangeOnResize, and cbNeverChange. By grouping variables in constant buffers, the application can minimize data bandwidth, which can optimize performance.

The effect from the D3D10 Textures demo, which is shown in Listing 6.17, has a vertex shader that transforms the vertex position and passes along the vertex texture coordinate to the pixel shader. The pixel shader samples the texture sampler using those texture coordinates, and the resulting color is used for the output. A screenshot from the D3D10 Textures demo is shown in Figure 6.9.

LISTING 6.17 THE TEXTURE MAPPING SHADER FOR THE DIRECT3D 10 TEXTURES DEMO

```
Texture2D decal;

SamplerState DecalSampler
{
    Filter = MIN_MAG_MIP_LINEAR;
    AddressU = Wrap;
    AddressV = Wrap;
};


cbuffer cbChangesEveryFrame
{
    matrix World;
    matrix View;
};

cbuffer cbChangeOnResize
{
    matrix Projection;
};


struct VS_INPUT
{
    float4 Pos : POSITION;
    float2 Tex : TEXCOORD;
};

struct PS_INPUT
{
    float4 Pos : SV_POSITION;
    float2 Tex : TEXCOORD0;
};


PS_INPUT VS(VS_INPUT input)
{
    PS_INPUT output = (PS_INPUT)0;
```

```
output.Pos = mul(input.Pos, World);
output.Pos = mul(output.Pos, View);
output.Pos = mul(output.Pos, Projection);

output.Tex = input.Tex;

return output;
}


float4 PS(PS_INPUT input) : SV_Target
{
    return decal.Sample(DecalSampler, input.Tex);
}


technique10 TextureMapping
{
    pass P0
    {
        SetVertexShader(CompileShader(vs_4_0, VS()));

        SetGeometryShader(NULL);

        SetPixelShader(CompileShader(ps_4_0, PS()));
    }
}
```

FIGURE 6.9   Screenshot from the D3D10 Texture demo application.

TEXTURE COMPRESSION

There are a few benefits of texture compression in video games. The first benefit is that it saves storage space. Today, memory is cheap, but it is also finite. On home consoles such as the Xbox 360 and the Nintendo Wii, DVD storage space is valuable when trying to store enough information to meet the demands of an AAA gaming product. Compression is a great way to help reduce storage space, thus allowing for more content to be stored and shipped with a game.

Another benefit of texture compression deals with hardware bandwidth and memory. The less data there is to send down the rendering pipeline, the faster the hardware can get the information it needs. If the hardware supports the use of compressed texture data, then it has less information to work with while the texture remains at the same resolution. Also, the amount of memory available in graphics hardware is limited. By using compressed textures developers have the option of having more space for higher-resolution textures, more textures, or both. For example, if the compression ratio is 6:1, the compressed size for a 32-bit 1024×1024 texture would be 700KB instead of the uncompressed size of 4.2MB.

In this chapter we talk about various compression algorithms and formats such as the DXTC, 3Dc, and A8L8. We also discuss the compression of color maps and normal maps in video games.

Color Map Compression

Decal textures that are composed of color data are a great candidate type to consider for texture compression. These types of textures can use lossless compression, which doesn't reduce quality, and lossy compression, which affects quality. Lossy compression is good to use for textures because most textures, with the right compression ratio, show no visible difference, or no major difference, between the uncompressed or the compressed versions of the texture. Reducing the amount of data used for a texture can allow for more bandwidth to be saved, which can increase the application's performance.

The DXTC image compression used by DDS texture images consists of texture compression formats that can get a compression ratio of 6:1 on color images using DXT1 and a 4:1 compression ratio using the other DXT formats. The DXTC compression formats use a lossy compression, so the quality of color maps can be less than the original, thus making them not the best choice for compressing normal map images.

It is important to know why lossy compression is not good to use for normal map textures. Normal maps store not colors but actual normal directions. To provide accurate lighting across a surface, the normals need to be relatively intact, or else the lighting will not be calculated correctly. The quality of a color map can be less than that of the original without many ramifications, but if normals are wrong, the results of lighting will stick out and can have a negative impact on the rendered surface. An example of a compressed texture compared to a noncompressed color map is shown in Figure 6.10, and an example of a compressed compared to a noncompressed normal map is shown in Figure 6.11.

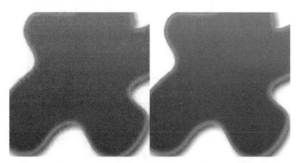

FIGURE 6.10   Color map compressed (left) and noncompressed (right).

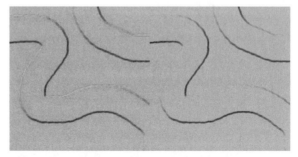

FIGURE 6.11   Normal map compressed (left) and noncompressed (right).

There are five DXTC formats: DXT1 through 5. DXT1 gives the lowest quality because it gives the greatest compression ratio out of the five formats. As the version moves closer to 5, the quality increases at the cost of compression size.

 When you save a DDS texture using an editor such as Photoshop, you can choose which DXTC version you want to use.

DXTC Normal Map Compression

Although DXTC uses lossy compression, which can have a negative impact on lighting quality, there are ways to minimize the negative impact of these compressed textures if you choose to use DXTC with normal maps. The challenge mostly lies in the fact that in a normal map there are often sharp changes across the surface that are used to give detail and variations for the lighting algorithms. Since normal maps are often not smooth across a surface, the compressed normals can be distorted in a way that changes the pattern necessary to create the desired detail. Also, the compressed values can cause the normal to become unnormalized. For lighting to be computed correctly we must use unit-length normals.

A few tricks can be used on normal maps to compress with DXTC formats while retaining an acceptable level of quality. These tricks include the following topics.

- Renormalizing normal values when reading from a texture
- Placing the X-axis (usually in the red component) of a normal in the alpha channel of a DXT5 compressed texture since the alpha channel is compressed separately and retains more quality
- Using the X- and Y-axis of the normal to generate the Z-axis instead of using the Z from the normal map, which can be combined with placing the X-axis in the alpha channel of the DXT5 texture for the most quality
- Using a normalization cube map, which is a fairly old trick used to normalize vectors without calculating the normal

Generating the Z-axis is a great option to use for normal maps that have been compressed. If a normal is lossy compressed, it can be changed in a way that causes it not to be unit-length. By generating the Z-axis the normal can always be unit-length without needing to renormalize the entire vector. A unit normal is a vector whose length equals 1. Because a unit-length vector must have a length of 1, and if we know what the X- and Y-axes are, we can essentially add those together, subtract that total from 1 (which is the length all normal vectors should be), and find the square root of the result, which tells us what the Z-axis must be. This can be done using the simple algebraic formula:

$$Z = square\_root(1 - (X * X - Y * Y))$$

Generating the Z-axis and using DXT5 with the X-axis stored in the alpha channel can give textures the best results when compressing normal maps using the DXTC formats, a screenshot of which is shown in Figure 6.12.

FIGURE 6.12 DXT5 and normal maps using various tricks.

The DXT1 format has the highest compression ratio of 8:1 but does not use an alpha channel, making it an RGB format. If you use the DXT1 extension format that does use an alpha, then you can get a 6:1 compression ratio. The DXT1 format uses 16-bit color values at R5G6B5, which was mentioned earlier in this chapter. The algorithm for the DXT1 format splits the image up into 4×4 pixel blocks where each block stores only two unique colors and uses a 16-bit palette. The pixels in each block reference an entry in the block's palette, allowing the colors to be represented using less data. Since the format uses 4×4 blocks, gradient information often becomes visibly blocky, and artifacts can be seen when information is compressed. A visual of these artifacts is shown in Figure 6.13.

FIGURE 6.13 Artifacts caused by DXT1 compression.

There are extensions to the DXT1 format to allow it to use a 1-bit alpha channel. Whether or not you use it depends on the level of acceptable results you are targeting for specific textures. The DXT1 format can give a compression ratio of 8:1, and its extension can give a compression ratio of 6:1.

The DXT2 format is similar to the DXT1 format, with the exception that the DXT2 format uses a 4-bit alpha that is premultiplied before the compression algorithm is executed so that more transparent pixels appear darker than opaque ones.

The DXT3 format is comparable to the DXT2 format, with the exception that the DXT3 format does not premultiply the data being compressed. The remaining formats, the DXT4 and DXT5 compression formats, are similar to DXT3, but the DXT4 alpha channel is premultiplied with the data that are to be compressed as it is with DXT2, and DXT5 interpolates the alpha channel when compressing the original image data.

It will take some experimenting to see which textures compress acceptably with which DXTC format, but, generally, using the DXT5 format with the X-axis in the alpha channel works the best if you are generating the Z-axis in a shader. Since the X- and Y-axes have the highest precision the formats offer when using DXT5, and since the Z-axis is generated to allow a unit-length vector, using that format can lead to acceptable results. Of course, using other formats might be acceptable in some situations as well.

DXTC stands for DirectX Texture Compression. In OpenGL it is known as S3TC or S3 Texture Compression.

3Dc Compression

3Dc texture compression was first created by ATI for their RADEON X800 series of graphics hardware and is a lossy compression format used for normal map images. Today, 3Dc is supported by OpenGL and Direct3D across all graphics hardware. DXTC is very effective at compressing three- and four-component textures such as RGB and RGBA images, while the visual quality of normal maps compressed using DXTC is lacking. 3Dc is ATI's solution for compressing normal maps, and it is very effective at two-component images. Since a normal's Z-axis can be easily calculated in a pixel shader, 3Dc is a great format to use for normal maps.

The 3Dc texture compression offers a compression ratio of 4:1 and is broken up into 4×4 blocks of pixels of 16 values each. Each of these values has two components that are compressed separately, and since there are only two, it is not practical to use 3Dc for RGB color maps since a blue value cannot be generated like the Z value of a unit-length normal. Since normals can have their Z-axis generated, the format only needs to rely on two components. A 3Dc compressed texture compared to an uncompressed and DXTC compressed texture is shown in Figure 6.14.

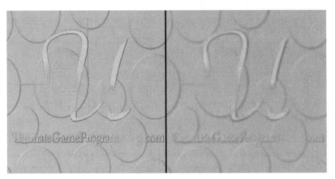

FIGURE 6.14   3Dc compressed texture compared to an uncompressed and DXTC compressed texture.

During compression of each block, the 3Dc algorithm finds a minimum and maximum pair of values, which is stored as 8-bit values. Once the minimum and maximum are found, the algorithms find six values between the minimum and maximum that are equally spaced in size. For example, if the minimum was 1 and the maximum was 14, the six values in between would be 2, 4, 6, 8, 10, and 12. This means each component can be 1 out of 8 values instead of 1 out of 256 values. Each component in each compressed pixel of each 4×4 block of pixels is then a 3-bit index into the table of eight values. This allows a single byte to be used for the representation of each pixel of the compressed texture since a byte is 8-bits, and two compressed component indexes are 3 bits (6 total) each.

3Dc is the compression of choice for normal map images. Although DXT5 can be a decent choice for normal map compression, its lossy compression scheme combined with the lack of bits per component makes it less favorable. Plus, 3Dc gives a 4:1 compression ratio just like DXT5 and is also lossy but gives much better rendering results for normal mapped surfaces.

A8L8 Format

The A8L8 format is not compression in the traditional sense. A8L8 works by allowing us to store normal maps using two components per pixel. Other than dropping the Z-axis of each normal, there is no actual compression. Since the Z-axis can be generated to rebuild the unit-length normal quickly, dropping a component from each pixel of a normal map image can add up for high-resolution textures. The Direct3D and OpenGL graphics API allows for two-component texture images to be created and used within an application. This feature allows us to load two-component data in this manner in our games, where a shader can be used to generate the necessary Z-axis. Since no compression algorithm is being run, there is also no loss of quality as with 3Dc and DXTC compression algorithms.

Although there is no lossy compression with A8L8, the results of using 3Dc for normal maps is much more beneficial because 3Dc gives a 4:1 compression ratio (i.e., a compressed image that is 25% the size of the original), and it gives great results when rendering. For older hardware that does not support 3Dc or DXTC, A8L8 might be an acceptable choice if no other solutions exist.

Using DDS Compressed Textures in Shaders

On the CD-ROM a demo application called GL Texture Compression is in the Chapter 6 folder. This demo application shows how to load a DDS decal texture image into OpenGL using the DDS loading code shown earlier in this chapter. The demo is exactly the same as the GL Textures demo, with the exception of the initialization function, which loads the DDS texture image that will be used.

The initialization function starts by setting the usual rendering states and loading the GLSL shaders that the demo uses, which are the same shaders as in the GL Textures demo. The function then loads the DDS image with the LoadDDS() function from earlier in this chapter before creating the OpenGL texture resource using glGenTextures().

To load a compressed texture directly into OpenGL, extensions are used, which depend on the image's format. For example, the DXTC image uses the GL_COMPRESSED_RGBA_S3TC_DXT1_EXT extension. The initialize function from the demo application determines which type of image is being loaded and determines the extension that needs to be used.

Once the format has been determined, the function loads each mipmap of the texture into memory. A DDS texture can have one or more mipmaps associated with the single texture. Each mipmap must be loaded if you want to use them. Technically, you only need to load the first mipmap level if you are not using the image's mipmap data. Compressed texture data are also loaded into the API using the OpenGL function glCompressedTexImage2DARB(), which is specifically designed to load compressed data.

Keep in mind that the size of each mipmap factor is 8 for DXT1 images and 16 for the rest. To calculate the mipmap size for each level you can use the following equation before attempting to load each mipmap level:

$$mipSize = ((w + 3) / 4) * ((h + 3) / 4) * mipFactor;$$

The width and height loaded from the image's header is used for the first mipmap level. Each mipmap level after that is half the size of the one that came before it. The initialization function from the GL Texture Compression demo is shown in Listing 6.18. A screenshot from the GL Texture Compression demo application is shown in Figure 6.15.

LISTING 6.18 THE INITIALIZATION FUNCTION FOR THE GL TEXTURE COMPRESSION DEMO

```
bool InitializeApp()
{
   glClearColor(0.0f, 0.0f, 0.0f, 1.0f);
   glShadeModel(GL_SMOOTH);
   glEnable(GL_DEPTH_TEST);
   glEnable(GL_TEXTURE_2D);


   if(!CreateGLSLShader("../vs.glsl", "../ps.glsl", g_shader))
   {
      if(!CreateGLSLShader("../../vs.glsl", "../../ps.glsl",
         g_shader))
         return false;
   }

   // Bind our shader variables.
   g_glslDecal = glGetUniformLocationARB(g_shader, "decal");


   // Load DDS image.
   ImageInfoDDS info;
   unsigned char *image = LoadDDS("../image.dds", info);

   if(image == NULL)
   {
      image = LoadDDS("../../image.dds", info);

      if(image == NULL)
         return false;
   }


   glGenTextures(1, &g_texture);
   glBindTexture(GL_TEXTURE_2D, g_texture);
```

```
int w = info.m_width;
int h = info.m_height;
int mipFactor = 0;

if(info.m_type == DDS_DXT1)
   mipFactor = 8;
else
   mipFactor = 16;

int mipSize;
int mipOffset = 0;

int type = 0;

switch(info.m_type)
{
   case DDS_DXT1:
      type = GL_COMPRESSED_RGBA_S3TC_DXT1_EXT;
      break;

   case DDS_DXT3:
      type = GL_COMPRESSED_RGBA_S3TC_DXT3_EXT;
      break;

   case DDS_DXT5:
      type = GL_COMPRESSED_RGBA_S3TC_DXT5_EXT;
      break;
}


for(int i = 0; i < info.m_numMipMaps; i++)
{
   mipSize = ((w + 3) / 4) * ((h + 3) / 4) * mipFactor;

   glTexParameteri(GL_TEXTURE_2D, GL_TEXTURE_MIN_FILTER,
                   GL_LINEAR);
   glTexParameteri(GL_TEXTURE_2D, GL_TEXTURE_MAG_FILTER,
                   GL_LINEAR);

   glCompressedTexImage2DARB(GL_TEXTURE_2D, i, type, w, h,
                             0, mipSize, image + mipOffset);

   // Half the image size for the next mip-map level...
   w >>= 1;
   h >>= 1;
```

```
        // Move the offset to the next mipmap.
        mipOffset += mipSize;
    }


    delete[] image;

    return true;
}
```

FIGURE 6.15 Screenshot from the GL Texture Compression demo application.

There are no Direct3D 9 or 10 versions of this demo on the CD-ROM, because Direct3D can use DXTC compressed textures in the API without any special setup by the application or programmer. Because of this, the same code used by the D3D9 Textures and D3D10 Textures applications can be used to load compressed DDS images that use DXTC formats. There is also nothing special that needs to be done in the shaders for these demos. Later in this book we use normal maps to perform normal mapping on surfaces.

SUMMARY

Texture mapping is a straightforward topic in computer graphics, but it is a fundamental and very important topic as well. Textures, and images in general, are the basis of many graphically rendered techniques in computer-generated imagery. The purpose of textures is to add detail to the less detailed. This is also true with nondecal textures such as height maps, bump and normal maps, reflection maps, alpha maps, and so forth, each of which are discussed later in this book.

In this chapter we briefly discussed some of the fundamentals of texture mapping that should serve as a review for experienced OpenGL and Direct3D coders for whom this book is intended. Throughout the remainder of this book we build upon what was discussed in this chapter to learn and implement effects common in modern video games. The following elements were discussed in this chapter:

- Texture mapping
- TGA images
- DDS images
- Texture filters
- Mipmaps
- Texture compression
- Run-length encoding
- Various image filters
- DXTC textures
- 3Dc textures
- A8L8 textures

CHAPTER QUESTIONS

Answers to the following chapter review questions can be found in Appendix A.

1. What is the primary goal of texture mapping?
    A. To add detail to the less detailed
    B. To reduce geometry requirements
    C. To reduce the work for artists who would otherwise add such detail using colored polygons
    D. All of the above
    E. None of the above
2. What does TGA stand for? What does DDS stand for?
3. Define texture compression. What are the two types of texture compression discussed in this chapter?
4. What is the difference between lossy and lossless compression?

5. What are the strengths and weakness of lossy and lossless compression when discussing normal maps?

6. Describe the DXTC compression format. What image file format discussed in this chapter uses DXTC compression for its image storage?

7. Describe the A8L8 format. How does it compress data, and what kind of images is it best suited for?

8. Describe the 3Dc compression format. List three benefits it has over the DXTC compression formats.

9. Describe the run-length encoding algorithm. What is the main reason that algorithm wasn't covered for TGA images even though the TGA file format supports it?

10. True or false: Run-length encoding textures are supported by today's graphics hardware.

11. True or false: Intel-based processors use big endian order.

12. True or false: Byte ordering affects only multibyte variables being read or written to a file.

13. True or false: Lossy compression is the best kind to use for normal map images but not for color map images.

14. True or false: Graphics hardware today supports DXTC and 3Dc compression formats internally using OpenGL and Direct3D.

15. True or false: Run-length encoding is a lossless compression algorithm.

16. True or false: A8L8 is a lossy compression format.

17. True or false: DXTC is more suitable for normal maps than color maps.

18. True or false: 3Dc is more suitable for normal maps than color maps.

19. True or false: DXTC and 3Dc are lossy compression algorithms.

20. True or false: 3Dc and DXTC are block-based compression formats.

CHAPTER EXERCISES

Exercise 1: Develop your own image file format. Create a simple application to read and write a file header and store the image information in RGB or RGBA format using uncompressed data.

Exercise 2: Build off of Exercise 1 and add RLE compression support to your image file format. Be sure you can uncompress the images so that they can be used in either OpenGL or Direct3D.

Exercise 3: Build off of Exercise 2 and add support for two-component normal maps along with RGB and RGBA images to your file format. Use a field in the file header that can be tested to determine which type of image is being loaded. You do not need to use RLE for the normal map data.

ADDITIONAL SURFACE MAPPING

In This Chapter

- Alpha Mapping
- Cube Mapping
- Reflections
- Refractions
- Render Targets
- Image Filters
- Additional Texture Mapping Techniques

The importance of textures in video games is not to be taken lightly. Textures, when it comes to graphics, are the most important resource, followed by programmable shaders for adding detail to virtual environments. Textures have many uses in video games that extend past using them for mapping color data onto surfaces.

The purpose of this chapter is to look at a few additional uses for texture mapping in video games. Topics in this chapter include using textures as rendering masks, using textures to render environments on objects, rendering scenes to surfaces that can be used as textures, and filtering algorithms for image data. Throughout this book we look at additional uses for textures as we progress to more advanced topics. These include using textures to calculate environment shadows, precompute a scene's radiance, simulate high polygon counts, and more.

ALPHA MAPPING

Not all textures need to be used as color images that are displayed on surfaces. One of the many uses for textures that we discuss in this book is as rendering masks. Anyone with experience with products such as Photoshop or Flash knows that a mask is a surface that is used to help control the rendering output of another surface. You can use a rendering mask to specify where on a surface you want color data to appear, blend, not appear, and so on. For example, if you had a mask of a circle and you had two images to be displayed on a surface, you could use the mask to dictate where on the surface the first image would appear and where on the surface the second image would appear. An example of this is shown in Figure 7.1, where the dark areas of the mask represent where the first image will appear and the white areas show where the second image will appear on the surface.

FIGURE 7.1   Using a rendering mask (left)
on two images (middle) to create the output (right).

In this section we use the alpha channel of an image as a rendering mask. This mask dictates what parts of the image are transparent and what parts are not. This type of rendering mask is known as alpha mapping, and it can be used to add controlled transparency on the pixel level to virtual objects.

The creation of an alpha map is fairly straightforward. In the image editor of your choice you can draw a pattern in the alpha channel that will act as the rendering mask. When you use the alpha channel, you have two choices to select from. The first choice is to treat each alpha component as a true or false value, which means any alpha that is 0 is invisible and anything greater than 0 is visible (or vice versa). The second option, and one that is commonly used for 8-bit components, is to use the alpha channel as a percentage of transparency. This can allow you to model surfaces such as glass or other semitransparent objects or parts of an object that is semi-transparent. In video games many types of objects are modeled using alpha mapping, including:

- Leaves on a tree branch
- Grass
- Particles
- Chain-link fences
- Some interface objects (buttons, life bars, etc.)
- Text
- Clouds
- Billboards (discussed later in this chapter)
- Glass that is not one unified transparent color
- Muzzle flashes from a gun

The purpose of alpha mapping is to dictate specifically which parts of a model or surface is fully or semitransparent. In complex models not all parts of an object need to be transparent. For example, for a plastic bottle the bottle might be semitransparent, but the label and cap might not be. Instead of expensive texture switching and rendering each part separately, something as simple as using the alpha channel as a mask for the object's texture is a faster solution.

The same idea can be used for the masking of any effect. In specular lighting it is possible to use a rendering mask to control which parts of an object are, for example, shiny and which parts are not. For a 3D character model of a medieval knight in shining armor, the armor might be shiny and semireflecting, but the character's skin is not. If one texture and shader was used for the entire model, the alpha channel or a separate texture could be used as a rendering mask to control the pixel-level details as necessary.

Another method that uses this idea is known as color-key transparency. With color-key transparency, instead of using the alpha channel of an RGBA image, you can use the RGB color of each pixel to determine transparency. This was commonly done in the old-school 2D games that we once enjoyed on gaming consoles such as Nintendo's NES, and it is still done commonly today. The technique works by choosing a single color as the transparent color. For example, if the color black was used (RGB [0, 0, 0]), any pixel that matched that color was not rendered, that is, it is transparent. For sprite images, especially those used in games, there is often a background color that is used as the color-key transparency value that is not rendered with the rest of the image. Often this color is one that is not used in the game, such as hot pink.

In the upcoming sections we look at alpha mapping in OpenGL, Direct3D 9, and Direct3D 10.

Implementing Alpha Maps in OpenGL

ON THE CD

On the CD-ROM a demo application called AlphaMappingGL in the Chapter 7 folder demonstrates how to perform alpha mapping in OpenGL. The Alpha testing feature must be enabled to perform hardware alpha testing in OpenGL. This can be done using the OpenGL functions glEnable(), which is used to enable states such as alpha testing with the flag GL_ALPHA_TEST, and glAlphaFunc(), which allows us to specify the comparison of the test. The comparison can be set to never, greater than a value, less than a value, not equal to a value, or always. The flags that can be used are

- GL_NEVER
- GL_LESS
- GL_GREATER
- GL_EQUAL
- GL_NOTEQUAL
- GL_LEQUAL
- GL_GEQUAL
- GL_ALWAYS

The demo application uses the code from the texture mapping demo called GL Texture from Chapter 6, "Mapping Surfaces," but adds a 32-bit image with an alpha channel and three lines of code to the rendering function, which are the OpenGL functions for enabling and disabling alpha testing as well as the comparison function. Since the code is already able to load an RGBA texture image, nothing else is necessary. The rendering function from the alpha mapping OpenGL demo is shown in Listing 7.1. The vertex and pixel shaders, for convenience, are shown in Listings 7.2 and 7.3. Figure 7.2 shows a screenshot of the application in action.

LISTING 7.1 THE RENDERING FUNCTION FROM THE ALPHAMAPPINGGL DEMO

```
void RenderScene()
{
    glClear(GL_COLOR_BUFFER_BIT | GL_DEPTH_BUFFER_BIT);
    glLoadIdentity();

    float vertices[]  = { -0.8f, -1, -6, 0.8f, -1, -6, 0.8f, 1, -6,
                          0.8f, 1, -6, -0.8f, 1, -6, -0.8f, -1, -6 };
    float texCoords[] = { 0, 0, 1, 0, 1, 1, 1, 1, 0, 1, 0, 0 };

    glEnableClientState(GL_VERTEX_ARRAY);
    glVertexPointer(3, GL_FLOAT, 0, vertices);

    glEnableClientState(GL_TEXTURE_COORD_ARRAY);
    glTexCoordPointer(2, GL_FLOAT, 0, texCoords);

    glUseProgramObjectARB(g_shader);
    glUniform1iARB(g_glslDecal, 0);

    glEnable(GL_ALPHA_TEST);
    glAlphaFunc(GL_GREATER, 0.5f);

    glBindTexture(GL_TEXTURE_2D, g_texture);
    glDrawArrays(GL_TRIANGLES, 0, 6);

    glDisable(GL_ALPHA_TEST);

    glDisableClientState(GL_VERTEX_ARRAY);
    glDisableClientState(GL_TEXTURE_COORD_ARRAY);

    glutSwapBuffers();
    glutPostRedisplay();
}
```

LISTING 7.2 THE VERTEX SHADER USED IN THE AlphaMappingGL DEMO

```
varying vec2 texCoords;


void main()
{
   gl_Position = gl_ModelViewProjectionMatrix * gl_Vertex;
   texCoords = gl_MultiTexCoord0.xy;
}
```

LISTING 7.3 THE PIXEL SHADER USED IN THE AlphaMappingGL DEMO

```
varying vec2 texCoords;

uniform sampler2D decal;


void main()
{
   gl_FragColor = texture2D(decal, texCoords);
}
```

FIGURE 7.2   The AlphaMappingGL demo screenshot.

In OpenGL you can also use `glBlendFunc()` to specify how the source and destination blend colors combine. The `glBlendFunc()` function takes two parameters: one for the source factor and one for the destination factor. In other words, this is that the source and destination determine the arithmetic used for the blending. The `glBlendFunc()` can be used not just for alpha testing, but for rendering in general. According to the Microsoft Developer Network (MSDN), it can also be used to draw anti-aliased points and lines using `GL_SRC_ALPHA` for the source factor and `GL_ONE_MINUS_SRC_ALPHA` for the destination factor. The function can also be used to optimize the rendering of anti-aliasing polygons by using `GL_ONE` for the source factor and `GL_SRC_ALPHA_SATURATE` for the destination factor. The `glBlendFunc()` function parameter can be one of the following values, where SRC is short for source and DST is short for destination.

- `GL_ZERO`
- `GL_ONE`
- `GL_DST_COLOR`
- `GL_ONE_MINUS_DST_COLOR`
- `GL_SRC_ALPHA`
- `GL_ONE_MINUS_SRC_ALPHA`
- `GL_DST_ALPHA`
- `GL_ONE_MINUS_DST_ALPHA`
- `GL_SRC_ALPHA_SATURATE`

Implementing Alpha Maps in Direct3D

In Direct3D we have the option of setting alpha testing in the High-Level Shading Language (HLSL) shader or in the application. In HLSL we can access Direct3D state features directly in the shader code. In pre–Shader Model 4.0 this can be done by setting the technique pass property `AlphaBlendState` to true to enable alpha testing and setting the source (`SrcBlend`) and destination (`DestBlend`) blend factors to use the source color's alpha (`SrcAlpha`) and inverse source alpha (`InvSrcAlpha`) or whatever combination gives you the results you are looking for.

ON THE CD

On the book's accompanying CD-ROM, in the Chapter 7 folder, there is a demo application called AlphaMappingD3D9, which performs alpha mapping using Direct3D 9. Alpha testing is set up and enabled in the technique's pass at the end of the demo's shader. In the setup, alpha testing is enabled, the source blend is set to the source's alpha color, and the destination blend is set to the inverse of the source's alpha color. The inverse is essentially 1 / `SrcAlpha`. This is a common way to set up alpha testing. Setting the destination with the inverse of the source alpha blends the transparent section with the rendering canvas (i.e., what is already rendered on the screen). The HLSL shader from the AlphaMappingD3D9 demo is shown in Listing 7.4. The demo is the D3D9Texture demo from Chapter 6 with the inclusion of enabling alpha testing, which is done in the shader's technique pass.

LISTING 7.4 THE ALPHAMAPPINGD3D9 DEMO'S SHADER

```
float4x4 worldViewProj : WorldViewProjection;

texture decal;

sampler DecalSampler = sampler_state
{
   Texture = (decal);
   MipFilter = LINEAR;
   MagFilter = LINEAR;
   MinFilter = LINEAR;
};


// Incoming vertex structure.
struct Vs_Input
{
   float3 vertexPos  : POSITION;
   float2 tex0       : TEXCOORD0;
};

// Output vertex information to the pixel shader.
struct Vs_Output
{
   float4 vertexPos  : POSITION;
   float2 tex0       : TEXCOORD0;
};

// Output from pixel shader.
struct Ps_Output
{
   float4 color      : COLOR;
};


Vs_Output VertexShaderEffect(Vs_Input IN)
{
   Vs_Output vs_out;
```

```
            vs_out.vertexPos = mul(worldViewProj,
float4(IN.vertexPos, 1));
            vs_out.tex0 = IN.tex0;

        return vs_out;
    }



    Ps_Output PixelShaderEffect(Vs_Output IN)
    {
        Ps_Output ps_out;

        ps_out.color = tex2D(DecalSampler, IN.tex0);

        return ps_out;
    }



    technique SimpleEffect
    {
        pass Pass0
        {
            Lighting = FALSE;
            AlphaBlendEnable = TRUE;
            SrcBlend = SrcAlpha;
            DestBlend = InvSrcAlpha;

            VertexShader = compile vs_2_0 VertexShaderEffect();
            PixelShader  = compile ps_2_0 PixelShaderEffect();
        }
    }
```

In Direct3D 10 using Shader Model 4.0 we have blend state (Blend-State) objects that can be used to enable blending. The blend state object can be created and set in the application using the D3D10_BLEND_DESC structure or inside a shader. Inside the blend state structure, with the HLSL BlendState matching the D3D10_BLEND_DES the application would have used if setting the blend state from inside the application's code, we can set the following properties.

- ALPHATOCOVERAGEENABLE
- BLENDENABLE
- SRCBLEND
- DESTBLEND
- BLENDOP

- SRCBLENDALPHA
- DESTBLENDALPHA
- BLENDOPALPHA
- RENDERTARGETWRITEMASK

The alpha-to-coverage (ALPHATOCOVERAGEENABLE) refers to multi-sampling. This is useful for overlapping polygons such as blades of grass.

The BlendEnable property can enable or disable blending using either true or false. The source blend (SRCBLEND) specifies the RGB value from the first source to be sampled, while the destination blend (DESTBLEND) specifies it for the second. The source and destination blend alpha properties (SRCBLENDALPHA and DESTBLENDALPHA) are the same but specify the operation for the alpha channel. Each of these properties can be one of the following values, where the values ending with _COLOR are not allowed for the alpha properties.

```
typedef enum D3D10_BLEND
{
    D3D10_BLEND_ZERO = 1,
    D3D10_BLEND_ONE = 2,
    D3D10_BLEND_SRC_COLOR = 3,
    D3D10_BLEND_INV_SRC_COLOR = 4,
    D3D10_BLEND_SRC_ALPHA = 5,
    D3D10_BLEND_INV_SRC_ALPHA = 6,
    D3D10_BLEND_DEST_ALPHA = 7,
    D3D10_BLEND_INV_DEST_ALPHA = 8,
    D3D10_BLEND_DEST_COLOR = 9,
    D3D10_BLEND_INV_DEST_COLOR = 10,
    D3D10_BLEND_SRC_ALPHA_SAT = 11,
    D3D10_BLEND_BLEND_FACTOR = 14,
    D3D10_BLEND_INV_BLEND_FACTOR = 15,
    D3D10_BLEND_SRC1_COLOR = 16,
    D3D10_BLEND_INV_SRC1_COLOR = 17,
    D3D10_BLEND_SRC1_ALPHA = 18,
    D3D10_BLEND_INV_SRC1_ALPHA = 19,
} D3D10_BLEND;
```

The blend operation (BLENDOP) and the alpha blend operation (BLENDOPALPHA) define how the RGB and alpha data are blended. These two properties can be one of any of the following values in this enumeration:

```
typedef enum D3D10_BLEND_OP
{
    D3D10_BLEND_OP_ADD = 1,
    D3D10_BLEND_OP_SUBTRACT = 2,
```

```
        D3D10_BLEND_OP_REV_SUBTRACT = 3,
        D3D10_BLEND_OP_MIN = 4,
        D3D10_BLEND_OP_MAX = 5,
    } D3D10_BLEND_OP;
```

The last property is the write mask for the rendering target (RENDER-TARGETWRITEMASK). This property allows you to specify which color component or components are allowed to be written to. By default, all components are written to during rendering. The write mask can be any one or any combination of the following flags:

```
typedef enum D3D10_COLOR_WRITE_ENABLE
{
    D3D10_COLOR_WRITE_ENABLE_RED = 1,
    D3D10_COLOR_WRITE_ENABLE_GREEN = 2,
    D3D10_COLOR_WRITE_ENABLE_BLUE = 4,
    D3D10_COLOR_WRITE_ENABLE_ALPHA = 8,
    D3D10_COLOR_WRITE_ENABLE_ALL =
      ( D3D10_COLOR_WRITE_ENABLE_RED |
D3D10_COLOR_WRITE_ENABLE_GREEN |
        D3D10_COLOR_WRITE_ENABLE_BLUE |
D3D10_COLOR_WRITE_ENABLE_ALPHA ),
    } D3D10_COLOR_WRITE_ENABLE;
```

ON THE CD

When specifying these properties within a shader instead of inside the application, you use the exact same names minus the D3D10_ prefix. In the Chapter 7 folder of the CD-ROM is a demo called AlphaMappingD3D10 that demonstrates alpha testing in Direct3D 10. A blend state object is created in the demo's shader and is set in the technique's pass. To set a blend state object, call the HLSL function SetBlendState(), which takes as parameters the blend state object, an array of blend factor colors (one for each component), and a sample coverage value that has the default of 0xffffffff. This function exists in the application as OMSetBlendState() and is a function of the Direct3D device object. The AlphaMappingD3D10 demo's shader is shown in Listing 7.5.

You can set the blend state in the application using OMSetBlendState() *or in the HLSL shader using* SetBlendState(), *which is the same function minus the* OM *prefix. You do not have to use both methods at the same time since that will only cause you to set the blend state twice, which is unnecessary.*

LISTING 7.5 THE ALPHAMAPPINGD3D10 DEMO'S SHADER

```
Texture2D decal;

SamplerState DecalSampler
{
   Filter = MIN_MAG_MIP_LINEAR;
   AddressU = Wrap;
   AddressV = Wrap;
};


BlendState AlphaBlending
{
   AlphaToCoverageEnable = FALSE;
   BlendEnable[0] = TRUE;
   SrcBlend = SRC_ALPHA;
   DestBlend = INV_SRC_ALPHA;
   BlendOp = ADD;
   SrcBlendAlpha = ZERO;
   DestBlendAlpha = ZERO;
   BlendOpAlpha = ADD;
   RenderTargetWriteMask[0] = 0x0F;
};


cbuffer cbChangesEveryFrame
{
   matrix World;
   matrix View;
};

cbuffer cbChangeOnResize
{
   matrix Projection;
};


struct VS_INPUT
{
   float4 Pos : POSITION;
   float2 Tex : TEXCOORD;
};
```

```
struct PS_INPUT
{
    float4 Pos : SV_POSITION;
    float2 Tex : TEXCOORD0;
};


PS_INPUT VS(VS_INPUT input)
{
    PS_INPUT output = (PS_INPUT)0;

    output.Pos = mul(input.Pos, World);
    output.Pos = mul(output.Pos, View);
    output.Pos = mul(output.Pos, Projection);

    output.Tex = input.Tex;

    return output;
}


float4 PS(PS_INPUT input) : SV_Target
{
    return decal.Sample(DecalSampler, input.Tex);
}


technique10 TextureMapping
{
    pass P0
    {
        SetBlendState(AlphaBlending, float4(0.0f, 0.0f, 0.0f, 0.0f),
                    0xFFFFFFFF);

        SetVertexShader(CompileShader(vs_4_0, VS()));
        SetGeometryShader(NULL);
        SetPixelShader(CompileShader(ps_4_0, PS()));
    }
}
```

CUBE MAPPING

Cube mapping is a type of texture mapping where six images, one for each face of the cube shape, are used to map a surface. Each of the faces of a cube map together create an actual cube, where each face of the cube is a different image of the (often) environment in a different direction. Cube maps are usually used for storing the images that make up an environment surrounding a point in space and are heavily used in modern video games. For example, the top of the cube map can be the sky, the bottom the ground, and the remaining sides can be the horizontal views of the entire environment. An example of a cube map is shown in Figure 7.3.

FIGURE 7.3   An example of a cube map.

Cube mapping is a common technique that is used as the basis for other techniques such as reflection mapping, which is used to perform reflections on shiny surfaces by using the information in the cube map to texture objects so that they appear to reflect their surroundings. A few common uses of cube maps include

- Reflection mapping
- Refraction mapping
- Lighting, which is more common using high-dynamic-range environment cube maps these days
- Vector normalizations using what is known as a normalization cub map, which is not as common with today's hardware

Since six images make up a single cube map, it is not enough to use 2D texture coordinates. When working with cube maps, we use 3D texture coordinates, that is, coordinates with three coordinate axes, instead of two in order to reference which one of the six images will be applied to a pixel within a surface's area. In the case of reflection and refraction mapping, which will be seen later in this chapter, the texture coordinates can be calculated by the shader, thus avoiding texture coordinates to be passed to the rendering API for the visual effect.

The 3D texture coordinates are often referred to as the S-, T-, and R-axes or the U-, V-, and W-axes.

Implementing Cube Mapping in OpenGL

ON THE CD

On the book's accompanying CD-ROM is a demo application called Cube-MappingGL that demonstrates cube mapping in OpenGL in a simple manner. The demo is a modified version of the GLTextures texture mapping demo from Chapter 6. In this demo a new function called LoadGLImage-Data() is used by the demo's initialization function. This new function simply wraps loading a single image file into OpenGL inside one function. This is done because the demo needs to load at least six images for the cube map, which is a lot of redundant code that can easily be placed inside a single function.

The demo's initialization function starts by setting the usual rendering states and loads the shader that will be used by the application for the effect. The function then loads each of the six images that are used to represent the cube map into a GL_TEXTURE_CUBE_MAP_ARB created texture object. To reduce redundant code the images are loaded by a loop. If all images have been loaded and added to the texture object, we can move on. When loading images into a cube map, we must first bind the cube map texture using glBindTexture(), and then we must specify to which face of the cube map we are loading the data. The face can be one of the following OpenGL flags.

- GL_TEXTURE_CUBE_MAP_POSITIVE_X_ARB
- GL_TEXTURE_CUBE_MAP_NEGATIVE_X_ARB
- GL_TEXTURE_CUBE_MAP_POSITIVE_Y_ARB
- GL_TEXTURE_CUBE_MAP_NEGATIVE_Y_ARB
- GL_TEXTURE_CUBE_MAP_POSITIVE_Z_ARB
- GL_TEXTURE_CUBE_MAP_NEGATIVE_Z_ARB

The initialization function from the CubeMappingGL demo is shown in Listing 7.6. Also in Listing 7.6 is the LoadGLImageData() function.

LISTING 7.6 THE CUBEMAPPINGGL'S LoadGLImageData() AND InitializeApp() FUNCTIONS

```
bool LoadGLImageData(char *imageFile, GLenum face)
{
    // Load TGA image.
    int width = 0, height = 0, comp = 0;
```

```
      unsigned char *image = LoadTGA(imageFile, width, height, comp);

      if(image == NULL)
         return false;

      int type = comp == 3 ? GL_RGB : GL_RGBA;

      gluBuild2DMipmaps(face, type, width, height, type,
                        GL_UNSIGNED_BYTE, image);

      delete[] image;

      return true;
}


bool InitializeApp()
{
   glClearColor(0.89f, 0.93f, 1.0f, 1.0f);
   glShadeModel(GL_SMOOTH);
   glEnable(GL_DEPTH_TEST);
   glEnable(GL_TEXTURE_CUBE_MAP_ARB);

   if(!CreateGLSLShader("../CubeMapVS.glsl", "../CubeMapPS.glsl",
      g_shader))
   {
      if(!CreateGLSLShader("../../CubeMapVS.glsl",
         "../../CubeMapPS.glsl", g_shader))
         return false;
   }

   // Bind our shader variables.
   g_glslDecal = glGetUniformLocationARB(g_shader, "decal");


   glGenTextures(1, &g_texture);
   glBindTexture(GL_TEXTURE_CUBE_MAP_ARB, g_texture);

   GLenum faces[] =
   {
      GL_TEXTURE_CUBE_MAP_POSITIVE_X_ARB,
      GL_TEXTURE_CUBE_MAP_NEGATIVE_X_ARB,
      GL_TEXTURE_CUBE_MAP_POSITIVE_Y_ARB,
      GL_TEXTURE_CUBE_MAP_NEGATIVE_Y_ARB,
      GL_TEXTURE_CUBE_MAP_POSITIVE_Z_ARB,
```

```
        GL_TEXTURE_CUBE_MAP_NEGATIVE_Z_ARB
    };

    char *fileNames1[] =
    {
        "../posx.tga", "../negx.tga",
        "../posy.tga", "../negy.tga",
        "../posz.tga", "../negz.tga"
    };

    char *fileNames2[] =
    {
        "../../posx.tga", "../../negx.tga",
        "../../posy.tga", "../../negy.tga",
        "../../posz.tga", "../../negz.tga"
    };

    // Load each texture for the cube map.
    for(int i = 0; i < 6; i++)
    {
        if(!LoadGLImageData(fileNames1[i], faces[i]))
            if(!LoadGLImageData(fileNames2[i], faces[i]))
                return false;
    }

    glTexParameteri(GL_TEXTURE_CUBE_MAP_ARB,
GL_TEXTURE_MIN_FILTER,
                        GL_LINEAR);
    glTexParameteri(GL_TEXTURE_CUBE_MAP_ARB,
GL_TEXTURE_MAG_FILTER,
                        GL_LINEAR);
    glTexParameteri(GL_TEXTURE_CUBE_MAP_ARB, GL_TEXTURE_WRAP_S,
                        GL_CLAMP_TO_EDGE);
    glTexParameteri(GL_TEXTURE_CUBE_MAP_ARB, GL_TEXTURE_WRAP_T,
                        GL_CLAMP_TO_EDGE);
    glTexParameteri(GL_TEXTURE_CUBE_MAP_ARB, GL_TEXTURE_WRAP_R,
                        GL_CLAMP_TO_EDGE);

    return true;
}
```

The last function with modified code from the texture mapping demo of Chapter 6 is the rendering function. In this function a rotating 3D cube is drawn to the screen, which is the only real difference in the function's code. Because the cube uses a maximum value of 1 for each of its coordinate axes, we do not need to specify texture coordinates for the object if each cube map image is supposed to fully map each of the sides of this 3D cube. The reason for this is that the texture coordinates would be the same as the vertex positions, which means we can use the vertex position for both attributes for this demo as a shortcut to having to specify and send texture coordinates. The rendering function from the CubeMappingGL demo is shown in Listing 7.7. Note that in the Update() function a pair of floating-point variables are incremented. This is used to rotate the object so that we can see all sides as the application runs.

LISTING 7.7 THE UPDATE AND RENDERING FUNCTIONS FROM THE CUBEMAPPINGGL DEMO

```
void Update()
{
   g_xRot += 0.25f;
   g_yRot += 0.5f;

   if(g_xRot >= 360)
      g_xRot = 0;

   if(g_yRot >= 360)
      g_yRot = 0;
}


void RenderScene()
{
   glClear(GL_COLOR_BUFFER_BIT | GL_DEPTH_BUFFER_BIT);
   glLoadIdentity();

   float vertices[]  = { -1, -1,  1,   1, -1,  1,   1,  1,  1,
                          1,  1,  1,  -1,  1,  1,  -1, -1,  1,

                          1, -1, -1,  -1, -1, -1,  -1,  1, -1,
                         -1,  1, -1,   1,  1, -1,   1, -1, -1,

                         -1, -1, -1,  -1, -1,  1,  -1,  1,  1,
                         -1,  1,  1,  -1,  1, -1,  -1, -1, -1,

                          1, -1,  1,   1, -1, -1,   1,  1, -1,
                          1,  1, -1,   1,  1,  1,   1, -1,  1,
```

```
                              -1,  1,  1,   1,  1,  1,   1,  1, -1,
                               1,  1, -1,  -1,  1, -1,  -1,  1,  1,

                               1, -1,  1,  -1, -1,  1,  -1, -1, -1,
                              -1, -1, -1,   1, -1, -1,   1, -1,  1};

    glEnableClientState(GL_VERTEX_ARRAY);
    glVertexPointer(3, GL_FLOAT, 0, vertices);

    glUseProgramObjectARB(g_shader);
    glUniform1iARB(g_glslDecal, 0);

    glTranslatef(0, 0, -10);
    glRotatef(-g_yRot, 1.0f, 0.0f, 0.0f);
    glRotatef(-g_xRot, 0.0f, 1.0f, 0.0f);

    glEnable(GL_TEXTURE_CUBE_MAP_ARB);
    glBindTexture(GL_TEXTURE_CUBE_MAP_ARB, g_texture);

    glDrawArrays(GL_TRIANGLES, 0, 36);

    glDisableClientState(GL_VERTEX_ARRAY);

    glutSwapBuffers();
    glutPostRedisplay();
}
```

The shaders from the CubeMappingGL demo are essentially the same as the GLTextures demo, with the exception of the texture coordinates being of the type vec3 instead of vec2, the texture's type being samplerCube instead of sampler2D, and the texture fetching function used being texture-Cube() instead of texture2D(). Again, since the vertex positions can be used to act as the texture coordinates in this simple demo, the shaders take advantage of this. The vertex shader from the CubeMappingGL demo is shown in Listing 7.8, and the pixel shader is shown in Listing 7.9. Figure 7.4 shows a screenshot from the CubeMappingGL demo. The background of the screen was set to match the sky color from the cube map so that the image of a terrain (the object in the cube map) looks like it is floating on screen. The Direct3D 9 and 10 versions of this demo create the same output, so the same screenshot applies to those as well.

LISTING 7.8 CUBEMAPPINGGL VERTEX SHADER

```
varying vec3 texCoords;


void main()
{
   gl_Position = gl_ModelViewProjectionMatrix * gl_Vertex;
   texCoords = gl_Vertex.xyz;
}
```

LISTING 7.9 CUBEMAPPINGGL PIXEL SHADER

```
varying vec3 texCoords;

uniform samplerCube decal;


void main()
{
   gl_FragColor = textureCube(decal, texCoords);
}
```

FIGURE 7.4 Screenshot from the GL, D3D9, and D3D10 cube mapping demos.

Implementing Cube Mapping in Direct3D

In Direct3D 9 cube map objects have the type LPDIRECT3DCUBETEXTURE9. When creating the actual cube map image, we also can use the DirectX Texture Tool, which is available in the DirectX SDK. In the Texture Tool you can create a new cube map texture and load individual images into each of the cube map faces. You can then save this image as a DDS, which can be loaded by Direct3D with no additional effort. Once you have the image saved, you can load it into Direct3D 9 using the cube map texture loading equivalent function that we've used for all demos so far. This function is called D3DXCreateCubeTextureFromFile(), and it has the following function prototype.

```
HRESULT D3DXCreateCubeTextureFromFile(
    LPDIRECT3DDEVICE9 pDevice,
    LPCTSTR pSrcFile,
    LPDIRECT3DCUBETEXTURE9 * ppCubeTexture
);
```

ON THE CD

On the CD-ROM in the Chapter 7 folder there is a demo sample called CubeMappingD3D9 that performs the cube mapping effect. The demo creates a Direct3D mesh of the type LPD3DXMESH and calls the D3DXCreateBox() function to generate a box model that can be rendered to the screen. Using Direct3D functions to generate geometry can save us time from having to either manually hard-code the data for an object and create a vertex buffer out of it or to load geometry from a file. The function prototype for the D3DXCreateBox() function is as follows, where the first parameter is the Direct3D 9 device object, the next three parameters are the size of the box in various dimensions, the fifth parameter is the mesh object that will store the geometry, and the last parameter can be used to store a list of each face's neighboring geometries, which can be set to NULL.

```
HRESULT D3DXCreateBox(
    LPDIRECT3DDEVICE9 pDevice,
    FLOAT Width,
    FLOAT Height,
    FLOAT Depth,
    LPD3DXMESH * ppMesh,
    LPD3DXBUFFER * ppAdjacency
);
```

In the demo's initialization function we load the cube map, which was created using the DirectX Texture Tool, we generate the box, and we load the shader. As for the OpenGL version of this demo, we use two global floating-point variables to rotate the object on screen. These variables are updated in the Update() function in the same way they were in the OpenGL version of this demo. Since the demo introduces a mesh object and a cube map texture, those resources must be released when they are no longer needed. This task is handled by the demo's Shutdown() function. The InitializeDemo(), Update(), and Shutdown() functions from the Direct3D 9 version of the cube mapping demo is shown in Listing 7.10.

LISTING 7.10 THE InitializeDemo(), Update(), AND Shutdown() FUNCTIONS FROM THE DIRECT3D 9 CUBE MAPPING DEMO

```
bool InitializeDemo()
{
   g_d3dDevice->SetRenderState(D3DRS_LIGHTING, FALSE);
   g_d3dDevice->SetRenderState(D3DRS_CULLMODE, D3DCULL_NONE);


   // Load the texture.

   HRESULT hr = D3DXCreateCubeTextureFromFile(g_d3dDevice,
                                      "cubemap.dds",
                                      &g_cubeMap);


   if(FAILED(hr))
      return false;


   // Load the geometry.

   hr = D3DXCreateBox(g_d3dDevice, 1, 1, 1, &g_mesh, NULL);

   if(FAILED(hr))
      return false;


   // Load shaders.

   LPD3DXBUFFER errors = NULL;

   hr = D3DXCreateEffectFromFile(g_d3dDevice, "effect.fx", NULL,
                             NULL, 0, NULL, &g_effect,
                             &errors);
```

```
    if(FAILED(hr))
    {
        LPVOID compileErrors = errors->GetBufferPointer();

        // Show the errors to the user.
        MessageBox(NULL, (const char*)compileErrors,
                "Shader Errors...", MB_OK |
MB_ICONEXCLAMATION);

        return false;
    }

    return true;
}


void Update()
{
    g_xRot += 0.05f;
    g_yRot += 0.01f;

    if(g_xRot >= 360)
        g_xRot = 0;

    if(g_yRot >= 360)
        g_yRot = 0;
}


void Shutdown()
{
    // Here we release the Direct3D objects.
    if(g_d3dDevice != NULL) g_d3dDevice->Release();
    g_d3dDevice = NULL;

    if(g_d3dObject != NULL) g_d3dObject->Release();
    g_d3dObject = NULL;

    if(g_cubeMap != NULL) g_cubeMap->Release();
    g_cubeMap = NULL;

    if(g_effect != NULL) g_effect->Release();
    g_effect = NULL;
```

```
        if(g_mesh != NULL) g_mesh->Release();
        g_mesh = NULL;
    }
```

The rendering function from the CubeMappingD3D9 demo creates a world matrix that combines the rotations that will be used to animate the main object. This world matrix is combined with the projection matrix and is sent as the model-view projection (MVP) matrix into the shader effect. Other than the MVP matrix, the shader requires the cube map to be set, which is done using the SetTexture() function of the effect object. Since we are using a Direct3D mesh object instead of a vertex buffer, to draw the geometry out we call the DrawSubset() function of the mesh object, which takes as a parameter which mesh index to draw. A model can be composed of many different meshes, so this parameter is used to specify which one you want to draw. If the model only has one mesh, like ours, we pass 0 to this function. The rendering function from the CubeMappingD3D9 demo is shown in Listing 7.11.

LISTING 7.11 THE RENDERING FUNCTION FROM THE CUBEMAPPINGD3D9 DEMO

```
void RenderScene()
{
    g_d3dDevice->Clear(0, NULL, D3DCLEAR_TARGET | D3DCLEAR_ZBUFFER,
                       D3DCOLOR_XRGB(227,236,255), 1.0f, 0);

    g_d3dDevice->BeginScene();

        // Calculate MVP.
        D3DXMATRIX world;
        D3DXMATRIX rotX, rotY;
        D3DXMatrixRotationX(&rotX, g_yRot);
        D3DXMatrixRotationY(&rotY, g_xRot);
        D3DXMatrixTranslation(&world, 0, 0, 3);

        D3DXMATRIX mvp = (rotX * rotY * world) * g_projMat;
        D3DXMatrixTranspose(&mvp, &mvp);


        // Draw the Model.
        g_effect->SetTechnique("CubeMap");
        g_effect->SetMatrix("worldViewProj", &mvp);
        g_effect->SetTexture("cubeMap", g_cubeMap);
```

```
        UINT totalPasses;
        g_effect->Begin(&totalPasses, 0);

        for(UINT pass = 0; pass < totalPasses; pass++)
        {
           g_effect->BeginPass(pass);
           g_mesh->DrawSubset(0);
           g_effect->EndPass();
        }

        g_effect->End();

     g_d3dDevice->EndScene();

     g_d3dDevice->Present(NULL, NULL, NULL, NULL);
  }
```

The shader used by the CubeMappingD3D9 demo (see Listing 7.12) is nearly identical to the texture mapping Direct3D 9 sample from Chapter 6. The only changes come from the fact that the texture coordinates use `float3` instead of `float2`, the vertex position is used as the texture coordinates, and the texture fetching function is `texCUBE()` instead of `tex2D()`.

LISTING 7.12 THE CUBEMAPPINGD3D9 DEMO'S SHADER

```
    float4x4 worldViewProj : WorldViewProjection;

    texture cubeMap;

    sampler CubeMapSampler = sampler_state
    {
       Texture = (cubeMap);
       MipFilter = LINEAR;
       MagFilter = LINEAR;
       MinFilter = LINEAR;
    };


    struct Vs_CubeMapInput
    {
       float3 vertexPos  : POSITION;
    };
```

```
struct Vs_CubeMapOutput
{
   float4 vertexPos   : POSITION;
   float3 tex0        : TEXCOORD0;
};

struct Ps_Output
{
   float4 color       : COLOR;
};


Vs_CubeMapOutput CubeMapVS(Vs_CubeMapInput IN)
{
   Vs_CubeMapOutput vs_out;

   vs_out.vertexPos = mul(worldViewProj, float4(IN.vertexPos, 1));
   vs_out.tex0 = IN.vertexPos;

   return vs_out;
}

Ps_Output CubeMapPS(Vs_CubeMapOutput IN)
{
   Ps_Output ps_out;

   ps_out.color = texCUBE(CubeMapSampler, IN.tex0);

   return ps_out;
}


technique CubeMap
{
   pass Pass0
   {
     Lighting = FALSE;

     VertexShader = compile vs_2_0 CubeMapVS();
     PixelShader  = compile ps_2_0 CubeMapPS();
   }
}
```

On the CD-ROM in the Chapter 7 folder is a Direct3D 10 version of the cube mapping demo. In the shader from the Direct3D 10 version of this demo it is important to use `TextureCube` as the texture type and to supply 3D texture coordinates. Other than that there is no change in this demo from the previous texture-based demos we've done in Direct3D 10. The Shader Model 4.0 shader from the Direct3D 10 demo is shown in Listing 7.13. Loading a cube map in Direct3D 10 can be done using the same function we've used to load 2D textures without any change.

Listing 7.13 The CubeMappingD3D10 Demo's Shader

```
TextureCube cubeMap;

SamplerState TextureSampler
{
    Filter = MIN_MAG_MIP_LINEAR;
    AddressU = Wrap;
    AddressV = Wrap;
};


cbuffer cbChangesEveryFrame
{
    matrix World;
};

cbuffer cbChangeOnResize
{
    matrix View;
    matrix Projection;
};


struct VS_CubeMapInput
{
    float4 Pos : POSITION;
};

struct PS_CubeMapInput
{
    float4 Pos : SV_POSITION;
    float3 Tex : TEXCOORD0;
};
```

```
PS_CubeMapInput CubeMapVS(VS_CubeMapInput input)
{
   PS_CubeMapInput output = (PS_CubeMapInput)0;

   output.Pos = mul(input.Pos, World);
   output.Pos = mul(output.Pos, View);
   output.Pos = mul(output.Pos, Projection);

   output.Tex = input.Pos;

   return output;
}


float4 CubeMapPS(PS_CubeMapInput input) : SV_Target
{
   return cubeMap.Sample(TextureSampler, input.Tex);
}


technique10 CubeMapping
{
   pass P0
   {
      SetVertexShader(CompileShader(vs_4_0, CubeMapVS()));
      SetGeometryShader(NULL);
      SetPixelShader(CompileShader(ps_4_0, CubeMapPS()));
   }
}
```

REFLECTIONS

Reflection mapping is a technique used to simulate reflections on objects by using cube mapping. In rasterization, real-time reflections are more difficult to represent than with ray tracing. In ray tracing we can use a vector equation to reflect the primary ray, which can be used to trace the scene to see what objects the reflected ray hits. The color that is chosen is combined with the color of the original object that was reflected upon, which gives you the appearance of reflections on ray traced objects. A visual of ray traced reflections is shown in Figure 7.5.

FIGURE 7.5   Ray traced reflection mapping.

In rasterization we cannot do that in the same manner in real time. One way around this limitation is to use a texture that is a 3D representation of the scene, for example, a cube map, and then use a set of equations to calculate the texture coordinates that are used to simulate the reflection effect. This can allow us to simulate reflections on objects in APIs such as OpenGL and Direct3D and is much cheaper than the ray tracing alternative.

In general, vector reflection can be done using the following equation, where `reflected_vec` is the reflected vector, `vec` is the vector being reflected, and `n` is a normal of which `vec` is being reflected.

$$reflected\_vec = ((vec \ dot \ n) * -2) * n + vec$$

Using this equation, for example, you can have `vec` represent the direction an object is moving, and `n` can be the normal of a surface such as a wall. If the object and wall collide, you can reflect the object's direction with the wall's normal so that the object appears to bounce off of it. Once the reflection occurs, the object will be traveling in a completely different direction. An example of this is shown in Figure 7.6. Reflection mapping is a very common technique used in modern video games to allow an environment to be reflected on shiny objects or on water surfaces, which we'll discuss in Chapter 14, "Water Rendering."

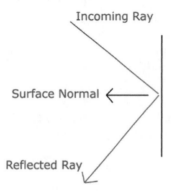

FIGURE 7.6   Reflecting a vector against another vector.

Cube mapping of an environment is known as environment mapping.

In reflection mapping using cube maps, the reflected ray can be used as a set of texture coordinates rather than to perform ray tracing on objects within a scene. This is what makes the technique cheap since a texture lookup is essentially what is required to perform reflection mapping.

Implementing Reflection Mapping in OpenGL

On the book's accompanying CD-ROM is a demo application called ReflectionsGL that demonstrates OpenGL reflection mapping. The demo builds off of the CubeMappingGL demo and uses the code from it. The only difference is the vertex shader and the rendering code. In the reflection mapping demo the object was replaced with a teapot, and a large square was rendered as a background so that the reflection-mapped object appears to be reflecting its environment. A teapot in OpenGL can be rendered in GLUT using the function `glutSolidTeapot()`, which takes as a parameter the size in units you want the teapot to be. A teapot is used because it is a more interesting shape than the box from the cube mapping demo, so its inclusion is strictly for visual effect.

The demo also separates the drawing into multiple functions so it is easier to read than all at once. The first function is `RenderBackground()`, which uses the negative Z cube map image (loaded into its own texture object) to render a large textured square to give the illusion that there is an actual environment. This isn't necessary, but it helps make the effect look more realistic than using an empty void like every other demo in this book. If there was no background, the illusion would have been somewhat lost, although the reflected object would appear the same. The background, like the teapot, is just for visual effect.

The teapot is rendered in a function called `RenderModel()`. The teapot is given its own rotations so that the object isn't just sitting there. This also allows us to see how the reflections look in a more dynamic situation. Both object rendering functions are called by `RenderScene()`. The three rendering functions are shown in Listing 7.14.

LISTING 7.14 THE RENDERING FUNCTIONS FROM THE REFLECTIONSGL DEMO

```
void Update()
{
    g_xRot += 0.25f;
    g_yRot += 0.5f;
```

```
   if(g_xRot >= 360)
       g_xRot = 0;

   if(g_yRot >= 360)
       g_yRot = 0;
}


void RenderBackground()
{
   float backVerts[]  = { -4, -4, -8,   4, -4, -8,
                           4,  4, -8,   4,  4, -8,
                          -4,  4, -8,  -4, -4, -8 };

   float backTexCoords[] = { 0, 1,  1, 1,  1, 0,
                             1, 0,  0, 0,  0, 1 };

   glEnableClientState(GL_VERTEX_ARRAY);
   glEnableClientState(GL_TEXTURE_COORD_ARRAY);

   glVertexPointer(3, GL_FLOAT, 0, backVerts);
   glTexCoordPointer(2, GL_FLOAT, 0, backTexCoords);

   glEnable(GL_TEXTURE_2D);
   glBindTexture(GL_TEXTURE_2D, g_background);
   glDrawArrays(GL_TRIANGLES, 0, 6);

   glDisableClientState(GL_TEXTURE_COORD_ARRAY);
}


void RenderModel()
{
   glUseProgramObjectARB(g_shader);
   glUniform1iARB(g_glslDecal, 0);

   glTranslatef(0, 0, -7);
   glRotatef(-g_yRot, 1.0f, 0.0f, 0.0f);
   glRotatef(-g_xRot, 0.0f, 1.0f, 0.0f);

   glEnable(GL_TEXTURE_CUBE_MAP_ARB);
   glBindTexture(GL_TEXTURE_CUBE_MAP_ARB, g_cubeMap);

   glutSolidTeapot(1.0);
```

```
        glDisable(GL_TEXTURE_CUBE_MAP_ARB);

        glUseProgramObjectARB(0);
    }


    void RenderScene()
    {
        glClear(GL_COLOR_BUFFER_BIT | GL_DEPTH_BUFFER_BIT);
        glLoadIdentity();

        RenderBackground();
        RenderModel();

        glutSwapBuffers();
        glutPostRedisplay();
    }
```

The last piece of modified code from the cube mapping demo is the vertex shader. In the vertex shader the texture coordinates for the cube map are calculated in real time. To calculate the texture coordinates we must create the reflection vector. The vector we are reflecting is the eye vector and the normal of the polygon we are currently rendering. The eye vector is essentially the direction we are looking. By reflecting this vector with the surface normal we will have a new vector that is pointing at the cube map pixel that is to be used at that point, which gives us the illusion of reflections on the object's surface. The eye vector is essentially the world-space vertex position subtracted by the camera's position. Since the camera is at (0, 0, 0) and doesn't move, this position was hard-coded in the shader. If you had a virtual camera system, you would use uniform variables to update the camera's position in the shader to match that of the application. To reflect the vector we call the GLSL function reflect(), which takes the two vectors involved in the reflection. This new vector is used as the texture coordinates for the cube map. The ReflectionsGL's vertex shader is shown in Listing 7.15. Figure 7.7 shows a screenshot of the demo. In the vertex shader the incoming vertex is in local-space, and it needs to be transformed by the model-view matrix to convert it to world-space. Transformed positions must be used since an object's local position isn't necessarily the same as its world position, especially if the object is dynamic, which ours is since it is rotating and has a translation position. You don't add projections to this transformation, because only the model-view matrix is needed, not the MVP matrix. Also, ftransform() in GLSL is the same as setting the output position to the incoming vertex position transformed by the MVP matrix.

LISTING 7.15 THE REFLECTIONGL'S VERTEX SHADER

```
varying vec3 reflectVec;


void main()
{
    vec3 pos = gl_ModelViewMatrix * gl_Vertex;
    vec3 norm = gl_NormalMatrix * gl_Normal;

    norm = normalize(norm);

    vec3 eyePos = vec3(0, 0, 0);
    vec3 incident = pos - eyePos;
    reflectVec = reflect(incident, norm);

    gl_Position = ftransform();
}
```

 Remember to use reflectVec *as the name of the texture coordinates in the pixel shader if you are using the code in Listing 7.15.*

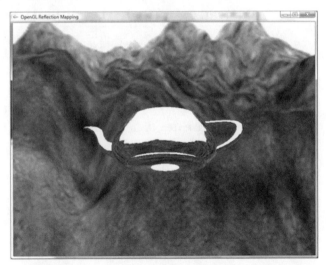

FIGURE 7.7   Screenshot of the ReflectionsGL demo.

 Remember that a normal must also be transformed into world-space like the position if the object is moving. This is because the normals have new positions as the object rotates. In OpenGL you can transform all normals by the gl_NormalMatrix *to keep them correct as an object moves.*

Implementing Reflection Mapping in Direct3D

ON THE CD

On the CD-ROM the Direct3D 9 and 10 versions of the reflection mapping demo, called ReflectionsD3D9 and ReflectionsD3D10, can be found in the Chapter7 folder. Since Direct3D shaders can have multiple shaders in one effect file, the Direct3D 9 and 10 demos specify two. The first shader is for a simple texturing mapping effect, and the second is for reflection cube mapping. The texture mapping effect is used for the shading of the background square that is rendered along with the object to make the scene look more believable. The Direct3D 9 and 10 effect files specify inputs, outputs, and variables that are used by at least one shader. To switch between shaders, set the technique to the one you want to use. Once a shader switch has been made, be sure to bind the variables specific for that shader so that it has the information necessary to work.

The Direct3D 9 version of the reflection mapping effect file is shown in Listing 7.16, and the Direct3D 10 Shader Model 4.0 version is shown in Listing 7.17. Like OpenGL's GLSL, HLSL specifies a built-in function called reflect() that can be used to reflect one vector off of another. Since the world-view matrix is needed to calculate the reflected vector, one is provided for the shader through a uniform variable in the same way the MVP matrix is supplied.

LISTING 7.16 THE REFLECTIONSD3D9 DEMO'S SHADER

```
float4x4 worldViewProj : WorldViewProjection;
float4x4 worldView : WorldView;

texture decal, cubeMap;

sampler DecalSampler = sampler_state
{
   Texture = (decal);
   MipFilter = LINEAR;
   MagFilter = LINEAR;
   MinFilter = LINEAR;
};

sampler ReflectMapSampler = sampler_state
{
   Texture = (cubeMap);
   MipFilter = LINEAR;
   MagFilter = LINEAR;
   MinFilter = LINEAR;
};
```

```
struct Vs_TexMapInput
{
   float3 vertexPos  : POSITION;
   float3 tex0       : TEXCOORD0;
};

struct Vs_TexMapOutput
{
   float4 vertexPos  : POSITION;
   float2 tex0       : TEXCOORD0;
};


struct Vs_ReflectMapInput
{
   float3 vertexPos  : POSITION;
   float3 normal     : NORMAL;
};

struct Vs_ReflectMapOutput
{
   float4 vertexPos  : POSITION;
   float3 reflectVec : TEXCOORD0;
};

struct Ps_Output
{
   float4 color      : COLOR;
};


Vs_TexMapOutput TextureMapVS(Vs_TexMapInput IN)
{
   Vs_TexMapOutput vs_out;

   vs_out.vertexPos = mul(worldViewProj, float4(IN.vertexPos, 1));
   vs_out.tex0 = IN.tex0;

   return vs_out;
}

Ps_Output TextureMapPS(Vs_TexMapOutput IN)
{
    Ps_Output ps_out;
```

```
      ps_out.color = tex2D(DecalSampler, IN.tex0);

   return ps_out;
}


Vs_ReflectMapOutput ReflectMapVS(Vs_ReflectMapInput IN)
{
   Vs_ReflectMapOutput vs_out;

   float3 pos = mul(worldView, float4(IN.vertexPos, 1));
   float3 norm = mul((float3x3)worldView, IN.normal);

   norm = normalize(norm);

   float3 eyePos = float3(0, 0, 0);
   float3 incident = pos - eyePos;

   vs_out.vertexPos = mul(worldViewProj, float4(IN.vertexPos, 1));
   vs_out.reflectVec = reflect(incident, norm);

   return vs_out;
}

Ps_Output ReflectMapPS(Vs_ReflectMapOutput IN)
{
   Ps_Output ps_out;

   ps_out.color = texCUBE(ReflectMapSampler, IN.reflectVec);

   return ps_out;
}


technique TextureMap
{
   pass Pass0
   {
      Lighting = FALSE;

      VertexShader = compile vs_2_0 TextureMapVS();
      PixelShader  = compile ps_2_0 TextureMapPS();
   }
}
```

```
technique ReflectMap
{
   pass Pass0
   {
      Lighting = FALSE;

      VertexShader = compile vs_2_0 ReflectMapVS();
      PixelShader  = compile ps_2_0 ReflectMapPS();
   }
}
```

LISTING 7.17 THE REFLECTIONSD3D10 DEMO'S SHADER

```
Texture2D decal;
TextureCube cubeMap;

SamplerState TextureSampler
{
   Filter = MIN_MAG_MIP_LINEAR;
   AddressU = Wrap;
   AddressV = Wrap;
};


cbuffer cbChangesEveryFrame
{
   matrix World;
};

cbuffer cbChangeOnResize
{
   matrix View;
   matrix Projection;
};


struct VS_TexMapInput
{
   float4 Pos : POSITION;
   float2 Tex : TEXCOORD;
};
```

```
struct PS_TexMapInput
{
   float4 Pos : SV_POSITION;
   float2 Tex : TEXCOORD0;
};


PS_TexMapInput TexMapVS(VS_TexMapInput input)
{
   PS_TexMapInput output = (PS_TexMapInput)0;

   output.Pos = mul(input.Pos, World);
   output.Pos = mul(output.Pos, View);
   output.Pos = mul(output.Pos, Projection);

   output.Tex = input.Tex;

   return output;
}

float4 TexMapPS(PS_TexMapInput input) : SV_Target
{
   return decal.Sample(TextureSampler, input.Tex);
}


struct VS_CubeMapInput
{
   float3 Pos     : POSITION;
   float3 normal  : NORMAL;
};

struct PS_CubeMapInput
{
   float4 Pos        : SV_POSITION;
   float3 reflectVec : TEXCOORD0;
};


PS_CubeMapInput CubeMapVS(VS_CubeMapInput input)
{
   PS_CubeMapInput output = (PS_CubeMapInput)0;

   float3 pos = mul(float4(input.Pos, 1), World);
```

```
   pos = mul(float4(pos, 1), View);
   output.Pos = mul(float4(pos, 1), Projection);

   float3 norm = mul(input.normal, (float3x3)World);
   norm = mul(norm, (float3x3)View);
   norm = normalize(norm);

   float3 eyePos = float3(0, 0, 0);
   float3 incident = pos - eyePos;

   output.reflectVec = reflect(incident, norm);

   return output;
}


float4 CubeMapPS(PS_CubeMapInput input) : SV_Target
{
   return cubeMap.Sample(TextureSampler, input.reflectVec);
}


technique10 TextureMapping
{
   pass P0
   {
      SetVertexShader(CompileShader(vs_4_0, TexMapVS()));
      SetGeometryShader(NULL);
      SetPixelShader(CompileShader(ps_4_0, TexMapPS()));
   }
}


technique10 CubeMapping
{
   pass P0
   {
      SetVertexShader(CompileShader(vs_4_0, CubeMapVS()));
      SetGeometryShader(NULL);
      SetPixelShader(CompileShader(ps_4_0, CubeMapPS()));
   }
}
```

REFRACTIONS

Refraction is a phenomenon that we see in everyday life. When light passes through two different materials that are made up of different densities, the direction of the light can change. As light passes through more dense materials, it moves slower. When this happens, the appearance of light in two different materials can take on a different look. For example, consider a straw in water. The refraction phenomenon can be seen when the straw leaves the air and enters the water. At the point of transition the straw appears to bend. Of course, the straw isn't bending, but the light is being refracted and is changing direction, giving the appearance of a bend as light goes from moving through air to moving through water.

A material in the context it is used in the discussion on refractions is not the same as a material in computer graphics.

Implementing Refraction Mapping in OpenGL

ON THE CD

On the book's accompanying CD-ROM, in the Chapter 7 folder, is a demo application called RefractionsGL that performs refraction mapping in OpenGL.

In refraction mapping we refract vectors and use them as texture coordinates just like we did for reflection mapping. Like reflections, we refract the incident vector calculated from the camera to vertex positions and the surface normal. This resulting vector is used in the pixel shader as a set of texture coordinates. In the RefractionsGL demo the pixel shader from the ReflectionsGL demo is used and nearly the same vertex shader as well. The difference lies with the vertex shader where the reflect() GLSL function is swapped with a refracting algorithm. This is shown in Listing 7.18.

LISTING 7.18 THE REFRACTIONSGL VERTEX SHADER

```
varying vec3 refractVec;


vec3 refract(vec3 incident, vec3 norm, float eta)
{
    float I = dot(-incident, norm);
    float I2 = 1.0 - eta * eta * (1.0 - I * I);

    vec3 r = eta * incident + ((eta * I - sqrt(abs(I2))) * norm);
```

```
    if(I2 > 0.0)
        return r;
    else
        return vec3(0, 0, 0);
}



void main()
{
    vec3 pos = gl_ModelViewMatrix * gl_Vertex;
    vec3 norm = gl_NormalMatrix * gl_Normal;

    norm = normalize(norm);

    vec3 eyePos = vec3(0, 0, 0);
    vec3 incident = pos - eyePos;
    refractVec = refract(incident, norm, 1.5);

    gl_Position = ftransform();
}
```

Snell's law describes what happens to light as it passes through different materials, and four variables are used in the algorithm in the demo's shader. These variables include the eye vector (camera to vertex), the surface normal, the refraction index (which is labeled as eta in the vertex shader), and the output vector (i.e., the refracted vector). The refraction ratio index specifies how a material affects light, where the higher the value, the slower light travels through it. You can search the Internet to find a lot of common indices for different materials that can be used. Examples include water, which is usually given 1.3333, air, which is usually given 1.003, and plastic, which is usually given 1.5. In the vertex shader from the demo we use a plastic ratio of 1.5 in the refract() function. If you run the application, the object does take on a plastic type of appearance. This is shown in Figure 7.8.

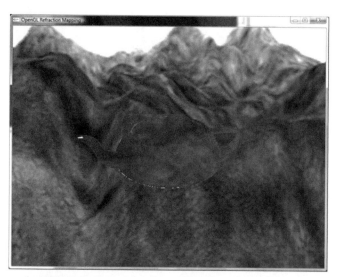

FIGURE 7.8 Screenshot from the RefractionGL demo.

The demo's vertex shader only refracts the vector once. Technically, the vector should be refracted when it enters the new material and when it leaves it, which can happen on and off for many different objects as a light ray passes through it. This can be quite difficult to get accurately and, generally, isn't necessary for games. Video games are about trade-offs between accuracy, quality, and what is acceptable.

The topic of refractions can become quite involved in the physics of light and real-world physics itself. The topic of complex physics is beyond the scope of this book. Because of this, the demo application simulates refraction but does not achieve true, accurate refraction. If you are knowledgeable about light physics, you can build off the demo to attempt to create the desired effect. In a game you'll most likely rely on a simulation such as the RefractionsGL demo rather than try to accurately recreate real-life refractions. The purpose of including refraction simulation in this chapter is as an example of how to create acceptable results instead of aiming for real-life accuracy.

ON THE CD

On the CD-ROM there are also Direct3D 9 and 10 versions of the refraction mapping demo, called RefractionsD3D9 and RefractionsD3D10. These demos have identical application code to the reflection mapping demos. The only difference is that the refraction code that was added to the OpenGL refractions demo exists in the Direct3D versions with the HLSL-specific data types (i.e., `float4` instead of `vec4`, etc.).

RENDER TARGETS

The ability to render scenes to textures is important for modern video games. For some effects it is necessary to render a scene that does not output immediately to the screen. The reasons behind this can be numerous. In today's games many scenes are rendered to off-screen surfaces known as render targets so they can be processed to add visual effects. A very popular example of this is the high-dynamic-range rendering effects that have become quite common in recent years. Some of the other uses for rendering to off-screen surfaces include the following.

- Dynamic cube mapping
- Rear-view mirrors in racing games
- Mirrors
- Virtual security cameras and TV monitors
- Post-processing effects such as depth of field and motion blur

In this section we briefly discuss how to create, render to, and use rendered data using rendering targets in OpenGL and Direct3D 9 and 10. Each API has its own way of doing this, even Direct3D 9 and 10. Rendering to an off-screen surface means rendering data to a texture. This texture can then be mapped onto surfaces like any other texture image.

OpenGL Frame Buffer Objects

There are numerous ways to render a scene to an off-screen surface in OpenGL. The most efficient, and the standard way to render to off-screen surfaces, is to use OpenGL frame buffer objects. OpenGL frame buffer objects were created to be a fast, standard method of rendering to surfaces. In the past developers had to use what are known as p-buffers (pixel buffers), which are not standard and are different depending on the operating system you are working on, or developers had to copy data from the back buffer and save it into a texture image. Copying from one buffer to another is tricky and is a very slow and inefficient option.

OpenGL frame buffer objects have the following benefits.

- Frame buffer objects' output can be read directly and quickly as a texture.
- They share a single context, which means no expensive context switching.
- They use less memory than p-buffers.
- They are system independent; in other words, they are part of the OpenGL standard.
- They are easy to set up.
- They can share depth buffers

To use frame buffer objects the hardware must support the EXT_frame-buffer_object extension. When this extension was first incorporated into OpenGL, it introduced two new objects: frame buffer and render buffer objects. A render buffer is a collection of buffers that are used during the rendering, which includes depth, stencil, and so on. A frame buffer is a texture that stores the results of the rendering. Render buffers can be attached to frame buffer objects, and when a frame buffer is bound to the rendering pipeline, all buffers attached to it are rendered too.

Binding, unbinding, creating, and destroying frame buffer objects are done in a similar fashion as for textures and shaders.

ON THE CD

On the CD-ROM is a demo called RenderTargetGL that demonstrates how to use OpenGL frame buffer objects to render to a texture. A frame buffer object, and a render buffer object, is a resource that can be represented by an ID much like textures using an unsigned integer. This is shown in the global section of the main.cpp source file from the RenderTargetGL demo application in Listing 7.19.

LISTING 7.19 GLOBAL SECTION OF THE RENDERTARGETGL DEMO

```
// OpenGL Texture.
GLuint g_texture;

// GLSLang objects.
GLhandleARB g_shader;

// Shader variables we will bind to.
GLuint g_glslDecal;

// FBO data.
GLuint g_fbo = 0;
GLuint g_db = 0;
GLuint g_renderDest = 0;
```

To generate a frame buffer object ID we use the OpenGL function glGenFrameBuffersEXT(), which takes as parameters the number of frame buffers to create and an array of unsigned integers to store the IDs of these buffers. This function looks exactly like the glGenTextures() function and works on the same principle. The function prototype for the glGenFrameBuffersEXT() function is as follows.

```
void glGenFramebuffersEXT(sizei n,
    unsigned int *framebuffers);
```

A render buffer can also be created in the same manner using the function glGenRenderbuffersEXT(), which has the same parameters. Binding a frame buffer, much like binding a texture, is done using the function glBindFramebufferEXT(). The function prototypes for these two functions are

```
void glGenRenderbuffersEXT(sizei n,
    unsigned int*renderbuffers);
```

```
void glBindFramebufferEXT(GLenum target,
    unsigned int framebuffer);
```

When you create a texture that will store the results of the rendering, which will be part of the render buffer, you can create it like any normal texture. Since there are no rendered data at the time of the texture's creation, it will not have any color data. This can be done by calling glTexImage2D() and sending NULL as the image data.

The OpenGL function glFramebufferTexture2DEXT() is used to bind a texture to a frame buffer. The function takes as its first parameter the target GL_FRAMEBUFFER_EXT, which is the only parameter that can be used for a frame buffer. The second parameter is what is being attached, which can be GL_COLOR_ATTACHMENT0_EXT through GL_COLOR_ATTACHMENTn_EXT, where n is the max color attachment unit, GL_DEPTH_ATTACHMENT_EXT, or GL_STENCIL_ATTACHMENT_EXT. The third parameter is the texture target type, which can be GL_TEXTURE_2D, GL_TEXTURE_RECTANGLE, GL_TEXTURE_CUBE_MAP_POSITIVE_X, GL_TEXTURE_CUBE_MAP_NEGATIVE_X, or any of the other cube map faces. The fourth parameter is the texture ID, and the last parameter is the mip map level. The function prototype for the glFramebufferTexture2DEXT() function is as follows.

```
void glFramebufferTexture2DEXT(enum target,
    enum attachment, enum textarget, uint texture,
    int level);
```

The status of a frame buffer's creation can be checked with a call to glCheckFramebufferStatusEXT(). The function takes a single parameter, GL_FRAMEBUFFER_EXT and can return any one of the following values:

- GL_FRAMEBUFFER_COMPLETE
- GL_FRAMEBUFFER_INCOMPLETE_ATTACHMENT
- GL_FRAMEBUFFER_INCOMPLETE_MISSING_ATTACHMENT
- GL_FRAMEBUFFER_INCOMPLETE_DUPLICATE_ATTACHMENT
- GL_FRAMEBUFFER_INCOMPLETE_DIMENSIONS_EXT

- GL_FRAMEBUFFER_INCOMPLETE_FORMATS_EXT
- GL_FRAMEBUFFER_INCOMPLETE_DRAW_BUFFER_EXT
- GL_FRAMEBUFFER_INCOMPLETE_READ_BUFFER_EXT
- GL_FRAMEBUFFER_UNSUPPORTED
- GL_FRAMEBUFFER_STATUS_ERROR

The last two functions to discuss are glRenderbufferStorageEXT() and glFramebufferRenderbufferEXT(), which have the following function prototypes.

```
void glRenderbufferStorageEXT(enum target,
    enum internalformat, sizei width, sizei height);

void glFramebufferRenderbufferEXT(GLenum target,
    GLenum attachment, GLenum renderbuffertarget,
    GLuint renderbuffer);
```

The function glRenderbufferStorageEXT() is used to set the pixel format and the dimensions of the rendering buffer, which we'll see an example of in the demo application later in this chapter. The second function, glFramebufferRenderbufferEXT(), is used to attach a render buffer to a frame buffer.

The creation of a frame and render buffer object from the RenderTargetGL demo is shown in Listing 7.20. The function generates the frame and render buffer, binds them, and creates a texture resource that will be rendered to. The function then attaches the texture resource to the frame buffer, sets up the properties of the render buffer, and attaches the render buffer to the frame buffer object.

LISTING 7.20 THE RENDERTARGETGL DEMO'S INITIALIZATION FUNCTION

```
bool InitializeApp()
{
    glClearColor(0.0f, 0.0f, 0.0f, 1.0f);
    glShadeModel(GL_SMOOTH);
    glEnable(GL_DEPTH_TEST);
    glEnable(GL_TEXTURE_2D);

    if(!CreateGLSLShader("../TextureVS.glsl", "../TexturePS.glsl",
        g_shader))
    {
        if(!CreateGLSLShader("../../TextureVS.glsl",
            "../../TexturePS.glsl", g_shader))
```

```
      return false;
}


// Bind our shader variables.
g_glslDecal = glGetUniformLocationARB(g_shader, "decal");


// Load TGA image.
int width = 0, height = 0, comp = 0;
unsigned char *image;

image = LoadTGA("../decal.tga", width, height, comp);

if(image == NULL)
{
   image = LoadTGA("../../decal.tga", width, height, comp);

   if(image == NULL)
      return false;
}

glGenTextures(1, &g_texture);
glBindTexture(GL_TEXTURE_2D, g_texture);

glTexParameteri(GL_TEXTURE_2D, GL_TEXTURE_MIN_FILTER,
               GL_LINEAR);
glTexParameteri(GL_TEXTURE_2D, GL_TEXTURE_MAG_FILTER,
               GL_LINEAR);

// Copy image data into OpenGL texture that is bound.
int type = comp == 3 ? GL_RGB : GL_RGBA;

gluBuild2DMipmaps(GL_TEXTURE_2D, type, width, height, type,
               GL_UNSIGNED_BYTE, image);


delete[] image;


// Generate frame buffer object and then bind it.
glGenFramebuffersEXT(1, &g_fbo);
glBindFramebufferEXT(GL_FRAMEBUFFER_EXT, g_fbo);
glGenRenderbuffersEXT(1, &g_db);
```

```
// Create the texture we will be using to render to.
glGenTextures(1, &g_renderDest);
glBindTexture(GL_TEXTURE_2D, g_renderDest);
glTexParameteri(GL_TEXTURE_2D, GL_TEXTURE_MIN_FILTER,
                GL_LINEAR);
glTexParameteri(GL_TEXTURE_2D, GL_TEXTURE_MAG_FILTER,
                GL_LINEAR);
glTexParameterf(GL_TEXTURE_2D, GL_TEXTURE_WRAP_S,
                GL_CLAMP_TO_EDGE);
glTexParameterf(GL_TEXTURE_2D, GL_TEXTURE_WRAP_T,
                GL_CLAMP_TO_EDGE);
glTexImage2D(GL_TEXTURE_2D, 0, GL_RGB, 800, 600,
             0, GL_RGB, GL_FLOAT, 0);

// Bind the texture to the frame buffer.
glFramebufferTexture2DEXT(GL_FRAMEBUFFER_EXT,
                          GL_COLOR_ATTACHMENT0_EXT,
                          GL_TEXTURE_2D, g_renderDest, 0);

// Initialize the render buffer.
glBindRenderbufferEXT(GL_RENDERBUFFER_EXT, g_db);
glRenderbufferStorageEXT(GL_RENDERBUFFER_EXT,
                         GL_DEPTH_COMPONENT24,
                         800, 600);
glFramebufferRenderbufferEXT(GL_FRAMEBUFFER_EXT,
                             GL_DEPTH_ATTACHMENT_EXT,
                             GL_RENDERBUFFER_EXT, g_db);

// Make sure we have no errors.
if(glCheckFramebufferStatusEXT(GL_FRAMEBUFFER_EXT) !=
   GL_FRAMEBUFFER_COMPLETE_EXT)
   return false;

// Return out of the frame buffer.
glBindFramebufferEXT(GL_FRAMEBUFFER_EXT, 0);

   return true;
}
```

Frame and render buffer resources can be freed when they are no longer needed. Frame buffers are released by calling the OpenGL function glDeleteFramebuffersEXT(), while render buffers are released by calling glDeleteRenderbuffersEXT(). These functions are called in the demo's ShutdownApp() function, which is shown in Listing 7.21.

LISTING 7.21 THE RENDERTARGETGL DEMO'S SHUTDOWN FUNCTION

```
void ShutdownApp()
{
    if(g_texture)
        glDeleteTextures(1, &g_texture);

    if(g_shader)
        glDeleteObjectARB(g_shader);

    if(g_db)
        glDeleteRenderbuffersEXT(1, &g_db);

    if(g_fbo)
        glDeleteFramebuffersEXT(1, &g_fbo);

    if(g_renderDest)
        glDeleteTextures(1, &g_renderDest);
}
```

Rendering to a frame buffer is as easy as binding a texture. To bind a frame buffer, which binds all render buffers, we call the function `glBind-FramebufferEXT()`, which was mentioned earlier in this chapter. Once a frame buffer is bound, you render to it by rendering geometry as normal. To return out of a frame buffer and back to the back buffer, we can send 0 as the ID to the `glBindFramebufferEXT()` function. In the rendering function from the demo a textured square is rendered to the frame buffer, and then the texture result is used as a texture to another square that is rendered to the screen. The rendering function is shown in Listing 7.22. Figure 7.9 shows a screenshot of the demo application.

LISTING 7.22 THE RENDERTARGETGL DEMO'S RENDERING FUNCTION

```
void RenderScene()
{
    float vertices[]  = { -0.8f, -1, -6, 0.8f, -1, -6, 0.8f, 1, -6,
                          0.8f, 1, -6, -0.8f, 1, -6, -0.8f, -1, -6};
    float texCoords[] = { 0, 0, 1, 0, 1, 1, 1, 1, 0, 1, 0, 0 };
```

```
// Bind the frame buffer so we can render to it.
glBindTexture(GL_TEXTURE_2D, 0);
glBindFramebufferEXT(GL_FRAMEBUFFER_EXT, g_fbo);

glClearColor(0, 0, 0, 0);
glClear(GL_COLOR_BUFFER_BIT | GL_DEPTH_BUFFER_BIT);
glLoadIdentity();

  glEnableClientState(GL_VERTEX_ARRAY);
  glVertexPointer(3, GL_FLOAT, 0, vertices);

  glEnableClientState(GL_TEXTURE_COORD_ARRAY);
  glTexCoordPointer(2, GL_FLOAT, 0, texCoords);

  glUseProgramObjectARB(g_shader);
  glUniform1iARB(g_glslDecal, 0);

  glBindTexture(GL_TEXTURE_2D, g_texture);
  glDrawArrays(GL_TRIANGLES, 0, 6);

  glDisableClientState(GL_VERTEX_ARRAY);
  glDisableClientState(GL_TEXTURE_COORD_ARRAY);

// Return out of render to texture mode.
glBindFramebufferEXT(GL_FRAMEBUFFER_EXT, 0);


glClearColor(0.6f, 0.6f, 0.6f, 0);
glClear(GL_COLOR_BUFFER_BIT | GL_DEPTH_BUFFER_BIT);
glLoadIdentity();

  glEnableClientState(GL_VERTEX_ARRAY);
  glVertexPointer(3, GL_FLOAT, 0, vertices);

  glEnableClientState(GL_TEXTURE_COORD_ARRAY);
  glTexCoordPointer(2, GL_FLOAT, 0, texCoords);

  glUseProgramObjectARB(g_shader);
  glUniform1iARB(g_glslDecal, 0);

  glTranslatef(0, 0, -2.5f);
  glBindTexture(GL_TEXTURE_2D, g_renderDest);
  glDrawArrays(GL_TRIANGLES, 0, 6);
```

```
        glDisableClientState(GL_VERTEX_ARRAY);
        glDisableClientState(GL_TEXTURE_COORD_ARRAY);

    glutSwapBuffers();
    glutPostRedisplay();
}
```

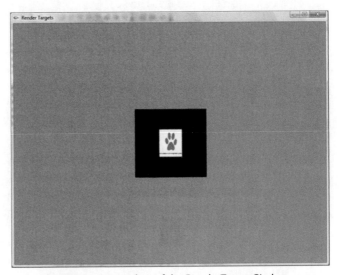

FIGURE 7.9 Screenshot of the RenderTargetGL demo.

Direct3D 9 Render Targets

Render targets in Direct3D 9 require three main objects, of types LPDIRECT3DSURFACE9, LPD3DXRENDERTOSURFACE, and LPDIRECT3DTEXTURE9. The LPDIRECT3DTEXTURE9 texture is used to store the results of the rendered scene to a texture object; LPDIRECT3DSURFACE9 object gives us access to the texture's surface to which we will be rendering; the LPD3DXRENDERTOSURFACE is the rendering target. Simply put, the texture is being rendered to, the surface gives us access to the texture's contents so that the results can be saved to the texture, and the render to the surface object is the rendering target.

When creating the texture, we can create an empty texture using the D3DXCreateTexture() function. When creating a texture that is used as the destination image of a rendering target, we must use the usage flag D3DUSAGE_RENDERTARGET. An example of how to create a texture that can be used as a rendering destination follows, where g_rtTexture is a normal LPDIRECT3DTEXTURE9 texture object:

```
hr = D3DXCreateTexture(g_d3dDevice, 800, 600, 1,
                       D3DUSAGE_RENDERTARGET, D3DFMT_A8R8G8B8,
                       D3DPOOL_DEFAULT, &g_rtTexture);
```

The surface of the texture can be obtained by calling the texture's `GetSurfaceLevel()` function, which takes as parameters the mip map level of the texture's surface to get the texture surface. Calling this function gives you access to the texture's surface when it is time to render to it. An example of getting the texture's surface can be seen here:

```
D3DSURFACE_DESC desc;
g_rtTexture->GetSurfaceLevel(0, &g_renderSurface);
g_renderSurface->GetDesc(&desc);
```

Once the texture and its surface are obtained, we can create the render target. In the preceding example we also get the surface's description. This allows us to create a rendering target that matches the dimensions and format of the texture to which it is rendering, which is necessary for compatibility between the two. If you don't use the description, you have to be sure to use the same information used to create the texture. To create the render target we call the function `D3DXCreateRenderToSurface()`, which takes as parameters the Direct3D device, the surface's width and height, the surface's format, a flag to enable depth and stencil buffer usage and its format, and the render target. An example of using this function is shown as follows.

```
hr = D3DXCreateRenderToSurface(g_d3dDevice, desc.Width, desc.Height,
                               desc.Format, TRUE, D3DFMT_D16,
                               &g_renderTarget);


if(FAILED(hr))
   return false;
```

It is easy to render to the texture in Direct3D 9 and requires us to use two functions of the rendering target's object: `BeginScene()` and `EndScene()`. Between these two functions we render the scene as we normally would. Once we call `EndScene()` of the render target, we return from rendering to the texture to "normal" rendering. An example of rendering to the texture is shown as follows.

```
g_renderTarget->BeginScene(g_renderSurface, NULL);

g_d3dDevice->Clear(0, NULL, D3DCLEAR_TARGET | D3DCLEAR_ZBUFFER,
                   D3DCOLOR_XRGB(0,0,0), 1.0f, 0);

...

g_renderTarget->EndScene(0);
```

Another way to think about it is to call `BeginScene()` and `EndScene()` on the rendering target's object instead of the Direct3D device, like we've done so far for all demos. On the book's accompanying CD-ROM there is a demo application called RenderTargetD3D9 in the Chapter 7 folder that demonstrates this technique. The demo uses each of the functions mentioned in this section, and it builds off of the texture mapping demo from Chapter 6.

Direct3D 10 Render Targets

So far we've been working with render targets in Direct3D 10 because that is the way things are rendered. In Direct3D 10 we can change the output of a rendering from the swap chain of a device to a texture. In Direct3D 10 a 2D texture has the type `ID3D10Texture2D`, as we already know. We can create an empty texture by calling Direct3D 10's `CreateTexture2D()`, which has the following function prototype:

```
HRESULT CreateTexture2D(
    const D3D10_TEXTURE2D_DESC *pDesc,
    const D3D10_SUBRESOURCE_DATA *pInitialData,
    ID3D10Texture2D **ppTexture2D
);
```

In the previous demos we obtained a texture's surface from the swap chain, but since we are rendering to a texture, we can create the empty texture ourselves. The only other thing we need to do to render to a texture is to create a render target description object when creating the rendering target. In previous demos this was set to `NULL` since the render target was targeting the swap chain. An example of creating a texture that can be rendered to and used as a texture for another surface, along with its rendering target, is shown as follows.

```
ID3D10RenderTargetView *g_offscreenRT = NULL;
ID3D10Texture2D *g_renderTexture;

D3D10_TEXTURE2D_DESC rtTextureDesc;
ZeroMemory(&rtTextureDesc, sizeof(D3D10_TEXTURE2D_DESC));

rtTextureDesc.ArraySize = 1;
rtTextureDesc.BindFlags = D3D10_BIND_RENDER_TARGET |
                          D3D10_BIND_SHADER_RESOURCE;
rtTextureDesc.Usage = D3D10_USAGE_DEFAULT;
rtTextureDesc.Format = DXGI_FORMAT_R8G8B8A8_UNORM;
rtTextureDesc.Width = 800;
rtTextureDesc.Height = 600;
```

```
rtTextureDesc.MipLevels = 1;
rtTextureDesc.SampleDesc.Count = 1;

hr = g_d3dDevice->CreateTexture2D(&rtTextureDesc, NULL,
                                  &g_renderTexture)


D3D10_RENDER_TARGET_VIEW_DESC rtDesc;
rtDesc.Format = rtTextureDesc.Format;
rtDesc.ViewDimension = D3D10_RTV_DIMENSION_TEXTURE2D;
rtDesc.Texture2D.MipSlice = 0;

hr = g_d3dDevice->CreateRenderTargetView(g_renderTexture, &rtDesc,
                                         &g_offscreenRT);
```

In Direct3D 10 the only real difference between rendering normally and rendering to a texture that can be used to texture objects is that we don't create the texture from the swap chain, but instead we create an empty texture ourselves manually. In the render target creation we also supply a description, with which we can tell Direct3D how the rendering target will be accessed. In our example we set the description for the rendering target to allow it to be accessed as a 2D texture. That is all that is necessary to render to a texture. Up to this point we had only one rendering target, which had a destination of the swap chain. To render to the texture we just use the rendering target we created specially for that, and the texture will store the results. Because Direct3D 10 forces us to use rendering targets for rendering in general, this turns out to be a very easy and natural step in the API.

ON THE CD

On the accompanying CD-ROM a demo called RenderTargetD3D10, in the Chapter 7 folder, uses the examples mentioned in this section to perform off-screen rendering in Direct3D 10, which is done by simply creating a texture and binding it to the target instead of a swap chain's texture.

IMAGE FILTERS

Image filters are pixel shader algorithms that can be applied to colors to create an effect. An image filter is often a post-processing effect that is applied to the rendered scene or to individual textures. *Post-processing* is a term used to describe an action that occurs after a rendering. For example, if you render a scene to a render target and then perform an effect on that rendered image, that is a post-processing effect.

Modern video games use post-processing effects a lot through the rendering of many different scenes. In this section we look at two very simple post-processing effects that can be performed on a scene. One effect turns any color data into black-and-white (luminance), and the other adds a sepia effect to color data.

A few of the most common post-processing effects in modern video games include:

- Depth-of-field
- Motion blur
- Light blooms and glow
- High dynamic range effects
- Night vision (e.g., like that seen in the *Splinter Cell* games from Ubisoft)
- Brightness and gamma correction
- Some anti-aliasing techniques

Luminance Filter

The first image filter we will look at is called the luminance filter. Luminance is used to describe a color as being gray-scale. Gray-scale means a color does not represent a color such as an RGB with varying intensities for its components but has the same value for all components. By having a color with matching component values you get a color that goes from black (RGB [0, 0, 0]), to white (RGB [1, 1, 1]). Anything between these two extremes is a shade of grey. This is what it means to be gray-scale. If an entire image is converted to gray-scale, it is essentially a black-and-white image.

You do not need to touch the alpha channel of a color image when turning it into a black-and-white image.

The algorithm for converting a color into a luminance value is fairly simple. It works by creating a single gray-scale floating-point value and using it for all color components in the final color. The calculation of the gray-scale value is computed by calculating the dot product between the color value and the luminance constant. The luminance constant equals the RGB color (0.30, 0.59, 0.11). Notice how the sum of these values equals 1. The dot product of any color against this luminance color constant converts it to gray-scale.

ON THE CD

The first demo we will look at that performs this luminance effect is the LuminanceGL OpenGL demo. The demo application is the same as the texturing mapping demo, but with a different pixel shader. Because of this, only the shaders are shown for all demos dealing with luminance and the upcoming sepia effect. You can find the LuminanceGL demo on the CD-ROM in the Chapter 7 folder.

The vertex shader from the demo application is shown in Listing 7.23, and the pixel shader is shown in Listing 7.24. The pixel shader calculates the gray-scale value of the color, which is then used to build the final output color.

LISTING 7.23 THE LUMINANCEGL GLSL VERTEX SHADER

```
varying vec2 texCoords;


void main()
{
   gl_Position = gl_ModelViewProjectionMatrix * gl_Vertex;
   texCoords = gl_MultiTexCoord0.xy;
}
```

LISTING 7.24 THE LUMINANCEGL GLSL PIXEL SHADER

```
varying vec2 texCoords;

uniform sampler2D decal;


void main()
{
   vec3 lumConst = vec3(0.30, 0.59, 0.11);

   vec3 color = texture2D(decal, texCoords);
   float dp = dot(color, lumConst);

   gl_FragColor = vec4(dp, dp, dp, 1);
}
```

ON THE CD

Just as the OpenGL luminance demo is essentially the OpenGL texture mapping demo with a new pixel shader, the Direct3D 9 and 10 demos are the same as their texture mapping demos except for their pixel shaders. The Direct3D demo is called LuminanceD3D9 and can be found on the CD-ROM in the Chapter 7 folder. The Direct3D 10 version of the demo is in the same folder and is called LuminanceD3D10.

In the Direct3D 9 and 10 demos the only change to the shader from the texture mapping demo from Chapter 6 lies in the pixel shader. The code is the same as the LuminanceGL demo for OpenGL, with the exception of the HLSL-specific data types, such as `float4`, and texture fetching functions, such as the `tex2D()` function, used in Shader Model 2 in the Direct3D 9 demo, and the `Sample()` function used by Shader Model 4.0 in the Direct3D 10 demo. The HLSL code used by the Direct3D 9 demo is shown in Listing 7.25. The Shader Model 4.0 version used by the Direct3D 10 demo is shown in Listing 7.26. Figure 7.10 shows a screenshot from the Direct3D demos.

LISTING 7.25 THE DIRECT3D 9 HLSL LUMINANCE EFFECT

```
float4x4 worldViewProj : WorldViewProjection;

texture decal;

sampler DecalSampler = sampler_state
{
   Texture = (decal);
   MipFilter = LINEAR;
   MagFilter = LINEAR;
   MinFilter = LINEAR;
};


struct Vs_Input
{
   float3 vertexPos  : POSITION;
   float2 tex0       : TEXCOORD0;
};

struct Vs_Output
{
   float4 vertexPos  : POSITION;
   float2 tex0       : TEXCOORD0;
};

struct Ps_Output
{
   float4 color      : COLOR;
};


Vs_Output VertexShaderEffect(Vs_Input IN)
{
```

```
   Vs_Output vs_out;

   vs_out.vertexPos = mul(worldViewProj, float4(IN.vertexPos, 1));
   vs_out.tex0 = IN.tex0;

    return vs_out;
}


Ps_Output PixelShaderEffect(Vs_Output IN)
{
   Ps_Output ps_out;

   float3 lumConst = float3(0.30, 0.59, 0.11);

   float3 color = tex2D(DecalSampler, IN.tex0);
   float dp = dot(color, lumConst);

   ps_out.color = float4(dp, dp, dp, 1);

   return ps_out;
}


technique SimpleEffect
{
   pass Pass0
   {
      Lighting = FALSE;

      VertexShader = compile vs_2_0 VertexShaderEffect();
      PixelShader  = compile ps_2_0 PixelShaderEffect();
   }
}
```

LISTING 7.26 THE DIRECT3D 10 HLSL LUMINANCE EFFECT

```
Texture2D decal;

SamplerState DecalSampler
{
   Filter = MIN_MAG_MIP_LINEAR;
```

```
   AddressU = Wrap;
   AddressV = Wrap;
};


cbuffer cbChangesEveryFrame
{
   matrix World;
   matrix View;
};

cbuffer cbChangeOnResize
{
   matrix Projection;
};


struct VS_INPUT
{
   float4 Pos : POSITION;
   float2 Tex : TEXCOORD;
};

struct PS_INPUT
{
   float4 Pos : SV_POSITION;
   float2 Tex : TEXCOORD0;
};


PS_INPUT VS(VS_INPUT input)
{
   PS_INPUT output = (PS_INPUT)0;

   output.Pos = mul(input.Pos, World);
   output.Pos = mul(output.Pos, View);
   output.Pos = mul(output.Pos, Projection);

   output.Tex = input.Tex;

   return output;
}
```

```
float4 PS(PS_INPUT input) : SV_Target
{
   float3 lumConst = float3(0.30, 0.59, 0.11);

   float3 color = decal.Sample(DecalSampler, input.Tex);
   float dp = dot(color, lumConst);

   return float4(dp, dp, dp, 1);
}


technique10 TextureMapping
{
   pass P0
   {
      SetVertexShader(CompileShader(vs_4_0, VS()));
      SetGeometryShader(NULL);
      SetPixelShader(CompileShader(ps_4_0, PS()));
   }
}
```

FIGURE 7.10   Screenshot from the OpenGL and Direct3D 9 and 10 Luminance demo.

Sepia Filter

The sepia image filter is used to add a brownish tone to color values. The algorithm builds on top of the luminance filter. The algorithm converts a color to luminance, uses that luminance value to interpolate between a light and a dark value, and then builds the final color value by interpolating between the original color, the sepia value, and the luminance color.

On the book's accompanying CD-ROM there is a demo application called SepiaGL that performs the sepia effect on an image in OpenGL. This demo builds off of the LuminanceGL demo application by using a different pixel shader. The vertex shader from the demo is shown in Listing 7.27, and the pixel shader is shown in Listing 7.28. The pixel shader performs the steps mentioned above to create the sepia effect. The interpolation is also performed using the GLSL function lerp(), which takes two values and a percentage. The percentage determines the blending amount from the first value to the second. The HLSL version of the effect used in the Direct3D 9 version of the demo, called SepiaD3D9, is shown in Listing 7.29, and the Direct3D 10 version, called SepiaD3D10, is shown in Listing 7.30. It is recommended that you see the effect in real time since a screenshot in black-and-white is unable to display the effect.

LISTING 7.27 THE SEPIAGL VERTEX SHADER

```
void main()
{
    gl_Position = gl_ModelViewProjectionMatrix * gl_Vertex;
    texCoords = gl_MultiTexCoord0.xy;
}
```

LISTING 7.28 THE SEPIAGL PIXEL SHADER

```
varying vec2 texCoords;

uniform sampler2D decal;


void main()
{
    vec3 lumConst = vec3(0.30, 0.59, 0.11);
    vec3 light = vec3(1, 0.9, 0.5);
    vec3 dark = vec3(0.2, 0.05, 0);

    vec3 color = texture2D(decal, texCoords);
    float dp = dot(color, lumConst);
    vec3 sepia = lerp(dark, light, dp);
    vec3 luminance = lerp(color, dp, 0.5);
    vec3 final = lerp(luminance, sepia, 0.5);

    gl_FragColor = vec4(final, 1);
}
```

LISTING 7.29 THE HLSL SHADER MODEL 2.0 SEPIA EFFECT USED IN DIRECT3D 9

```
float4x4 worldViewProj : WorldViewProjection;

texture decal;

sampler DecalSampler = sampler_state
{
   Texture = (decal);
   MipFilter = LINEAR;
   MagFilter = LINEAR;
   MinFilter = LINEAR;
};


struct Vs_Input
{
   float3 vertexPos  : POSITION;
   float2 tex0       : TEXCOORD0;
};

struct Vs_Output
{
   float4 vertexPos  : POSITION;
   float2 tex0       : TEXCOORD0;
};

struct Ps_Output
{
   float4 color      : COLOR;
};


Vs_Output VertexShaderEffect(Vs_Input IN)
{
   Vs_Output vs_out;

   vs_out.vertexPos = mul(worldViewProj, float4(IN.vertexPos, 1));
   vs_out.tex0 = IN.tex0;

   return vs_out;
}
```

```
Ps_Output PixelShaderEffect(Vs_Output IN)
{
   Ps_Output ps_out;

   float3 lumConst = float3(0.30, 0.59, 0.11);
   float3 light = float3(1, 0.9, 0.5);
   float3 dark = float3(0.2, 0.05, 0);

   float3 color = tex2D(DecalSampler, IN.tex0);

   float dp = dot(color, lumConst);
   float3 sepia = lerp(dark, light, dp);
   float3 luminance = lerp(color, dp, 0.5);
   float3 final = lerp(luminance, sepia, 0.5);

   ps_out.color = float4(final, 1);

   return ps_out;
}


technique SimpleEffect
{
   pass Pass0
   {
      Lighting = FALSE;

      VertexShader = compile vs_2_0 VertexShaderEffect();
      PixelShader  = compile ps_2_0 PixelShaderEffect();
   }
}
```

LISTING 7.30 THE SEPIAD3D10 HLSL 4.0 EFFECT

```
Texture2D decal;

SamplerState DecalSampler
{
   Filter = MIN_MAG_MIP_LINEAR;
   AddressU = Wrap;
   AddressV = Wrap;
};
```

```
cbuffer cbChangesEveryFrame
{
   matrix World;
   matrix View;
};

cbuffer cbChangeOnResize
{
   matrix Projection;
};


struct VS_INPUT
{
   float4 Pos : POSITION;
   float2 Tex : TEXCOORD;
};

struct PS_INPUT
{
   float4 Pos : SV_POSITION;
   float2 Tex : TEXCOORD0;
};


PS_INPUT VS(VS_INPUT input)
{
   PS_INPUT output = (PS_INPUT)0;

   output.Pos = mul(input.Pos, World);
   output.Pos = mul(output.Pos, View);
   output.Pos = mul(output.Pos, Projection);

   output.Tex = input.Tex;

   return output;
}


float4 PS(PS_INPUT input) : SV_Target
{
   float3 lumConst = float3(0.30, 0.59, 0.11);
   float3 light = float3(1, 0.9, 0.5);
   float3 dark = float3(0.2, 0.05, 0);
```

```
float3 color = decal.Sample(DecalSampler, input.Tex);

float dp = dot(color, lumConst);
float3 sepia = lerp(dark, light, dp);
float3 luminance = lerp(color, dp, 0.5);
float3 final = lerp(luminance, sepia, 0.5);

return float4(final, 1);
}


technique10 TextureMapping
{
    pass P0
    {
        SetVertexShader(CompileShader(vs_4_0, VS()));
        SetGeometryShader(NULL);
        SetPixelShader(CompileShader(ps_4_0, PS()));
    }
}
```

ADDITIONAL TEXTURE MAPPING TECHNIQUES

As you should be aware of, texture mapping goes further than the topics discussed so far in this chapter. Throughout the remainder of this book we look at texture-based graphical techniques that are fairly common in modern commercial video games. Two of these techniques are discussed briefly in this section, while the rest are discussed throughout the upcoming chapters. These topics include but are not limited to:

- Billboards
- Anti-aliasing
- Gloss mapping
- Bump and normal mapping
- Parallax mapping
- Shadow mapping
- Light mapping
- Various post-processing effects

Billboards

Billboards is an old and still useful effect in video games. A billboard is a flat surface, often rectangular, that is textured and always faces the camera. Regardless of your orientation and regardless of whether you attempt to circle around a billboard, it always faces the camera. A very popular example of this can be seen in the original *Doom* PC video game.

In the early days of 3D video games not all objects in the scenes were actually 3D. This can be seen in games such as *Doom* and *Duke Nuke'em*. Today, objects and characters can be fully 3D. Even though billboard objects are not used in all of the same ways they once were, they still have value. Today, billboard objects are mostly used in effects such as particle systems. Particle systems and billboards are discussed in more detail and implemented in Chapter 12, "Special Effects: Additional Effects." Particle systems can be used to create effects such as:

- Fire
- Smoke
- Explosions
- Dust
- Weapon effects
- Weather effects (e.g., rain, snow)

Super Sampling

Aliasing is the term used to describe images that have been distorted by jagged edges. The problem is that the images on computer monitors are composed of pixels. These pixels are square and are either shaded or not. In other words, you cannot half shade a pixel. If fine lines need to be displayed and if those lines do not take up the entire area of a pixel, the pixels are fully shaded anyway, and a staircase affect can often be seen in areas of an image that has sharp changes. An example of aliasing is shown in Figure 7.11.

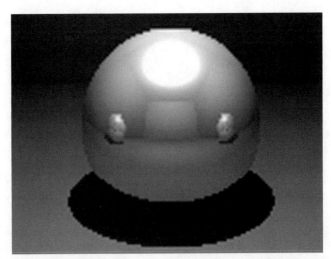

FIGURE 7.11 Aliasing effects seen in an image that was rendered to a monitor.

One method to reduce aliasing artifacts is to increase the resolution of the rendered scene. The downside is that this does not solve the problem, but, depending on the resolution change, it can minimize the visible effects. Often, the smaller the resolution, the more obvious the jagged edges in an image are.

Increasing the size in itself is not the solution to aliasing artifacts, but if you render at an increased resolution and then down-sample the results to the resolution you want displayed, you can eliminate the appearance of jagged edges. This process is known as super sampling. Super sampling allows each pixel to, instead of being sampled at the center, be averaged with the colors around it, which is what happens if you take a higher-resolution image and render it onto a surface that has a lower resolution. This allows sharp jagged edges to be essentially blurred, which eliminates their visible effect. Another way you can blur a rendered image is to go through each pixel and manually blur it with the pixels around it. This is usually done as a post-processing effect that uses a full-screen or partial screen blur.

There are different types of super sampling, for example, super sampling that adaptively samples pixels based on the areas that need it most. Super sampling is expensive and requires a fair amount of video memory and processing. By anti-aliasing only the areas that need it by sampling neighboring pixels, you can reduce the need to up-sample and down-sample resolutions of a rendered scene. One straightforward way to accomplish this is to use a pixel shader of a full-screen square texture mapped with the rendered scene and only blur pixels that have sharp changes from their neighbors.

Anti-aliasing is a term used for algorithms that attempt to eliminate or reduce aliasing artifacts. Super sampling is an anti-aliasing technique.

So far, grid super sampling has been discussed. Grid sampling is the simplest form of super sampling, and it works by averaging a grid of pixels around the pixel in question and averaging the results (blur). There are also:

- Random super sampling
- Poisson disc super sampling
- Jitter super sampling

Random super sampling, also known as stochastic super sampling, randomly samples pixels around a center pixel instead of doing it in a uniform grid. Since the sampling is random, some areas can lack the necessary samples, while others might receive more than they visually need. The plus side to random sampling is that grid sampling can still lead to some aliasing if the number of subpixels is low, which can be minimized in some cases with a random distribution of samples.

Poisson disc sampling uses random samples with the additional overhead of checking that each sample is not too close to another. If they are, then the sample is not used in the algorithm. This has the advantage random sampling has over grid sampling but is more expensive to process since it introduces additional steps.

Jittering is a very common way to perform anti-aliasing, especially in ray tracing. With jittering you take a grid of pixels, but you alter each grid position by a random set of deltas. With random and Poisson disk sampling the pixels chosen are completely random and can be very close or relatively far from the pixel that is being anti-aliased. With jittering you have a uniform grid of samples that are randomly moved within a finite range. Jittering has the benefits of using a random type of sampling instead of a strict grid, plus pixels are not too close or too far because of the maximum distance they can move from their original grid position.

Direct3D and OpenGL support hardware multi-sampling. This is used to tell the graphics API how many times a pixel is to be sampled during the rendering of geometry. The more samples that are used in multi-sampling, the better the output. Multi-sampling is hardware-optimized super sampling.

Blurring an image using an anti-aliasing technique can be considered an image filter. In a post-processing effect this image filter can be applied to a textured square, where the square is full-screen in size and the texture is the rendered scene, which could have been created using rendering targets.

Dynamic Cube Mapping

Earlier in this chapter we discussed cube mapping and off-screen render targets. Cube mapping is a technique that can be used to texture-map an environment onto an object, which could further be used for effects such as reflections and refractions. The earlier discussion was limited to static scenes. If another object was moving closely around the object displaying reflections, for example, the object would not appear on the reflection, and the illusion could be lost.

One solution to this is to extend the effect to dynamic cube mapping. By combining off-screen render targets and cube mapping, it is possible to take "snapshots" of the environment around a position and then use those images as a cube map for reflections. This has the added benefit of including everything around a point, even dynamically moving objects such as characters, particles, and vehicles.

Dynamic cube mapping is not cheap, as it requires cube maps to be updated often enough to retain the level of quality and accuracy desired. Also, multiple objects that need dynamic cube maps might appear in a scene. The object being rendered depends on what cube map is used. For example, if an object is a perfectly reflective mirror, it will need a cube map at its position since accuracy is important for that kind of object. If the object is slightly reflective but is not a highly reflective object, such as a plastic bottle, general cube maps placed in an area can be used and shared among similar objects. This is commonly done, and anyone viewing a *Half-Life 2* map within Valve's Hammer level editor can see many of these cube map objects placed in general areas and used by objects that get close enough to them.

 DirectX 10's geometry shader allows a dynamic cube map to be updated in one pass instead of six.

SUMMARY

Texture mapping is the basis of many effects and techniques used in modern video games. In this chapter we looked at a few common techniques that can be found in modern games that all use texture mapping to display their results. Along with texture mapping, lighting and shadows are also highly important topics when creating the scenes in highly successful commercial games. Lighting and shadows are discussed in detail in the following three chapters.

The following elements were discussed throughout this chapter:

- Alpha mapping to create surfaces with transparent or semitransparent areas using a masking texture
- Cube mapping
- Reflections and refractions
- Off-screen rendering to textures
- Luminance image filter
- Sepia image filter
- Billboards
- Anti-aliasing
- Dynamic cube mapping

CHAPTER QUESTIONS

Answers to the following chapter review questions can be found in Appendix A, "Answers to Chapter Questions."

1. What is the purpose of alpha mapping? How does it work?
2. What is the purpose of cube mapping? How does it work?
3. A cube map has how many sides?
    - A. 4
    - B. 6
    - C. 8
    - D. None of the above
4. What is reflection mapping? How does it work in rasterization rendering?
5. What is refraction mapping? How does it work in rasterization rendering?
6. What are render targets, and what purpose do they have in video games? List at least three uses for rendering targets that were discussed in this chapter.
7. What are image filters, and what is their purpose in the rendering of a scene?
8. Discuss the luminance image filter algorithm. What does it output?
9. Discuss the sepia image filter algorithm. What does it output?
10. What is the main property of a billboard?
11. In the early days of 3D games what were billboards used for? What are they mostly used for today?
12. Describe anti-aliasing. What is its purpose in computer graphics?
13. Describe why aliasing occurs on rendered scenes.
14. Discuss super sampling. List three types of super sampling discussed in this chapter.

15. Discuss how dynamic cube mapping works. What effect is it often attempting to create in modern video games?
16. True or false: Billboards are used to create 3D models.
17. True or false: Reflections and refractions are based on cube mapping.
18. True or false: Render targets allow us to choose which window a scene is rendered to.
19. True or false: An alpha map can be considered a surface mask for opacity.
20. True or false: Dynamic cube mapping combines cube mapping and off-screen rendering.

CHAPTER EXERCISES

Exercise 1: Use your knowledge of how you can use the alpha channel as a mask to create an application that allows you to define the blend percentage of two textures. Use multi-texturing to texture-map a surface, but use the alpha channel in the first image as a blend percentage of how much of the first and second image should be combined. Masking using the alpha channel was discussed in the alpha mapping section of this chapter.

Exercise 2: Use your knowledge of cube mapping and rendering targets to implement dynamic cube mapping. Have one reflective object in the scene and two objects, one at each side, next to the main object. Render the scene six times at the location of the main reflective object for each face of the cube map, but don't render the reflective object when creating the cube map.

Exercise 3: Implement a simple anti-aliasing post-processing shader. Have this shader sample the four pixels above, four pixels below, and four pixels to each side of the current pixel being shaded. Average the colors of the nine pixels and use that color for the final pixel color.

DIRECT AND GLOBAL ILLUMINATION

LIGHTING AND MATERIALS

In This Chapter

- Lighting Overview
- Materials
- Implementing Lighting
- Extensions to Per-Pixel Lighting
- Additional Lighting Techniques

In computer graphics of all kinds lighting has long been a very important aspect of creating realistic imagery. Lighting, along with shadows, is used to gives scenes a sense of realism and authenticity. Without lighting, many 3D scenes can appear flat and dull, and the absence of variations between light and dark might not always look as appealing as most gamers would like. Lighting and shadows can also be used to set the atmosphere of the scene, thus drawing the player deeper into the feel and the story that the designers were after.

This chapter discusses a few of the different lighting algorithms commonly used in modern video games. This chapter also discusses materials in general and how they have evolved along with 3D graphics in video games. Lighting can become quite a complex subject, and it is often a large focus of many 3D scenes. As scenes become more realistic, so do the different environment elements that are used to represent current and next-generation video games. The purpose of this chapter is to learn how to take a lighting algorithm and implement it in shader source code.

LIGHTING OVERVIEW

Lighting in video games is an acceptable simulation that can be performed in real time or can be performed offline and loaded at run-time. The physics of light is very complex and requires some in-depth knowledge of the subject. In video games an understanding of real-world light is not needed or even used in the virtual world. Because video games are real-time applications, the calculations used for lighting in modern video games are not true to nature in the scientific and mathematical sense. What is seen is an acceptable approximation and a solution to a complex problem that can be quickly calculated on today's hardware.

In the earlier days of 3D video games the lighting, if lighting existed in a game, was represented by preprocessed data. Often, these data were stored in what is known as a light map, which is discussed in Chapter 9, "Advanced Lighting and Shadows," and rendered using common multitexture mapping solutions. Today, preprocessed lighting and shadowing information is still highly important and is a topic that will be discussed in upcoming chapters of this book.

Lighting in video games often boils down to calculating a surface's color and brightness. This information can be used to simulate a light's contributions on each surface in the scene. This chapter examines a few very popular and common algorithms along with their implementations in OpenGL and Direct3D 10. In computer graphics lighting is not synonymous with shadowing, unlike in nature. The topic of real-time shadows will be discussed in more detail in Chapter 9.

Direct3D 9 implementations can be found on the CD-ROM. Since Direct3D 9 and 10 both use HLSL, only Direct3D 10's implementation is discussed since the differences are negligible.

Lighting in Computer Graphics

The addition of lighting effects to realistic 3D scenes is an important feature in today's games. The difference between a scene with no lighting and shadowing effects and a scene with them can be drastic in their visual look and feel. An example of the difference is shown in Figure 8.1.

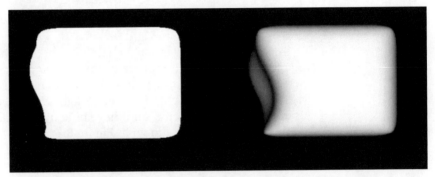

FIGURE 8.1   No lighting (left) compared to lighting (right) in a scene.

Lighting can be represented in a video game in one of three ways. The lighting can be preprocessed using an offline tool and texture-mapped onto the geometry in the scene, the light can be computed in real time, or the lighting can be a combination of both options. Modern video games often use a combination of real-time and preprocessed lighting to allow for a balance of quality and performance.

Types of Light Sources

Many types of lights can exist in a virtual scene. The most common types of lights include point, spot, and directional lights. A directional light is a light in computer graphics that comes from a particular direction and whose distance is considered infinite. With directional lights it does not matter how far away a light is, or if a position is even defined, because the light shines on the scene's objects regardless. An example of directional lighting is shown in Figure 8.2. In nature, directional lights do not exist since light has an origin and is not infinite in its distance of effect. For example, a candle's light can only reach a small radius of distance, whereas the sun has a much greater reach and intensity.

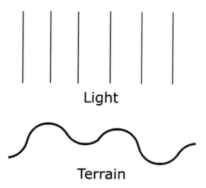

FIGURE 8.2 Directional light.

A point light is similar to a directional light but with light that fades as the distance between the source of the light and the point being shaded increases. This is known as distance attenuation, and, in computer graphics, it gives the point light effect. Point lights have a position in space, a distance attenuation factor, and they shine light in all directions. An example of a point light is shown in Figure 8.3.

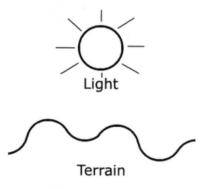

FIGURE 8.3 Point light.

A spot light is similar and closely resembles a point light, but a spot light only shines light in a specific direction within a cone volume. A real-world example of a spot light is lights such as flashlights that point light where light is blocked in some but not all directions. Taking a flashlight as an example, there is only one section of the flashlight from which light can escape, which creates the spot light effect in addition to the shade of the object. An example of a spot light in computer graphics is shown in Figure 8.4.

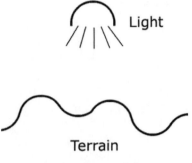

FIGURE 8.4   Spot light.

Per-Vertex and Per-Pixel Lighting

In computer graphics there are usually two levels of calculations when computing lighting: per-vertex and per-pixel. When calculations are made for the per-vertex level, they are made for each vertex of a mesh. The results of the per-vertex lighting are combined with the vertex color, or act as the color, and are interpolated across the surface. The useful feature of per-vertex level calculations is that they are limited to the total number of vertices involved during the operation, which, using standard lighting algorithms, is fairly cheap on today's hardware. The downside to per-vertex lighting, ironically, is that the lighting quality is directly tied to the vertex count, which requires a large number of vertices to obtain the best quality. Adding more geometry to a model is not ideal in a video game that must run in real time.

Per-pixel lighting involves lighting calculations performed on each raster pixel that makes up the surface. Since there are more pixels that make up a surface than vertex points, this gives a tremendous amount of quality regardless of polygon or vertex count. Since each pixel of a rendered surface is involved, the screen resolution plays a larger role in the final quality. On the plus side, low resolutions can still produce nice-quality renderings with lighting. A comparison of per-vertex and per-pixel lighting is shown in Figure 8.5.

FIGURE 8.5   Per-vertex (left) and per-pixel lighting.

Light Models

A lighting model refers to an algorithm that is used to perform lighting. In video games, and computer graphics in general, many different types of lighting models have been developed throughout the years. Two of the most popular types of lighting, as well as the ones supported in OpenGL's and Direct3D 9's fixed-function pipeline, are the Lambert diffuse and Phong lighting models. This chapter examines the Lambert diffuse, Phong, and Blinn-Phong, which is a variation of Phong, lighting models. Phong and its variation Blinn-Phong are used for the calculations of highlights on shiny objects and can be used to add subtle detail to shiny materials.

Lighting Terms

Several lighting types, when combined, provide the total illumination of each vertex (per-vertex light) or each pixel (per-pixel light) being rendered. The calculation of some of these types depends on which lighting model (algorithm) is chosen. The lighting terms used commonly in modern video games include the following.

- Emissive
- Ambient
- Diffuse
- Specular
- Attenuation
- Visibility

The term *emissive* is used to represent how much light is given off by a surface. In video games this term is often a constant color in the form of:

Emissive = e

In video games, using a constant color is a cheap way to approximate how much light is leaving a surface. This approximation is not a true calculation since such a calculation would be very expensive to perform and would require the code to calculate the light leaving and entering each surface throughout the scene several times to calculate this one light. This is often done in global illumination algorithms, which traditionally are reserved for preprocessed lighting algorithms such as radiosity. Global illumination and the various algorithms that fall within that category are discussed in Chapter 10, "Global Illumination Techniques," in more detail. The idea behind global illumination is to calculate the light that is bouncing off of all the surfaces throughout the scene and to determine how such factors affect the scene's surfaces. The opposite of global illumination is local illumination, which is local lighting that doesn't take into consideration the light's global effect on all surfaces, which is the type of lighting discussed in this chapter. Since global illumination is extremely expensive to do in a real-time application, emissive lighting is often not used or is a small constant value.

Ambient light is light that has bounced around the scene globally and is entering the surface. The difference between emissive and ambient light is that emissive light leaves the surface, while ambient light is incident light coming into the surface. Ambient light, like emissive light, falls under global illumination and is expensive to calculate. In video games this light is often a constant color used for all objects of the scene. An example of an object rendered with only ambient light using the constant color approximation is shown in Figure 8.6. Since a constant color is used, objects rendered with it do not look realistic.

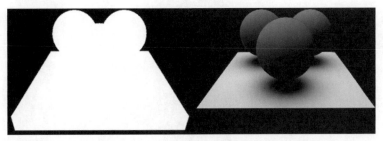

FIGURE 8.6   Ambient light as a constant compared to ambient occlusion.

A more realistic approach to using ambient light is to use what is known as ambient occlusion. Ambient occlusion is the calculation of per-vertex or per-pixel visibility terms that is multiplied by the ambient color to create a more realistic effect. The topic of ambient occlusion is discussed along with global illumination in Chapter 10, and it is a technique that is being used in some next-generation video games. Ambient light can take the following form, where *ka* is a material term (discussed in more detail in the next section) used to describe how the light interacts with the surface.

*Ambient = ka * ambient_constant*

The ambient constant color does not change per surface like the other types.

The term *diffuse* refers to light that has reflected and scattered after hitting a surface in many different directions. A diffuse surface is microscopically rough, where the roughness causes light to reflect in directions that do not mirror the incoming light ray's direction. Because light is scattered essentially all around each point of the surface, the viewing angle at which a diffusely lit surface is viewed does not affect how the surface looks. An example of a diffusely lit object is shown in Figure 8.7. Diffuse light is represented by the following, where *diffuse_cal* is calculated by a chosen lighting model (light algorithm) and *kd* is the material's diffuse property.

$$Diffuse = kd * diffuse\_cal$$

FIGURE 8.7   Diffuse light.

Specular light is similar to diffuse light, with the exception that the specular light has reflected in the, or near the, mirror (opposite) direction of the incoming light. Surfaces that are able to reflect light sharply in the mirror direction are very smooth microscopically. Mirrors are so smooth that they nearly perfectly reflect light, creating a direct mirror image on the surface. An example of specular light is shown in Figure 8.8, where the specular contribution was calculated using the Phong lighting model. Specular light can be represented as:

$$Specular = ks * specular\_cal$$

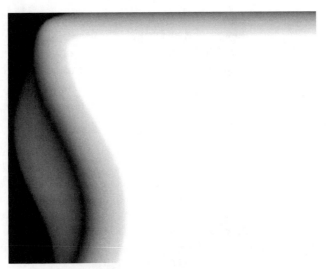

FIGURE 8.8   Specular light.

The last two terms are *attenuation* and *visibility*. Visibility is a Boolean flag used to represent if a light ray is being blocked by another piece of geometry. In this case there would be some part of another surface between the surface being rendered and the light source. By taking visibility into account, shadows can appear in the rendered scene. Shadows are often calculated in this manner using a preprocessed algorithm because of this expense, but in real-time shadowing techniques other approaches are often used to quickly calculate shadows in a scene. Shadows are discussed in more detail in Chapter 9. Ambient occlusion is a technique used to calculate visibility in a preprocessed manner.

Attenuation is used to represent how light loses intensity over distance. This is used to represent light sources such as point and spot lights, which were discussed earlier in this chapter. Assuming the light does not become more intense as it travels through distance, this value is often between 0 and 1.

All the lighting terms combined can take on the following representation, where the attenuation only affects the diffuse and specular lights:

Light = Emissive + Ambient + Visibility * (Diffuse + Specular) * Attenuation

If visibility is 0, then the attenuation, diffuse, and specular light would not need to even be calculated since visibility will zero them out during the multiplication.

These lighting terms are used in computer graphics such as in video games to attempt to simulate light seen in real life. In the natural world there are no different terms. There are just light rays striking surfaces, which are then either absorbed, reflected, or a combination of both. The physics of real-life light is not necessary for the types of simulations and approximations seen in video games and the terms discussed in this chapter are commonly accepted terms for calculating virtual light.

MATERIALS

A material defines how a surface is rendered in computer graphics and is usually a collection of properties and assets that collectively creates a specific effect. In recent years the definition of a material has changed to include programmable shaders and other resources. Materials in modern video games have become quite complex sub-systems. In today's games materials drive how surfaces look, and some commercial game engines have dedicated material management systems.

Every factor that contributes to how a surface looks can be considered a part of the surface's material. A material is commonly made up of but is not limited to the following items.

- Decals
- Bump and normal maps
- Height maps
- Gloss (specular) maps
- Alpha maps
- Displacement maps
- Programmable shaders
- Diffuse material (kd)
- Ambient material (ka)
- Specular material (ks)
- Emissive material

One thing to note about these items is that the diffuse, ambient, and specular material properties are the *kd*, *ka*, and *ks* values that are multiplied by the light's diffuse, specular, and global ambient calculated terms. The surface material equivalent of these terms is used to modify the lighting terms to account for how the surface interacts with the lights. This is used to mimic objects that absorb more light than they reflect, for example, or vice versa.

A material essentially represents a real-world surface type. For example, an artist can create a brick wall material that uses a brick wall decal texture, a bump map created from the texture's height values, and light properties for the diffuse, specular, and ambient lights that allow the surface to look like a real brick wall when rendered in a game. Other examples of materials are tree bark and the surface of the game's water.

Today's games are driven by the game's data and assets. The creation of a material system can be an important asset for a game engine and can prove very useful. Each of the major commercial game engines that exist today have some type of material system built into their rendering component.

Game engine *is a term used to refer to an abstract game framework. These frameworks are used to create games. A game engine can be thought of as a software development kit (SDK) of sorts, providing high-level and convenient features that a game could use.*

IMPLEMENTING LIGHTING

In this section the focus turns to implementing various common light models for the diffuse and specular contributions. These common lighting models provide practice and experience turning an algorithm into working code. Two of the lighting models implemented are the ones used internally by Direct3D 9 and OpenGL. Since Direct3D 10 does not have a fixed-function pipeline, lighting models must be implemented manually using programmable shaders. Since learning to call a few OpenGL and Direct3D 9 functions will not teach anyone about how to implement any of the lighting models that are discussed, this chapter implements all effects using programmable shaders.

Lambert Diffuse

ON THE CD

On the book's accompanying CD-ROM are demo applications called LambertGL, LambertD3D9, and LambertD3D10 that demonstrate how to perform diffuse lighting. The demos use Lambert's law to compute the diffuse light. Lambert's law states that the diffuse contribution of the lighting equation can be calculated using two vectors: the vertex normal and the light vector. The light vector is calculated by subtracting the light's position from the vertex position and normalizing the results. Since the only two properties used are the light and normal vectors, the camera's position and orientation would not affect how a diffuse surface appears.

If the angle between the normal vector and the light vector is equal to 1, the two vectors are perpendicular. This is essentially saying that the normal is pointing at the light's position. Assuming no obstacles are blocking the light from reaching the surface, the light would be fully illuminated at this point. As the angle between the two vectors decreases, so does the amount of light that reaches that point. For example, as the surface turns away from the light source, the light's contribution across the surface can diminish.

The angle between two vectors that are unit-length (normalized) can be calculated by using the dot product as follows.

Angle = dot(normal, light_vec)

Using the dot product on two unit-length vectors gives the cosine angle between them, and this value's maximum is 1 for unit-length vectors. The angle value can be multiplied by the light's color to calculate the diffuse contribution as follows.

*Diffuse = light_color * Angle*

If this calculation is made on the pixel level, a smooth gradient can be calculated across a surface whose normal is not perpendicular to the light vector. If the angle between the two vectors is less than 0, that means the light source is behind the surface. This also means that anything less than 0 can be clamped to 0, which when multiplied by the light's color effectively zeros it out. In HLSL and GLSL a shader function called `saturate()` can be used to clamp a value between the 0 and 1 range.

The OpenGL implementation can be found in the LambertGL folder. In it an object is loaded from a file. Each vertex of the object specifies the positional and vertex normal properties, which are essential to the diffuse light model that is being used. The model that is loaded is an .obj model. Loading and rendering an .obj model in OpenGL, Direct3D 9, and Direct3D 10 is covered in Appendix D, "The OBJ File Format."

Each of the lighting demos in this chapter creates per-pixel lighting effects. As mentioned earlier, the difference between per-pixel and per-vertex lighting lies in which shader the light color is calculated. The creation of a per-vertex and a per-pixel version of the same demo is unnecessary because of this minor difference.

To convert the demos to per-vertex lighting all that needs to be done is to calculate the diffuse color in the vertex shader and pass that to the pixel shader, which is set as the output pixel color.

In the LambertGL GLSL vertex shader the final output position is calculated, the world space position is calculated, the normal is rotated, and the light vector is calculated. The world space position must be calculated because the light position is specified in world space. If the two pieces of data were specified in different spaces, then the correct light vector could not be computed. The light vector is essentially the world-space position minus the world-space light position. The normal must be rotated because the object is moving in the demo. The normal is just a direction, so scaling and translation information is not needed during the vector transformation. Because of this, the model-view matrix, which is represented by `gl_NormalMatrix` in GLSL, is used to ensure that the normals are rotated as the model is rotated. If this was not done, the normals being used rather than the real normals after the object has been rotated would be different, thus giving incorrect lighting results. The vertex shader for the LambertGL demo is shown in Listing 8.1.

LISTING 8.1 THE LAMBERTGL VERTEX SHADER

```
varying vec3 normal;
varying vec3 lightVec;

uniform vec3 lightPos;


void main()
{
    gl_Position = gl_ModelViewProjectionMatrix * gl_Vertex;
    vec4 pos = gl_ModelViewMatrix * gl_Vertex;

    normal = gl_NormalMatrix * gl_Normal;
    lightVec = lightPos - pos;
}
```

Listing 8.2 shows the pixel shader for the LambertGL demo. In the pixel shader the interpolated light vector and normal, which were passed to the pixel shader by the vertex shader, are renormalized. This is done because the two vectors are being interpolated across the surface, which can denormalize the vectors. It is important to use unit-length vectors for the dot product calculation, making this step important. The diffuse value is calculated from the dot product (cosine angle) of the light and normal vectors, which is clamped between 0 and 1 using `saturate()`. This diffuse value is multiplied by the light's color to get the diffuse contribution, which is hard coded as a white light. Since this demo is an example of diffuse lighting, the entire diffuse contribution is used as the pixel's output color. Note that the `diffuse` variable is the cosine angle and the actual diffuse contribution is the result of the color being multiplied by the angle.

LISTING 8.2 THE LAMBERTGL PIXEL SHADER

```
varying vec3 normal;
varying vec3 lightVec;


void main()
{
   normal = normalize(normal);
   lightVec = normalize(lightVec);

   float diffuse = saturate(dot(normal, lightVec));

   gl_FragColor = vec4(1, 1, 1, 1) * diffuse;
}
```

The Direct3D 9 and Direct3D 10 shaders both use HLSL, and because of this, only the Direct3D 10 version is listed to avoid unnecessary code listings. In the LambertD3D10 shader, shown in Listing 8.3, the same steps are used as in the OpenGL version of the demo. Because the matrices for Direct3D are not provided to the shader like they are in OpenGL, a new uniform variable has been added to store the model-view matrix along with the model-view projection matrix so that the incoming vertex normal can be correctly rotated for the lighting equation. The OpenGL and both Direct3D demos use the same scene for the applications, which is shown in Figure 8.9, and each demo loads the same .obj model.

LISTING 8.3 THE LAMBERTD3D10 SHADER

```
float4 lightPos;


DepthStencilState DepthStencilInfo
{
   DepthEnable = true;
   DepthWriteMask = ALL;
   DepthFunc = Less;
};


cbuffer cbChangesEveryFrame
{
```

```
    matrix World;
    matrix View;
};

cbuffer cbChangeOnResize
{
    matrix Projection;
};


struct VS_INPUT
{
    float4 Pos : POSITION;
    float3 Norm : NORMAL;
    float2 Tex : TEXCOORD;
};

struct PS_INPUT
{
    float4 Pos : SV_POSITION;
    float3 Norm : NORMAL;
    float3 LightVec : TEXCOORD0;
};


PS_INPUT VS(VS_INPUT input)
{
    PS_INPUT output = (PS_INPUT)0;

    float4 Pos = mul(input.Pos, World);
    Pos = mul(Pos, View);
    output.Pos = mul(Pos, Projection);

    output.Norm = mul(input.Norm, World);
    output.Norm = mul(output.Norm, View);

    output.LightVec = lightPos.xyz - Pos.xyz;

    return output;
}


float4 PS(PS_INPUT input) : SV_Target
{
```

```
        float3 normal = normalize(input.Norm);
        float3 lightVec = normalize(input.LightVec);

        float diffuse = saturate(dot(normal, lightVec));

        return float4(1, 1, 1, 1) * diffuse;
    }


technique10 LambertDiffuse
{
    pass P0
    {
        SetDepthStencilState(DepthStencilInfo, 0);

        SetVertexShader(CompileShader(vs_4_0, VS()));
        SetGeometryShader(NULL);
        SetPixelShader(CompileShader(ps_4_0, PS()));
    }
}
```

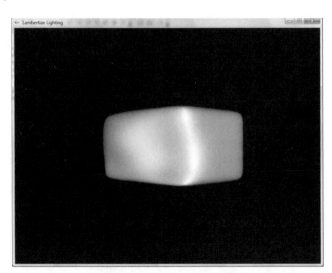

FIGURE 8.9   Lambertian lighting.

Phong

The specular reflectance, unlike diffuse light, is dependent on the view. This can be seen in nature when observing any object with a shiny highlight. As the object moves or the eyes move around the object, the highlight changes. The two specular lighting models discussed in this chapter are the Phong model and the Blinn-Phong model. The Phong model was developed by Bui Tong Phong in 1975, and the Blinn-Phong model, developed by Jim Blinn, is a variation of the Phong model.

Like diffuse light, the Phong specular model uses two vectors, view vector and the reflected light vector, to compute the specular contribution. The view vector is calculated by subtracting the camera's position from the vertex position. The reflected light vector is the light vector reflected off of the surface normal. As the view and reflected vectors become more perpendicular, the highlight looks brighter. This is equivalent to saying that if the light is shining directly on the surface, the shine of the surface is brighter. The dot product of these two vectors is often raised to an exponent to simulate surface roughness. This can be seen as follows.

$$Specular = power(dot(V, R), 8)$$

If the diffuse value is 0, the calculation of the specular value can be avoided since there would be no specular contribution if there is no diffuse contribution. When calculating the reflected vector, the following equation can be used, where R is the reflected light vector, the dot product can be reused from the diffuse calculation, *normal* is the vector being reflected off of, and *light_vec* is the light vector:

$$R = 2 * (dot\ normal,\ light\_vec) * normal - light\_vec$$

The `reflect()` *shader function can also be used to reflect a vector in GLSL and HLSL.*

When calculating the final light color using diffuse and specular light, the two are added together as follows.

$$Final\_col = Diffuse\_final + Specular\_final$$

Where the diffuse is:

$$Diffuse\_final = light\_color * dot(normal,\ light\_vec)$$

And the specular, assuming a specular power of 8 is used, is:

$$Specular\_final = light\_color * power(dot(V, R), 8)$$

The output from the OpenGL and both Direct3D versions of the Phong lighting demo are shown in Figure 8.10. In both of these demos the specular highlight changes dynamically as the application is running.

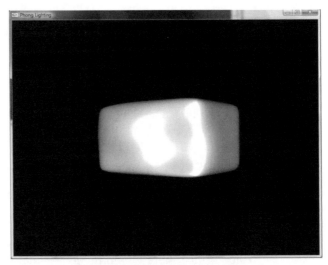

FIGURE 8.10   Phong Specular light.

ON THE CD

The OpenGL version of the Phong demo is called PhongGL, and the Direct3D versions are called PhongD3D9 and PhongD3D10. Each of these samples are on the accompanying CD-ROM in the Chapter 8 folder. In each of the samples the shaders build off of the Lambert diffuse lighting shaders. In the vertex shader the view vector is calculated and passed to the pixel shader, and in the pixel shader the specular contribution is calculated after the diffuse shader. Again, like the Lambert demos, a light color of white is assumed, although this can be changed to any color desired. The OpenGL Phong vertex and pixel shaders are shown in Listing 8.4 and Listing 8.5, and the Direct3D 10 HLSL version is shown in Listing 8.6.

LISTING 8.4 THE PHONGGL VERTEX SHADER

```
varying vec3 normal;
varying vec3 lightVec;
varying vec3 viewVec;

uniform vec3 eyePos;
uniform vec3 lightPos;


void main()
{
   gl_Position = gl_ModelViewProjectionMatrix * gl_Vertex;
   vec4 pos = gl_ModelViewMatrix * gl_Vertex;
```

```
    normal = gl_NormalMatrix * gl_Normal;
    lightVec = lightPos - pos;
    viewVec = eyePos - pos.xyz;
}
```

LISTING 8.5 THE PHONGGL PIXEL SHADER

```
varying vec3 normal;
varying vec3 lightVec;
varying vec3 viewVec;


void main()
{
    normal = normalize(normal);
    lightVec = normalize(lightVec);
    viewVec = normalize(viewVec);

    float diffuse = saturate(dot(normal, lightVec));

    vec3 r = normalize(2 * diffuse * normal - lightVec);

    float specular = pow(saturate(dot(r, viewVec)), 8);

    vec4 white = vec4(1, 1, 1, 1);

    gl_FragColor = white * diffuse + white * specular;
}
```

LISTING 8.6 THE PHONGD3D10 SHADER

```
float4 lightPos;
float4 eyePos;


DepthStencilState DepthStencilInfo
{
    DepthEnable = true;
    DepthWriteMask = ALL;
    DepthFunc = Less;
};
```

```
cbuffer cbChangesEveryFrame
{
   matrix World;
   matrix View;
};

cbuffer cbChangeOnResize
{
   matrix Projection;
};


struct VS_INPUT
{
   float4 Pos : POSITION;
   float3 Norm : NORMAL;
   float2 Tex : TEXCOORD;
};

struct PS_INPUT
{
   float4 Pos : SV_POSITION;
   float3 Norm : NORMAL;
   float3 LightVec : TEXCOORD0;
   float3 ViewVec : TEXCOORD1;
};


PS_INPUT VS(VS_INPUT input)
{
   PS_INPUT output = (PS_INPUT)0;

   float4 Pos = mul(input.Pos, World);
   Pos = mul(Pos, View);
   output.Pos = mul(Pos, Projection);

   output.Norm = mul(input.Norm, World);
   output.Norm = mul(output.Norm, View);

   output.LightVec = lightPos.xyz - Pos.xyz;
   output.ViewVec = eyePos.xyz - Pos.xyz;

   return output;
}
```

```
float4 PS(PS_INPUT input) : SV_Target
{
    float3 normal = normalize(input.Norm);
    float3 lightVec = normalize(input.LightVec);
    float3 viewVec = normalize(input.ViewVec);

    float diffuse = saturate(dot(normal, lightVec));

    float3 r = normalize(2 * diffuse * normal - lightVec);

    float specular = pow(saturate(dot(r, viewVec)), 8);

    float4 white = float4(1, 1, 1, 1);

    return white * diffuse + white * specular;
}


technique10 PhongSpecular
{
    pass P0
    {
        SetDepthStencilState(DepthStencilInfo, 0);

        SetVertexShader(CompileShader(vs_4_0, VS()));
        SetGeometryShader(NULL);
        SetPixelShader(CompileShader(ps_4_0, PS()));
    }
}
```

Blinn-Phong

The Phong specular model is very impressive to watch. The downfall to the Phong algorithm is that it is expensive to calculate the reflection vector. The purpose of Jim Blinn's variation of the Phong model is to replace that expensive calculation with a cheaper one. On today's hardware the expense of the Phong model is not as high as it once was.

In the Blinn-Phong model the dot product between the reflected light vector and the view vector was replaced with the dot product between the normal and a different vector called the half vector. The half vector lies between the light vector and the surface normal at the halfway point. To calculate the half vector the shader only has to add the light vector to the view vector. The angle between the half vector and the normal gives the highlight's value. As with the Phong model, the Blinn-Phong model still raises the specular value by a power.

A Blinn-Phong sample screenshot is shown in Figure 8.11. The results of the Blinn-Phong model are not quite what they are with the traditional Phong model. Because the Blinn-Phong model is considerably faster to compute than the Phong model, this sacrifice is often considered minor. This is especially true since the differences in the reflected highlights are hard to notice with some objects. Chances are that most, if not all, gamers would not notice the difference between many of the approximations that are displayed in virtual scenes, which makes them more than appropriate to use.

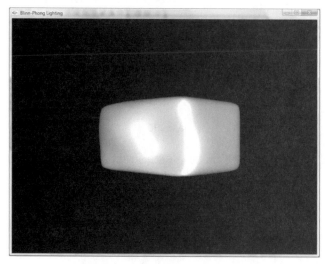

FIGURE 8.11   Blinn-Phong specular light.

ON THE CD

On the accompanying CD-ROM, in the Chapter 8 folder, are Blinn-Phong samples called BlinnGL, BlinnD3D9, and BlinnD3D10. When compared to the Phong samples, the vertex shaders are the same in the Blinn-Phong versions. In the pixel shader the R dot V operation is replaced with the N dot H operation, where H, the half vector, is calculated in the pixel shader. To achieve results similar to the Phong model, a higher specular power is used. There are still differences in the highlight if the two are compared, but to the untrained, or even the trained, eye the differences would be hard to detect in most cases. The OpeGL pixel shader for the BlinnGL demo is shown in Listing 8.7, and the Direct3D 10 version is shown in Listing 8.8.

LISTING 8.7 THE BLINNGL PIXEL SHADER

```
varying vec3 normal;
varying vec3 lightVec;
varying vec3 viewVec;


void main()
{
   normal = normalize(normal);
   lightVec = normalize(lightVec);
   viewVec = normalize(viewVec);

   vec3 halfVec = normalize(lightVec + viewVec);

   float diffuse = saturate(dot(normal, lightVec));
   float specular = pow(saturate(dot(normal, halfVec)), 50);

   vec4 white = vec4(1, 1, 1, 1);

   gl_FragColor = white * diffuse + white * specular;
}
```

LISTING 8.8 THE BLINND3D10 PIXEL SHADER

```
float4 PS(PS_INPUT input) : SV_Target
{
   float3 normal = normalize(input.Norm);
   float3 lightVec = normalize(input.LightVec);
   float3 viewVec = normalize(input.ViewVec);
   float3 halfVec = normalize(lightVec + viewVec);

   float diffuse = saturate(dot(normal, lightVec));
   float specular = pow(saturate(dot(normal, halfVec)), 25);

   float4 white = float4(1, 1, 1, 1);

   return white * diffuse + white * specular;
}
```

EXTENSIONS TO PER-PIXEL LIGHTING

Per-pixel lighting has always proven to be a very useful technique when performing real-time lighting in video game scenes. Over the years, a few different techniques have become standard in next-generation video games that are extensions to per-pixel lighting. The most popular techniques deal with bump mapping and its extensions that further add upon per-pixel lighting.

Bump Mapping

In per-pixel lighting the interpolated vertex normal is used by the pixel shader to calculate the diffuse and specular values. The interpolated normal is smooth across the surface, which creates a gradient of color.

Bump mapping is a technique that extends upon per-pixel lighting. In bump mapping instead of using the interpolated normal, the algorithm uses a normal retrieved out of a texture image known as a bump map. The pixels in a bump map image allow a per-pixel level of normal vector specification in the image. By altering these normal vectors from one another, the lighting can be changed on a pixel level. This change in lighting can be used to create patterns and detail that isn't actually there. These patterns are then used to simulate detail on the surface that can have real-time lighting applied to it without adding more polygons. These details can include but are not limited to:

- Cracks
- Bumps
- Roughness
- Gaps
- Words
- Various patterns

The purpose of the bump map is to specify the per-pixel normal vectors of a surface instead of using an interpolated normal. The great feature of bump mapping is that it is a cheap and easy way to represent very small and fine detail on surfaces without adding geometry. For some surfaces, such as a bumpy brick wall, the amount of geometry that would be necessary to represent such objects would be enormous, even for one surface.

The benefits to using bump mapping are clear and straightforward. The technique is a form of per-pixel lighting, which means the lighting and the surface's interaction with that light is fully dynamic. This is especially evident when lights and views move around bump mapped objects. The additional benefits to bump mapping include:

- Easy to create the detail and store it in a bump map
- Cheap to process on today's hardware
- Allows games to have a higher sense of visual complexity without additional geometry
- Allows detailed per-pixel materials to be easily created, such as brick walls, cracked stones, rusted metal, and more
- Can look fantastic in video games

Creating Bump Map Textures

A bump map image is essentially a color map image. Earlier in this book it was mentioned that textures can store information that was not used as colors. In bump mapping the image data represent normal vectors instead of colors. In a bump map each vector has a length of 1. When using the color value of 255 as a representation of 1.0, it is easy to represent a normal in a color image using color values, although the precision is not that of floating-point variables since images often use single bytes per component.

 Some graphics hardware has support for floating-point components, which can be used for storing bump map data.

The data in images are stored as unsigned values, which means they have a range of (0, 1). Normal vectors, on the other hand, are signed and have a range of (−1, 1). When reading a normal vector from the bump map in the pixel shader, it must be converted to the signed range. To convert it to the signed range the following equation can be used in a pixel shader, where *Normal* is the value read from the image.

$$Normal = 2 * (Normal - 0.5)$$

To turn the signed vector into an unsigned one, which can be useful when calculating and storing normal vectors in a bump map, the following equation can be used.

$$Normal = 0.5 * Normal + 0.5$$

Normal vectors can be stored in an image by using the image's red, green, and blue channels for the vector's X, Y, and Z axes after they have been converted to the unsigned range. A bump map is often created from a height map. A height map is a grayscale image that represents heights, where the darker the color, the lower the height. To create a bump map out of any image, the steps for the algorithm include:

- Convert the image to black and white.
- For each pixel in the height map sample the current pixel, the pixel to the right, and the pixel above the current pixel.

- Create two edge vectors by subtracting the above pixel from the current pixel (edge 1) and the right pixel from the current pixel (edge 2).
- Calculate the cross product of the two edges.
- Normalize the cross product.
- Convert the normal to the unsigned range.
- Store the normal in the image.

Because height maps represent height and because normal vectors are being created, normal map images often have a bluish tone to them. This happens because the normal is pointing in the Z axis, which if stored in an RGB or RGBA image is the blue component. By converting a texture into black and white, the colors can then act as a height value. Height maps can be created by other means or even calculated algorithmically when creating a bump map out of an existing image; this is an easy step in the algorithm.

Once the image is grayscale, each pixel can be treated as a vertex where the current pixel, pixel to the right, and pixel above the current pixel form a triangle. This triangle can be normalized, and that normal vector is stored in the bump map. The triangle normalization algorithm requires that two edge vectors be created, the cross product between those edges be found, and the cross product be normalized to create the triangle normal. The algorithm to calculate a bump map from an existing color image is shown in the following pseudo-code.

```
function CreateBumpMap(Color[] color_image, Color[] bump_map)
{
    color_image = ConvertToGrayScale(color_image);

    foreach(Color pixel in color_image)
    {
        Color above_pixel = GetPixelAbove(pixel, color_image);
        Color right_pixel = GetPixelRight(pixel, color_image);

        // Grayscale images have the same value for the
        // red, green and blue so it wouldn't matter which
        // was sampled.  Below the red is used...

        Vector edge1(1, 0, above_pixel.r - pixel.r);
        Vector edge2(0, 1, right_pixel.r - pixel.r);

        Vector cross = CrossProduct(edge1, edge2);
        cross = Normalize(cross);

        Color normal = ConvertToUnsigned(cross);
```

```
    StoreInImage(normal, bump_map);
  }

  SaveImage(bump_map, "bump_map.dds");
}
```

Although a tool can be coded to calculate bump maps, many existing tools are available for download over the Internet. One such tool is NVIDIA's Normal Map Filter, which is a plug-in for Adobe's Photoshop CS.

Bump maps are often RGB or RGBA images. It is possible and is very common in the games industry to store bump and normal maps as a two-component compressed image. This is discussed in more detail in Chapter 15, "Optimization," since its use is for optimization of both performance and disk space storage.

Implementing Bump Mapping

There are two types of bump mapping: object space and texture (tangent) space. Object-space bump mapping uses object-space-defined normal vectors with an object-space light vector to calculate the lighting terms. In an object-space bump mapping application, if the normal vectors are stored in object space into the bump map, the per-pixel lighting shaders from earlier in this chapter can be used with the slight addition of taking the normal from the image instead of from the vertex shader. This type of bump mapping is pretty straightforward. The problem with object-space bump mapping is that the bump map created for a specific object can only be used for that object. In object-space bump mapping the normal vectors in the bump map are tied to where they would be on a specific object. This means the same bump map cannot be shared between surfaces that use the same material. It also means a UV-mapped object must not have triangles that share UV coordinates since each normal vector must be specific for the exact pixel for which it will be rendered. This makes creating an object-space bump map complicated and difficult.

 Object-space bump maps have more variations of color than texture-space normal vectors. This occurs because the object-space vectors are not necessarily pointing through the Z-axis like they are in texture-space bump maps, where all normals are pointing primarily through the Z-axis.

Texture-space, also known as tangent-space, bump maps require some additional data and operations but are easier to create. In texture-space bump mapping the normal vectors are stored in their own local coordinate space. Using the pseudo-code algorithm from earlier in this chapter to create a bump map image will create a bump map in texture-space since a specific object's geometry is not being applied to the normal vectors that were being saved. In other words, the normal vectors are in their own space outside of object- or world-space. The benefits to using texture-space bump mapping include:

- You can use the same bump map for different objects and surfaces.
- You can have surfaces that share UV coordinates.
- It is easier to create texture-space bump maps than to attempt to store object-space normal vectors in the bump map.

The problem with texture-space vectors is that they are in a different space than the light and other vectors used during lighting. One solution is to convert the light vector, as well as the other used vectors, to texture-space before calculating the light terms. For an application to have the correct lighting, all pieces of information must use the same space.

Texture-space bump mapping is a very popular style of bump mapping. A 3×3 rotation matrix can be created that can be used in the vertex shader to transform any vector into texture-space. This matrix is known as the TBN matrix, where T represents the S tangent, B represents the bi-normal, and N represents the vertex normal. The TBN matrix takes the following form:

```
column 1 [T.x, B.x, N.x]
column 2 [T.y, B.y, N.y]
column 3 [T.z, B.z, N.z]
```

The normal is the vertex normal that is easy to supply to the vertex shader. The bi-normal can be calculated in the vertex shader by taking the cross product between the S tangent and the normal. The S tangent requires more work to calculate. In Appendix D the .obj loading code calculates each S tangent for every vertex in the model. The S tangent calculation requires the directional change in the texture coordinates to be determined. The S tangent is a vector that describes the change in direction of the U coordinates, while the bi-normal is the V coordinate. The TBN vectors together form the 3×3 matrix that can be used to transform vectors in the vertex shader into texture-space. The S tangent can be passed to the vertex shader through a free texture coordinate unit. Since the S tangent calculation code is a major part of the .obj loader, a discussion of its algorithm is presented in Appendix D.

On the CD-ROM are bump mapping demos called BumpMappingGL, BumpMappingD3D9, and BumpMappingD3D10 for OpenGL and Direct3D 9 and 10. In the vertex shader for these demos the S tangent is passed through an empty texture coordinate since OpenGL and Direct3D do not offer dedicated channels for this property like they do for the vertex position, vertex normal, and so on. In the vertex shader the TBN matrix is calculated, the light vector is transformed into texture space, and the light vector is passed along to the pixel shader. In the bump mapping demos only diffuse lighting is performed, although specular light can be added if desired. If specular light is added, the view vector must also be transformed into texture-space. The BumpMappingGL vertex shader is shown in Listing 8.9.

LISTING 8.9 THE BUMPMAPPINGGL VERTEX SHADER

```
varying vec2 texCoords;
varying vec3 lightVec;

uniform vec3 lightPos;


void main()
{
    gl_Position = gl_ModelViewProjectionMatrix * gl_Vertex;
    vec4 pos = gl_ModelViewMatrix * gl_Vertex;

    vec3 normal = gl_NormalMatrix * gl_Normal;
    vec3 sTangent = gl_MultiTexCoord1.xyz;
    vec3 bTangent = cross(sTangent, normal);

    mat3 tbnMatrix = mat3(sTangent, bTangent, normal);

    texCoords = gl_MultiTexCoord0.xy;
    lightVec = lightPos - pos;

    // Convert light direction to texture space.
    lightVec = tbnMatrix * lightVec;
}
```

In the pixel shader the light vector is normalized because denormalization while being interpolated across the surface is possible. Next, the normal from the normal map is fetched and converted to a signed range of $(-1, 1)$. This value is also normalized to ensure that the normal remains unit-length. Once the normal is ready, the diffuse lighting algorithm proceeds as it did in the per-pixel lighting demo. The BumpMappingGL pixel shader is shown in Listing 8.10, and the Direct3D 10 version of the demo is shown in Listing 8.11. Figure 8.12 shows a screenshot from the bump mapping demos.

LISTING 8.10 THE BUMPMAPPINGGL PIXEL SHADER

```
varying vec2 texCoords;
varying vec3 lightVec;

sampler2D decal;
sampler2D normalMap;


void main()
{
   lightVec = normalize(lightVec);

   vec3 normal = texture2D(normalMap, texCoords);
   normal = (normal - 0.5) * 2;
   normal = normalize(normal);

   float diffuse = saturate(dot(normal, lightVec));

   gl_FragColor = texture2D(decal, texCoords) * diffuse;
}
```

LISTING 8.11 THE BUMPMAPPINGD3D10 SHADER

```
float4 lightPos;

Texture2D decal;
Texture2D normalMap;

SamplerState DecalSampler
{
   Filter = MIN_MAG_MIP_LINEAR;
   AddressU = Wrap;
   AddressV = Wrap;
};


DepthStencilState DepthStencilInfo
{
   DepthEnable = true;
   DepthWriteMask = ALL;
   DepthFunc = Less;
};
```

```
cbuffer cbChangesEveryFrame
{
   matrix World;
   matrix View;
};

cbuffer cbChangeOnResize
{
   matrix Projection;
};


struct VS_INPUT
{
   float4 Pos : POSITION;
   float3 Norm : NORMAL;
   float2 Tex : TEXCOORD;
   float3 STan : TANGENT;
};

struct PS_INPUT
{
   float4 Pos : SV_POSITION;
   float2 Tex : TEXCOORD0;
   float3 LightVec : TEXCOORD1;
   float3 ViewVec : TEXCOORD2;
};


PS_INPUT VS(VS_INPUT input)
{
   PS_INPUT output = (PS_INPUT)0;

   float4 Pos = mul(input.Pos, World);
   Pos = mul(Pos, View);
   output.Pos = mul(Pos, Projection);

   output.Tex = input.Tex;

   float3 normal = mul(input.Norm, World);
   normal = mul(normal, View);

   float3 bTangent = cross(input.STan, normal);

   float3x3 tbnMatrix = float3x3(input.STan, bTangent, normal);
```

```
        output.LightVec = lightPos.xyz - Pos.xyz;
        output.ViewVec = eyePos.xyz - Pos.xyz;

        output.LightVec = mul(output.LightVec, tbnMatrix);
        output.ViewVec = mul(output.ViewVec, tbnMatrix);

        return output;
    }


    float4 PS(PS_INPUT input) : SV_Target
    {
        float3 normal = normalMap.Sample(DecalSampler, input.Tex);
        normal = (normal - 0.5) * 2;
        normal = normalize(normal);

        float3 lightVec = normalize(input.LightVec);
        float3 viewVec = normalize(input.ViewVec);

        float diffuse = saturate(dot(normal, lightVec));

        return decal.Sample(DecalSampler, input.Tex) * diffuse;
    }


    technique10 BumpMapping
    {
        pass P0
        {
            SetDepthStencilState(DepthStencilInfo, 0);

            SetVertexShader(CompileShader(vs_4_0, VS()));
            SetGeometryShader(NULL);
            SetPixelShader(CompileShader(ps_4_0, PS()));
        }
    }
```

FIGURE 8.12   Screenshot from the bump mapping demo.

Normal Mapping

Normal mapping is bump mapping used for a specific application. This application involves using the normal map as a means to add detail to a low-resolution model so that it appears to resemble the higher-resolution version of the model. The idea behind bump mapping is to add detail to surfaces without adding polygons. Where normal mapping differs from bump mapping is that the bump map is created from a height map (grayscale image), while a normal map, which is essentially the same thing, is created from the difference between a low- and high-resolution model.

Normal mapping can be seen in many of today's games such as *Gears of War*, *Halo 3*, *Metal Gear Solid 4*, and *Call of Duty 4*. Normal mapping is becoming a standard feature in today's realistic video games because of the amount of detail that can be added to geometry without additional polygons. In normal mapping it becomes possible to have low or medium polygon counts for objects while rendering them to appear as if they have hundreds of thousands or even millions of polygons.

The same shaders created for a bump mapping effect can be used for normal mapping. The only real difference is how the normal map is originally calculated. When creating a normal map, it is important to have the following items:

- Low-resolution model
- High-resolution model
- Smooth normal vectors for each vertex of the low-resolution model
- Smooth normal vectors for each vertex of the high-resolution model
- UV texture coordinates for the low-resolution model

Note that the high-resolution model does not need to have UV texture coordinates—just the low-resolution mesh. Smooth normal vectors are not face normals but are interpolated normals across the surfaces of the mesh. Face normals point in one direction for all vertices that are part of the polygon. Vertices that share triangle edges need to have smooth interpolated normals instead of the normal for whichever face is being processed. This means some vertices will have a normal that is a combination of the different faces to which it is attached.

The normal map creation algorithm works by casting rays from each vertex in the low-resolution model in the direction of that vertex's interpolated normal. This ray is intersected against the high-resolution model to find the point of intersection. The normal at the point of intersection is the normal that is stored in the normal map, whose position in the normal map is defined by the low-resolution model's UV texture coordinate. The position of the point of intersection is used to find the Barycentric coordinates, which are used during the interpolation of the normals of the three vertices in the high-resolution model's intersected triangle.

To recap, to create a normal map a low- and high-resolution model is created. For each vertex in the low-resolution model a ray is created from the vertex position pointing in the direction of the smooth vertex normal and is intersected against the high-resolution model. Once the point of intersection is found, the point of intersection along with the vertices of the intersected high-resolution model's triangle are used to find the Barycentric coordinates. These coordinates are used to interpolate between the high-resolution model triangle's normal vectors to find the normal that would correspond to the point of intersection. This normal is stored in the normal map. The algorithm can be defined as follows.

```
function NormalMap(lo_res, hi_res, normal_map)
{
   CalculateSmoothNormals(lo_res);
   CalculateSmoothNormals(hi_res);

   foreach(vertex in low_res)
   {
      ray = CreateRay(vertex.pos, vertex.smooth_normal);

      intersect = IntersectModel(ray, hi_res);
```

```
    bar_coords = GetBarcentric(intersect.point,
                               intersect.hi_res_tri);

    normal = Interpolate(bar_coords, intersect.hi_res_tri);

    StorePixel(normal, normal_map, vertex.UV);
  }

  SaveImage(normal_map, "normalmap.dds");
}
```

Because triangle-to-ray intersection is so expensive, the generation of a normal map is often a preprocessing step where the game's run-time is only aware of the normal map image and the low-resolution model. Various tools can be downloaded from the Internet to compute the normal map of two models instead of manually writing a custom tool. One such tool is NVIDIA's Melody, which is available for free from their developer Web site. Plenty of tools exist that can perform this task if the creation of an in-house tool is not desired, just as many free tools are available to compute a bump map without having to roll out a custom tool.

When creating a normal map, it is very important that the UV coordinates are correct, or else incorrect results can appear. Also, if face normal vectors are used instead of smooth normal vectors, the normal mapped object's quality will not be as high. This loss of quality is a result of discontinuities that are created as a result of using face normal vectors instead of smooth vectors. This discontinuity occurs when surfaces face in directions that cause their normal vectors to cross paths, which is not what is desired since normal mapping is essentially simulation of curvature. Simulation of curvature uses the smooth normal vectors since they smoothly run along the curvature of the geometry.

Parallax Mapping

Parallax mapping is an extension of bump and normal mapping that is used to add detail and dimension to 3D objects in a virtual scene. Parallax appears in areas of the surface that is being rendered in which sections appear to move in relation to one another as the view or object's orientation moves. An example of parallax mapping in a modern video game is shown in Figure 8.13 from the DirectX SDK sample *Parallax Occlusion Mapping*.

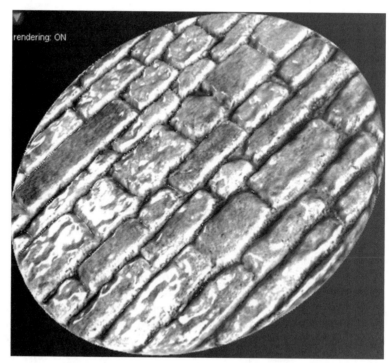

FIGURE 8.13   Screenshot of the parallax mapping effect.

In Figure 8.13 the parallax effect of the brick wall can be seen as the view moves from one location to another. This gives the impression that the brick wall has 3D bricks, when in reality it is a flat bump mapped surface. The effect is an illusion that has tremendous results on some surfaces and materials.

Parallax mapping works by dynamically distorting the textures that are used by the material. This includes any decals, bump and normal maps, and so forth. The distortion occurs in the pixel shader where a new set of texture coordinates is calculated based on the view information.

Using the parallax effect shown in the *Perfect Dark Zero* screenshot, if those bricks are real 3D objects, they will be composed of 3D data. Assuming that a highly detailed grid with various heights can be used to create that shape (i.e., a displacement map), this would mean the surface has a series of varying heights associated with it. If that same 3D look is to be represented on a surface that is flat instead of having varying heights, a height map can be used to store such height information on the pixel level. This height map is used to displace the vertex that gives it its final position. Displacing a vertex position is commonly done for geometry such as terrains and is known as displacement mapping. In parallax mapping the vertex positions are not being displaced, but the texture coordinates are, so that a 3D simulation can occur on a flat surface. In other words, parallax mapping requires the following resources.

- A height map
- A bump or normal map
- Any other decals or textures the material uses

Displacement mapping is a technique where a direction vector is read from a texture known as a displacement map and is added to the vertex position. This moves the vertex position into a new place, thus changing the shape of the object.

Bump or normal mapping alone is not enough to represent significant depth on a pixel level, which is why the height map is needed. To create a new set of texture coordinates that are used to access the texture information, an offset must first be calculated. This offset allows for high heights to be shifted away from the viewer and the low heights to be shifted toward the viewer. This offset is combined with the texture coordinates, and a new set is created. This new set gives the appearance of parallax on surfaces in a 3D scene.

The offset texture coordinates are created using the tangent-space view vector and the height from the height map to displace the surface's original texture coordinates. The steeper the viewing angle, the more displaced the texture coordinates. As the texture coordinates are displaced, this gives the illusion of depth. For surfaces such as stone walls this can be used to give the appearance of gaps between the stones or gaps (concert) between the bricks of a brick wall.

Parallax mapping is also known as offset mapping, offset limiting, and virtual displacement mapping.

ON THE CD

On the book's accompanying CD-ROM there is a demo called ParallaxMappingGL in the Chapter 8 folder. The vertex shader for this demo, which is shown in Listing 8.12, is the same as the bump mapping demo with the addition of a tangent-space view vector.

LISTING 8.12 THE PARALLAXMAPPINGGL VERTEX SHADER

```
varying vec2 texCoords;
varying vec3 lightVec;
varying vec3 viewDir;

uniform vec3 lightPos;
```

```
void main()
{
   gl_Position = gl_ModelViewProjectionMatrix * gl_Vertex;
   vec4 pos = gl_ModelViewMatrix * gl_Vertex;

   vec3 normal = gl_NormalMatrix * gl_Normal;
   vec3 sTangent = gl_MultiTexCoord1.xyz;
   vec3 bTangent = cross(sTangent, normal);

   mat3 tbnMatrix = mat3(sTangent, bTangent, normal);

   vec3 camPos = vec3(0, 0, 0);

   texCoords = gl_MultiTexCoord0.xy;
   lightVec = lightPos - pos.xyz;
   viewDir = camPos - pos.xyz;

   // Convert to texture space.
   lightVec = tbnMatrix * lightVec;
   viewDir = tbnMatrix * viewDir;
}
```

In the pixel shader most of the parallax effect operations are being carried out. The first step is to retrieve the height from the height map. The next step is to add a scaling and bias to the height map, which can be used to adjust the effect for different types of materials. Since parallax mapping is an approximation and is not true displacement mapping, it is not always going to be exact. With the height value a new texture coordinate can be calculated by multiplying the height with the texture-space view vector, which is then added to the original texture coordinates. These texture coordinates can then be used to sample the normal map and the decal texture, thus creating the parallax effect. The pixel shader for the ParallaxMappingGL demo is shown in Listing 8.13.

LISTING 8.13 THE PARALLAXMAPPINGGL PIXEL SHADER

```
varying vec2 texCoords;
varying vec3 lightVec;
varying vec3 viewDir;

sampler2D decal;
sampler2D normalMap;
sampler2D heightMap;
```

```
void main()
{
   float scale = 0.03;
   float bias = 0.01;

   lightVec = normalize(lightVec);
   viewDir = normalize(viewDir);

   // Get the height value and calculate the new texture coord.
   float heightVal = texture2D(heightMap, texCoords).x;
   float height = scale * heightVal - bias;
   vec2 newTexCoord = height * viewDir.xy + texCoords;

   vec3 normal = texture2D(normalMap, newTexCoord).xyz;
   normal = (normal - 0.5) * 2.0;
   normal = normalize(normal);

   float diffuse = saturate(dot(normal, lightVec));

   gl_FragColor = texture2D(decal, newTexCoord) * diffuse;
}
```

Taking the height at the current pixel, multiplying it by the view vector, and adding it to the texture coordinates performs a sort of virtual ray tracing operation where the result is a texture coordinate at the next approximated intersected height. As mentioned earlier, this technique is an approximation and, although it will give impressive results, is not true to how the surface would look if that detail was geometric. This trade-off is usually acceptable, and the results can work in games for a number of different types of surface materials.

ON THE CD

Also on the accompanying CD-ROM are Direct3D 9 and 10 versions of the demo called ParallaxMappingD3D9 and ParallaxMappingD3D10. The shader for the Direct3D 10 version of the demo is shown in Listing 8.14.

LISTING 8.14 THE PARALLAXMAPPINGD3D10 VERTEX AND PIXEL SHADER INPUTS AND SHADERS

```
struct VS_INPUT
{
   float4 Pos : POSITION;
   float3 Norm : NORMAL;
   float2 Tex : TEXCOORD;
   float3 STan : TANGENT;
};
```

```
struct PS_INPUT
{
   float4 Pos : SV_POSITION;
   float2 Tex : TEXCOORD0;
   float3 LightVec : TEXCOORD1;
   float3 ViewVec : TEXCOORD2;
};


PS_INPUT VS(VS_INPUT input)
{
   PS_INPUT output = (PS_INPUT)0;

   float4 Pos = mul(input.Pos, World);
   Pos = mul(Pos, View);
   output.Pos = mul(Pos, Projection);

   output.Tex = input.Tex;

   float3 normal = mul(input.Norm, World);
   normal = mul(normal, View);

   float3 bTangent = cross(input.STan, normal);

   float3x3 tbnMatrix = float3x3(input.STan, bTangent, normal);

   output.LightVec = lightPos.xyz - Pos.xyz;
   output.ViewVec = eyePos.xyz - Pos.xyz;

   output.LightVec = mul(output.LightVec, tbnMatrix);
   output.ViewVec = mul(output.ViewVec, tbnMatrix);

   return output;
}


float4 PS(PS_INPUT input) : SV_Target
{
   float3 lightVec = normalize(input.LightVec);
   float3 viewVec = normalize(input.ViewVec);

   float scale = 0.03;
   float bias = 0.01;
```

```
float heightVal = heightMap.Sample(DecalSampler, input.Tex);
float height = scale * heightVal - bias;
float2 newTexCoord = height * viewVec.xy + input.Tex;

float3 normal = normalMap.Sample(NormalMapSampler,
                                 newTexCoord);
normal = (normal - 0.5) * 2;
normal = normalize(normal);

float diffuse = saturate(dot(normal, lightVec));

return decal.Sample(DecalSampler, newTexCoord) * diffuse;
}
```

ADDITIONAL LIGHTING TECHNIQUES

Several additional techniques are used in modern video games to add detail and realism to 3D scenes. A few of these techniques are briefly discussed in this section. These techniques include the following.

- Point lights
- Light blooms
- Lens flare
- Light shafts

Point Lights

ON THE CD

On the CD-ROM are demo applications called PointLightGL, Point-LightD3D9, and PointLightD3D10 that perform point lighting. In the point lighting demos the purpose is to create a point light source that has its light intensity attenuate over distance. The point lighting demos add the attenuation term to the Blinn-Phong lighting demo.

To create a point light effect, an attenuation term is calculated and is multiplied with the diffuse and specular contributions. To calculate the attenuation factor, a commonly used equation is as follows, where d is the distance from the light position to the vertex.

Attenuation = 1 / d2

The distance between two vectors can be calculated by subtracting the two vectors and finding the length (magnitude) of the result. The further the distance becomes, the less intense is the lighting contribution. In GLSL there is a function called distance() that performs this in the shader. In

Direct3D's HLSL, since the light vector is calculated anyway (light pos − vertex pos), finding the length of the light vector returns the distance. The attenuation term is 1 over this value. In the demos a floating-point variable of 0.05 is multiplied with the equation to allow for control over the light's range. The smaller the value, the brighter the light will be. The vertex and pixel shader from the OpenGL version of the demo is shown in Listing 8.15. The Direct3D 10 version is shown in Listing 8.16 where only the inputs and the vertex and pixel shaders are listed.

LISTING 8.15 THE POINTLIGHTGL VERTEX AND PIXEL SHADER

```
// VERTEX SHADER


varying vec3 normal;
varying vec3 lightVec;
varying vec3 viewVec;
varying float attenuation;

uniform vec3 eyePos;
uniform vec3 lightPos;
uniform float lightRange;


void main()
{
   gl_Position = gl_ModelViewProjectionMatrix * gl_Vertex;
   vec4 pos = gl_ModelViewMatrix * gl_Vertex;

   normal = gl_NormalMatrix * gl_Normal;
   lightVec = lightPos - pos.xyz;
   viewVec = eyePos - pos.xyz;

   float d = distance(lightPos, pos.xyz);

   attenuation = 1 / (lightRange * d * d);
}


// PIXEL SHADER
```

```
varying vec3 normal;
varying vec3 lightVec;
varying vec3 viewVec;
varying float attenuation;


void main()
{
    normal = normalize(normal);
    lightVec = normalize(lightVec);
    viewVec = normalize(viewVec);

    vec3 halfVec = normalize(lightVec + viewVec);

    float diffuse = saturate(dot(normal, lightVec));
    float specular = pow(saturate(dot(normal, halfVec)), 25);

    vec4 white = vec4(1, 1, 1, 1);

    gl_FragColor = (white * diffuse + white * specular) *
                        attenuation;
}
```

Listing 8.16 The PointLightD3D10 Demo's Vertex and Pixel Shaders

```
struct VS_INPUT
{
    float4 Pos : POSITION;
    float3 Norm : NORMAL;
    float2 Tex : TEXCOORD;
};

struct PS_INPUT
{
    float4 Pos : SV_POSITION;
    float3 Norm : NORMAL;
    float3 LightVec : TEXCOORD0;
    float3 ViewVec : TEXCOORD1;
    float attenuation : TEXCOORD2;
};
```

```
PS_INPUT VS(VS_INPUT input)
{
   PS_INPUT output = (PS_INPUT)0;

   float4 Pos = mul(input.Pos, World);
   Pos = mul(Pos, View);
   output.Pos = mul(Pos, Projection);

   output.Norm = mul(input.Norm, World);
   output.Norm = mul(output.Norm, View);

   output.LightVec = lightPos.xyz - Pos.xyz;
   output.ViewVec = eyePos.xyz - Pos.xyz;

   float d = length(output.LightVec);

   output.attenuation = 1 / (0.05f * d * d);

   return output;
}


float4 PS(PS_INPUT input) : SV_Target
{
   float3 normal = normalize(input.Norm);
   float3 lightVec = normalize(input.LightVec);
   float3 viewVec = normalize(input.ViewVec);
   float3 halfVec = normalize(lightVec + viewVec);

   float diffuse = saturate(dot(normal, lightVec));
   float specular = pow(saturate(dot(normal, halfVec)), 50);

   float4 white = float4(1, 1, 1, 1);

   return (white * diffuse + white * specular) *
            input.attenuation;
}
```

Bloom

Really bright light sources or objects can create a sort of glow around an object while being lit. This glow is a light bloom that appears around objects that resembles a halo-like effect. Blooming occurs when the eyes or the camera is suddenly viewing a very bright object.

Blooming in computer graphics can be created by first rendering a scene to a render target. The next step is to draw to another render target a blurred version of the scene, which can be done by drawing a full-screen quad using the rendered scene render target as a texture and using blurring shaders. The last step is to draw another full-screen quad while using both textures as a blended image. This series of steps is often done by artists in applications such as Photoshop when attempting to soften or add a glowing effect to images, and the same can be done in computer graphics in real time.

Blooming is very popular in high-dynamic range rendered scenes, which are discussed in Chapter 11, "Special Effects: High Dynamic Range." By combining blooming with a dynamic brightness adjustment system, a game can simulate what the human eye goes through when suddenly moving from a dark space to a very bright space and vice versa. An example of this is walking outdoors on a very bright day from a dark indoor setting or waking up in the middle of the night and turning on a light after the eyes have adjusted to the dark.

Blooming in games often uses a down-sampled render target for the blurring pass of the algorithm. Down-sample means to use a smaller resolution than the original. Since the render target is blurred, the details are not different enough that the original size would be needed. Using a smaller resolution for the blurring can be faster to process while giving the same results.

To recap, blooming is performed by rendering the scene to a texture, rendering a full-screen square with the rendered scene as a texture so that a blurred version can be created, and blending the blurred image with the original rendered scene. The blurred contents will give a glow around objects in the scene. In order not to have a full-screen blurred effect, which would only soften the look of the rendered scene, the only pixels that are blurred are the bright ones. In high-dynamic range rendering this can be any pixel that is brighter than the (1, 1, 1) white color. In non-high-dynamic range rendering this can be any value above any threshold chosen, such as 0.8. An example of bloom appears in the *Post Process* sample from the DirectX SDK, as shown in Figure 8.14.

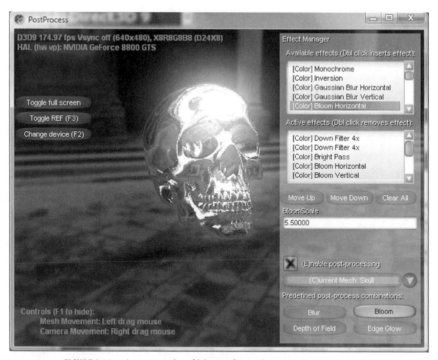

FIGURE 8.14 An example of bloom from the *Post Process* sample.

Lens Flare

Lens flare is an artifact of light hitting the camera lens. This flare is actually scattered light as it is reflected from within the camera's lens. In video games this effect is created to simulate this optical artifact, which is not always desired in TV and film like it is in games. Adding a lens flare gives the impression that the virtual viewer is an actual camera.

In games lens flare is often created by drawing 2D elements to the screen. The elements start at the visible light source and move more in the direction toward the middle of the screen. As the distance between the projected light source (e.g., the sun) and the middle of the screen decreases, so does the distance between the elements.

Lens flare is easy to do in computer graphics. The position of the light source causing the flare can be transformed into screen space using vector and matrix mathematics, the middle of the screen is easily determined as half the width and height resolution, and the drawings of the elements are 2D alpha texture-mapped squares. When drawing the elements, the only trick is deciding how far apart the elements should be to achieve the best results. If the distance between the projected light source and the middle of the screen are determined, the elements can be spaced evenly along that 2D vector; the distance acts as a radius, and the diameter of the range for the effect is twice that size. An example of a lens flare is shown in Figure 8.15. Today a flare effect can be created using a high-dynamic range rendering algorithm that differs from the traditional lens flare technique discussed here, which is discussed in Chapter 11.

FIGURE 8.15   Lens flare in a blank environment.

Light Shafts

As light enters and exits glass, such as a window, or another medium, a light shaft can appear. A light shaft is the result of rendering lights and shadows in participating media. In nature a light shaft appears because light is hitting suspended particles that are reflected in a different direction. Shadows appear because the object in the suspended particles is further blocking light rays from passing. Objects that are in this field of particles, when lit from a direction, can create the light shaft effect.

Many different light shafts can be created in games. These shafts can come from windows, clouds (also known as god rays), being under water, fog, dust particles suspended in the air, spot lights, and so forth.

Light shafts can be created many different ways in games. The easiest way is to draw polygons coming from the light source and use additive blending. This can be seen in the *Legend of Zelda: The Wind Waker*. As the polygon's vertices become more distant from the source, it becomes more transparent, giving it a more realistic look.

This same idea can be extended to using extruded polygons from a window or any other object within the field. This tends to not lead to the best results, as the view angle changes for some objects, but can be easily done in real time. Many games are starting to add light shafts, fake or not, to add more realism to their scenes.

SUMMARY

Lighting is a very complex topic in computer graphics, especially when video games are concerned. In this chapter the discussion covered a large range of topics from the basics to more intermediate lighting techniques. Throughout the next few chapters more advanced lighting techniques and shadowing algorithms will be examined in more detail. Lighting is a great way to add detail to scenes, and all modern commercial video games use lighting. This chapter focused on beginner- and intermediate-level lighting algorithms and techniques in video games. Each of these techniques, especially normal mapping, has become standard in the gaming industry.

The following elements were discussed in this chapter.

- Diffuse light
- Specular light
- Ambient light
- Attenuation
- Visibility terms
- Light models
- Lambert
- Blinn
- Phong
- Directional lights
- Point lights
- Spot lights
- Per-vertex and per-pixel lighting
- Bump mapping
- Normal mapping
- Parallax mapping
- Height maps
- Bloom
- Lens flare
- Light shafts

CHAPTER QUESTIONS

Answers to the following chapter review questions can be found in Appendix A, "Answers to Chapter Questions."

1. What is a lighting model?
2. What is a surface material?
3. List five terms and assets that can be part of a surface's material.
4. Describe a directional light and its purpose in computer graphics.
5. Describe a point light and its purpose in computer graphics.
6. Describe a spot light and its purpose in computer graphics.
7. What is ambient light? Why is it used in graphics?
8. What is diffuse light? Why is it used in graphics?
9. What is specular light? Why is it used in graphics?
10. Describe the Lambert diffuse lighting model.
11. Describe the Phong specular lighting model.
12. Describe the Blinn-Phong lighting model and how it differs from the Phong model.
13. What is bump mapping? Describe its purpose in video games.
14. What is normal mapping? How does it differ from bump mapping?
15. Describe parallax mapping. What added benefits does it offer to game developers?
16. Describe lens flare. How can it be achieved in a video game?
17. What are light shafts? Name one game that uses light shafts.
18. What is blooming, and how is it achieved?
19. What is a height map? How are they used in computer graphics? How does a height map differ from a displacement map?
20. True or false: Lambert diffuse uses three vectors to compute its lighting terms. These vectors are the light vector, the view vector, and the normal vector.
21. True or false: The Phong specular model uses a half vector and the normal raised to a power to calculate the specular contribution.
22. True or false: Attenuation is used to decrease light intensity over distance.
23. True or false: The visibility term is used in the point light effect to give the illusion that the light has a radius.
24. True or false: Parallax mapping is known as virtual displacement mapping.
25. True or false: Parallax mapping is a type of per-pixel lighting.
26. True or false: Ambient occlusion is used to add shadows to geometry.
27. True or false: Phong lighting is cheaper than Blinn.
28. True or false: Lens flare is an optical artifact that exists in real-world cameras.
29. True or false: The main purpose of blooming is to brighten the scene.
30. True or false: The diffuse light models are view dependent.

CHAPTER EXERCISES

Exercise 1: Expand on the bump mapping demo application to include specular lighting.

Exercise 2: Implement lens flare in a 3D application using the steps discussed in this chapter.

Exercise 3: Write a custom tool that is able to take a .tga image as input and create a bump map out of it. Use the algorithm discussed in this chapter.

ADVANCED LIGHTING AND SHADOWS

In This Chapter

- Shadows in Games
- Projection Shadows
- Shadow Volumes
- Shadow Mapping
- Soft Shadows
- Light Mapping
- Deferred Shading

Lighting and shadows are used to add realism to rendered scenes. This realism can be photorealistic or nonphotorealistic in appearance. Lighting is used to shade surfaces that are illuminated by sources of light, while shadows represent the absence or lack of light at a point. Shadows are very important when you are attempting to represent a scene, both for aesthetics and to highlight spatial relationships between surfaces and objects. Many video games that strive for realism pay a lot of attention to the lighting and shadows in the rendered scenes.

The purpose of this chapter is to examine the role shadows play in modern video games. Lighting is used to add a great deal of detail to a rendered scene, but without shadows, a lot of potential is lost during the output. There is no denying the impact shadows have in computer graphics, and they are very important. In computer graphics, shadows are not free, and separate algorithms exist for calculating them in real-time applications.

SHADOWS IN GAMES

In video game graphics, shadows are not created as a result of lighting or an absence of it. In video games, surfaces are illuminated based on the surface and light properties. Because of this, most real-time lighting algorithms do not take into account surrounding surfaces while shading. Taking into account surfaces other than the one being lit is very expensive to compute and is not done in real time. This practice was first discussed in Chapter 8, "Lighting and Materials," and is known as *visibility*. Visibility is usually a Boolean flag representing whether or not a point on a surface can be seen by the current light that is being processed. Visibility can also be a percentage ranging from 0 to 1 (100%) that can be used to create soft shadows that have a gradual fall-off from their centers.

Since a surface is lit without taking into account additional surfaces, the surface is lit as if there is a straight line-of-sight between it and the light source, assuming the surface being rendered is not facing away from the light. By rendering all surfaces in this manner, it is possible to fully light a scene in real time, but shadows will not be present. This is shown in Figure 9.1, where light is not being blocked by the surrounding objects when lighting each individual surface.

FIGURE 9.1   A lit scene with no shadows. Notice the absence of a shadow on the ground.

In video game graphics, to account for shadows within the scene it is important for the game to determine if a surface, or point on a surface, being shaded has its visibility to the light source blocked by another surface. This allows some points on the surface to be lit differently based on visibility information. This is what causes shadows to form using the rendering techniques seen in modern video games. An example of this is shown in Figure 9.2.

FIGURE 9.2   An example of lighting and shadows.

Taking visibility into account can add a great deal to the rendered scene. More advanced lighting and shadowing algorithms take into account light that has bounced off of other surfaces around the scene. This can cause hard and sharp shadows to appear softer as well as allow light to absorb some of the color of a surface and reflect it back into the scene, so that a surface takes on a small amount of the color of another surface near it. In general, this is known as global illumination, and it will be discussed in more detail in Chapter 10, "Global Illumination Techniques."

Real-Time Versus Preprocessed Shadows

Shadows are computed in real time or offline as a preprocessing step. Both real-time and offline shadow calculations attempt to account for the visibility of the lighting equation. In real-time algorithms, the goal is to do this as quickly as possible given the scene depth complexity. This can be a challenge in video games due to the traditionally high cost of calculating visibility.

This chapter examines real-time shadows. Chapter 10 discusses preprocessed shadowing topics and techniques in more detail. Real-time shadows pose an interesting challenge. They must appear realistic in a real-time application. With preprocessed algorithms, because the calculations are done offline, the time the algorithms take to calculate the lighting and shadows is far less restrictive than with a real-time approach.

The calculation of shadows can become quite involved. In many games, the following conditions can arise in 3D scenes.

- Static objects casting shadows on other static objects
- Static objects casting shadows on dynamic objects
- Dynamic objects castings shadows on static objects
- Dynamic objects castings shadows on other dynamic objects
- An object casting a shadow upon itself (for example, a character's arm above its head causing a shadow of the arm to project onto the character)
- An object lying inside multiple shadows (multiple objects casting a shadow on one area or object)
- Multiple light sources causing each object to potentially cast multiple shadows at multiple angles

Most real-time shadowing techniques attempt to solve many of these problems while also performing at an interactive rate. Static shadows are more forgiving than dynamic shadows because they can be calculated once and used during run-time. This is often in the form of a light map that stores both lighting and shadowing information for static geometry, which is discussed later in this chapter. Because static shadows do not change, they often can be represented by textures that were computed with very expensive shadow and lighting algorithms, which is what most realistically rendered 3D games do.

Popular Types of Shadows

There are two main types of shadows and many different shadowing algorithms that are used to compute them. In computer graphics there exist hard and soft shadows. Hard shadows are sharp and made up of a solid color. Many games use hard shadows, and they are faster to compute than their soft shadow counterparts. An example of a hard shadow is shown in Figure 9.3.

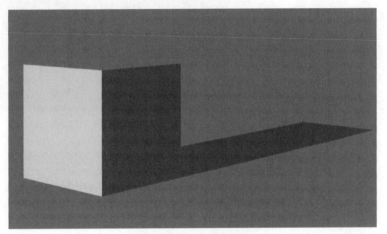

FIGURE 9.3   A hard shadow.

Soft shadows have a softer appearance, with a gradual fall off from the center of the shadow to its outer edge. Soft shadows are more realistic because the real world is full of soft shadows. In the past in video games, soft shadows were too expensive to be performed on most hardware in real time. Today, many games use soft shadows in their scenes, with one example being Crytex's *Crysis*. An example of a soft shadow is shown in Figure 9.4.

FIGURE 9.4 A soft shadow.

In this chapter, the main shadowing techniques discussed include projection shadows, shadow mapping, and shadow volumes. Games today mostly use shadow mapping for shadow generation, which has long been a popular choice among game developers.

Shadow Imposters

Many early 3D video games used simple objects to represent shadows in scenes. These simple objects were often very basic shapes, such as a flat circle. An example of a game that uses shadows in this manner is *Super Mario 64* for the Nintendo 64.

Representing shadows in this manner usually involves rendering the flattened object underneath the object casting the shadow. To further add to its representation, the circle can get smaller as the object moves away from the surface. An example of this is if the player jumps off the ground and into the air. Although this type of shadowing is not realistic and is hardly used in high-budget video games, at one time they were common, when gaming machines had more limited resources and processing power than today.

PROJECTION SHADOWS

One of the easier and more straightforward shadowing algorithms is known as projection shadows. Projection shadows are created by rendering flattened objects (original or simplified objects such as a circular imposter) from either the perspective of a light source or in some general direction.

Many early 3D video games use projection shadows. These shadows can be simple imposters or they can mimic the object. In the game *Super Mario 64* for the Nintendo 64, the shadow was a simple flattened circle that was projected downward to appear underneath the character. In the game *Resident Evil* for the PlayStation game console, the shadows take more complex form that more closely resembles the characters than a simple circle but are not as complex as the character model itself.

 A shadow imposter such as a flat circle can be used instead of the original mesh or even a simplified mesh and can be rendered quickly due to the small amount of information (e.g., two triangles if used for an alpha-mapped textured square of a circle).

When it comes to using projection shadows the pros include the following.

- It is easy to implement.
- It does not require special hardware support like other techniques such as shadow mapping.
- Shadows can be created out of any object, or an imposter can be used if necessary.

Cons include the following.

- Shadows are not soft and realistic (which can be simulated by slightly moving the light source many times, blending the results, but this is highly inefficient and in many cases impractical).
- Projecting the shadows so that they appear to lie on a surface can be difficult with surfaces that are not completely flat, such as terrains.
- It does not allow for objects to self-shadow themselves at all or shadow other complex objects realistically.
- Projecting every surface onto every other surface is not practical for complex scenes.
- Projection shadows do not work well with specular surfaces.
- Because a projected shadow is essentially just a flat version of a rendered object, it cannot be used to shadow a volume (for example, an object above a statue and shadowing the entire model)

Essentially, projection shadows are created using a shadow-projection matrix. This matrix is created so that it scales anything that is rendered using it to a completely flat shape. A light direction can be used to control the direction from which the shadows will appear once rendered. To create the shadow, all one needs to do is to use the matrix to render an object that is casting the shadow using no materials (i.e., no textures, no lighting, etc.). This will render the object flattened.

Rendering Projected Shadows

To display shadows on surfaces that are not completely flat, such as terrain, the polygons that make up the surface receiving the shadow can individually clip and orient the flattened geometry acting as the shadow. This means additional overhead must be used to display the shadow so that it actually looks like a shadow on the ground. Depending on how large the shadow is and how many nonflat surfaces it covers depends on how much overhead is involved. This process is discussed more in Chapter 12, "Special Effects: Additional Effects."

Another option that can be used instead of clipping polygons to one another is to use the stencil buffer of the graphics API. Using the stencil buffer for shadows is discussed in more detail in the "Shadow Volumes" section of this chapter, but the general idea is to use the stencil buffer to mask where surfaces are so that the shadow can appear only where "receiver" surfaces are, instead of being a piece of geometry floating in space. An example of this is shown in Figure 9.5.

FIGURE 9.5   A projected shadow not clipped (left) and clipped (right).

When rendering coplanar surfaces, a problem with the depth buffer can occur. This problem is known as z-fighting, which is rendering artifacts that occur when surfaces that occupy the same plane are being rendered. An example of z-fighting is shown in Figure 9.6.

FIGURE 9.6 Z-fighting.

To overcome this, one option is to render the objects close to one another so that they appear to occupy the same location but far enough apart to not use an offset. The depth buffer has a limited precision that does not help matters. Another option is to allow the hardware to take care of the offset by enabling what is known as polygon offset. Both OpenGL and Direct3D have this feature, which can easily be enabled at any time. For OpenGL this is as easy as calling the OpenGL functions `glEnable(GL_POLYGON_OFFSET_FILL)` and `glPolygonOffset(GLfloat factor, GLfloat units)`.

The Shadow Matrix

The last topic to discuss when talking about projection shadows is the creation of the shadow-projection matrix. This is done using a plane specified as A, B, and C with a distance *d* and a light position. The light's position is specified as an X, Y, and Z position. An additional property, usually stored in a W component of a 4D vector can be 0 or 1. A value of 0 causes the calculations of the shadow matrix to be based on a directional light, while 1 is for a positional light source. The pseudo-code for creating the shadow matrix is as follows:

```
function CreateShadowMatrix(Plane plane, Vector4D lightPos)
{
    float dp = plane.Dot(lightPos);
    float matrix[16] = 0;
```

```
matrix[0]  = dp - lightPos.x * plane.a;
matrix[4]  = 0  - lightPos.x * plane.b;
matrix[8]  = 0  - lightPos.x * plane.c;
matrix[12] = 0  - lightPos.x * d;

matrix[1]  = 0  - lightPos.y * plane.a;
matrix[5]  = dp - lightPos.y * plane.b;
matrix[9]  = 0  - lightPos.y * plane.c;
matrix[13] = 0  - lightPos.y * d;

matrix[2]  = 0  - lightPos.z * plane.a;
matrix[6]  = 0  - lightPos.z * plane.b;
matrix[10] = dp - lightPos.z * plane.c;
matrix[14] = 0  - lightPos.z * d;

matrix[3]  = 0  - lightPos.w * plane.a;
matrix[7]  = 0  - lightPos.w * plane.b;
matrix[11] = 0  - lightPos.w * plane.c;
matrix[15] = dp - lightPos.w * d;

return matrix;
}
```

The matrix returned by this function can be set to the rendering API, and any object rendered afterward will appear flat. To give it a shadow appearance, as mentioned earlier, it is important to consider rendering the shadow object with no lighting or materials like textures and so on.

ON THE CD

On the CD-ROM is a demo called Shadow Projection in the Chapter 9 folder that demonstrates a simple implementation of this shadowing technique. The demo application renders two objects: a square that acts as the ground and a 3D box.

Shadow Volumes

The next type of shadowing technique that will be discussed is known as a shadow volume. Shadow volumes have been used in a number of games, most popularly in the game *Doom 3* to perform shadowing throughout the entire scene. Shadow volumes share some slight similarities with projection shadows while solving many of the issues that projection shadows have. Shadow volumes do not suffer from rendering artifacts like shadow mapping does, which is discussed in more detail in the next section.

When rendering a shadow volume, the idea is to project the outline of an object into the scene based on the light position or direction. In projection shadows, a matrix is used to create a flat object that is projected in a direction. In shadow volumes, new geometry is created using the silhouette (outline) of an object. This works by finding the edges of an object that define the object's outline based on its orientation to the light and creating quads that extend from those edges into the scene in the direction of the light vector.

An edge is defined by two points. With the light vector's direction, another set of two points can be calculated (i.e., projected from the first two), causing all four points to form a quad. A visual example of this is shown in Figure 9.7.

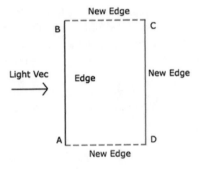

FIGURE 9.7 Creating quads from an object's edges.

The creation of a shadow volume must be done once for all lights and objects in the scene that can cast shadows. Since this can become quite expensive for large scenes and many lights, most games do not allow some light sources to be considered in the shadow rendering. These types of lights can be very small light sources, while lights that would be used in the shadowing include sources such as sunlight, large point and spot lights, and so forth.

This brings up an interesting problem. Significant overhead is involved in the creation of shadow volumes. If an entire scene can cast shadows, then essentially every edge that is part of the scene must be examined, and those that lie on the silhouette must be projected to create the shadow volume. This process must happen for every light source that can affect an object and create shadows. This also means that if the object or the light source moves, then all shadow volumes affected must be recalculated. Since shadows can be cast by objects outside the view frustum, it would not always be acceptable to correctly shadow a scene while only doing so with objects and edges that can are visible. The main pros of shadow volumes are as follows.

- Shadow volumes can allow objects to self-shadow themselves.
- Shadow volumes do not suffer from aliasing artifacts like shadow mapping does.
- Shadow volumes can be used to render all shadows for all objects in a scene.
- Shadow volumes are easy to implement once you understand the technique.
- Shadow volumes use the stencil buffer (discussed later in this chapter), which is a very common feature in graphics hardware.

The cons include the following.

- There can be significant overhead when computing shadow volumes for all outline edges of a scene, especially when multiple lights that can cast shadows are involved as well as moving objects and light positions (and object orientations).
- Shadow volumes are traditionally hard shadows, although with some effort it is possible to soften them, but this is expensive and not always practical or efficient.
- Shadow volumes can take up a lot of fill rate on graphics hardware when shadowing a scene fully.
- It requires additional data for the quick determination of silhouette edges so that shadow volumes can be calculated (e.g., keeping a list of all the edges in an object and then testing these edges to determine which are part of the object's outline).

Finding the Silhouette Edges

The most important step in the shadow volume algorithm is to find the edges that compose the outline of the model. A silhouette outline edge is determined by one major condition. This condition states that if an edge is part of only one polygon and if that polygon is facing the source, or in this case the light source since the volumes must extend from that, then it is part of the silhouette. If the edge is shared by two polygons, with one polygon facing the source while the other is facing away, then it is part of the silhouette.

In cartoon rendering (cel-shading), the silhouette is determined by the viewer's position, while in shadow volumes it is determined by the light position.

To calculate the silhouette, you must get all edges of every polygon of an object. For a triangle, this would mean creating three edges per polygon, where one edge goes from point A to point B, another goes from point B to point C, and the third goes from point C to point A. An example of this is shown in Figure 9.8.

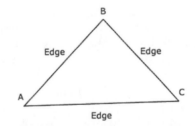

FIGURE 9.8   Finding the edges of a polygon.

Once you know how to get the edges, the next step is to create an edge list for the entire object. In this list you record the edge and which polygons it is part of. One way to do this is to create an array (or better yet, a kd-tree if you are familiar with them) and insert each edge into this container. While inserting, you first check to see if the edge is already in the container, which would have occurred if another polygon already sharing that same edge already inserted it. If the edge is not in the container, it is added, and a reference (possibly an index if the polygons were stored in an array) to the polygon that owns that edge is included as well. If the edge already exists, a reference to the polygon that attempted to insert the edge is added to the already-existing edge. In other words, you create a list of edges where each edge element has a list of which polygons share that edge. The creation of the edge list is fairly simple and only needs to be performed once, possibly as a preprocessing step.

During the construction of the shadow volume, the light vector is calculated and the edge list is examined. Every edge that has only one polygon, which is facing the light, is used to create a quad that will be part of the shadow volume. Every edge that has multiple polygons where one is facing the source and the others are not is used to create a quad. To create the quad, you take the two points that make up the edge, which will be used as the first two points of the quad, and add them to the light vector multiplied by some large distance. This gives you two new point positions that, when combined with the edge points, form a quad. If you do this for all silhouette edges of the object, the shadow volume will be created. The quad calculation is as straightforward as the following:

Point_3 = Edge_Point_1 + Light_Vec * Some_Large_Distance
Point_4 = Edge_Point_2 + Light_Vec * Some_Large_Distance

Once the shadow volume is calculated, it is stored in its own vertex buffer so that it can be rendered in a later stage, which will be discussed in the next section. When creating the edge list, you can use tree and array data structures. For example, a kd-tree (short for k-dimensional tree) can be used first to allow you to quickly insert and search for edges, and it is important to be able to quickly search if an edge is already added to the list. If an edge is not found, it is added to the tree along with the polygon of which it is a part. If an edge is found, the polygon that attempted to add the edge is added to the already-existing edge's polygon list. Once all edges and polygons have been added to the kd-tree, then all elements of the tree can be removed and inserted into an array. Since the array does not need to be searched for later steps, this can be very useful, especially when saving the array to a file that is much easier and convenient than using a node-based data structure. For those of you who are familiar with data structures, this process will seem fairly easy. If you are not familiar with data structures, we recommend the book *Data Structures and Algorithms for Game Developers*, which covers these two data structures in detail along with many others that are highly useful in programming.

Rendering the Shadow Volume

When you are determining if a point is in shadow or not, a vector is created that goes from the viewer to the point. This vector is the direction property of a ray, where the origin is the camera's position. If the ray intersects a front-facing shadow volume quad, then a counter, let's call it volume counter, is incremented. When a back-facing shadow volume is intersected, that means the ray is leaving a shadow volume, and the volume counter is decremented. This means that if the volume counter is greater than or equal to 1 when the ray strikes the object, the point on that object's surface is in shadow. if the volume counter is less than 1, the point is not in shadow. In video games, the stencil buffer is used to perform this volume counting in the hardware, and the steps to render using it are as follows.

1. Render the scene without color write or materials (i.e., no per-pixel lighting, no textures, etc.) to fill the depth buffer.
2. Enable the stencil buffer and render the front-facing quads of the shadow volumes to it (i.e., render with back-face culling on). The shadow volumes are not displayed (unless you want them to be), so color and depth writing should be disabled since only the stencil buffer is needed. Set the stencil buffer to increment for every surface rendered.
3. Render the shadow volumes again, but this time render the back-face polygons (front-face culling on) and decrement the stencil buffer for every surface rendered. Since the depth buffer was filled before, any back-face shadow volume polygon that is behind a scene object will not decrement the counter. Thus, if an object is within a shadow volume, after these two stencil write tests, the stencil buffer will have a value of 1 or higher at the end of this pass.

4. Render the scene normally but use the results of the stencil test to only render to screen pixels that are set to 0. If the canvas was cleared to black before the rendering frame began, the shadowed areas would not be changed, making them solid black with no additional effort needed. We only need to render to where the stencil pixels are set to 0, which will give us our fully shadowed scene.

When rendering shadow volumes, one major problem can be encountered. If the camera is inside a shadow volume, the counting scheme can be incorrect and pixels that should be 0 will not be. In *Doom 3*, John Carmack (a game industry legend) came up with a rather simple yet effective solution. In his version of the algorithm, the polygons of the shadow volume are rendered by culling front-facing polygons first instead of back-facing geometry and incrementing the stencil buffer whenever the depth test fails. During the second pass, the front-facing polygons are rendered and the stencil buffer is decremented every time the depth test fails. This version of the shadow volume algorithm is known as *Carmack's reverse* and can be used to avoid the volume counter issues that can arise when either the near clipping plane clips volume geometry or if the camera is in the shadow volume.

On some hardware, it is possible to combine the two passes of the shadow volume rendering into one by using a two-sided stencil. When a two-sided stencil is enabled, you can render polygons without culling, and the hardware will increment and decrement as needed based on the direction the volume polygons are facing. Performing a one-pass approach in hardware can lead to performance benefits.

ON THE CD

On the CD-ROM in the Chapter 9 folder is a demo application called Shadow Volumes that demonstrates how to render a scene using shadow volumes. These demos (one for each API discussed in this book) use Carmack's reverse.

SHADOW MAPPING

The next type of shadowing is by far the most popular way to create shadows in video games. Shadow mapping is used in many 3D video games. Shadow mapping looks at the scene from the point-of-view of the light source. Anything the light is shining on can cast and receive shadows, while anything outside this volume can be ignored by the current light. In shadow mapping, a depth texture is created based on this information, and this texture is used to determine which pixels in the final render are in shadow and which are not.

When rendering the scene from the point-of-view of the light source, only the depth values are stored in a rendering target. When the scene is rendered again, it is rendered normally, but it uses the depth values from the render target to determine which pixels are in shadow and which are not. This rendering target is known as the shadow map but also goes by the names shadow buffer and depth texture.

The shadow mapping algorithm uses texture projections to project the shadow map image over the scene. For creating the shadow map, the following steps are used during the algorithm.

1. Bind the rendering target that will be used to store the depth values that make up the shadow map.
2. Set the view-projection matrix so that the view is seen from the light's perspective.
3. Render the scene with no color writes and only store the depth values.

The shadow map will need to be calculated every time the light or an object that is affected by the light moves. The precision of the shadow map rendering target is important because using too many bits is a waste, while using too few can lead to rendering artifacts. Usually, experimentations can be performed to find which rendering target format gives you the best visual result at a performance level that is acceptable for the game.

Another thing to note is that the larger the shadow map texture, the more overhead is involved in calculating it for each light. If the shadow map is too small, aliasing artifacts will become obvious. These artifacts can be minimized by increasing the resolution of the shadow map texture, which doesn't solve the problem but can decrease how noticeable it is, or by blurring the texture's pixels. Blurring the shadow map will soften its edges, allowing lower-resolution images to be used to avoid performance issues.

When you create the shadow map, a perspective projection can be used for point and spot light sources, and an orthogonal projection can be used for directional lights. For performance reasons, it is important to disable color writes and rendering states because the only relevant information in the shadow map is the depth values. Also, when using multiple shadow casting lights, you must create a different shadow map for each light source.

Rendering with the Shadow Map

Once the shadow map is created, it can be used in the scene. To do so, follow these steps to render a scene with shadows using the shadow map.

- Render the scene normally.
- While rendering, project the shadow map into the scene using a technique known as projection texturing. This is done by transforming the vertex in the vertex shader by the light matrix and sending that down to the pixel shader.

- In the pixel shader, test if the pixel being shaded for the light-space vertex has a depth that is larger (farther) than the depth from the shadow map. If it does, the pixel is in shadow. Otherwise, it is not.

When you are rendering with the shadow map, stitching artifacts can appear when the depth value of a shadow is the same or very close to that of a surface. One option is to offset the depth value a little bit, but this will not always fix the problem. Another way to minimize this artifact is to render only back faces of the scene when generating the shadow map.

To test the depth of a pixel with the depth out of the shadow map, the depth of the pixel being shaded must be transformed into what it would be if it were being viewed from the light's perspective, not the camera. This is accomplished by transforming the point into light-space by using a matrix that defines the light's information. This transformation occurs in the vertex shader and is passed down and interpolated by the pixel shader for all points of the primitive. The light matrix uses the light's position as the translation. It usually uses a scale and bias of 0.5 to map from −1 to 1 into 0 to 1 to better match the range of depth values (which are usually between 0 and 1), and it uses the light's view-projection matrix, which was discussed earlier. Combining the light's view-projection, translation, and scaling and bias matrices gives you the light matrix. This matrix does not change unless the light changes in some way, which means it can be calculated once whenever you need to. An example of a depth texture and its use for shadow mapping are shown in Figure 9.9.

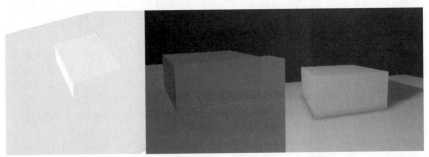

FIGURE 9.9   Shadow map (left), unshadowed scene (middle), and shadowed scene (right).

When performing the texture lookup in the pixel shader, the transformed light-space position is used for the 3D texture coordinates. Specific shader functions exist for using a 2D texture for a texture projection lookup with 3D coordinates, such as tex2Dproj() in HLSL.

On the CD-ROM in the Chapter 9 folder are demo applications for shadow mapping called Shadow Mapping. The demos use rendering targets for the creation of the shadow map texture.

SOFT SHADOWS

Hard shadows can have a negative effect on the realism of a scene. In nature, shadows can be soft, and in computer graphics, using softened shadows can lead to a more realistic look.

Soft shadows can be computed in a number of ways. One general method is to fake soft shadows by blurring the shadow's contents. In the case of shadow mapping, you can apply a blur to the shadow map texture to give the shadow a softer look. Faking soft shadows in this manner won't give a game physically correct soft shadows, but it is a simple and straightforward solution, especially if performance is an issue.

With projected or shadow volumes, soft shadows can be faked by jittering. Jittering is rendering an object more than once. Each time an object is rendered, it is rendered at a slightly different position, and the results are blended with the previous jitter pass. In the case of a shadow volume, the volume can be moved a little bit and the shadows can be rendered using blending. This, of course, is not efficient or practical in many cases and will not be realistic.

To calculate more realistic soft shadows, we have to use some approximations in video games because soft shadows in reality are a result of light bouncing around the world and reflecting off of many objects extremely quickly. One way to do this is to calculate the umbra and penumbra. The umbra defines the region that is completely in shadow and is fully occluded by some object. The penumbra is the area outside the umbra that gradually softens with distance. The penumbra defines the region that is not fully blocked or visible to the light source. Using shadow volumes as an example, a volume can be created that defines the area of the umbra, and another volume can be created that is the penumbra. Any pixels within the umbra are solid, while the penumbra gradually gets lighter as it moves outward. The volumes for both of these regions depend on the light's position in relation to the object: The closer the object is, the larger the umbra and smaller the penumbra are, while the farther away the source is, the larger the penumbra and smaller the umbra are.

Soft shadows resulting from global illumination are discussed in Chapter 10. Real soft shadows based on the umbra and penumbra can be quite expensive to calculate for an entire scene. Most games fake soft shadows by, for example, blurring the shadow map using an algorithm the game developers feel works best for the game being developed. In most cases, the players will not know that the shadow is soft because it was blurred, unless they are knowledgeable in computer graphics and are playing with the light sources in a way to see if the softness changes dynamically.

LIGHT MAPPING

Light mapping is the use of a texture image and multi-texturing to simulate lighting and shadows. Light maps store lighting gradients for each surface in the scene. When the light map is computed, very expensive lighting and visibility calculations are used to create the texture data. In a video game, the lighting and shadows can be highly realistic at the expense of only being used for static scenes. When the light map is created, the visibility value of the lighting equation is often calculated and contributes to the light map's texture data. An example of light mapping is shown in Figure 9.10.

FIGURE 9.10 No light mapping (left) and light mapping (right).

A light map essentially stores intensities of light, and because of this a light map is often a luminous image. The pixels of a light map that is luminous are called lumels. If a light map is not luminous, for instance, if it stored colors such as color bleeding (discussed in Chapter 10) or if the lights were a different color outside of gray-scale, then it can be an RGB color image.

For rendering light maps, hardware multi-texturing is often used to blend the light map texture with the other material information of a surface (e.g., decal texture, bump map, etc.). Using light maps is the easy part. The difficult part is the calculation of the light map images themselves. Which lighting and shadowing algorithm is used determines how long it takes to calculate the light map. Light map creation is often done as a preprocessing step and usually uses very CPU-expensive calculations to create the detail.

Calculating Light Map Coordinates

Creating a light map starts by creating light map texture coordinates for each surface that is to be light mapped. The purpose of these texture coordinates is to help with the calculation of the light map and to be used in the application when the light maps are applied to the surface. Light map coordinates start out as the vertex's position and are projected into UV texture coordinates to be used during run-time and for the calculation of the light map. Usually, the texture coordinates between light maps and other textures, such as decal images, differ, so light-mapped scenes have multiple texture coordinates for their objects.

The projection of the light map coordinates into UV coordinates can be done using a technique known as planar texture mapping (or some other form of texture coordinate generation). Planar texture mapping projects coordinates onto one of the three coordinate axes. The axis that is used is determined by which axis has the largest absolute value. If the X-axis is the largest value, then the YZ plane is used; if the Y-axis is the largest, then the XZ plane is used; if the Z-axis is the largest, then the XY plane is used. For example, if we are projecting three vertices of a triangle onto the YZ plane, the planar projection would look like the following.

```
// YZ Plane Projection

lightmap_coord[0].u = vertex[0].y;
lightmap_coord[0].v = vertex[0].z;

lightmap_coord[1].u = vertex[1].y;
lightmap_coord[1].v = vertex[1].z;

lightmap_coord[2].u = vertex[2].y;
lightmap_coord[2].v = vertex[2].z;
```

To transform these coordinates to texture-space so that they are between 0 and 1, the minimum and maximum U and V values are determined and the edge (delta) between them is calculated. With this information you need to subtract each vertex of the triangle's coordinate by the minimum value and then divide that by the edge delta to transform it to texture-space. This can look like the following pseudo-code.

```
// Assuming lightmap_coord is an array of Vector2D,
// with one for each vertex.

Vector2D min_coord = min(lightmap_coord);
Vector2D max_coord = max(lightmap_coord);

Vector2D delta = max_coord - min_coord;

// Assuming this is a struct holding U and V...

lightmap_coord[0] -= min_coord;
lightmap_coord[0] /= delta;
```

```
lightmap_coord[1] -= min_coord;
lightmap_coord[1] /= delta;

lightmap_coord[2] -= min_coord;
lightmap_coord[2] /= delta;
```

The next step is to get edge vectors so that the original vertex positions can be interpolated to determine the world-space position of each pixel in the light map image. To do this, we can use the following pseudo-code, where the polygon's plane, a point on the plane (for example, the first vertex of the triangle), and the polygon's normal can be used to get the edge directions between the minimum and maximum UV information that was computed in an earlier pseudo-code example.

```
d = distance(plane, point);

Vector3D minUminV, maxUminV, minUmaxV;

// Polygon normal = n;

minUminV.x = -(n.y * min_coord.u + n.z * min_coord.v + d) / n.x;
minUminV.y = Min_U;
minUminV.z = Min_V;

maxUminV.x = -(n.y * max_coord.u + n.z * min_coord.v + d) / n.x;
maxUminV.y = Max_U;
maxUminV.z = Min_V;

minUmaxV.x = -(n.y * min_coord.u + n.z * max_coord.v + d) / n.x;
minUmaxV.y = Min_U;
minUmaxV.z = Max_V;

Vector3D edge1 = maxUminV - minUminV;
Vector3D edge2 = minUmaxV - minUminV;
```

Calculating Lumels of a Light Map

Once each of the light map UV coordinates and the edge vectors are calculated, the light map texture image can be created. This is done by looping through the width and height of the desired light map and interpolating the vertex positions of the triangle. This gives us the world-space position for each light map pixel. With this world space position and normal, which can be the polygon's normal, it is possible to perform lighting. This can be done using the Lambert diffuse lighting model that was first discussed in Chapter 8. In a real game, it would be more beneficial to use a much more expensive algorithm such as radiosity, but in this chapter, we use the Lambert diffuse model as a simple example so we can focus on how to create the light map rather than on the lighting and shadowing algorithms. Technically, you can use any lighting model you want for the light map.

When you calculate the lighting, a ray from the light map pixel toward the light sources can be calculated, and the resulting ray can be used to test for visibility. This allows simple shadows to form. Again, most games use more expensive and complex lighting and shadowing solutions for light mapping, which is discussed in Chapter 10. The pseudocode for the creation of the light map image data can be seen as follows.

```
const int lightmap_width = lightmap_height = 16;
const int max_lights = 32;

Color3 lightmap_image[lightmap_width * lightmap_height];
Light lights[max_lights];


for(int y_index = 0; y_index < lightmap_height; y_index++)
{
   for(int x_index = 0; x_index < lightmap_width; x_index++)
   {
      // edge1 and edge2 were computed in an
      // earlier pseudo-code example.

      // Example: edge2 * (y_index / lightmap_height) gives
      // us a value between 0 and 1.

      Vector3D edge1a = edge1 * (x_index / lightmap_width);
      Vector3D edge2a = edge2 * (y_index / lightmap_height);

      // minUminV is from the previous pseudo-code example.
      // Used to get interpolated position.

      Vector3D lightmap_pos = minUminV + edge2a + edge1a;

      // Loop through all lights and get their contributions.

      for(int l_index = 0; l_index < max_lights; l_index++)
      {
         Color3 color = Color3(0, 0, 0);
```

```
    // Visibility allows for shadows to form.
    // Global illumination will create better soft shadows.

    if(VisibleToLight(lightmap_pos) == true)
    {
        Vector3D light_vec = lights[l_index].pos - lightmap_pos;
        light_vec.Normalize();

        // Lambert diffuse.  n is the polygon normal.
        diffuse = Dot3(n, light_vec);

        // Assumes this light is a directional light.
        // i.e., no attenuation is used in this example.

        color += lights[l_index].color * diffuse;
    }
}

    // Would cap to 255 unless allow HDR light maps.

    lightmap_image[x_index][y_index] = color;
    }
}

SaveToFile(lightmap_image, "lightmap.dds");
```

ON THE CD

On the CD-ROM is a demo application called Light Mapping that demonstrates how to perform light mapping in OpenGL and Direct3D 9 and 10. The demos use Lambert diffuse lighting from Chapter 8. In Chapter 10, we discuss much more complex and advanced lighting and shadowing algorithms that can be used in light mapping instead of something like the Lambert model, which is more than suitable for real-time rendering. The power of light mapping comes from using it for the representation of lighting and shadowing using algorithms that are far too complex for real-time graphics hardware. In this chapter, we use a simple lighting model to demonstrate that the light maps were created correctly.

Note that in a game, it is common to batch light map textures into texture atlases to make rendering with them more efficient. If the scene of a gaming level was split up using a data structure such as a binary space partitioning (BSP) tree, for example, then each BSP tree node can have its own light map. BSP trees are discussed in more detail in Chapter 15 "Optimizations."

DEFERRED SHADING

Deferred shading is a method of shading a scene that makes the number of lights irrelevant or not as important when rendering the scene. Outside of deferred shading, a scene's lighting is done by rendering all geometry for a single light. Multiple lights can be calculated in one shader, but the number of registers that are available is very limited, which limits the number of lights. In addition, this is a challenge because the number of lights that affect an object might change from object to object. Another issue deals with the calculations themselves because if many lights are needed, there must be enough instructions available for the shader to execute. For earlier shader models, this instruction count is severely limited. If a multipass approach is taken, the scene will need to be rendered once for each light, which is highly inefficient for most game scenes, especially for a large number of visible lights.

The idea behind deferred shading is to shade the scene after it has been rendered. This works by rendering the information necessary for a scene to an off-screen buffer known as the G-buffer. The G-buffer stores the rendered positions, normals, and other attributes of the rendered geometry. This information is used during a later stage to shade the pixels of the scene, for example, by rendering quads to the screen that represent the area of influence of a visible light source. Generally speaking, this makes the cost of rendering a light, using a quad as an example, the same as the cost of rendering two triangles instead of the cost of rendering the entire scene. Rendering the 2D screen-space quad to the screen the pixel shader uses the G-buffer and the light's information to shade the pixels that make up the region correctly. If 100 small light sources are visible, the cost, polygon-wise, of rendering these lights is only 200 triangles, which is very small by today's standards. If the lights are large, this can start to affect the fill rate, like it would for many directional lights, but for most point or spot lights, this is not always an issue.

Creating the G-Buffer for Deferred Shading

The format of the G-buffer is very important because it determines the precision and quality of the information that it can store. If one rendering target is used for the G-buffer, many bits per component will be needed to hold all of the common information. One hundred and twenty-eight bits for each four components might give a lot of precision, but it also might be wasteful. Not only is it wasteful, but performance can suffer when rendering to such a large buffer, not to mention the amount of video memory necessary to store the information on the graphics hardware.

A common solution is to use multiple rendering targets (MRTs) for deferred shading. With MRTs, developers can create one rendering target to hold all of the positions, one for the normals, another for the decal colors (e.g., those read from textures), and so forth. MRTs make it possible to render to multiple rendering targets at the same time in a pixel shader so that multipass rendering is not necessary. This can lead to performance benefits over trying to use one extremely large format for a single rendering target buffer. It must be noted that some hardware might not be able to create G-buffers past a certain size, so using multiple rendering targets that are of a common size (for example, 32 bits) can scale better.

Using MRTs requires that each buffer use the same bit depth. This can be a challenge because a balance must be maintained to get the best results and performance. For example, using 128 bits would provide a lot of precision for positions and normals, but what about colors? Using 128 bits for colors that can be stored in 32 bits is excessive. The same is true for the reverse situation, where the positions and normals will not have enough bits but the color buffer will.

The format that is used depends on the application and the needs of the developer. Using positions, normals, and colors as an example, it is possible to use 32-bit rendering targets for the job if the quality is acceptable. Using 32 bits for colors is no different than what is usually done for RGBA images. For normals this might not be enough precision, but one option can be to use the first 16 bits for the X and the next 16 bits for the Y. That way, the Z-axis can be calculated on the fly, allowing a little more precision, which might be acceptable. As for the position, the 32 bits can be used to store the depth of the rendered position. That way, the world-space position can be calculated using the view vector and the depth value, allowing for some increased quality instead of trying to fit the components of a position in 32 bits.

Rendering with the G-buffer

Filling in the G-buffer is straightforward. The following steps are used to fill in the G-buffer using MRTs.

1. Bind all buffers that are used to represent the G-buffer.
2. Render the scene without color writes. Store the necessary information in the correct render target of the G-buffer that corresponds to it.
3. Return to rendering to the back buffer.
4. Bind the G-buffer textures to the texture units of the API.
5. For every light, render a 2D quad that represents the area of influence for it.

The shader these lights use depends on the light source type. Shaders can exist to render directional lights, point lights, spot lights, or, if branching is used (discussed in Chapter 15, "Optimization"), it might be possible to use one uber shader and use conditional statements to determine what type of light is rendered.

The quad can be calculated by transforming the bounding rectangle of a light source and its area of influence to screen-space. For directional lights, the entire screen is used, so the area of influence will not need to be calculated. Another option instead of creating a quad is to create a bounding box or sphere and render it around the light source. That way, the shader that is used only examines pixels that make up the bounding box or sphere, and the pixels within that range are lit properly.

Deferred shading is fairly straightforward if the hardware supports multiple rendering targets. The trick is to choose the best bit depth. Because of the nature of deferred shading, it is difficult to render multiple types of materials at the same time. In most deferred shaded scenes, only one type of material is used. In some games, this is not a problem, but in others it can be.

ON THE CD

On the CD-ROM in the Chapter 9 folder are demo applications called Deferred Shading for each of the supported APIs covered of this book. These demos create many different directional light sources and render a 3D scene using the technique. The demo uses multiple 32-bit rendering targets to create the G-buffer.

SUMMARY

Shadows are an important part of realistically rendering 3D gaming environments. Shadows are not free in video games, and rendering techniques exist to create them. Performing shadowing in a scene that is already being lit efficiently in real time is not always a trivial task for game developers.

This chapter discussed common shadowing techniques and additional lighting topics in detail. In video game graphics, no one technique is perfect for all situations because each technique has its own strengths and weaknesses. Through experimentation and planning, it is possible to come up with a hybrid implementation for reading shadows and lighting with acceptable quality in real time.

The following elements were discussed throughout this chapter.

- Shadows in general
- Projection shadows
- Shadow mapping
- Shadow volumes
- Soft shadows
- Light mapping
- Deferred shading

Chapter Questions

Answers to the following chapter review questions can be found in Appendix A.

1. Describe the shadow projection technique. What is the main mathematical object that is used during the rendering of shadows? In pseudo-code, show what this matrix looks like when taking into account a light and a plane's surface.
2. List the methods of rendering projected shadows onto surfaces that are not flat. How can the rendering of a shadow for a complex object be simplified instead of using the original geometry?
3. List at least three pros and three cons of using projection shadows.
4. Describe the shadow volume technique. Describe what has become known as Carmack's reverse.
5. Describe the algorithm for rendering and extruding a silhouette for the rendering of a shadow volume.
6. List at least three pros and three cons of using shadow volumes.
7. What are soft shadows? Describe them in detail.
8. What is the difference between soft and hard shadows? Why is the topic of soft shadows important in video games?
9. What is shadow mapping? Describe the shadow mapping algorithm in detail.
10. How can aliasing artifacts be minimized when rendering shadows using a shadow map?
11. Describe cascading shadow mapping.
12. Describe one technique that can be used to calculate a soft shadow.
13. What is deferred shading? What are its main advantages, and what are its main disadvantages?
14. What is the G-buffer? How is a G-buffer created in computer graphics?
15. If one large buffer is not used for the G-buffer, what alternative exists?
16. Describe light mapping and its use in video game graphics since the early days of 3D games.
17. How are light maps calculated? Describe the general algorithm for creating a light map (not including any specific lighting algorithms).
18. Instead of creating a light map for each surface, what can be done to make working with light maps more efficient?
19. What are the pixels of a luminous light map called?
20. Describe planar texture projections.
21. True or false: Shadows form naturally in computer graphics while lighting a scene.
22. True or false: The shadow-projection matrix is used to project a shadow map onto a scene.

23. True or false: A shadow volume is used to describe geometry that is extruded from an object's silhouette into the scene.
24. True or false: Shadow volumes take advantage of the stencil buffer.
25. True or false: Shadow projection does not allow for self-shadowing.
26. True or false: A soft shadow is a sharp color, usually black, that is blended into the scene.
27. True or false: A light map refers to a texture that is often computed during the preprocessing stage.
28. True or false: A light map and a shadow map are the same thing
29. True or false: Deferred shading refers to shading a scene later rather than sooner.
30. True or false: Deferred shading allows for multiple lighting algorithms to be processed quickly.

CHAPTER EXERCISES

Exercise 1: Build off of the deferred shading demo and add specular lighting and normal mapping.
Exercise 2: Build off of Exercise 1 and add point lighting.
Exercise 3: Build off of Exercise 2 and add spot lights to your deferred shading implementation.

GLOBAL ILLUMINATION TECHNIQUES

In This Chapter

- Overview of Global Illumination
- Ambient Occlusion
- Path Tracing
- Radiosity
- Photon Mapping
- Precomputed Radiance Transfer

When realism is the goal of a rendered scene, it is important to consider many different factors that are used to light and shadow surfaces. This information includes diffuse and specular light contributions, object-to-light visibility, and the interaction of light as it bounces off of surfaces onto other surfaces throughout the scene being rendered.

Throughout this book, lighting was done locally and was directly applied to surfaces based on their relationship to the light. In this chapter we will discuss what is known as global illumination, which is used in computer graphics to increase the rendering quality of a scene by increasing the level of realism used in the lighting and shadowing calculations.

OVERVIEW OF GLOBAL ILLUMINATION

Global illumination attempts to solve the lighting equation for both direct and indirect light sources. In global illumination the light bounces around the scene by striking objects and having part of its energy absorbed while the rest reflected. In computer graphics we do not need to know how much energy is absorbed but rather how much is reflected back into the scene.

Global illumination has always been a very expensive way to compute lighting and shadows in a scene. Because of this, algorithms that are used for global illumination often store the results of their calculations in light maps. Because light maps are used, scenes that use global illumination are static. Dynamic objects in these static scenes often have non-global illumination algorithms executed on them since real-time global illumination isn't quite ready for real-time applications.

Direct Lighting versus Indirect Lighting

Direct lighting is the type of lighting seen in Chapter 8, "Lighting and Materials," where only the surface being rendered and the current light source are evaluated in the equation. This means the visibility and the light bouncing off of nearby objects were not considered. An example of direct lighting in a 3D scene is shown in Figure 10.1.

FIGURE 10.1   Direct lighting only.

With indirect lighting, the surfaces of a scene become light sources themselves. Indirect lighting calculates the light that has reflected off of surfaces onto other surfaces. The distance between the surfaces and the materials of the surfaces determines how much light bleeds onto a surface. Color and light bleeding describes light that has reflected off of one surface and has affected another surface to the point where some of its color can be seen on the new surface. An example of indirect lighting is shown in Figure 10.2.

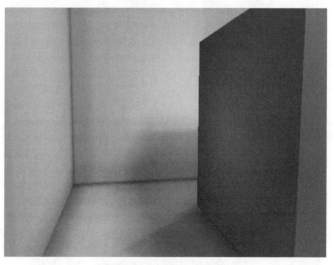

FIGURE 10.2   Indirect lighting.

Global illumination computes direct, indirect, and the geometry and visibility terms of the lighting equation. Both the visibility and geometric terms were discussed in Chapter 8. In the following sections of this chapter we will briefly discuss a few global illumination techniques that are common in computer graphics today.

AMBIENT OCCLUSION

Ambient occlusion is a global illumination technique that is used to define the occlusion amount of a point in a scene. The idea behind ambient occlusion is that each point shoots multiple rays into the scene, and each ray is tested for intersection against all geometry in the scene. The ratio of ray hits and misses is added up and an average is found that represents the occlusion. This number is then multiplied by the ambient light value to give it a more realistic look, which ambient light traditionally lacks. An example of ambient occlusion is shown in Figure 10.3. Ambient occlusion is often calculated by testing a point for occlusion with the scene's geometry, or it can be calculated by looking for occlusions with just the model to which it belongs. This can be used to precalculate the ambient occlusion for soft self-shadowing of a model instead of global occlusion.

 Ambient occlusion calculates a visibility factor (term) that is applied to the ambient light.

FIGURE 10.3   Ambient light (left) and ambient occlusion (right).

In theory, ambient occlusion is a fairly simple technique and can be done on the vertex-level or pixel-level (using light maps, for example). If the ambient occlusion was being performed on the vertex level, each vertex would be evaluated for every mesh in the scene. For each vertex, a defined number of rays are cast in different directions pointing away from the surface. As more rays are used, this often leads to better quality at the expense of increased time to calculate every point's ambient occlusion value. The ambient occlusion value itself is a floating-point value between 0 and 1 (i.e., 0 to 100%), where 0 is fully shadowed, 1 is fully visible, and anything between is a variation of the two extremes.

When calculating ambient occlusion, you simply get the average of how many rays intersect the scene geometry versus those that do not intersect for each point. This is done by generating a set number of rays in a hemisphere around the point being calculated. Because of how ambient occlusion works, it is suited for outdoor or large areas where objects are not always going to be occluded by geometry that doesn't include sky polygons. Since the ambient light is an extremely simple approximation of global fill light from light sources such as the sun, ambient occlusion is used with the ambient term to attenuate the constant color value.

Ambient occlusion creates soft shadows throughout a scene and soft self-shadows on the individual meshes. It is an approximation of the global visibility term that can be multiplied by the light contribution to increase the realism in a scene. More and more games are using ambient occlusion to increase realism in 3D scenes.

Ambient occlusion uses the Monte Carlo method, which is an algorithm that uses random or pseudo-random inputs (in this case the hemisphere of rays) on a set of input points. In other words, the Monte Carlo method relies on a repeated random sampling of input to calculate some output.

Ambient occlusion can be quite expensive to calculate and is usually done as a preprocessing step. Some game developers have developed techniques for performing it or a variation of it in real time, which we'll discuss later on in this chapter.

Alternative Method for Calculating Ambient Occlusion

Ambient occlusion can be calculated using the ray tracing method. Ray tracing, discussed in Chapter 3, "Ray Tracing," is a very effective yet expensive way to calculate values in computer graphics. In pseudo-code, using the ray tracing method can look like the following, assuming that the ambient occlusion is being calculated per vertex:

```
function AmbientOcclusion(Scene scene)
{
    hemisphere = CalculateHemiSphere();

    for each(mesh in scene)
    {
        for each(vertex in mesh)
        {
```

```
        transformed_hemisphere = Orient(vertex.normal, hemisphere);
        hit_count = 0;

        for each(ray in transformed_hemisphere)
        {
          if(Intersect(ray, scene) == true)
          {
            hit_count++;
          }
        }

        vertex.ao = hit_count / transformed_hemisphere.ray_count;
      }
    }
  }
```

Another way to calculate ambient occlusion is to use hardware acceleration. This is typically done by rendering a cube map around a point by rendering polygons as black against a white rendering buffer. The ambient occlusion at that point is essentially the sum of all pixels in the hemi-cube (cube equivalent of the hemisphere) averaged out by taking the weighted average. This can be done by down-sampling the rendering targets until you get to a 1 × 1 down-sample, which stores the average luminance.

A down-sampled rendering target is essentially a smaller resolution of the original. By rendering to down-sampled rendering targets until you get to a rendering target with a width and height of 1, you are left with a single color value that represents the average color value of the original rendering, which in this case can be used as the ambient occlusion value.

Bent Normal

When you use ambient occlusion with diffuse irradiance maps, artifacts can appear on the rendered surfaces. This occurs because the vertex normal might point toward an object that occludes it, and since ambient occlusion takes occlusion values into account, so should the lookup into the diffuse irradiance map.

A diffuse irradiance map is a cube map that stores diffuse lighting colors. If you are using a cube map for diffuse lighting, it is recommended that you use the bent normal when calculating the diffuse term rather than the vertex normal. A bent normal is the average normal of the entire unoccluded ray directions used during the ambient occlusion calculation. The bent normal can be used instead of the vertex normal and can give better results to the rendered scene. The altered pseudo-code for calculating ambient occlusion and calculating the bent normal can be seen in the following example:

```
function AmbientOcclusion(Scene scene)
{
    hemisphere = CalculateHemiSphere();

    for each(mesh in scene)
    {
        for each(vertex in mesh)
        {
            transformed_hemisphere = Orient(vertex.normal, hemisphere);
            hit_count = 0;
            miss_count = 0
            bent_normal = Vector3D(0, 0, 0);

            for each(ray in transformed_hemisphere)
            {
                if(Intersect(ray, scene) == true)
                {
                    hit_count++;
                }
                else
                {
                    bent_normal += ray.direction;
                    miss_count++;
                }
            }

            bent_normal /= miss_count;
            bent_normal.Normalize();

            vertex.ao = hit_count / transformed_hemisphere.ray_count;
            vertex.bent_normal = bent_normal;
        }
    }
}
```

The bent normal is used for diffuse irradiance maps. With a diffuse irradiance map, the vertex normal is used as the cube map texture coordinate to look up the diffuse color of a point. If you are performing ambient occlusion, it is recommended that you test using the bent normal to see how the final results change. Some of these changes might be minor and harder to detect, while others might appear more obvious.

If a vertex normal is pointing toward occluded geometry, using it with an irradiance map can lead to incorrect lighting since the point is supposed to be occluded by other geometry. The bent normal is a simple way to alter the radiance of a point slightly to limit this, but the bent normal is just an approximation that points in a direction that is closer to where light would be coming from into the point instead of using a normal that could potentially be pointing right at an occluding surface.

Implementing Ambient Occlusion

ON THE CD

On the CD-ROM, in the Chapter 10 folder, is a set of demos for OpenGL, Direct3D 9, and Direct3D 10 that perform ambient occlusion. The demos are called Ambient Occlusion GL, Ambient Occlusion D3D 9, and Ambient Occlusion D3D 10, respectively.

In the ambient occlusion demos on the CD-ROM the ambient occlusion term is calculated on a vertex level. The ambient occlusion term is represented as vertex colors and is passed to the vertex and pixel shaders for rendering. Another option that can be used is to perform the ambient occlusion on the pixel level by using a light map, which was first discussed in Chapter 9, "Advanced Lighting and Shadows."

SSAO

Screen-space ambient occlusion (SSAO) was developed by Crytex and is used in the 2007 game *Crysis*. SSAO is a screen-space technique that calculates ambient occlusion in real time for an entire frame. The benefits of SSAO include the following:

- Does not depend on scene complexity
- Can be done using constant memory
- Can be done using constant time
- Can be added to existing frame works that use programmable shaders

SSAO uses the information in a depth rendering target, which is discussed for the depth-of-field effect in Chapter 12, "Special Effects: Additional Effects," to determine the ambient occlusion factor for each pixel. Generally, the algorithm uses a rendering target to store each depth value for the entire rendered scene. In a postprocessing stage this depth value is used to compute the eye space position of that pixel. Pixels surrounding the current pixel are sampled randomly around a sphere surrounding the current point. The depth values of these points are then compared and used to calculate the ambient occlusion factor. On the plus side, if the depth rendering target is used for other techniques such as depth of field, then the rendering target can be reused effectively multiple times.

One thing to note about this algorithm is that it is entirely in screen space. This means that occluding objects outside of the screen are not considered. Also, the algorithm creates an approximation based on nearby pixels. This means that not only is it not true ambient occlusion, but it only affects pixels that are close to one another, not pixels far apart or surfaces that are not visible. If many pixels are considered in an attempt to make SSAO more accurate, there is still the inevitable performance issue.

Regardless, the technique does offer some impressive results and is used in Crysis to add to the visuals of the rendered scene.

PATH TRACING

Path tracing is an extension of ray tracing that also provides global illumination for a rendered scene. In Chapter 3, we discussed primary, reflected, refracted, and shadow rays, each of which are the main rays used to compute scenes using ray tracing. When using these rays with lighting, it is possible to calculate a scene with direct lighting and shadowing.

Path tracing extends ray tracing by adding rays that are used to gather the contribution of the influences from nearby surfaces so that the indirect lighting for global illumination can be obtained. In the ambient occlusion section earlier in this chapter a hemisphere is used to create rays that are traced throughout the scene to detect the percentage of them that intersects scene geometry. In path tracing the same general idea is used by placing a hemisphere around the original point of intersection and using those new rays to determine how much color from nearby surfaces influences the original point of intersection's color.

The major disadvantage of path tracing is that the rendering times can become substantially longer since many new rays are being generated and traced thousands, if not millions, of times for one rendered image, which is in addition to the original rays used for ray tracing. Also, when performing path tracing, if too few rays are used for the hemisphere of rays, you can end up with what appears as noise in the final image. Noise is rendering artifacts that have fine grains of color throughout the image.

Setting its disadvantages aside, path tracing offers a simple and realistic way to create global illumination in ray tracing. In general, if you have a ray tracer, you already have everything needed for path tracing. The main extension that needs to be made is that for every point of intersection that is found during normal ray tracing, create a number of new rays forming a hemisphere around the point and use those rays to calculate the indirect lighting of nearby surfaces.

Path tracing is a Monte Carlo sampling technique.

Extending the Ray Tracing Algorithm

In Chapter 3, the pseudo-code for backward ray tracing took on the following form:

```
function Backward_RayTracing(scene)
{
   foreach(pixel in image)
   {
      ray = Calculate_Ray(pixel);
      closestObject = null;
      minDist = "Some Large Value";

      foreach(object in scene)
      {
         if(ray->Intersects(object) && object->distance < minDist)
         {
            minDist = object->distance;
            point_of_intersect = ray->Get_Intersection();
            closestObject = object;
         }
      }

      if(closestObject != null)
      {
         foreach(light in scene)
         {
            Shade_Pixel(point_of_intersect, light, closestObject);
         }
      }
   }

   Save_Render("output.jpg");
}
```

The pseudo-code for path tracing that extends the backward ray tracing example can be seen in the following:

```
function PathTracing(scene)
{
   foreach(pixel in image)
   {
      ray = Calculate_Ray(pixel);
      closestObject = null;
      minDist = "Some Large Value";

      foreach(object in scene)
      {
         if(ray->Intersects(object) && object->distance < minDist)
         {
            minDist = object->distance;
            point_of_intersect = ray->Get_Intersection();
            closestObject = object;
         }
      }

      if(closestObject != null)
      {
         foreach(light in scene)
         {
            Shade_Pixel(point_of_intersect, light, closestObject);
         }

         Hemisphere = CreateHemisphereAround(point_of_intersection);

         foreach(ray in hemisphere)
         {
            AddClosestIntersectedObjectColor(ray, scene);
         }
      }
   }

   Save_Render("output.jpg");
}
```

When you perform path tracing, some attenuation is used for nearby surfaces so that color influence from a close object is stronger than that of a farther away object. In the pseudo-code example the function AddClosestIntersectedObjectColor() traces through the scene again, gets the color of the closest intersected object, then attenuates that color by distance and adds the results to the point we were originally shading. If many samples around the hemisphere are used, this can give a path tracer a great deal of realism while increasing the rendering time dramatically. Attenuation was first discussed with point lights in Chapter 8.

RADIOSITY

Radiosity is a very popular global illumination algorithm used to solve the lighting equation for diffuse surfaces. Radiosity in computer graphics was developed in 1984 by Goral, Torrance, and Greenberg of Cornel University. The main idea behind radiosity is that light leaves the original light source and is transferred throughout the scene. The light that a surface receives is also transferred throughout the scene to calculate the indirect lighting of global illumination. In 3D video games radiosity is used for diffuse surfaces since the diffuse term is view-independent and can be precalculated and stored by an offline tool, unlike the specular term, which is view dependent and is calculated in real time in games.

Radiosity has been used in the game industry for quite some time. One popular game that used it is *Half-Life 2*, which stores the results in light maps, a common practice for any global illumination algorithm used in video games.

Radiosity is used to represent the direct and indirect lighting of surfaces throughout the scene. Since indirect lighting is used, soft shadows and light and color bleeding are common features of scenes rendered with the radiosity algorithm.

Radiosity is an algorithm that simulates the transference of energy (i.e., light) between diffuse surfaces of a scene.

Calculating Radiosity

In theory, radiosity is a very simple global illumination technique. The scene is divided up into what are known as patches. To aid in the visualization, imagine that these scene patches are simply the scene represented by many small polygons. In other words, a patch is essentially a polygon. The algorithm works by taking a small amount of energy from the light sources throughout the scene and transferring that energy between all of the patches of the scene. That is known as the first bounce in progressive radiosity, a type of radiosity. During the second and additional rendering bounces, the light is transferred not only from the original light sources to the patches but also from the patch to patch. During progressive radiosity the amount of energy that is transferred is usually very small and adds up over the additional iterations (bounces). Eventually, after a certain number of bounces, the amount of energy added by additional bounces can become negligible. When light is transferred, the value leaving a surface is equal to the light that has come into the surface multiplied by a reflection property of the material's surface.

In radiosity everything is considered a light source, and every surface can potentially light another surface. No distinction is made between light sources and patches at this level. During the first bounce the only patches with energy are the original light sources or surfaces that have been set up as light emitters (e.g., the polygons of light bulbs, the polygons of the sky dome, etc.). Therefore the patches that make up the scene's geometry that are not original light sources have a starting light energy of 0. During the transfer of lighting from the light sources into the scene, you are literally looping through the patches, or in this example, the polygons, and are calculating how much energy the patch is receiving from the light source (i.e., how bright it is). This includes the visibility term that describes whether the patch sees the light source, determining the angle the patch is from the light source (which is commonly done using N dot L in diffuse lighting, for example) and calculating the differential angles, which is done by finding the dot products between the vector of the two surfaces and the surface normals and then determining the difference between them.

The combined properties and terms that describe a patch's relationship between it and another patch are known as a form factor. A form factor takes into account the distance, angle (differential angle), geometric relationship, and visibility one patch has in relation to another. When calculating the relationship between patches, it is possible to create a table, essentially a 2D array, that stores the form factor relationships between the patches on time before the radiosity calculations begin. This is commonly known as a radiosity matrix.

For large scenes the radiosity matrix can grow so huge that its memory requirements become an issue. A radiosity matrix for a scene with N number of patches has a size of N2. It is possible to calculate form factors when they are needed instead of creating the radiosity matrix. This avoids the memory requirements of one large table in favor of calculating these terms each time they are needed. Since radiosity is a preprocessing technique done using an offline tool in computer graphics, it might not be an issue if a tool spends extra processing time due to the overhead of always having to recalculate terms. This is especially true for scenes that are so large that the radiosity matrix memory requirements must be considered.

 One of the main purposes of progressive radiosity is to allow results to show without needing to calculate the full radiosity solution progressively. This is also known as the progressive refinement method.

Form Factors

In radiosity we calculate the form factor, which is a single floating-point value that represents the relationship between two patches, and we calculate a patch's incident and emissive value. Incident light is light coming into a patch from other patches, and emissive light is light leaving the patch in the direction of another patch in the scene.

The form factor, which is the relationship between two patches that are currently being examined, is multiplied by the patch's incident light value to calculate its emissive light to another patch. Therefore, if a patch is not receiving light, it is not giving light. One way of looking at this is to consider how diffuse lighting works in general. In diffuse lighting you can think of the N dot L equation as a type of simplified form factor that describes the relationship between a surface and a light, which is multiplied by the light and surface color to create the final emissive (output) color that is actually rendered. We use the term *simplified form factor* because in the real-time diffuse lighting algorithms we discussed in Chapter 8, the fact that other surfaces don't act as light sources is not taken into consideration. Form factors in radiosity are far more complex and are not as simple as calculating N dot L. Keep in mind that the term *form factor* represents a value that takes into account the geometric, visibility, and physical relationship between patches that is used to determine how much energy is transferred between the two patches.

When you calculate radiosity for a scene, the patches need to be small for quality purposes because large surfaces do not distribute lighting as well, can cause aliasing artifacts, and do not distribute light to surfaces with smaller areas well. In 3D scenes large polygons are often subdivided into smaller polygons for the radiosity calculation. This can increase the memory requirements considerably by dynamically increasing the polygon count. If a radiosity matrix is used, this is additional memory overhead that cannot be ignored, especially for the high polygonal scenes we see in animated movies such as *Shrek*. Therefore, instead of subdividing patches, light map pixels can be used as the patches. That way, the quality depends not on the polygon count and polygon area size but on the light map resolution. It also means that you do not have to deal with subdivision of large polygons because the artifacts are now caused by texture resolution when using light maps. If you don't use light maps to store the calculated colors but instead you choose to store it at the vertex level, then you'll have to deal with subdivision or risk a decrease in graphical quality.

 Radiosity was first developed in the 1950s by engineers working in thermometry.

Implementing Radiosity

Let's assume you have a scene that is to have its illumination stored in a light map. The light map is set up (discussed in Chapter 9), and the light map pixels are considered the patches. Progressive radiosity is used to transfer the light that exists in the scene throughout the scene. In other words, you loop through the patches, and for each patch you create an inner loop that loops through all patches (except the current patch since a patch can't light itself), calculate its relationship (form factor) with the second patch, combine the color from the surface emitting light by this form factor, and store it in the patch (second patch) receiving the light. Once you've done this for all patches, you have completed a single bounce. The number of bounces used depends on what quality you are after. In progressive radiosity the first bounce often has the scene looking dark, while additional bounces tend to brighten up the scene. Usually, once a certain number of bounces have been completed, additional bounces won't affect the scene and would therefore be considered unnecessary. There is no one universal number of bounces, and in progressive radiosity it is possible to view the results after each bounce until the scene is lit satisfactorily.

Although radiosity has traditionally been viewed as a difficult algorithm to understand, in reality its theory is fairly straightforward. The real difficulty for those without the math background lies in the mathematics of calculating the form factor. If you assume that the polygons of a scene are considered the patches, and if you assume that subdivision does not need to occur (to make the example easy to visualize), then a simple radiosity algorithm consists of looping through the patches and calculating the lighting between them by combining its form factor with the outgoing light from surface A and storing it in surface B. In pseudo-code this can take on the following form using the example that assumes subdivision is not necessary and the polygons are acting as the patches:

```
function Radiosity(scene, total_bounces)
{
    // Assumes that all patches that are original light sources
    // has their incident term set to its starting energy level.

    // Also this assumes the light sources are represented as
    // geometry in the scene, such as a sky dome for example.

    for(bounce = 0; bounce < total_bounces; bounce++)
    {
        foreach(polygon_a in scene)
        {
            foreach(polygon_b in scene)
```

```
            {
                // Remember a patch can't light itself.
                if(polygon_a == polygon_b)
                    skip;

                factor = CalculateFormFactor(polygon_a, polygon_b);

                polygon_a.emissive = polygon_a.incident *
                                        polygon_a.reflectivity;

                polygon_b.incident = polygon_a.emissive * factor;

                polygon_a.color += polygon_a.emissive;
            }
        }
    }
}
```

Using progressive radiosity, you can build the color for a patch through iterations. When calculating the visibility term, you can use a single ray between the patches and test for intersection with the scene, but this leads to hard shadows. To create soft shadows, many rays can be used surrounding the hemisphere around the patch. This is similar to what is done for ambient occlusion, and the use of multiple rays turns the visibility term from a Boolean flag to a percentage of occlusion.

The visibility term can add a tremendous amount of calculation time to your algorithms, To give you a quick example, I once developed a tool to calculate global illumination using spherical harmonics a number of years ago, which will be discussed later in this chapter. The original implementations did not use any optimizations and were more of a learning experience at the time than anything else. The test scene consisting of just under 8,000 polygons using the un-shadowed diffuse spherical harmonics algorithm (with 100×100 coefficient samples) took only a few minutes. When the visibility term was added to create soft shadows, the same scene took over 8 hours to fully compute. Waiting eight hours to calculate the lighting and shadowing of a scene with essentially four objects, without even considering indirect lighting (known as spherical harmonics inter-reflections), was simply out of the question. I decided to use an octree (discussed in Chapter 15, "Optimization") to speed up the ray intersection test by quickly rejecting as many tests as possible. This reduced the 8 hour calculation time to just under 12 minutes. Although the code was far from optimized other than quickly throwing together an octree into the sample, it is clear that the visibility term, if left unchecked, can cause calculation times that are unacceptable, even for an offline tool. Therefore, it is important to understand data structures that can be used to speed up calculations such as octrees, BSP trees, and so on, if implementing a global illumination algorithm that uses expensive visibility term calculations. For my simple scene of four objects, I would have had to wait over 8 hours just to add shadows, but what if the scene was as complex as the scenes in modern video games? What if the scene was as complex as scenes seen in animated movies such as *Shrek*?

Currently, a lot of research is being done in real-time radiosity. Because of the way radiosity works, many researchers are attempting to use hardware acceleration with the Z-buffer to perform radiosity in real time. Radiosity is a very expensive algorithm to compute, but advances in hardware are getting researchers closer to their goal of real-time calculations with every generation that passes. Most variations of real-time radiosity render the scene from a patch into a hemi-cube and use the rendering results as a fast way to attempt to gather the incoming illumination for that patch.

PHOTON MAPPING

Photon mapping is another technique that extends the ray tracing algorithm to incorporate global illumination of a scene. Photon mapping is a two-pass technique in which the first pass is used to build the photon map and the second uses the photon map to illuminate the scene.

The photon map is not an image as its name implies. A photon map is a data structure, often implemented as a kd-tree. The photon map is used to store the entire direct and indirect illumination of a scene so that the second pass can use that when shading the pixels of the final rendered image.

The *kd*-Tree

A *kd*-tree is a binary tree data structure with *k* dimensional keys in it. In the binary tree data structure each node is made up of a key and two child nodes. Usually this key is a single value (i.e., single dimension), but with a *kd*-tree it can be made up of multiple values for a single key, such as a 3D vector.

A *kd*-tree can be used for range searches, nearest neighbor searches, space partitioning, and so forth. Using a range of values for a single key allows a *kd*-tree to find all nodes that fall within that range or that match it. Thus, for example, if we wanted to look for a range of values that is a close or exact match to the 3D vector (20, 4, 85), we could use this data structure for a fast way to compute it.

In photon mapping the *k*d-tree is used to store the color of a tracing for each location a photon strikes (which will be discussed in the next section). During the second pass of the photon-mapping technique when rendering the image, the point of intersection is used as the search key, and the element in the photon map that is closest to that point is used.

For more information about *k*d-trees, refer to the book *Data Structures and Algorithms for Game Developers* (Charles River Media).

Calculating Photon Maps

The calculation of a photon map is performed in the first rendering pass. During this pass rays are traced from the light source into the scene, and they bounce around until a certain condition is met. This is similar to combining path tracing with forward ray tracing.

As each ray leaves each light, it bounces off of surfaces. Every time a ray, which is called a photon in photon mapping, strikes a surface, a small amount of its energy is left at that point before it is bounced back into the scene. This continues until a recursive depth level is met, until a photon has no more energy, or based on whatever condition meets your needs.

In forward ray tracing the direct lighting is used to render the scene. In path tracing a hemisphere of rays is created for each point of intersection during the normal ray tracing algorithm, and the rays are allowed to bounce around to gather the indirect contributions of nearby surfaces for each point of intersection. In photon mapping rays leave the light and bounce around the scene. Each time they bounce off of a surface, that point of intersection and the amount of color striking that point are stored in the *k*d-tree. Before reflecting back into the scene, the photon absorbs a small amount of the color of that surface as well. This continues until all rays have been traced from all lights. Once the photon map is created, it is ready for the second and final rendering pass.

Applying Photon Maps to a Ray-Traced Scene

The second pass of the photon mapping technique uses normal ray tracing to render the scene. The difference in photon mapping is that the point of intersection of each ray strike is used as the search key into the photon map (*k*d-tree) to retrieve the color that point should have. This color after the first pass represents the direct and indirect contributions of that point. The nearest-neighbor searching algorithm is used for the *k*d-tree since the points of intersection might not match 100% to the photo hit locations from the first pass.

To review photon mapping, you start by tracing many rays from each light source of the scene. Every time a ray (which is called a photon) hits a surface, the color that is calculated is stored at that point of intersection in the photon map (*k*d-tree), which happens for each ray bounce. A bounce simply means reflecting off of surfaces. Once a ray has bounced its maximum number of bounces (used to avoid infinite loops or to limit calculations for performance) or until there is no more energy in the photon, it is done and we move on to the next ray. This happens for all rays of a light and for all lights of a scene. When you are done, you have the photon map. The second pass requires you to perform ray tracing as usual, but when a ray hits a surface, you use the point of intersection to look up the color that will be used in the photon map.

Photon maps are very expensive to calculate because not only are many rays being traced from each light source, but expensive calculations are being done on the colors. This includes lighting, caustics, anti-aliasing, reflections, refractions, and any other material properties you choose to support. Even after the photon map is done, the image still has to be rendered using ray tracing of its own, which was already expensive itself.

On the up side, photon mapping allows polygonal and nonpolygonal surfaces to be used within the same scene without any compatibility issues and can extend ray tracing to solve for the entire lighting equation for many types of materials. Photon mapping is also good with materials such as smoke and fog and the interactions light has with them.

PRECOMPUTED RADIANCE TRANSFER

Precomputed radiance transfer is an algorithm that precomputes the radiance information of a scene so that it can be used during an application in a separate phase. Scenes that are rendered using area light sources (for example, outdoor sunlight) can have a lot of their information precomputed offline so you can avoid having to attempt to calculate them in real time, which is not practical for complex algorithms based on global illumination. During run-time this information is often used to render scenes efficiently using the encoded complex lighting solutions.

In this chapter we will briefly discuss spherical harmonics for lighting for those without much of a background in mathematics. Spherical harmonics is a form of precomputed radiance transfer and has been used in computer graphics over the past few years.

Overview of Spherical Harmonics

Spherical harmonics in computer graphics is a way to encode a scene's lighting using area light sources in a way that can be decoded in real time using basic mathematical operators such as adding and multiplying coefficients together. Spherical harmonics have many uses in mathematics, but recently the technique has been applied to computer graphics to encode and represent highly realistic and complex lighting information.

Spherical harmonics for lighting works by projecting the lighting information into the spherical harmonics basis, which is expensive and is done using a preprocessing tool offline. Because the information is precomputed and stored for run-time use, it is often used to store diffuse lighting information for 3D game scenes. The information can be stored on the per-vertex or per-pixel level. Per-vertex spherical harmonics lighting looks great, as you will see later in this chapter, because the interpolation of color values between vertex points using an API such as OpenGL or Direct3D is enough to approximate the lighting of many different types of surfaces.

The major advantage to using spherical harmonics is that in run-time, using the coefficients that were calculated offline, you can apply lighting and shadows to a 3D scene using hardware performance that is comparable to rendering objects with vertex colors. We'll see how this is done in an upcoming section in this chapter.

Three types of methods of spherical harmonics are used for lighting a scene. In the first method the spherical harmonic coefficients are calculated and are used to encode the diffuse lighting model. This method is commonly known as spherical harmonics diffuse un-shadowed because there is only diffuse light, with no shadowing or indirect light.

In the second type of spherical harmonics the visibility term is added along with the geometric term to account for occluded surfaces. In other words, rays are traced by the spherical harmonic samples into the scene to test if an object is in shadow or not. This is known as spherical harmonics diffuse shadowed, and it builds directly off of the un-shadowed version.

The third type of spherical harmonics used for lighting builds off of the second type and adds to the rendering equation the indirect lighting contributions from nearby surfaces. Like the calculation for the visibility term, this step is usually done using old fashion ray tracing. Taking into account the indirect light of a scene makes the third form a global illumination model for lighting known commonly as spherical harmonics diffuse inter-reflected. This step is usually done after the second step has completely finished, while the second step is added directly into the algorithm of the first. This means you can calculate the indirect light after you have finished calculating the scene's direct lighting.

Calculating Spherical Harmonics Data

The most difficult part of spherical harmonics for lighting is the mathematics behind the calculation of the spherical harmonic coefficients and samples. Spherical harmonics allows for a way to store all the light that reaches a point over a hemisphere. Since this can lead to a tremendous amount of information, spherical harmonics also offers a way to compress that information into a more compact form.

Information is compressed by using a basis function to create a compact representation of information, which in this case is the spherical harmonic transfer function. In general, the basis function used depends on what type of information you are trying to represent. Let's say you have 1,000 pieces of information (exactly what is irrelevant at this moment) that you can represent more compactly using 50 pieces of information. To manipulate this information to create some desired output, you only need to work with the compact representation of 50 pieces of information, not the original 1,000. The compact pieces of information are known as the coefficients and, performance-wise, this difference can be huge. This is the purpose of spherical harmonics—to take an entire hemisphere of light around a point in 3D space and represent it in a way that is more compact.

Spherical harmonics in computer graphics is a set of basis functions used to encode light. Coefficients are used to scale the basic function to closely recreate the original information. Complex information can be represented as different basis functions if necessary. In lighting, the goal is to use spherical harmonics to compress a hemisphere of light. In spherical harmonics we use spherical coordinates to represent a point over a unit sphere.

Spherical Harmonics Un-Shadowed

ON THE CD

As mentioned previously, the hardest part of spherical harmonics is encoding the lighting data. Unfortunately, understanding the complex math requires a great deal of background information that is beyond the scope of this book. On the CD-ROM in the Chapter 10 folder is a demo application called SH Diffuse Un-Shadowed that demonstrates performing spherical harmonics, without shadowing, in a graphical application for readers who are comfortable with the mathematics.

Once you have the coefficient information, it is easy to use it in a gaming application. Assuming that you already have the coefficients for an object's vertex and the spherical harmonic coefficient samples, to calculate the vertex color you just need to loop through the coefficients, multiply them together, and sum the results. This is shown in Listing 10.1 from the SH Diffuse Un-Shadowed demo, where the coefficients are represented as three values in a Vector3D object.

LISTING 10.1 SUMMING THE COEFFICIENTS TO CALCULATE THE VERTEX COLOR

```
Vector3D ShLighting(Vector3D *coeffs, Vector3D *vertexCoeffs,
                    int totalCoeffs, double scale)
{
    Vector3D col;

    for(int i = 0; i < totalCoeffs; i++)
    {
        col.x += coeffs[i].x * vertexCoeffs[i].x * scale;
        col.y += coeffs[i].y * vertexCoeffs[i].y * scale;
        col.z += coeffs[i].z * vertexCoeffs[i].z * scale;
    }

    return col;
}
```

Since scenes with their lighting encoded using spherical harmonics are often static, you can use the function from Listing 10.1 to calculate the vertex colors once and apply them to the object as it is saved to a file. That way you can have full lighting and shadowing in your scene that executes as fast as rendering geometry, using nothing more than vertex colors. No light maps are needed unless you plan on storing this information in the pixel-level and this requires no complex shaders other than just outputting the interpolated vertex color as the pixel color's output. A screenshot of the demo application is shown in Figure 10.4.

FIGURE 10.4 Spherical harmonics diffuse un-shadowed.

Spherical Harmonics Shadowed

The second type of spherical harmonics we will discuss adds soft shadows to the algorithm. In theory and in implementation this is fairly straight-forward if you have already implemented spherical harmonics un-shadowed. An example of spherical harmonics diffuse shadowed is shown in Figure 10.5.

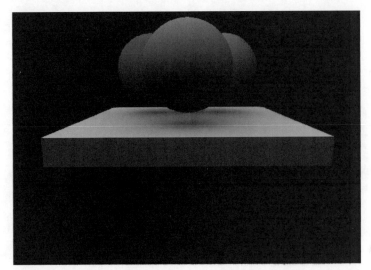

FIGURE 10.5   An example of spherical harmonics diffuse shadowed.

To add soft shadows to the algorithm, you only need to take the ray for each spherical sample that is being used to calculate the lighting coefficient and test that ray for intersection throughout the scene. This test will result in a Boolean value for each sample. Since the samples combine to create the color of the vertices, and since each vertex has a large number of samples, soft shadows naturally form as a result of this because we are dealing with a hemisphere of light, so the visibility is combined to create a result similar to ambient occlusion, minus the ambient part.

Spherical Harmonics Inter-Reflected

The next type of spherical harmonics for lighting adds indirect lighting to the algorithm, thus making it a global illumination technique. This algorithm is known as spherical harmonics inter-reflected lighting, and it is performed after the diffuse-shadowed method.

As with all indirect lighting methods discussed in this chapter, the idea is to take a small amount of color from nearby triangles and apply it to the surfaces to account for indirect light. The steps to perform spherical harmonics inter-reflected are as follows.

1. Perform spherical harmonics using the diffuse shadowed method. You can use diffuse un-shadowed, but then you will not have the shadows in the final lighting result.
2. Loop through the vertices of the scene and trace a hemisphere of rays from each vertex into the scene. For each ray hit, take the spherical harmonics coefficients of all of the triangle vertices at the point of intersection using barycentric coordinates and use them as the light contribution.
3. Scale the light contribution by the dot product of the triangle's normal that was intersected with the ray's direction. Scale this by the total number of samples.
4. Doing this for all vertices is considered one bounce of inter-reflected light. As with progressive radiosity, you can perform a number of bounces to get the desired quality.

SUMMARY

Global illumination is a very important topic for computer graphics. In video games global illumination is often preprocessed and used during run-time to create scenes that look highly realistic. Usually, these results are stored in light maps, which have long been a popular way to light and shadow scenes using complex methods such as global illumination.

The following elements were discussed throughout this chapter.

- Global illumination in general
- Ambient occlusion
- Path tracing
- Radiosity
- kd-trees
- Photon mapping
- Spherical harmonics

CHAPTER QUESTIONS

Answers to the following chapter review questions can be found in Appendix A, "Answers to Chapter Questions."

1. What is global illumination?
2. What is the purpose of global illumination in video games?
3. Define direct lighting.
4. Define indirect lighting.
5. What is ambient occlusion?

6. How does ambient occlusion increase the quality of rendered objects?
7. What form of ambient occlusion does the game *Crysis* use?
8. Generally describe radiosity.
9. What is path tracing?
10. How does path tracing differ from traditional ray tracing?
11. Generally describe photon mapping.
12. Which tree data structure is often used for photon mapping?
13. Describe precomputed radiance transfer in general.
14. What is one technique (mentioned in this book) that can be used to calculate precomputed radiance transfer?
15. What type of texture image is usually used for storing the pre-processed information of a globally illuminated scene?

CHAPTER EXERCISES

Exercise 1: Modify one of the ambient occlusion demos to calculate and apply ambient occlusion using a light map.

Exercise 2: Extend the basic ray tracer from Chapter 3 to include path tracing as described in this chapter.

SPECIAL EFFECTS

SPECIAL EFFECTS: HIGH DYNAMIC RANGE

In This Chapter

- Overview of HDR
- Implementing HDR
- HDR Special Effects and Additional Topics

Ａs information moves through the rendering pipeline, it is affected by the different stages that operate on it. During the rendering pipeline data can be lost, and the lack of precision with the rendering buffer formats can cause artifacts to be seen on the final rendered result. These artifacts can be amplified by using effects such as in-game lighting, which can cause rendered objects to not look as good as they can because of the color contrast and other issues associated with using low color ranges like what has been done up until this point in the book. Recently, the importance of working with a higher range of values and precision in video games has emerged and is quickly becoming standard.

The purpose of this chapter is to discuss high–dynamic range (HDR) rendering in terms of what it is, how it is used, and its importance in modern video games. HDR rendering is fast becoming a standard feature in many realistic 3D video games, especially first-person shooters such as *Halo 3*, *Crysis*, *Splinter Cell: Conviction*, and *Project Gotham Racing*. It is important to understand what high–dynamic range rendering in computer and game graphics is.

OVERVIEW OF HDR

Traditionally, in computer games the graphics used unsigned 8-bits for the color range. This gives games the ability to store up to 256 different values for each color component, ranging from 0 to 255. In games this range of values was enough to represent many of the scenes that existed in top-of-the-line video games. Today, as gaming graphics evolves, so does the amount of precision and range that is required to retain quality in the effects that are used.

Eight-bit values used in the traditional range allowed for a 256:1 contrast ratio. HDR is used to surpass that to preserve detail.

Graphics in the past used what can be referred to as low–dynamic range (LDR) rendering. This means there is a low range of possible values for each component. While working with colors, this book has mostly used 8-bit unsigned char variables, especially when loading image data from a TGA or DDS file. With HD resolutions and more complex and realistic graphics algorithms being performed in games, using only 256 values for each color component does not give a large enough range of colors to retain enough quality for many game scenes. Graphics have long been a major selling factor in video games, and HDR rendering can be used to help increase a game's graphics if used properly and efficiently.

What Is HDR?

In games, HDR rendering starts with using a texture format for the rendering buffers that utilize a higher range than 8-bit variables. This is commonly done by using floating-point formats. By using floating-point buffers the precision of the values are far higher than bytes because fractions of values can be stored instead of just whole numbers. The more bytes that are used for each floating-point component, the higher the range of values. Floating-point formats allow for different color component values to appear as follows:

Red = 100.001, Green = 100.0015, Blue = 100.003

Using bytes, the differences cannot be fractions of a number. Floating-point formats are useful because by using multiple bytes per component a graphics engine can have both a higher range of values and higher precision. This precision is important for things such as lighting and dynamic contrast, which are discussed later in this chapter. Figure 11.1 shows an example of non-HDR compared to HDR.

FIGURE 11.1   Without HDR (left) and with HDR (right).

More than 8 bits for the components using integer formats are also possible. This gives a higher range but not a higher precision. On today's graphics hardware floating-point buffers are fairly common.

Using LDR the upper limit of the color range is white, and anything under it is a shade of gray. The problem is that objects that are bright cannot be accurately modeled in this range. Take, for instance, two very bright objects, where one is brighter than the other. If the objects are clamped to the LDR range, they will appear to have the same intensity. For the brighter of the bright objects to appear brighter, the other object must be a value under 1.0. This means the other bright object is no longer bright but is instead a shade of gray, which is not accurate. When mapping final values (discussed later in this chapter) to a form so that it can be displayed to the screen, this will need to happen, but during the rendering pipeline as lighting and colors are being calculated, the values being used will quickly become inaccurate. This and the other issues with LDR rendering keep scenes from looking as realistic as they can, even on today's standard display devices.

IMPLEMENTING HDR

To implement HDR rendering in a video game the steps can be fairly straightforward. Assuming no special HDR effects are added, which is discussed later in this chapter, all that is really needed is a floating-point format to be used for the rendering targets and a tone-mapping shader so that the HDR results can be mapped to the displayable range. The general steps to performing HDR are as follows.

- Create floating-point rendering targets.
- Render the scene and perform all lighting, special effects, and so forth that are needed in the scene to the render target.
- Render any HDR special effects such as light blooms and streaks.
- Render a full-screen square using the rendering results from the render target as a texture and perform tone mapping to convert the image into a displayable one.

Creating Floating-Point Buffers and Rendering HDR Data

The main requirement for HDR rendering is to create and use floating-point formats for the rendering destinations. Using floats allows for a higher precision of values. Using more bytes for each component allows for a higher range of values.

What format to use depends on how much information is necessary to achieve the desired results. This can be determined through experimentation during the development of a game. For example, a format that uses 16 bits for each component requires half the amount of data of one that uses 32 bits and is even less than one that uses 64 bits. If the differences between them are negligible, memory requirements can be lessened using the lower bit depth versus using the higher ones.

In Chapter 7, "Additional Surface Mapping," render targets were covered in detail. When creating a rendering target that can be used to store HDR data, a floating-point buffer is created instead of an unsigned char buffer. The hardware dictates what formats are supported and what ones are not. As long as a floating-point buffer is chosen and is supported, the rendering target can be used as-is for HDR values and precision. Keep in mind that HDR values are essentially values over 1.0, and the clamping of LDR values is a result of the limitation of the data type used for the buffer, not the graphics API. Since the rendering target can handle the higher range, the values are not clamped, which before would cause saturation in the rendered scene for bright colors and banding artifacts for darker areas. For simple HDR rendering the buffers used can look like the ones in Figure 11.2.

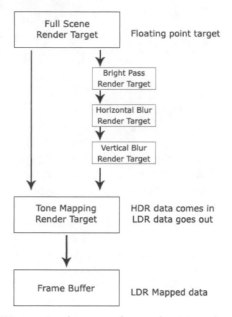

FIGURE 11.2   Render targets for simple HDR rendering.

Tone Mapping

When rendering HDR data, the information eventually will need to be displayed to some device. These devices, which are often television sets or computer monitors, have a fixed brightness that they can project. This means the brightness of a rendered scene can be much brighter than the device can display. Other outputs include printouts and media projectors, which also are limited in what the brightest point of the display can be viewed as. An example of tone mapping is shown in Figure 11.3.

FIGURE 11.3   HDR data (left) and tone-mapped data (right).

This limitation is overcome by using a technique known as tone mapping. Tone mapping essentially maps the RGB colors from one space to another. In this case the HDR data are converted to the LDR range so that the computer monitor or television is able to display the images properly. Without tone mapping, very bright rendered images are clamped at the display's brightest point, which causes rendered scenes to be saturated. Very dark areas within the rendered scene are also clamped, and much of the detail is lost during the display.

Tone mapping takes the brightest and lowest values within the HDR rendered imaged and dynamically maps them to the 0 to 255 range. This process is dynamic because how the values are mapped depends on these two extreme values. In other words, the brightest point in the HDR image becomes the new "white" point, and all other points are adjusted to that. During the conversion, some loss of detail occurs when tone mapping the HDR data into LDR, but this is a necessary step to display the rendered scene on standard devices. When using HDR rendering, the important idea is to preserve detail as the scene is being generated, so that the final output, when mapped to LDR, looks more realistic than if the detail was lost throughout the rendering process (i.e., during the lighting, blending, etc.).

Detail loss traditionally occurs with data that are clamped during each operation. For example, if a pixel has a red, green, and blue value of 3.0, it would be clamped to 1.0 in an LDR rendering target. If another lighting operation is performed using that data, the rendering process will use the 1.0 instead of the original HDR value of 3.0. Every time light and colors are added, the clamped data, not the real data, are used. If, let's say, 5.0 was added to each component for some operation, instead of having 8.0, the device will be still working with a clamped 1.0. If a scalar was multiplied by this color, let's say 0.5, then instead of having 4.0, the device would have 0.5. The difference between a standard TV or monitor's medium gray of 0.5 (128) is far different from the 4× bright white value of 4.0. The purpose of rendering throughout the pipeline in HDR is to preserve this detail so that the tone-mapping pass can convert it into a displayable range after all lighting and colors have been fully calculated and the scene looks more like what it should look like. A very simple example of tone mapping a color value with a given exposure is shown in the following pseudo-code:

```
float4 ToneMap(float4 col, float exposure)
{
    col = col * exposure;

    return pow(col, 0.55);
}
```

Assume here that `col` is the color being tone-mapped and `exposure` is used to increase the exposure level (brightness) of the color being processed. The power function `pow()` is used to take the color value and map it to the 0 to 1 range. As far as tone mapping is concerned, this would be a fairly straightforward and simple technique that can be used in an application in a pixel shader. Another option that can be used is the following pseudo-code, which is based loosely on an equation that can be found in the MSDN for the Direct3D 9 HDR Lighting sample:

```
float4 ToneMap(float4 col, float exposure)
{
    col = col * exposure;
    col = col / (1 + col);

    return col;
}
```

ON THE CD

Once tone-mapped, the results are displayed normally to the screen. By specifying an exposure value, it is possible to control the brightness from within the application. On the book's accompanying CD-ROM are demo applications called HDRGL, HDRD3D9, and HDRD3D10. These demo applications displays a room lit by a bright point light source in the middle of the scene. The exposure of the scene can be controlled by the up and down arrow keys on the keyboard. Each of these demos renders the scene to a floating-point render target and performs the simple tone-mapping operation described in this section during the display. The light color for the light source is above the traditional white point of 1.0 and can be controlled by the left and right arrow keys. A screenshot of the running demo application is shown in Figure 11.4.

FIGURE 11.4   A screenshot from the HDR demos.

HDR Special Effects and Additional Topics

HDR rendering has a minimum requirement of a multi-byte, and preferably a floating-point format for precision, used during the calculation of the rendered scene. Once complete, the results are tone mapped as they are displayed to the screen. In modern commercial video games the HDR data have additional optional effects applied to them. These effects can be used to add to the final rendered result in interesting ways. This section discusses a few of the more common effects along with other topics. These include:

- Light blooms
- Light streaks
- Dynamic tone mapping

Bloom

Light blooming is a camera artifact that appears on bright objects and causes a halo or bloom of light to appear. As a camera's lens tries to focus on a brightly lit object, the light reflecting off of the object can appear to bleed beyond the object itself. In computer graphics, in this case video game graphics, like lens flare, the idea of light blooms is to create this artifact so that rendered scenes look as if they were captured using a real camera. An example of a light blooming effect is shown in Figure 11.5.

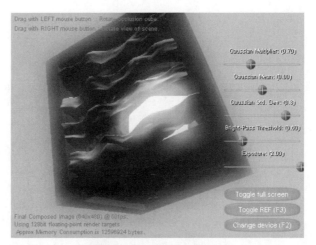

FIGURE 11.5 Light blooming.

Light blooming is usually done using HDR rendering. It is possible to reproduce light blooming in a non-HDR format, but the nature and effect of light blooming requires really bright objects for quality. In an LDR setting the range of values is very low, leading to quality that is not as good as the HDR version. Also, the low range of values limits the look of the light bloom effect on objects. This occurs because the amount of brightness affects the bloom effect, and if LDR is capped at a maximum of 1.0 (255), this effect outside of HDR is not the same.

Light blooms can be created in the following series of steps.

- Render the scene to a floating-point render target with the higher range of lighting values.
- Render the scene (full-screen quad textured with the original scene image) to a down-sampled version, for example, a render target that is $^1/_{16}$ the size of the screen resolution and only store values considered bright (e.g., any pixels brighter than white).
- Perform a horizontal blur on the down-sampled data.
- Perform a vertical blur on the down-sampled data.
- Blend the blurred result with the original rendered scene.

Performing the horizontal and vertical blur separately assumes a two-pass blurring approach.

Rendering to a render target that uses a format suitable for HDR allows for the scene to retain all its data and precision. Rendering to a down-sampled version of the scene is used as a speed boost since near-accurate results can be achieved without using the full resolution. In the second step, when the down sampled version is being created, only pixels that are considered bright are stored. This is done by rendering a full-screen quad using the original render target as a texture. In the shader it will test every pixel from the incoming texture to see if it is above whatever is considered the bright threshold. If the pixels pass the test, then those pixels are saved to the down-sampled render target, or else black is saved. This process is known as a bright-pass filter. The bright-pass values are the original HDR bright colors scaled by the luminance of the HDR colors. This can be done using the following pseudo-code:

```
float4 GetBrightPassVal(float4 col)
{
   float4 lum_const = float4(0.30, 0.59, 0.11, 1);
   float luminance = dot(col, lum_const);

   return col * luminance;
}
```

Once the bright information has been filtered and stored in the down-sampled render target, this information is then blurred. This blurring is known as a blur pass and is usually done by using a Gaussian blur. Blurring along the horizontal and vertical directions of the blur-pass render target creates a result that represents the blooms that will be added to the scene. In the final step the original render target texture is combined with the blur-pass texture to create the final result. The final result is tone mapped and displayed to the screen.

In standard APIs such as OpenGL and Direct3D this technique can be done using four rendering targets. The first target stores the results of the original render, the second stores the results of the bright-pass filter, the third stores the results of the horizontal blur, and the fourth stores the results of the vertical blur. The tone-mapped blending of the original render target and the final blur-pass render target creates HDR light blooms when the blur-pass results are used as an overlay on top of the original scene.

Another way to calculate the luminance is to use the average scene luminance. This can be done by rendering to a down-sampled 16×16 render target, using that to render to a 4×4 render target, and then using that to render to a 1×1 render target. The last render target, the

1×1 target, has a single color value in it that can be used as the average scene luminance, which can be sampled from a pixel shader. This can lead to better results than using the luminance of the current pixel.

Streaks

Light streaks are similar to light blooms, but while light blooms use a Gaussian blur overlay, light streaks do not. Light streaks can require as many as three or more passes to create. A light streak takes the bright-pass filtered image and heavily blurs the data in a specific direction. For each pass a different direction is chosen for the blur. When all passes are done, the passes are combined by taking the average color of each pixel in each render target. The results of the combination are the light streaks that can be overlaid over the bloom pass and the original scene to create the final rendered scene. An example of light streaks is shown in Figure 11.6. Figure 11.7 shown an example of using light streaks in a virtual scene.

FIGURE 11.6   Streaks of light.

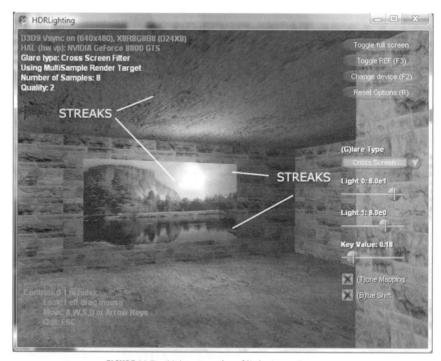

FIGURE 11.7 Using streaks of light in a 3D scene.

Light streaks can be used to simulate light as it passes by the sides of objects. If light streaks are done correctly, this can give subtle visual cues that can increase the realism of the rendered scene. Like light blooms, the use of light streaks depends on what is desired out of the rendered scene and how adding such an effect affects game-play.

Dynamic Tone Mapping

In the human body the eyes do not instantly adapt to dramatic changes in the brightness of the environment's lighting. In other words, there is time between the eyes's ability to adjust to sunlight after it has spent considerable time in a dark environment or vice versa.

Recently, many HDR-supported video games have used a dynamic tone-mapping technique to simulate the eye having to adjust to sudden changes in brightness. Most recently this can be seen in *Halo 3* by Bungie Studios, as shown in Figure 11.8. In *Halo 3* the dynamic tone mapping is kept to a minimum so that it is noticeable but does not have a negative impact on the game-play, which is important for online multiplayer games.

FIGURE 11.8   Dynamic tone mapping. The image on the left is taken in the dark and the one on the right occurs after the virtual eye adjustment to the light.

In Microsoft's DirectX SDK there is a sample that performs dynamic tone mapping to produce this effect. Instead of using the average scene luminance, the technique uses what is known as the adapted scene luminance. This is calculated using the following equation by the SDK sample:

```
float new_lum = adapted_lum + (current_lum - adapted_lum) *
                (1 - pow(0.98f, 30 * time));
```

In the equation used by the SDK sample, HDR Lighting, the dynamic luminance is calculated by subtracting the current adapted luminance from the pixel luminance, multiplying that by 1 minus the power of 0.98 and a time delta, and adding that to the current adapted scene luminance. The time delta is used to control how slow or fast the virtual eyes adjusts to the scene. In most types of video games this must occur faster than it does for the human eye since gamers would not want to wait long for the camera to adjust just to see what they are doing, especially if they are engaged in a fierce fire-fight in a game like *Halo 3*.

Dynamic tone mapping that is used to simulate the virtual eye adjusting to the scene's brightness is becoming very common in Xbox 360 and PlayStation 3 video games. The adaptation must be balanced so that it does not have a negative impact on the player's ability to play the game.

SUMMARY

HDR rendering is important in the preservation of detail as lighting and colors are calculated throughout the rendering of a scene. HDR rendering requires floating-point multibyte formats and tone mapping to convert the HDR data into a displayable range. Additional effects can be added, such as bloom and flare, but these effects are optional in the HDR process.

The following elements were discussed in this chapter.

- LDR
- HDR
- Tone mapping
- Dynamic tone mapping
- Bloom
- Streaks

CHAPTER QUESTIONS

Answers to the following chapter review questions can be found in Appendix A, "Answers to Chapter Questions."

1. What does LDR stand for?
   A. Low dynamic rendering
   B. Low definition rendering
   C. Low dynamic range
   D. None of the above
2. What does HDR stand for?
   A. High dynamic rendering
   B. High definition rendering
   C. High dynamic range
   D. None of the above
3. List two of the main benefits to using HDR data throughout the rendering process. Why is each of those benefits important?
4. What contrast ratio does LDR typically get?
   A. 1:256
   B. 256:1
   C. 255:1
   D. 1:255
   E. None of the above
5. How is HDR data displayed to the screen?
   A. By using floating-point buffers
   B. Tone mapping
   C. Down sampling
   D. None of the above
6. Why is HDR important for the progression of video game graphics?
7. Describe the tone mapping technique.
8. Describe the dynamic tone mapping technique. How is it used in some modern video games?
9. Describe the light blooming technique.
10. Describe the light streaks technique.
11. True or false: Bloom can be performed in LDR rendering.

12. True or false: Light streaks are caused as a result of tone mapping very bright objects.
13. True or false: Higher range can be obtained without necessarily using floating-point buffers.
14. True or false: Storing HDR values in a separate buffer is known as a bright-pass filter.
15. True or false: Light streaks can only be performed on HDR data.

CHAPTER EXERCISES

Exercise 1: Build off of one of the HDR demos and add four additional lights, each with varying brightness.

Exercise 2: Build off of Exercise 1 and add light blooms to the HDR demo using the steps and algorithms described in this chapter. Create a blur shader that allows the direction of the texture coordinate offsets for the color samples to be passed in as a uniform variable. That way only one shader is needed and the horizontal and vertical directions can be specified by the application.

Exercise 3: Build off of Exercise 2 and add support for light streaks. Use the blur shader to specify four directions for the blue (e.g., top-left, top-right, bottom-left, and bottom-right). When combining each of the streak passes into one, be sure to use the average color of each of the passes. This can look like the following.

```
col = tex2D(StreakPass1, texCoord);
col += tex2D(StreakPass2, texCoord);
col += tex2D(StreakPass3, texCoord);
col += tex2D(StreakPass4, texCoord);

col /= 4;
```

SPECIAL EFFECTS: ADDITIONAL EFFECTS

In This Chapter

- Blurring
- Depth of Field
- Motion Blur
- Particle Systems
- Additional Effects

Every modern 3D video game employs some form of special effects when rendering the scenes in the game. These special effects range from simple effects to more complex rendering algorithms. Special effects have the primary goal of adding visual flare to the rendered scenes. Some effects, although seemingly unimportant, can add greatly to any video game.

In this chapter we will look at a few of the more common special effects in modern 3D video games. This chapter will focus on effects used in many upcoming next-generation video games. Special effects as a whole can require a book on their own. Many special effects already discussed in this book include:

- Lighting, HDR lighting, and light blooms
- Time and day-night cycles
- Shadows
- Ambient occlusion
- Reflections
- Refractions
- Frensel
- Light beams and shafts
- Lens flare

BLURRING

Blurring is the basis for many different rendering effects used in modern video games. In Chapter 11, "Special Effects: High Dynamic Range," we discussed blurring as a means to create a blooming effect in high–dynamic-range rendering. Blurring can be used for other things in computer graphics, most notably, motion blur and depth of field. Motion blur and depth of field are starting to be used more and more in current and upcoming video games as a way to increase realism and add a cinematic feel to the rendered scenes.

There are various blurring algorithms such as Gaussian blur, radial blur, and so forth. Blurring essentially boils down to sampling a set number of pixels and averaging the result. For example, if you had a pixel that you wanted to blur using its neighboring pixels in a 3 × 3 grid (see Figure 12.1), you could use a pixel shader to fetch each texel, add them all together, and divide the result by 9. Doing this for all pixels in the image will blur it. This type of blurring is fairly straightforward and simple to write out in a pixel shader. Examples of some blurring algorithms include:

- Average
- Motion
- Gaussian

- Box
- Surface
- Sharp
- Smart
- Radial
- Lens

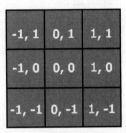

FIGURE 12.1 Blurring a pixel using a 3 × 3 grid around it.

Depth of Field

Modern games that strive for realism are starting to embrace effects that are common to the motion picture industry. These effects are used to enhance the rendered scene to give it a natural or expected feel that acts in a way the user would expect its real-life counterpart would act. One of these techniques is known as depth of field, which will be described in more detail in this section.

Depth of field is an artifact of real-life camera lenses that is caused when objects that are out of the focal range appear blurred. When an object is in focus it appears clear to the camera lens, but the camera has a harder time displaying objects outside of the range. This includes objects in the background as well as objects in the foreground. As objects move past the focal range, they gradually become more blurred, or defocused.

Some video games have started to use this camera artifact to increase the realism of video games. Like other techniques, such as lens flare, this technique is used to give gamers what they expect from a real-life camera in the virtual world. Also, by using depth of field, the developers are able to place in focus objects that the player should be concentrating on. An example of this can be seen in the game *Crysis*.

Depth of field is used throughout *Crysis* and can be seen in everything from cut-scenes to the weapon modifying screen to the in-game first-person view and so on. During the game, the object you are looking at marks the focal point. Anything outside of the focal range is blurred.

Blurring is not just caused by distance but also can be caused by motion, which is known as motion blur.

Depth-Based Blurring

Depth of field can be performed as a postprocessing effect that is applied to a scene that has already been rendered. Postprocessing effects are very common in today's games. The postprocessing effects commonly seen in games include the following.

- Depth of field
- Bloom
- Deferred shading for lighting
- Motion blur
- Screen-space ambient occlusion (discussed in Chapter 10, "Global Illumination Techniques")
- Heat vision
- Night vision

One way to perform depth of field is to use rendering targets. The pixel-based algorithm is fairly straightforward and consists of the following steps:

1. Render the scene normally. During the rendering, store the depth values out to an off-screen rendering target. This target can be, for example, R16F, which makes it a single-component 16-bit floating point buffer. The actual format depends on the desired results and what is acceptable to the application.
2. Render the scene to a down-sample rendering target one-quarter (or more) the size of the original.
3. With the down-sampled version, perform a blur on the entire image. This can be done using a Gaussian, radial, average, or another type of blurring algorithm. It can even be done using a Poisson-disk filter, which was discussed in Chapter 9, "Advanced Lighting and Shadows."
4. For the final render, use the original scene render target, depth target, and blurred target textures to create the depth of field effect. The depth value is used to create the depth factor. This factor is a value between 0 and 1 that is used to interpolate linearly between the original render and the blurred version of it. The depth factor is a percentage that is calculated based on the focal range in which the depth lies. Depths outside the focal range can be fully blurred, which essentially means using the blurred rendering target's color fully.

The rendering overview is shown in Figure 12.2. Keep in mind that the format of the depth render target will play a role in the output. More bits means more precision but also more memory. Also, when performing depth of field in this manner, it is important to use point sampling instead of some form of linear filtering. This is because linear texture filtering (i.e., bilinear and trilinear) use averaged colors for each pixel. In depth of field the average depth is not what is desired—you need the pixel's true depth value. One major reason for this is that the depths between pixels can change drastically when moving from one primitive to another.

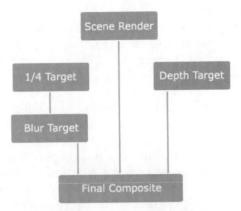

FIGURE 12.2   Depth of field overview.

By performing depth of field in this manner, the depth rendering target can be used for other postprocessing effects, such as motion blur. One thing to note is that performing a Gaussian blur can lead to color bleeding, which is when colors are being affected by neighboring pixels. One method to combat this is to use a different blurring algorithm, such as the Poisson-disk filter and what is known as a circle of confusion. The *acceptable circle of confusion* is a term used to describe a circle that is indistinguishable from a point. As this circle gets gradually bigger, more blurriness is seen on the rendered result. Therefore, depth of field is not a sharp change from normal to blurred, although such a simple method could be used if the results were acceptable. Using the Poisson-disk filter and an algorithm that is based on the circle of confusion can help remove color leaks as well as improve blur quality.

ON THE CD

On the book's accompanying CD-ROM is a demo application called DOF that performs depth of field (DOFGL for OpenGL and DOFD3D9 and DOFD3D10 for Direct3D). In this demo, blurring the rendering result as described earlier in this chapter is used to achieve the desired results. The algorithm presented in this section is used to create an interpolation value for each pixel that is used to blend between the original render and the blurred version.

Direct3D 10 allows depth texture contents to be read as a shader resource, or, in other words, a texture. If the shader makes use of this, this can avoid the need to create an entirely different rendering target for storing depth values.

MOTION BLUR

A picture represents light captured over a small amount of time. This time is determined by many factors, such as shutter speed, which deal with topics outside the scope of this book. If objects are moving when the picture is taken, a blurring effect can be captured and stored. The faster the object is moving, the more blur can be observed, depending on the camera speed.

Motion blur is an artifact that can be seen in any action movie as the camera and scene objects move at fast rates. In video games motion blur is used to simulate this effect to create a more cinematic appearance. Examples of modern video games that use motion blur include *Halo 3*, *Crysis*, *Metal Gear Solid 4*, and many more.

The purpose of motion blur in computer graphics is make the animation be perceived as continuous. Without motion blur, each scene is a sharp instance of time, even for objects moving at high speed. Motion blur gives rendered scenes a much more cinematic appearance, similar to depth of field.

In computer graphics some special effects are purposely implemented for visual impact. In television and movies these artifacts are not always as welcomed as they are by game developers.

Fast Motion Blur

There are many different ways to perform motion blur. One of the simplest methods is to use the accumulation buffer of the graphics API. The algorithm can be performed in the following steps:

1. Set up the accumulation buffer.
2. Render the scene into the accumulation buffer once for each time frame, which includes the current object's position and its last X number of positions (for example, four).
3. Each time the scene is rendered, only accumulate a percentage of its output to the accumulation buffer.
4. Use the results of the accumulation buffer as the final output for the motion blur effect.

The accumulation buffer is easy to set up and use, and rendering objects is nothing new, which is an upside, but this process has many downsides. For starters, the accumulation buffer is traditionally fairly slow. Also, to use this buffer for motion blur, the application has to render the scene multiple times per frame. If the effect used four time frames for the motion blur, then the scene would be rendered four times, more if more frames were needed. Other downsides include having to store and manage all of the necessary data to be able to render the scene at the correct transformations multiple times.

Using OpenGL as an example, the function glAccum(GL_LOAD, fraction) (where fraction is a floating-point variable between 0 and 1) can be used to start the accumulation buffer, which takes an operation flag of what the function would be doing and a percentage to accumulate. The flag GL_LOAD is used to start the accumulation buffer, and the flag GL_ACCUM is used to add to the accumulation buffer. Using glAccum(GL_RETURN, 1.0) returns the entire contents of the accumulation buffer and sets them to the back buffer. Thus, after every scene rendering, calling glAccum(GL_ACCUM, fraction) with the amount to acculmulate will give you the motion blur effect for objects in motion. It is very simple to do, but there are better techniques for performing the motion blur effect.

ON THE CD
On the book's CD-ROM is a simple OpenGL demo application called Accumulation Blur that demonstrates using the accumulation buffer to perform simple motion blur. This demo shows a rotating cube with a slight motion blur effect.

Geometry-Based Motion Blur

Geometry-based motion blur is motion blur that is performed by using extruded geometry. This technique is described in the DirectX SDK for the sample called "Motion Blur 10" for Direct3D 10, which uses geometry shaders to generate the extruded geometry. The idea behind the technique is that a triangle strip is generated based on the direction of movement for the geometry that is being rendered. This is done by sending in an array of matrices to the shaders so that the current position as well as positions forward and backward through time can also be used. As each triangle strip is created, it is given an alpha value that is based on how much time has elapsed in relation to the current time frame.

Geometry-based motion blur is independent of frame rate, but it also requires additional information to be stored and passed to the graphics hardware for each frame. For dramatic motion blur effects this can add up to quite a bit of information, especially for effects that are to include information that lasts for seconds rather than a fraction of a second (the total time of a few frames).

Pixel-Based Motion Blur

There are various ways motion blur can be achieved using a postprocessing effect. One method is to create and maintain a series of off-screen rendering targets, where one target is the current frame and the others are previously rendered frames. Because memory is finite and very valuable for GPU devices, these additional targets can be the one-quarter resolution versions, for example, of the previous original rendered scenes. For rendering motion blur, each rendering target can be blended using varying percentages to create the final composite. An example of motion blur performed in this manner is shown in Figure 12.3. Blurring in this manner is similar to the idea behind the motion blur described in the Fast Motion Blur section of this chapter, but instead of rendering the scene multiple times each frame, it keeps past rendered scenes in down-sampled rendering targets.

FIGURE 12.3   Motion blur by blending multiple targets that represent past frames.

On the plus side, motion blur performed in this manner is fairly simple and straightforward. On the downside, this type of motion blur is very limited because of the number of frames used and the amount of video memory it consumes for all of those rendering targets. The more frames that are used, the better the final result will be, but it also consumes much more video memory.

Another method is to take the previous approach and to remove the need for multiple rendering buffers, instead using just one to accumulate the blending from the current and previous frames. This way, when it is time to create the final render, one motion blur rendering target is blended using a weighted value with the back-buffer. This is very simple to do, but when using low-precision formats and high percentage values, ghost images may appear. These are images from previous frames that appear slightly on the current frame to create a ghost-like image. This can be minimized by using low percentages and higher-precision formats for the buffers, but the effect is not perfect. An example of this is shown in Figure 12.4.

FIGURE 12.4   Motion blur by blending one target that represents many past frames.

Another motion blur technique is to use velocity motion blur. This is different from the other types of motion blur described so far in this chapter. With velocity motion blur, the screen-space velocity of each surface is stored in an additional rendering target. Velocity is a physics term that describes the rate of change between two positions. If you know the rate of change between a vertex's last and current positions, you can calculate its velocity, which can be as simple as the difference between the two positions.

The 2D vector that represents the velocity is stored in a rendering target. Since the effect is a postprocessing effect, it is essentially a 2D effect, which means that only the rate of change in X and Y would be used. When building the velocity buffer, the algorithm takes into account not only the geometry velocity but also the camera's velocity. This can be seen in *Crysis*, where moving the camera really fast causes a strong motion blur to appear on the scene, even when the objects around the player are relatively still.

The next step in velocity-based motion blur is to take the originally rendered scene and the velocity buffer (render target) and create the final image by using the velocities to dictate the direction of the blur effect. The pixels in that direction are added up and summed—the larger the velocity value, the more pixels are used.

Motion blur in this fashion is very powerful and convincing in its output. The major obstacle that needs to be avoided is situations where fast-moving background objects bleed color onto slow-moving or stationary foreground objects. To avoid this, depth information can also be stored and used to detect where a background object in motion is bleeding into a foreground object. This can be as simple as using a depth test to make sure the pixel being used in the blur is one that is not for a foreground (closer to the camera) object.

PARTICLE SYSTEMS

A particle in computer graphics is a small geometric object that is used to represent something very small that exists in nature. Like real-life particles, the particles in a particle system can collectively be used to create an effect. These effects can be dust in the sunlight, smoke, rain drops, and so forth. Particles in a particle system tend to have these following characteristics:

- Particles typically act independent of one another, although they can be allowed to affect one another if the developers want them to.
- Particles are often represented as billboard quads or point sprites (which are hardware-accelerated billboards).

- Particles tend to share many attributes, such as texture, for example, but each particle has its own set of properties that define its behavior once released into the world.

A particle system is an object that holds a list of particles and effect attributes and updates the particles as necessary. A particle is an object with a list of properties that define how it is to be rendered and moved throughout the game world. These properties can include the following elements.

- Position
- Velocity
- Life span or energy level (which can double as the alpha transparency value)
- Mass
- Color
- Texture
- Size

A structure for a particle can be as straightforward as the following.

```
struct Particle
{
   Vector3D position;
   Vector3D velocity;
   float mass;
   float size;

   Color3 color;
   float engergy;
}
```

A particle system, in addition to storing a list of particles, can have the following attributes.

- Area of affect
- Starting location
- Maximum number of particles that can be released at one time
- External forces (e.g., gravity, wind, etc.)
- State (e.g., on or off)

A particle system can have the following structure, minus member functions if represented as a class:

```
class ParticleSystem
{
      Vector3D position;
      BoundingBox area;
      Vector3D forces;
```

```
    bool systemOn;

    List<Particle> particles;
    int maxReleasedParticles;
}
```

Particle systems can be hard coded specifically for a purpose (e.g., to create smoke, rain, etc.) or can be coded as generic systems that can be used to create any type of particle effect. A generic system would require more work and would be trickier to implement than a straightforward implementation for a specific purpose, but it does have the added benefit of flexibility. With a generic system, an external editor can be used to create the particle effect, which can then be saved to a file and loaded by the particle system during a game. This is great because different effects can be quickly and easily put together using a visual tool, as well as being easy to tweak and adjust.

For an object-oriented approach, a particle system class would need to initialize all particles and update them. Updating refers to moving the particles based on their physics attributes. When a particle is considered dead (e.g., energy is 0, the particle has moved past a certain area, a certain amount of time has passed), then, if the particle system is looping the effect, a new particle can be created by re-initializing the dead particle back to the start.

Earlier we saw that position and velocity, among other elements, are common properties of a particle. These two elements can be used to refer to what is known as a point mass in game physics.

Point Masses

Point mass is a physics term used to describe an object that can be linearly translated throughout an environment but whose orientation is irrelevant or negligible. This is different from a rigid body, which is similar, with the exception that its orientation and the forces that affect it are considered.

Point mass physics is perfect for particles because a particle in a video game is often a simple textured surface that is always facing the camera. In other words, the orientation is nonexistent. In nature the particles are so small that their orientations cannot be observed with the naked eye. Thus, it would be a waste of processing cycles to take orientation into account.

In game physics acceleration is the rate of change in velocity. Velocity is used to describe the rate of change in position, and the position is a stationary location in the 3D universe, as shown by Equation 12.1. Acceleration is the current force acting on the object, and mass can be thought of as the object's weight. Note that mass is a scalar (floating-point value), while force, acceleration, velocity, and position are vectors.

$$acceleration = force / mass$$
$$velocity = velocity + acceleration * time$$
$$position = position + velocity * time$$
Equation 12.1

Time is used in physics to represent the rate of change in time, also known as the time delta. If we know all the forces acting on an object, we can calculate the acceleration, which means the velocity and position of the object can also be calculated. But what if we know how much acceleration we want to add and would like to get the force acting on the object? Force is calculated as mass multiplied by acceleration (Equation 12.2).

$$force = mass * acceleration$$
Equation 12.2

Using straightforward algebra by replacing the terms allows for the possibility of calculating any unknown variable as long as all of the variables are not unknown. In a video game you would know either the force you want to have acting on an object or its acceleration. If a car was being represented, the acceleration could be determined by how hard and long the user pressed the "gas" button. Force can be anything from gravity to wind. Force is a vector whose direction and strength are specified by the axes. The larger the value for each axis of the force vector, the harder the force in that direction.

When a point mass is updated, the velocity acts as both the direction of the movement and its speed. Because the velocity is not unit-length, the larger it is, the faster the object will move. Also, when updating in game physics, it is important to clear the force variable (set to 0) after the update. This is done because the total force of an object is usually calculated for each frame and applied to the object, or however often physics calculations take place. If an object is in motion and the force that was driving it goes away, the object gradually comes to a stop. This assumes that other physics properties are added, such as friction or buoyancy, which would decrease the velocity until it was 0, making any position updates stationary.

For particle systems, a full-blown physics system is not needed. In fact, for most particle systems, the position and velocity are all that is needed. Assuming forces cannot act on the particles, such as gravity, once a particle is unleashed upon the game world, it usually goes about its direction until either a certain about of time has passed, it collides with the game world in a way that it would cause no additional need for its update (e.g., a snowflake hitting the ground), or until its energy level is diminished and thus it can no longer be seen. When it comes to energy, this can decrease a specific amount over time until it is 0.

If velocity is not changed by either acceleration or by some other method, it is known to be constant. This is called constant velocity. Unless a particle in a particle system must be acted upon by external forces, such as gravity or wind, for example, constant velocity is usually all that is used.

Billboards and Point Sprites

In Chapter 7, "Additional Surface Mapping," we mentioned that a billboard is a texture-mapped quad that is always facing the camera. Because orientation is not part of a billboard, they are perfect for use with particle systems. A particle system with hundreds or thousands of particles can be rendered with not a lot of geometry.

Point sprites are hardware-accelerated billboards in which the geometry is created on the GPU. The only thing the application needs to do besides enable the feature through the API being used is to render a list of points and specify the point sprite size. The points of each point sprite represent its center. This makes drawing a lot of billboards easy by rendering out a list of points and allowing the hardware to handle generating the geometry so that it is facing the viewer.

ON THE CD

On the CD-ROM in the Chapter 12 folder are point sprite demos for each of the graphical APIs covered in this book. These demos are called PointSpriteGL, PointSpriteD3D9, and PointSpriteD3D10. In Direct3D 10 the geometry can be generated using a geometry shader, while the other APIs have specific API functions and flags that are used to set up the point sprite feature.

A particle system's starting location and starting area is known as an emitter. The emitter is the area from which particles start.

Sparks

Sparks are a very common particle effect in 3D video games. A spark can be generated from firing a weapon, striking a surface with an object or projectile, a downed electrical wire, an emergency flare, and so forth. Sparks are very nice-looking effects that can be used effectively in a video game.

Sparks can be created similarly to the particle system demo that will be implemented later in this chapter. The sparks themselves are usually oval in shape, and their colors tend to be fairly bright and vibrant. A spark's color can be changed a bit throughout its life span by using a property known as a color delta (change in color over time). The direction of the particles depends on the object generating and using the effect. If the sparks are coming from a fuse for a stick of dynamite, then particles would be generated to move in a spherical area from the starting location, like in the particle system demo for this chapter. If the spark was caused by a bullet hitting a metal surface, it might have more of a hemispherical movement. If the effect comes from a road flare, it will most likely be generated to move in an upward cone. It all depends on what looks right and what is the most effective route to take for the effect and object being represented in the game world.

Fire

Fire can be created different ways in a video game. One method is to use a particle system that generates particles within a small range and moves them in an upward direction. This direction would vary among the particles to add volume to the fire effect. An example of this is shown in Figure 12.5, where the particles are close enough to give the impression of one flame rather than obviously individual textured polygons.

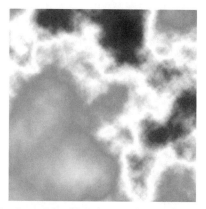

FIGURE 12.5   A particle effect that can be used for simple fire.

Another way to create fire is to use a particle system that places an animated textured billboard somewhere within the game world. This way, only one particle is used for a small patch of fire, and the fire can be made to look photorealistic. For example, in *Halo 3* the player can use a flamethrower weapon. Fire appears on surfaces that this weapon strikes. Fire like this can be recreated by using an animated billboard that is placed by the game at the point where the fire from some source strikes a surface. The animation of the billboard is used to give the fire a very realistic look and feel.

Smoke

The smoke particle effect is similar to the fire effect, but smoke particles usually have a longer life span and a larger area of effect (e.g., if used with fire, the smoke particles can rise higher than the fire). Smoke can be used together with a fire effect to create a more realistic combination, or it can be used on its own. Games use smoke in many clever ways. In *Ghost Recon Advance War Fighter 2* players can use smoke grenades to mask their movements and positions from enemy sight.

When smoke is represented as a particle system, the particles can grow larger in size over time. Their transparency can fade with time too, to create a more natural look and feel similar to how people expect smoke to behave. An example of this is shown in Figure 12.6.

FIGURE 12.6   A particle effect that can be used for smoke.

Additional Particle Effects

The number and types of particles that can be created are almost limitless. If the developer spends time creating a generic particle system, he can create new effects by adjusting various properties and parameters. These properties can include the particle's texture, life-span, initial movement direction, initial position, and so forth. A few of the most common types of particle effects used in modern video games include the following.

- Water splashes
- Water drips
- Smoke
- Fire
- Sparks
- Dust (e.g., in a driving game dust can appear under the tires on a dirt road)
- Rain
- Snow

Particle System Demo

ON THE CD

On the CD-ROM in the Chapter 12 folder is a demo application called Particle System (ParticleSystemGL, ParticleSystemD3D9, and ParticleSystemD3D10). This demo creates a simple particle explosion effect using point sprites. The particle system starts each of the particles at the origin (0, 0, 0). The particles are then moved in random velocities, and their energy is decreased over time. Once a particle's energy is at 0, the particle is reinitialized back at the origin with a new random velocity.

The demo allows users to exit by pressing the escape key or to change how the particle system emits using the spacebar. By default, the particle system will keep creating new particles whenever one dies. If the spacebar is pressed, the state will switch to tell the particle system to wait until there are no more particles with energy before recreating them. This allows two different types of particle effects to be created with the one particle system. An example of this demo is shown in Figure 12.7.

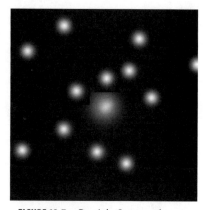

FIGURE 12.7 Particle System demo.

ADDITIONAL EFFECTS

Many different effects can be observed in a video game. Several of these effects will be discussed in the remainder of this book. Two of these effects are weapon effects and geometric decals. For the rest of the book the following effects will be discussed and examined.

- Frensel
- Caustics
- Reflections and refractions for water
- Shorelines

Weapon Effects

Special effects tied to weapons can be seen in every 3D game on the market. Weapon effects are used mainly to add visual feedback that an action is taking place. When it comes to guns in video games, the most common effect is the muzzle flash. In many shooters this effect is implemented as a billboard that is rendered facing the camera at the location from which the weapon is firing. This can be seen in games such as *BioShock*, *Gears of War*, and *Halo 3*.

Other in-game weapon effects include bullet casings falling from a gun's barrel and smoke from the barrel of a gun after it fires, both of which can be done with a particle system. Many effects can be applied to the weapon, whether it is a traditional weapon, alien weapon, or something in between. Most of these effects are very easy and basic in their makeup.

In addition to effects being applied visually to the weapon themselves, effects can also be applied to the projectiles the weapons shoot. For example, rockets from a rocket launcher can leave contrails of smoke as they travel through the environment, lightening bolts can extend from magic wands, and bullets can leave trails that extend from the point where the gun shoots to the point of collision.

One popular game that uses bullet trails is *Halo 3*. In *Halo 3* and many other games, the trails are created by using two alpha-textured quads in the shape of a cross. This allows the trail to be defined in 3D using 2D elements, as shown in Figure 12.8. With alpha transparency, the two quads together can look like a 3D volume.

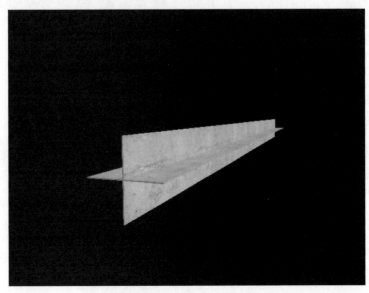

FIGURE 12.8   Two quads form a trail.

Sometimes the best solution is the easiest solution. By using two quads, you can cheaply create a convincing weapon trail. This can be used efficiently for many different effects, and because of their size, shape, and look, it would be hard to tell that they are so simple in their geometry. Much like particles in a particle system, it is possible to create effects without a lot of data.

Dynamic Decals on Surfaces

Many shooting games allow the player to fire upon the geometry in a game's environment. When a bullet or some other projectile strikes these surfaces, it leaves a mark in its wake. For a bullet, this is usually a bullet hole. For explosions, this is usually a scorch mark of some kind. An example of this from *Gears of War* for the Xbox 360 is shown in Figure 12.9.

FIGURE 12.9   Dynamic decals applied to surfaces.

These decals are dynamic and are generated during game-play based on the user's actions. For objects that lie flat along a plane, such as a wall, generating these decals is fairly easy. The first step is to determine where the collision occurred between the projectile (a bullet in this example) and the surface (a wall in this example). With the point of intersection in hand, the wall's surface normal is used to orient the decal that will be generated. The surface normal and the point of intersection, as well as the size of the bullet hole, are used to generate the decal's mesh. This mesh is rendered to the screen like any other mesh.

Games usually have a set number of these decals that can be placed throughout the game world. In a game like *Gears of War* it is possible to see decals disappear once a certain threshold is reached. Decal geometry can be used for many types of things, including the following common items.

- Bullets holes
- Scorch marks from explosions
- Foot prints
- Blood
- Tire tracks and skid marks

Although it is simple to generate these types of meshes from relatively flat surfaces, it becomes more of a challenge for curved surfaces. With curved surfaces, the surrounding polygons that can be affected by the decal need to be examined. For each polygon on the surface that is affected by the decal, the decal is clipped to that polygon, and new geometry information must be generated. This allows decals to wrap with the surface of a curved object. Without this, the decal can seem to float around its edges, which breaks the illusion that the decal is actually damage that has been caused to the object's surface.

Also, clipping must be done for decals that exist off the edge of a polygon, such as the edge of a wall. Again, without polygon clipping, the illusion can be lost, and the decal will look like a piece of paper glued to the surface of whatever was hit instead of looking like a bullet, or some other projectile, struck and impacted the surface. An example of this is shown in Figure 12.10.

FIGURE 12.10   Decal without clipping (left) and with clipping (right).

SUMMARY

Special effects can be seen throughout any modern 3D video game. In the next generation of video games many special effects are being used to give games a more cinematic look to help bridge the gap between them and the visuals seen in motion pictures.

The following elements were discussed throughout this chapter.

- Blurring
- Depth of field
- Motion blur
- General particle systems
- Point sprites
- Sparks
- Smoke
- Fire
- Weapon effects
- Geometric decals

CHAPTER QUESTIONS

Answers to the following chapter review questions can be found in Appendix A, "Answers to Chapter Questions."

1. List at least three types of blurring algorithms.
2. Describe depth of field. What is its purpose in next-generation video games?
3. Describe the focal range that was discussed during the section on depth of field. What happens to objects outside of this range?
4. What is the circle of confusion? How does it relate to depth of field?
5. Describe motion blur. What is its purpose in next-generation video games?
6. Describe geometry-based motion blur. What are its benefits and what are its disadvantages?
7. Describe pixel-based motion blur. What are its benefits and what are its disadvantages?
8. What is a particle system? Describe each of the particle effects discussed in this chapter.
9. What are point masses? How do they differ from rigid bodies? Why do particle systems use point masses?
10. If we know the acceleration of a point mass, how can we calculate the force being applied to it?
11. Why would a developer create a generic particle system?

12. Describe geometric decals? List at least five ways they can be used in a video game.
13. Describe what it would take to display a geometric decal on a flat surface, such as a wall. What about a curved surface?
14. How do 2D elements combine to create weapon effects that appear to be 3D?
15. True or false: Depth of field blurs the scene based on the camera's depth.
16. True or false: The accumulation was used earlier in this chapter to perform depth of field.
17. True or false: The purpose of motion blur, besides adding cinematic quality to rendered scenes, is to give the impression that motion is continuous.
18. True or false: A point sprite is an animated texture.
19. True or false: A particle system uses some point mass physics.

CHAPTER EXERCISES

Exercise 1: Implement a particle effect that looks like sparks shooting in an upward cone direction. Build off of the particle system demo from this chapter to implement the effect.

Exercise 2: Implement a particle effect for very simple fire and smoke. Use both in a single application.

Exercise 3: Implement velocity-based motion blur. Use a simple scene object such as a rotating cube for the effect. Use the previous and current rotation matrices as a way to build the velocity in the vertex shader. Use the direction and amount to determine how the pixels are sampled for the blur.

RENDERING NATURE

SKY AND TERRAIN RENDERING

In This Chapter

Many 3D video games use environments that have an outdoor setting. When you are trying to realistically render these outdoor settings, a lot of assets and resources are often required to create the desired effect. Management of these resources can become complex within the game or game engine. In video games the environments are highly important aspects of a game that should not be taken lightly.

The purpose of this chapter is to cover on a high level the rendering of general outdoor environments. This chapter covers rendering skies and terrains as well as other objects in nature such as clouds, trees, plants, and grass. Much of the outdoor rendering scenery in many modern realistic games requires a great deal of artistic ability as well as the technology to drive it. Because of the nature of the subject, this chapter takes a high-level look at these topics since each one could require a book of its own dealing with both programming and art.

SKY RENDERING

The sky is a very important visual cue that exists in outdoor environments in video games. The way the sky looks can depend on a lot of factors such as how much detail is desired, how visible the sky is, how important it is for the sky to look a certain way, and so forth. Without the sky, most environments, especially outdoor areas, do not look realistic. If realism is the goal of a game, attention must be given to how the sky is represented, managed, and rendered.

This chapter discusses a few straightforward methods of rendering a sky in video games. Some of these methods are very simple, while others require more resources to achieve more realism. There is no one perfect option since the game's environment itself can lend more to the decision than personal preference.

Sky Planes

A sky plane is a large textured quad that hovers above the scene. At a minimum, a sky plane can be represented by two large triangles that have either a stationary position or are positioned to always have their middle above the player. In early games the sky was simulated by rotating textures, which gave the appearance of dynamic clouds. In early games, such as *Goldeneye* for Nintendo 64, representing a sky in this manner was sufficient and impressive to look at.

 Dynamically altering the texture coordinates to make the texture appear to be animated is called rotating textures. This texture is usually a tiling image. The rotation can be applied to the texture matrix.

Figure 13.1 shows an example of a sky plane. Because the sky plane is so simplistic in shape and geometry, it often lacks the visual realism that modern games employ today. When looking at a sky plane at an angle, the realism it was trying to achieve can be lost. The disadvantage to using a sky plane can be minimized considerably if the environment itself had lots of other environment geometry that blocked the viewer's ability to see the sky plane's limitations. Examples of these additional pieces of geometry are mountains, large buildings, large trees, and so forth. If the sky plane's extents and limitations can be blocked, a game could potentially have some usefulness when using a sky plane.

FIGURE 13.1   Sky plane.

ON THE CD

On the CD-ROM are demo applications that display a sky plane in a 3D scene. These demos (one each for OpenGL, Direct3D 9, and Direct3D 10) display a ground plane along with the sky plane to give the viewer more reference to how an empty scene that uses a sky plane might look.

Although the scene is simplistic, it should be evident why sky planes might not be the best option in all situations. In nature we are able to see the sky as it passes over the horizon. With the sky plane there is no horizon, and thus the illusion that the geometry is the sky can be lost. If a game can place enough objects around the environment to block the horizon, this is not so bad, but in many games, the view distance of outdoor scenes is very important. In games like *Halo 3* a lot of work is put into the horizon of outdoor environments, even for areas the player cannot explore but can see. If a game like *Halo* used a sky plane, a lot of detail, realism, and immersion would be lost in the large outdoor settings in which the game primarily takes place.

Even if the horizon issue was resolved using geometry that makes up the gaming environment, the sky plane still has the limitation of being flat. This occurs because both the texture and the sky plane itself are 2D. One way to get around this limitation is to use multiple layers of textures. By using multi-texture techniques and by using different animation speeds for the cloud textures, it is possible to fake depth in the sky in a way that makes it look more realistic and interesting. This can also be seen in the demo application for the sky plane technique where two textures are used for the sky and both textures are moving at different speeds.

Sky Boxes

Sky boxes are used as an alternative to sky planes. With a sky box it is possible to not only cover the horizon with interesting imagery but also to give players the illusion that there is more to the world around them than what actually exists. All outdoor scenes in major video games like *Halo 3*, *Crysis*, *Metal Gear Solid 4*, and so forth use some form of bounding geometry for the sky and horizon. This bounding geometry can be as simple as a box (i.e., sky box) or a dome (i.e., sky dome). Using a dome for the bounding geometry that represents the sky and horizon is discussed in more detail in the next section. In the early days of 3D games sky boxes were the standard. Today, sky domes with complex layers of textures have become the norm and can be seen in many, if not all, professionally made games.

A sky box is literally a box that is extremely large and is centered on the player's view or surrounding the game level. A sky box texture can be thought of as a cube map where each side of the box represents a different direction. A sky box does not need to be represented by many triangles since the sides of the box are flat. This makes using sky boxes fairly cheap compared to sky domes.

One limitation to the sky box is that the edges of the box's polygons can often be seen. Also, depending on the textures and how close the box is, it is possible to see the sharp direction turns that make up the box edges. This limitation has to do with not only the shape of the box, but also with texture filtering that is applied to the images that make up the bounding scenery. In some cases these artifacts can break the illusion that the sky box was designed to create, which is to give players the illusion that there is an actual world around them that is alive and present.

There are two easy ways to fix this limitation. One way is to use edge clamping when setting up the texture filtering modes that are used on the sky box's textures. Another option is to place a border around the image, for example, a five-pixel border, and adjust the texture coordinates so that only the image pixels that make up the actual image to be displayed are mapped, and the border is ignored. Since the main problem is texture filtering when using linear interpolation, placing this border around the image and adjusting the texture coordinates so that they don't reference the edges (borders) can be done to avoid artifacts that are common with sky box textures. This assumes that edge clamping for the texture filter is not used.

A benefit to sky boxes, and bounding geometry for scenery in general, is that they cover the entire screen, so it is not necessary to clear the color buffer between frames. This is true because every pixel of the screen is rendered to by the bounding scenery or game objects, so the clearing of the color buffers is an operation that proves useless. A series of games that appears to avoid clearing the color buffer is *Halo 1*, *2*, and *3*. Anyone able to glitch past the game's invisible barriers that are used to keep players from going places they are not intended to go can move to a location where the sky dome and visible geometry do not cover the entire screen. This causes many rendering artifacts of duplicate geometry appearing on the screen, smearing, and so forth. Since players are not supposed to be able to access these areas, these visual errors caused by not clearing the color buffer can be ignored. Of course, this would be a different situation if the artifacts appeared in the legal gaming area.

ON THE CD

On the CD-ROM in the Chapter 13 folder are demo applications for OpenGL and the two versions of Direct3D used in this book that use the sky box method. The skybox uses linear interpolation without edge clamping so that the artifacts associated with them can be better seen and witnessed visually in real time.

Sky Domes

There are benefits to using bounding geometry in video games. The most obvious benefit is that it allows artists to extend the game world and create the illusion of a world beyond where the player can navigate. A great example of this can be seen in *Alan Wake* for the PC, as shown in Figure 13.2. The bounding environment is so well done that it is hard to differentiate between where the game level ends and the backdrop begins.

FIGURE 13.2 Extending past the game world in *Alan Wake*.

Sky planes and sky boxes are really good to use for indoor environments that have views of the outside or environments where there are many geometric occluding objects around the game player. Most modern games that have outdoor settings where the view distance is important use what are known as sky domes. A sky dome is a literal dome where half of a sphere is used for the shape. Since most games have some ground geometry, it is not necessary to have a full sphere shape since only the top half would be visible. For games that do need something under the sky dome that does not include the ground, a plane or a flat circle is often used to retain the illusion. This is commonly done in the *Halo* series, where the player is able to look off of a cliff into the distant bounding scenery (sky dome) and down at the distant bottom geometry.

 If the sky dome is all that is used, it is possible to make the clear color the same as the fog color if fog is used. The downside to this is that clearing of the color buffer would need to be enabled if it was possible to look at a region of the game where no geometry existed.

Sky domes offer many benefits over sky planes or boxes. The first benefit is that they allow for a smooth transition from the top of the sky into the horizon. The second benefit is that they give a spherical shape to the sky, which is more realistic. In the game *Ratchet and Clank: Tools of Destruction* the bounding scenery has a smooth and natural look as the view circles around the player.

Another benefit can be seen in the game *Alan Wake*, where the sky dome allows colors to be blended in a way that gives the appearance of a smooth transition from day to night (see Figure 13.3). Day-to-night cycles are becoming very popular in video games that provide open worlds. In video games like *Saint's Row* and *Grand Theft Auto IV*, the progression from day to night and the illusion of a living and constant game world is very important.

FIGURE 13.3   *Alan Wake's* day-to-night cycle with the sky dome.

Additional benefits to using sky domes are that they allow for more realistic atmospheric effects. These effects include sun rays, 3D clouds, more realistic texture layering, and so forth. The major downside to using a sky dome is that it requires far more polygons than the other methods mentioned in this chapter. Games that do not take advantage of what the sky dome has to offer might be perfectly suitable for a sky box instead. This depends on the game's environment and what is suitable for the desired look. Another downside to using sky domes is that it is harder to create impressive high-quality textures for them. Even with its downsides, though, the sky dome is probably the best choice to use for many different types of games, especially open outdoor games.

On the CD-ROM in the Chapter 13 folder are demo applications called SkyDomeGL, SkyDomeD3D9, and SkyDomeD3D10 that use the sky dome method. The sky dome is a geometric model loaded from an .obj file and is textured with a simple sky image.

Clouds

Clouds are a very important feature of the sky. With clouds the level of realism of bounding sky geometry can be increase substantially. Several different methods can be used to create clouds. The first method is to use a texture for the clouds. This texture can be created by an artist, captured by a photographer, or generated mathematically.

One method for the generation of clouds using noise uses an algorithm known as Perlin noise. Perlin noise is a set of data that is somewhat but not completely random. An example of completely random data is white noise such as that of a TV screen displaying static. Perlin noise is smoother than white nose but has random properties. When implemented, Perlin noise is a 3D data set of (X, Y, Z) or a 4D data set of (X, Y,

Z, time), where time can be used to interpolate the data. This interpolation can lead to the appearance of animations within the data set. If Perlin noise is used for clouds, it is possible to interpolate the data to give the clouds motion. Perlin noise can also be tilable, which can make it an interesting choice for game graphics.

It is possible to also use geometry to represent clouds. This geometry can be 2D imposters such as billboards or 3D geometric shapes. If shadow mapping is used on the 3D clouds, it is also possible to allow the shadows to be cast onto the environment in real time. An example of using 3D geometry for clouds in a modern video game can be seen in *Crysis*. In *Crysis* the clouds are created using volumetric layering. It uses this same technique to realistically create the fog in the game as well.

Clouds can be created using simplistic methods or more complex methods. Which method is used depends on how the clouds are viewed. If the player can fly (e.g., using a plane, a character's special ability, etc.), then faking clouds that are part of the bounding scenery's geometry might not be enough. In *Crysis* the clouds and fog are so well done that they add a new level of cinematographic look when viewing the game world from above and around the clouds.

TERRAINS

Terrains in video games are used to represent the roughness and nature of the Earth's surface. To realistically model the outdoors, some level of terrain has to be used to retain realism. Without the rough and varying nature of terrains, outdoors scenes can appear flat and unrealistic. In early games this was enough because terrain is hard to realistically represent without a certain level (count) of geometric polygons. Terrains that have smooth rolling hills require even more polygons, which would have been difficult to manage on early gaming hardware.

There are various ways to create and represent terrains in video games. This chapter only briefly discusses terrains since the topic, including the real-time management of terrains, can fill a book on its own. When done correctly, the terrain of an environment, in combination with distance scene geometry (e.g., sky domes) can create a vast and compelling atmosphere. An example of this can be seen in the newly released game *Assassin's Creed*.

Brute Force Rendering Terrains

Terrain is essentially a complex geometric model, and like any model this geometry can be rendered all at once in a video game. This is known as the brute force style of rendering a terrain. Whether or not the terrain can be rendered in one call depends on the graphics hardware and the number of polygons in the terrain model. In modern video games the terrains are so complex and huge that it is not practical or possible to render the entire terrain all at once in real time.

In most cases the terrain is rendered in small pieces, and only the pieces that are visible are rendered. Within those rendered pieces most game engines further optimize the rendered data by using varying levels of detail, which is the process of rendering geometry at lower resolutions as objects move farther from the viewer. By drawing distant geometry at a low resolution, it is possible to save processing operations without much of a visual difference to the player. Since the ability to notice detail decreases with distance, using level of detail is and has been a tremendously useful technique for game developers.

Chapter 15, "Optimization," discusses various management techniques that can be used for rendering environments such as terrains in more detail. These topics include level of detail, data partitioning, and other very useful topics to game developers.

Height Map Terrains

A height map is an image that stores height values rather than color values. A terrain can be thought of as a highly geometric grid where the height values of each of these grid edge points vary from one to the other. These varying heights can be stored and read from a height map, which is what some terrains do. The heights in a height map can be controlled so that rolling hills and mountains are represented visually in an image editor such as Adobe Photoshop. An example of a terrain created from a height map is shown in Figure 13.4.

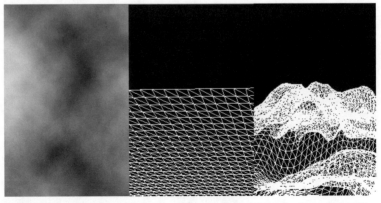

FIGURE 13.4   Height map (left), flat grid (middle), and the final terrain (right).

Using a height map to displace the vertices of a grid that is acting as the environment is a technique known as displacement mapping. If the terrain is static, the displacement mapping can either occur once when the terrain is being loaded and prepared for use, or, better yet, it can be done offline so that the ready terrain can be loaded more quickly. Real-time displacement mapping on the GPU can also be performed, but it can be considered useless if the terrain is static. Displacement mapping does not affect the amount of geometry that makes up the terrain.

Terrain Generation

Terrains can be generated algorithmically using a number of different methods. The benefit to using an algorithm to calculate the terrain includes being able to quickly create a series of models using the CPU by changing various parameters. One option with terrains created in this manner is to modify them after the algorithm has created a starting mesh to work with. Two very popular algorithms used to generate terrain that we discuss in this chapter are the midpoint displacement and fault formation algorithms.

Midpoint displacement is also called the diamond-square algorithm as well as the plasma fractal algorithm. The midpoint displacement algorithm creates a line between two points that lie on the edge of a square. This square initially is the edges of the entire terrain model. An example square is shown in Figure 13.5.

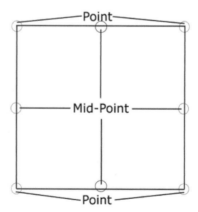

FIGURE 13.5   An example of a starting square with four corners.

The midpoint of the square, let's call it point E, is calculated by averaging each of the corners of the square and adding a random value between $-d/2$ and $d/2$. The value d can be any starting value. An example of d can be the length between the two extreme points of the square. Initially, since all heights are 0 (assuming the grid is not given initial height values), the first midpoint is essentially the random value. Once point E is set, the algorithm recursively performs the same process for the subsquares until a specific level of detail is reached. This is shown in Figure 13.6.

Original   First Pass   Second Pass

FIGURE 13.6 After one pass (left), two passes (mid), and three passes (right).

After each pass, d is multiplied by 2^{-r}, where r is a value that can be used to determine the detail of the terrain. The smaller r is, the more roughness will appear in the terrain. If you are starting with a grid with a set number of vertices, the edges that make up the grid and the middle of the entire terrain are processed in the first pass; the subsquares between each edge and the first-pass's midpoint are processed in the second pass. This continues recursively until no more subsquares can be processed.

The second algorithm, fault formation, starts off with a grid for the terrain. This grid can be flat or have initial height values, which is also the case for the midpoint displacement algorithm. The algorithm creates a random line from one edge of the terrain to the other. For every vertex on one side of the terrain, their heights are lowered, while on the opposite side their heights are raised. The amount that is raised or decreased is determined by d, where d can start off as the length between the two extreme points of the terrain, for example. After every pass, d is decreased. This occurs for as many passes as are specified. The more passes that are specified, the rougher the terrain will appear. An example of fault formation is shown in Figure 13.7. With each pass that is executed, the value of d should be decreased but never made equal to or less than 0.

FIGURE 13.7   After one pass (left), two passes (mid), and three passes (right).

Terrain Box Filtering

Some terrains, especially those generated algorithmically, can appear to have rough edges that cause them not to look like natural terrain. One solution to this is to use a smoothing filter to smooth out the edges of the terrain to create more natural-looking hills, valleys, and so forth.

A straightforward and effective algorithm is to average each height with its neighbors. Up to eight vertex heights surround each vertex and can be added together and averaged to get the new height of the current vertex. This assumes a 3×3 filter is being used, where the middle of the 3×3 area is the current vertex, there is one vertex on each side of the current vertex, and there are three vertices above and below the current vertex's row. The filter simply adds up all nine heights and averages them out to create the new height. Once all vertices have been processed, the terrain will appear smoother. Vertices that appear on the edge of the terrain will not be averaged with nine vertices but with however many vertices surround them. An example of a box filter that can be used to filter out an array of heights follows.

```
unsigned char *BoxFilter(int w, int h, unsigned char *heightMap)
{
    if(heightMap == NULL || w <= 0 || h <= 0)
        return NULL;
```

```
unsigned int size = w * h;
unsigned int startWidth = 0;
unsigned int startHeight = 0;
unsigned int endWidth = w - startWidth;
unsigned int endHeight = h - startHeight;

unsigned char *filteredMap = new unsigned char[size];

if(filteredMap == NULL)
   return NULL;

for(unsigned int z = startHeight; z < endHeight; z++)
{
   for(unsigned int x = startWidth; x < endWidth; x++)
   {
      float heightSum = 0.0f;
      float totalHeightsFound = 1.0f;

      // Sample top row of heights (row 1 col 1, 2, 3).
      if((x - 1) + (z - 1) * w >= 0 && (x - 1) + (z - 1) * w < size)
      {
         heightSum += heightMap[(x - 1) + (z - 1) * w];
         totalHeightsFound++;
      }

      if(x + (z - 1) * w >= 0 && x + (z - 1) * w < size)
      {
         heightSum += heightMap[x + (z - 1) * w];
         totalHeightsFound++;
      }

      if((x + 1) + (z - 1) * w >= 0 && (x + 1) + (z - 1) * w < size)
      {
         heightSum += heightMap[(x + 1) + (z - 1) * w];
         totalHeightsFound++;
      }


      // Sample first height in mid row of map (row 2, col 1).
      if((x - 1) + z * w >= 0 && (x - 1) + z * w < size)
      {
         heightSum += heightMap[(x - 1) + z * w];
         totalHeightsFound++;
      }
```

```
                // Sample this height in mid row of map (row 2, col 2).
                heightSum += heightMap[x + z * w];


                // Sample first height in mid row of map (row 2, col 3).
                if((x + 1) + z * w >= 0 && (x + 1) + z * w < size)
                {
                    heightSum += heightMap[(x + 1) + z * w];
                    totalHeightsFound++;
                }


                // Sample last row of map (row 3 col 1, 2, 3).
                if((x - 1) + (z + 1) * w >= 0 && (x - 1) + (z + 1) * w < size)
                {
                    heightSum += heightMap[(x - 1) + (z + 1) * w];
                    totalHeightsFound++;
                }

                if(x + (z + 1) * w >= 0 && x + (z + 1) * w < size)
                {
                    heightSum += heightMap[(x    ) + (z + 1) * w];
                    totalHeightsFound++;
                }

                if((x + 1) + (z + 1) * w >= 0 && (x + 1) + (z + 1) * w < size)
                {
                    heightSum += heightMap[(x + 1) + (z + 1) * w];
                    totalHeightsFound++;
                }

                // Average for this new height.
                filteredMap[x + z * w] = (unsigned char)(heightSum /
                                        totalHeightsFound);
            }
        }

    return filteredMap;
}
```

If you are using an array of heights as the height map, the preceding function above can be used to smooth it out before applying it to a terrain. Another option that uses the code is to copy the new heights to the parameter array. If the temporary array is deleted, then calling this function will take care of filtering the heights without any additional work outside of the function. This assumes you do not want to have a separate filtered array returned from the function.

Although the code looks complex, it is actually fairly simple. The code just loops through the entire array element by element. For each vertex it adds up all heights that surround it and averages them out. The new result is stored in the filtered array, and once all heights have been processed, the algorithm is complete.

Texturing Terrains

There are a few ways to texture a terrain. The first method is to use a large texture that can be stretched across the surface of the terrain. This method is straightforward, but the textures need to be huge to preserve a decent level of visual quality with the surface-mapped image. Generating the texture coordinates for a terrain in this matter is pretty straightforward. If the minimum texture coordinate is 0 and the maximum is 1, the texture coordinate for each vertex is its grid position width and height percent. This is calculated by dividing the vertex's X-axis by the width of the terrain and dividing the Z-axis by the length of the terrain. The heights of each vertex would not affect the texture coordinates—just the X and Z.

The second option is to use tiled images. One potential downside to using tiled images is that patterns can appear or seams can be seen, but if the tile image is good or if a set of tiles is used, the quality of the terrain's texture can be improved. Creating texture coordinates that can be used for a texture that is to be tiled is fairly easy. If you are using the method described earlier for calculating the texture coordinates of the terrain, all you would need is to multiply the maximum width and height of the terrain by however many times the texture should repeat in that direction when dividing them by one of the axes to get the texture coordinate percent. For example, if the terrain's width is 256 and the current vertex has an X-axis position of 100, if the texture is to be repeated four times across the terrain, the following equation could be used, which gives the result of 0.09 for the TU texture coordinate:

$$tex\_coord\_u = 100 \; / \; (256 * 4)$$

Terrain textures often display some blurriness. Increasing texture resolution can help improve this but at the cost of increased bandwidth requirements and memory. Another option is to use a detail texture, which is a grayscale texture that is stretched across the surface of the terrain. The contents of the detail texture often have small cracks and bumps within them. When multi-textured on the surface of the terrain, the detail texture adds enough visual detail that the terrain appears sharper than without it. An example of this is shown in Figure 13.8.

FIGURE 13.8   Decal texture (left), detail texture (middle),
and decal with a detail texture (right).

Some terrain textures are created by using a series of tiles, where each tile represents the terrain texture at a different elevation. In many modern games different textures are blended together to create a mixture between rock and grass, grass and snow, rock and sand, and so forth (see Figure 13.9). A tile can be an image of any material that can be used on the terrain's surface. Snow, for example, can appear more on the top of mountains, while below, near the bottom, grass and rock can be used. A texture for the terrain that has these elements can be generated by mixing these tiles based on the height at which they are suppose to appear.

FIGURE 13.9   Textures blended based on elevation.

In a straightforward implementation this would work, but in some cases additional parameters are used to control the terrain texture generation. This includes slopes, cliffs, and other things of that nature that can affect the appearance of a terrain's tile mixture. This is ideally an artistic question. When creating an algorithm that is able to generate an entire terrain's texture from a set of tiles, it is important to consider what rules are needed to ensure that the textures are created in a specific manner.

In its simplest form texturing using blended tiles is fairly straightforward and can be broken into the following steps.

- Set a maximum elevation for each tile.
- For each vertex that is rendered determine which two tiles the vertex's height falls between.

- Use the lower tile as the minimum height, use the higher tile as the maximum height, and use the vertex's height to find the percent that the vertex height falls within that range.
- Use that percent as the blend amount when performing multi-texturing.

If the terrain is static, this process can be performed offline to create one large texture or a series of textures that has the final results of the elevation blending.

Terrain Patches

Sometimes the terrain is broken up into smaller pieces that can be individually processed by the game engine. One idea that can be done in a game is to split the terrain into patches. A patch is a small square of geometric primitives. When placed side by side, these patches, collectively, represent the entire terrain. An example of a patch is shown in Figure 13.10.

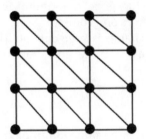

FIGURE 13.10   A terrain patch.

By splitting the terrain into patches it is possible to perform the following tasks.

- Render only the patches that are visible.
- Render the patches at a lower level of detail as they move further from the camera.
- Texture each patch with its own texture, which could also come from a texture atlas.

Earlier in this chapter we mentioned that most common game terrains are too large to be rendered using a brute force approach. Terrains in modern video games are often broken up into smaller pieces, where each of these pieces can be tested for visibility. When rendering, only the pieces that are visible are sent to the graphics hardware. This idea falls under terrain management, and it can become quite complex for a lot of the next-generation gaming titles that are starting to hit the market.

Culling sections of the terrain is often left to other data structures and algorithms, some of which is discussed in Chapter 15. By using terrain patches it is easy to vary the level of detail for the patch as the view moves further away from it. In the example in Figure 13.11 the indices that are used to draw the patch vary for each level of detail, and some levels have more triangles than others.

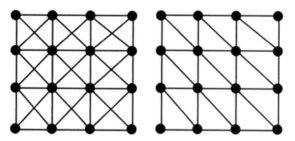

FIGURE 13.11 Level of detail on a terrain patch.

Terrain level of detail can suffer detail "pop-ins" as the view gets close enough for a higher level to be used. This is often seen in games, and a lot of effort goes into minimizing the player's ability to notice level-of-detail changes on geometry. Most level-of-detail changes won't be noticed unless the change is large enough to cause an obvious shift on screen. Chapter 15 includes a discussion about how to minimize this behavior for terrains.

ADDITIONAL TOPICS

There are many additional topics concerning the creation, management and rendering of a terrain. Many of these topics are based on art and resources that are used to make an environment seem more natural and realistic. In most games the terrains are not empty, and they often include many other objects, each of which needs to be managed by the game engine as well. Some of the more common game objects include the following entities.

- Trees
- Plants
- Grass
- Rocks
- Roads and other paths

Atmospheric effects also can be used to great effect with outdoor terrains. Nature has a lot going on, and to realistically render it a game scene needs to simulate many different things at once. These things can include some of the following, and many of these items require a lot of effort by game artists.

- Fog
- Clouds

- Dust
- Sun rays
- Debris (e.g., leaves blowing in the wind)
- Day and night cycles
- Weather effects (e.g., rain, snow, heat haze)

The terrain itself can become quite complex. Not only does terrain have rolling hills, mountains, and other properties, but they also have many other properties that are needed to capture the authentic look of real-life terrain. These objects include the following.

- Caves
- Cliffs
- Islands
- Water (e.g., rivers, oceans)
- Ditches
- Craters
- Canyons

Terrains and the other entities in an outdoor environment can require a tremendous amount of detail and resources when creating a realistic modern video game. In Chapter 15, a number of the various data structures and algorithms that have been development throughout the years are examined. These data structures and algorithms have the primary purpose of speeding up the rendering of complex environments, whether they are indoors or outdoors. Every game engine has the challenge of finding the best solution for the types of games that will be built using it. A few of these topics that are discussed in Chapter 15 include the following.

- CLOD
- ROAM
- Quad-trees
- Octrees

TERRAIN DEMO

ON THE CD

On the book's CD-ROM are demo applications called TerrainGL, TerrainD3D9, and TerrainD3D10. In these demos the application creates a high polygonal grid that acts as the terrain. The demo then loads a height map image and uses the green color component as the vertex height. The width and height of the height map image dictates the width and height of the terrain. Since the height map is a grayscale image, any one of the color components could have been used since they are all the same value.

In the terrain demos there is also a sky dome surrounding the terrain. The arrow keys can be used to move throughout the terrain, and the escape key is used to quit the application. The terrain demo is nothing new or special compared to the demos seen throughout this book. The only thing it does is adjust the height values of the grid that it creates in a loop with the values from within an image created in Photoshop. In Chapter 15, more complex terrains are created for the discussions on terrain rendering optimizations and management. In this chapter the terrain is small enough to be rendered like any other 3D model.

Summary

The discussion of terrains and everything that is included with them can easily span a book on its own. This is especially true when it comes to the artwork that is created for modern video games. When creating a realistic terrain, a lot of time and effort goes into not only making the terrain look as good as it can, but also in getting the technology as efficient as possible so it can manage the terrain and all of the game world's objects.

The following elements were discussed in this chapter.

- General terrains
- Height maps for terrains
- Displacement mapping
- Terrain generation
- Terrain texture mapping
- Terrain texture generation
- Sky planes
- Sky boxes
- Sky domes
- Clouds

Chapter Questions

Answers to the following chapter review questions can be found in Appendix A, "Answers to Chapter Questions."

1. List three ways a sky can be represented in a video game.
2. What can be used with the sky plane to make it more realistic?
3. What is an advantage to using a sky box? What is a disadvantage to using a sky box?
4. List one method that can be used to minimize the limitation of the sky plane not crossing the horizon.

5. List three advantages to using a sky dome in a video game. What is one disadvantage to using a sky dome in comparison to a sky box?
6. List two general ways clouds are presented in video games.
7. How does *Crysis* render clouds and fog?
8. What is brute force rendering when it comes to terrains? Are terrains usually rendered using this technique? Why or why not?
9. Describe terrain patches.
10. Describe the midpoint displacement algorithm. How does the value of *r* affect the terrain?
11. Describe the fault formation algorithm. Why is it important that the value *d* never reaches 0?
12. What are texture tiles for terrains? How can they be blended together to simulate natural changes in elevation?
13. List four techniques briefly mentioned that can be used to manage environment data.
14. How can images be used to manipulate the height of terrain vertices?
15. Describe the box filtering algorithm. What is its purpose when working with terrains?

CHAPTER EXERCISES

Exercise 1: Build off of the sky dome demo and allow for a color to be specified that is combined with the texture. Use this to create a very simple simulation of a day-to-night cycle where the arrow keys can be used to move from night to day.

Exercise 2: Build off of the terrain demo and create a piece of geometry that can be placed under the sky done. When creating the terrain, create edges around the terrain that go far downward toward the bottom of the sky dome to give the illusion that the sky dome and the terrain are one. Try your best artistically when creating the geometry and textures.

Exercise 3: Build off of the previous exercise and add layered textures to the sky dome. Perform this by using alpha mapping and multi-texturing. Allow each layer to move at slightly different speeds to give the appearance that one layer of clouds is farther from the other. Try your best artistically when creating the geometry and textures.

WATER RENDERING

In This Chapter

- Examining Water in Modern Games
- Additional Water Effects
- Water Rendering Demo

Rendering water realistically has long been a goal of many outdoor rendered scenes. In the early days of 3D video games, hardware limited the amount of detail that could appear in outdoor scenes. As technology advanced, so did the realism and complexity of all types of scenes, especially outdoor environments. This advancement can be seen in the detail of terrain complexity; the sky, trees, and grass; and especially in the visual quality and representation of water. The advanced use of water can have a tremendous impact on the visual realism in a game's environment, and today, many games use this once overlooked part of outdoor environments.

In this chapter we briefly discuss the rendering of water in 3D video games. On today's hardware, water can be rendered more naturally and realistically than in the past. The rendering and simulation of water will continue to grow in complexity as the hardware allows. Water can breathe new life into any outdoor scene, especially when combined with game physics.

EXAMINING WATER IN MODERN GAMES

Water can be seen in many games throughout the history of 3D gaming. In the beginning, water was essentially a very simplistic model that acted as water but did not use any type of simulation that is associated with water. Today, water gets a lot of attention, and the games that use it are showing the industry how much water can add to an outdoor game. The game *BioShock*, from 2K Games, uses water as its main element for the gameplay and atmosphere.

In this chapter we examine how water is rendered in various popular games. At the end of the chapter, we present the chapter's water rendering demo. There are many different ways water can be represented in a game. The important thing to take from this chapter is that a game should use a method that works best for it, the hardware, and the types of environments trying represented in the game.

Goldeneye 007: Nintendo 64

In Rare's *Goldeneye 007* for the Nintendo 64, water was used in some of the many game environments to add to the outdoor scenery. *Goldeneye 007* is a legendary game that redefined home gaming console graphics and first-person shooting gameplay on a system other than a PC. When it was first released in 1997, it became one of the best-selling titles for Nintendo's N64 (the console's nickname) gaming system. Today, *Goldeneye 007* remains one of the most beloved games of all time.

Goldeneye 007 used the most simple approach to rendering water in a game. When this game was released, hardware limitations kept outdoor scene complexity relatively low compared to today's games. Because of this, water in the game did not possess any properties of water other than its color and that the player could not walk on it.

To render water, *Goldeneye 007* essentially used a large textured square that was placed in the game world to act as the environment's water. To give the water surface more of a distinct look and feel, the game developers used moving texture coordinates to simulate the water moving. In addition to using dynamic texture coordinates for the water's surface, they also used them for the sky plane. This gave the appearance of moving clouds as well as moving water.

At the time, rendering water in this manner was acceptable. We performed the process of rendering water, and the sky for that matter, in the Sky Plane demo application in Chapter 13, "Sky and Terrain Rendering." This method is as easy as rendering water can get in a video game.

Perfect Dark: Nintendo 64

Rare's 2000 game *Perfect Dark* was the follow-up title to their blockbuster hit *Goldeneye 007* for the Nintendo 64. *Perfect Dark* was built using a modified version of the framework (game engine) used in *Goldeneye 007*. *Perfect Dark* not only proved itself a worthy follow-up to Rare's *Goldeneye 007*, but it used improved graphics and rendering techniques. This was in part thanks to the Nintendo 64 expansion RAM add-on, which was used to boost the graphical quality in many Nintendo 64 games that supported its use.

Water in the original *Perfect Dark* still used the same generally simple idea as *Goldeneye 007*. In *Goldeneye 007* the water's animation movement was linear and constant. This means that the speed at which the animation was viewed did not change, and neither did the direction of its movement. In practice this is very easy, but when implemented, it doesn't truly look like water. On hardware such as the Nintendo 64, there was only so much that could have been done anyway when compared to today's hardware.

In *Perfect Dark* the water's animation was modified so that it changed direction and speed as it was being viewed. This gave it a more believable water-like appearance using the game console's hardware at a relatively cheap cost. To create the style of water seen in *Goldeneye 007*, a matrix can be used on the texture coordinates to rotate them in a specific direction. To implement the style of water seen in *Perfect Dark*, the direction and speed can be dynamically adjusted for each frame. This can be as simple as taking a velocity vector and using a sine wave that is based on time to move the vector forward and backward. Since velocity is being used, the speed decreases as each axis reaches 0 and increases as they move farther away in either the positive or negative direction. This can be seen using the following equation if the water is moving only in the direction of the X-axis:

New_Velocity = Velocity_Constant * Vector3D(sin(time), 0, 0)

The sine waves more within the −1 to 1 range. Alternatively, the equation can be expanded to use each axis of the vector. If the original velocity constant was given different values for each axis, the look of the water using this method would appear more dynamic. Also, axis modifiers can be used by using random values to adjust the vector being multiplied by the velocity to give it an even more dynamic look that does not appear like canned animations.

Dragonball Z Budokai Tenkaichi 2: Nintendo Wii

In the Nintendo Wii game *Dragonball Z Budokai Tenkaichi 2 (DBZBT 2)*, the water used is slightly more complicated than that seen in *Goldeneye 007* and *Perfect Dark*. In *DBZBT 2* it was important for the water to have a more realistic look and feel while also being friendly to render on the Wii's hardware. It was also important that the players and objects be able to interact with the water by freely moving in and out of it.

In *DBZBT 2* the water is essentially a large square. To give the water a more water-like appearance, the translation location of the water moves slightly up and down to simulate water movement. This transforms the entire water surface, which is as easy as using a sine wave to modulate the Y-axis of the surface's position. Some other games, a few of which will be discussed later in this chapter, take that general idea and apply it to a grid of height values to simulate water waves much more realistically.

The water in *DBZBT 2* is also semi-transparent. In *Goldeneye 007* and *Perfect Dark*, the water surface was a solid texture. In *DBZBT 2*, alpha is used so that objects under water can be seen from above and vice versa. This gives the water a much more natural feel, but it requires more work for the artist because the terrain under the water must be present, whereas in a game like the original *Perfect Dark*, it does not have to actually be there.

The water's texture is simple and can be recreated by either using an animated sprite or by using multi-texturing where the game interpolates between two or more textures based on time. Both methods give the illusion that the water is alive and active, and they are both pretty simple to implement.

In a game like *DBZBT 2*, no special techniques need to be applied to objects that are rendered under water. By using textures for static surfaces under the water whose tints match the overall water color, it is possible to render surfaces that look like they are truly underwater without any complex graphical techniques. The job, in this case, is moved from the programmers to the artist.

Half-Life 2 Lost Coast: PC

Half-Life has been responsible for helping to shape and redefine the first-person shooter genre in the video game industry. *Half-Life 2* boasts some of the most impressive PC game graphics of its time. Since its release, *Half-Life 2* expansions and additions, including *Episode 1*, *Episode 2*, *Portal*, and *Team Fortress 2*, have continued the tradition of great games that not only play well, but look fantastic.

Water can be seen throughout *Half-Life 2*. One game level in particular, called *Lost Coast*, uses a host of different graphical techniques to render the game's water, which include using high–dynamic range rendering and lighting. In *Half-Life 2* the goal was to render water that looked and acted more like what people would expect from water. In the games examined previously, this means that using a large flat surface such as a solid textured square would not be enough to achieve the desired effect. When *Half-Life 2* was released, the PC hardware was advanced enough to render water using much more complicated formulas and techniques that really pushed water rendering in video games to new heights.

The water in *Half-Life 2* uses many more graphical techniques than the previously examined games. For starters, the game uses reflections for the water's surface. Reflections allow the scene around the water to realistically appear on the water's surface. The same can be said for refractions. Reflection and refraction mapping were discussed in Chapter 7, "Additional Surface Mapping," and their implementation is fairly straightforward.

The water surface in *Half-Life 2* uses multiple texture images. Among these images are moving normal map images. Normal mapping on the surface of water can be used to create the illusion of very small waves being formed and moving throughout the scene. By using multiple texture layers, it is possible to create some really interesting small waves of water on a large-scale surface that represents something like the ocean. Even if the surface is a large square, like in the games examined up to this point, a normal map can be used to give the water a much more realistic appearance without large amounts of geometry and animation processing.

Half-Life 2 also uses the Frensel effect for the rendering of water to combine refection and refraction contributions based on the angle at which a surface is being rendered. As light strikes water in nature, some of the light is reflected and some is refracted. What is ultimately seen depends greatly on the viewing angle. When viewing water directly downward from above, it is possible to see through water because you are mostly seeing refracted light that went through the water, hit some surface, and then made its way back up to the eyes. When looking at water from an angle, you mostly see the light rays that have reflected off of the water's surface and toward the eyes. This makes sense because reflected rays do not reflect in the mirror direction on water that is in motion, so when looking at water straight downward what is being seen are mostly refracted bounced rays rather than reflected. The same can be said about seeing the surface at an angle where more reflected light rays reach the eye, but the refracted rays don't.

The Frensel effect can be used in computer graphics to give water a much more realistic appearance. To implement the Frensel effect, it is important to determine the viewing angle of the surface. This is represented by the viewing incident vector (discussed in Chapter 7). In real life, Frensel is a very complex topic in the fields of physics and optics. In video game graphics it can be approximated using the following formula:

Coefficient = max(0, min(1, bias + scale * (1 + I dot N) power))

In the equation used to calculated the coefficient for the effect, the vector I is the incident vector and N is the surface normal. When combining reflection and refraction using this coefficient, the following equation can be used:

Color = Coefficient * Reflected_Color + (1 − Coefficient) *
Refracted_Color

The reflected and refracted colors are the colors calculated using the reflection and refraction mapping shaders (discussed in Chapter 7). The scale, bias, and power variables can be used to modify the output of the rendered effect. By using Frensel, water rendered in video games look far more realistic. In *Half-Life 2* this is combined with reflections and refractions, bump mapping to create small animated waves and movements on the water's surface, and transparency. Also, in *Half-Life 2* some objects, such as rocks and mountain sides, are partially rendered using a higher specularity than objects that are dry to simulate wet surfaces. This small touch adds an even higher level of realism because it gives the impression that the objects around the water are indeed wet.

Using reflection, Frensel, and refraction on each color component where red is refracted more than green and blue gives you chromatic dispersion. This effect is used to simulate light entering a surface like a prism.

Crysis: PC

In *Far Cry*, a game by Crytex, the water was initially a simple disk mesh that followed the player around. This mesh used reflections and transparencies to get more of a water feel, but the mesh itself was fairly simple. The game developers wanted to have real 3D waves, which required a more complex mesh than the simple disk.

The game used screen-space tessellation. This worked by projecting the mesh data onto the water surface by using a precomputed screen-space quad. The mesh data were clipped to the bounds of the screen as well. Although artifacts existed, which made physics calculations with the water more difficult, the developers made it work.

 The graphics behind Crysis, *with some mention of* Far Cry, *can be read about in the paper "Finding Next Gen—CryEngine 2." More information on this resource can be found in Appendix B, "Compiling Sample Code."*

The game *Crysis*, also from Crytex, uses a host of additional methods not seen in *Far Cry* or other games such as *Half-Life 2*. For starters, the game used underwater god rays, which are light shafts that appear under the water to give it a more realistic effect. Light shafts are also used above water to show sunlight shining through the trees, for example.

Crysis also uses a technique known as caustics for rendering of water. Caustics describe an envelope of reflected and refracted light as it strikes a curved surface, or, in this case, the water's surface. This can cause light to be more concentrated in some directions than others. See Figure 14.1 for an example.

FIGURE 14.1   Caustics with a glass of water.

The mesh of the water is based on a grid. To animate the grid realistically, the game *Crysis* uses the fast Fourier transform. The fast Fourier transform is an algorithm used to process the information, which is the discrete Fourier transform and its inverse. Essentially, the fast Fourier transform is used to quickly compute large sets of data, which in this case is animation for the water surface.

Crysis uses this information to dynamically change the water animation so that it is based on the wind and wave directions. This can be very computationally expensive, and the game allows the feature to be disabled if desired. In *Crysis* shorelines also appear, as the water and the terrain are in the near distance. Shorelines are discussed in more detail later in this chapter.

BioShock: PC and Xbox 360

2K Games' blockbuster hit, *BioShock*, used water to a degree that has set it apart from many other games being released during its time. In *BioShock* the water was used not just for visual quality but also as part of the gameplay. The developers of *BioShock* had a challenge on their hands with getting the water looking and interacting just right.

In *BioShock* there is a lot going on in terms of its water. Many different particle systems in the game world are water-based. These include leaks, drips, splashes, and so on. The water itself takes on two major forms. First, there is the water that cannot be directly interacted with, which exists outside of the player's immediate environment (the game takes place largely underwater). When the player looks out of windows, the water animations wave in a way to make it appear like the player is truly in an underwater city that is drowning itself.

The second form water takes on is the actual bodies of water that exist throughout many of the rooms in the game. This water not only acts as a visual object, but can be used as a weapon. When enemies are in the water and the player drives electricity through it, the enemies are electrocuted. This makes water a gameplay tool as well as a visual feature. In addition, the water can be used as an aid. For example, if a character is on fire, he can jump in the water to extinguish the flames.

The water used in *BioShock* has many characteristics. Like *Crysis*, it uses caustics simulation for real-time use in addition to reflections, refractions, and per-pixel light. The game developers put in a lot of effort both technically and artistically to create a game world that truly did feel like it was covered with and surrounded by water, which is no easy task.

ADDITIONAL WATER EFFECTS

Many games use additional effects and techniques to add to the water in the gaming scene. Many games require interaction with water. One great example of this is in *BioShock*, where the water has a very important gameplay purpose along with visual importance.

In this section we discuss a few of these additions that can be used to enhance the water in video games.

Optimizations

Large bodies of water like the kind seen in games such as *Crysis* require more complex management systems than in many other games. Water can be managed using the same or similar data structures and algorithms that are used for terrains. Water can be represented using a large flat surface or using a grid of surfaces. The way water is rendered (reflections, refractions, Frensel, etc.), the way it is animated, and the small differences in vertex-to-vertex height values are what makes water different from terrain. With water, level-of-detail is important for far view distances to avoid rendering geometry using more primitives than is necessary. When using physics-based objects and water animations, optimizations become unavoidable in modern video game graphics when large bodies of water can be seen at a given time and orientation from within the environment.

The exact optimizations that are performed are usually based on what the game needs. *DZBT2* would have vastly different management requirements than games like *Crysis* or *BioShock*.

Underwater Rendering

How objects are rendered underwater can be very important when realism is the goal. For most games, this topic is less important depending on the environments and what the game developers feel is acceptable. For games that place importance on how objects underwater are rendered there are various things to take into consideration.

Water is a medium, and how light interacts with it is different from a medium like air. This means visibility will be affected, as well as lighting and shadowing. When light enters water, rays of light can be seen. These rays have various names, but one common name is god rays.

Audio Underwater

Audio has long played an important role in video games of all types. In nature sounds take on a different form when they cross through different media such as air and water. When underwater, the sound can be distorted. In games this phenomenon can be used to add a very subtle but realistic effect within the game environment.

One game that uses this, for example, is *Halo 3*. When the player's camera is under water, the sound effects are altered to simulate what they would sound like when heard underwater. The main purpose of such an effect is to add a touch of realism and give credibility to the game's water.

Water Splashes and Interaction

Sometimes it is important to allow the user of a game to interact with the game's environmental water. When the player does interact with the water in some manner, the player expects certain audio and visual cues. These cues can include the following:

- Footstep sounds that simulate what walking on water would sound like
- Splash sounds when forceful enough collisions occur with the water
- Splashes as an object forcefully enters or exits the water
- Sound of waves hitting the shore for large bodies of animated water
- Expected damage while interacting with water (for example, adding electricity to the water and damaging all players and enemies standing in it)

The purpose of each of these elements is to give credibility to the game's water system. In *BioShock* players can interact with the water by using it as a weapon. If an enemy is standing in the water the player can freeze water into ice to severely damage and restrict the enemy's movements. The player can also ignite oil using fire to damage enemies that are standing on the liquid. This not only adds realism to the game's water, but it also serves as a very useful gameplay tool that the player can control whenever the situation allows.

Another example can be seen in *DZBT2*, where the players can enter and exit the water rapidly, causing a splashing effect. This effect is usually simple to create and requires using textured, animated quads to appear at the location of collision with the water. This small visual effect makes the water more believable since without it, the illusion and credibility of the water can suffer, especially with the forceful collisions that occur in that game.

Water Particle Systems

Particle systems have many uses in video game environments. They can be used for various special effects such as blood splatter, smoke, fire, weather effects, and much more. Many common types of particles are used to add to the environment's water. These common water-based particle effects can include:

- Rain
- Leaks (e.g., leaky pipes)
- Fountains
- Waterfalls
- Splashes
- Wet footprints
- Water-based weapons and tools (e.g., the water backpack gun in *Super Mario Sunshine* for the GameCube)

Water-based particles are used to add elements and features to the game's water that would be difficult to model. Particle systems are an easy way to add these visually useful effects without complex geometry or, in most cases, management systems. *BioShock* made heavy use of water-based particle systems for everything from leaky pipes to water entering the environment through cracks.

Water Physics

The use of physics is becoming standard in the video game industry. Because of the increased emphasis on physics in video games, water physics too are gaining a lot of attention. When players interact with the game environment's water, the response to that interaction can help give the player the feeling that the water is actually real.

Physics is beyond the scope of this book and deals with topics such as buoyancy and rigid bodies. Today, many games use physics with their water management systems to add realism.

Shorelines

Shorelines are a great graphical addition that can be used to increase the realism of rendered water. Shorelines usually appear with large bodies of water such as oceans and lakes. Many games, including *Crysis*, use shorelines with water and terrain.

One method of rendering shorelines is to render them using multitexturing based on the water's surface depth to the terrain height. For patches of water that are close enough to the terrain for shorelines to appear, developers can take advantage of the effect to boost the water's realism for large bodies of water.

Not every scene or every body of water would need to use shorelines in the rendered outdoor scene. For large bodies of water, such as oceans, it might be a great visual touch for those players that can move close to the shore. An example of using shorelines in a 3D video game can be seen in *Crysis*.

Water Rendering Demo

ON THE CD

On the book's accompanying CD-Rom is a demo application for OpenGL, Direct3D 9, and Direct3D 10 called Water (WaterGL, WaterD3D9, and WaterD3D10). The demo application renders a semitransparent water surface using simple water animations based on moving textures and vertex positions. A terrain is also used so that geometry can be seen under the water as well as above it.

The water mesh is based on a grid of polygons. The mesh is animated using a sine wave to move the heights of the water up and down during the application's execution. At the end of this chapter are some exercises that can be followed to add to the realism and detail of the demo, which can make for a fun set of practice exercises.

Summary

Water can have a profound affect on a rendered scene. Water can have an impact on not only outdoor scenes but also on indoor scenes as proven by the game *BioShock*. Water rendering can become fairly complex when realism is the goal. As games become more realistic, game developers often give more attention and resources to the area of water in game graphics.

The following elements were discussed throughout this chapter:

- Water used in various popular 3D video games
- Reflections and water
- Refractions and water
- The Frensel effect
- Bump mapping with water
- Water-based effects

Chapter Questions

Answers to the following chapter review questions can be found in Appendix A, "Answers to Chapter Questions."

1. Describe how water is rendered in the game *Goldeneye 007*. How does it differ from *Perfect Dark*?
2. Describe how the water was rendered in *Dragonball Z Budakai Tenkaichi 2*. What separates it from a game like *Perfect Dark*?
3. Describe how water was rendered in *Half-Life 2*. List four graphical techniques that were used for the rendering of its water.
4. Describe how water was rendered in *Crysis*.

5. Describe how water was rendered in *BioShock*. What did *BioShock* do that was different than the games that came before its release?
6. Describe the Frensel effect. What purpose does it have for water rendering, and how does it affect reflections and refractions?
7. Describe the purpose of using bump maps on the water's surface. What purpose could it have for flat or nearly flat surfaces?
8. How did the water generally work in *Far Cry*?
9. What is the purpose of caustics in computer graphics?
10. What are shorelines, and would a developer determine where they should appear?

CHAPTER EXERCISES

Exercise 1: Add bump mapping to the water's surface to simulate small waves. Use a moving bump map texture to create this effect.

Exercise 2: Build off of Exercise 1 and add reflections with the semi-transparent water surface.

Exercise 3: Build off of Exercise 2 and add refractions and the Frensel effect.

OPTIMIZATIONS AND CONCLUSIONS

OPTIMIZATION

In This Chapter

- Culling Geometry
- Far Plane Culling
- Scene and Space Partitioning
- Geometry Instancing
- Additional Optimization Techniques

The video games that are being released today use highly complex technology to drive the simulations being presented. All next-generation games use a series of optimizations to aid in managing and processing all of a game's resources. Without these optimizations many 3D games would not be practical to operate in real-time. For developers to get the most out of the hardware they develop for, they must implement clever solutions to the various issues that can affect the game's performance.

This chapter examines many of the common optimizations that video game developers use today. Optimizations are a huge topic, and the information discussed in this chapter will give you an idea of a few of the challenges and issues game developers of all types face when creating games. Because this is a book on game graphics, these topics pertain to a game's visuals. Some of the information in this chapter, specifically, the information on scene and space partitioning, can also be used with great success in other areas of a video game such as physics and artificial intelligence.

CULLING GEOMETRY

In complex 3D video game environments there is often more geometry that is not visible to players than what they can see. In rendering, this can lead to an unnecessary amount of geometry being passed to and processed by the graphics hardware. Today's games have more complex scenes than the hardware can handle all at once. Because of this, game developers must develop code that can efficiently render their complex gaming worlds to get the most out of the hardware being used.

The avoidance of rendering unnecessary geometry by only rendering what can be seen is known as geometry culling. Culling is removing geometry from the pipeline that would have otherwise been passed down to it and, in the case of computer graphics, can be used to significantly boost the performance of an application. As gaming environments grow in size, so does the necessity of culling geometry that the player can't see. Culling is also known as hidden-surface removal, and all complex 3D video games implement the technique in code. In this chapter we discuss many of the techniques that are common to video game graphics.

 The Z-buffer is a simple type of visibility determination where the buffer is used to determine if the surface being rendered is in front of, on, or behind geometry that has already been rendered.

FAR PLANE CULLING

In computer graphics there exists a far plane that is part of the clipping process. Far-plane culling, essentially, is not rendering geometry that is past the far plane divide. This type of culling is fairly simple and straightforward to do in real-time applications such as video games.

The technique uses a classification operation on the geometry and the plane. Objects that are completely behind the plane are rejected from rendering, objects completely in front of the plane are accepted, and objects that span the plane can be dealt with based on the needs of the application and the geometry. Usually, objects can be rendered as long as they span or are in front of the far plane. It is possible to clip the geometry to the far plane, but in a video game this operation would most likely prove more expensive than it would be to just render out spanning geometry. This is especially true in the complex 3D video games that are being released today.

Although this technique can be used to avoid the processing of geometry that is far away, it does have the slight disadvantage of allowing objects to disappear from view with distance. Depending on the environment, this might be acceptable, but if the visibility of the disappearance of objects needs to be minimized, one option is to use fog to mask this affect. Using fog to hide the point where objects disappear behind the far plane can maintain the illusion that the game world is consistent. Many modern games use fog with outdoor environments and, at some point, objects can be so far from the viewer that they are easily occluded (i.e., blocked from view by other objects) or very difficult to see in the game.

Back-Face Culling

Polygons are flat surfaces that can be rendered in a 3D scene. Regardless how many vertex points make up a surface, the surface has only one plane. Because of this fact, a polygon that can be rendered in 3D is either facing straight on toward the viewer, at an angle, parallel to the viewer, or away from the viewer at some angle. When dealing with hollow geometry, that is, 3D geometry that isn't completely flat, the back facing polygons are not visible to the viewer since the front facing polygons occlude them from view.

The idea behind back-face culling, and front-face culling, is to avoid rendering geometry that is not facing the viewer. Take, for example, a 3D character model where, let's say, half the polygons are facing the viewer at any given time and the other half is not. If the character is facing the viewer, the character's back is not visible. When you use back-face culling, the rendering API does not draw any polygons that are not facing the viewer. This means the polygons that make up the back of the character in this example are not rendered since they cannot be seen.

Back-face culling is a simple idea. Any polygon whose normal is pointing away from the viewer is rejected from the rendering process. The dot product between the view vector and the normal can be used to determine which direction the normal is pointing. In common graphics APIs such as OpenGL and Direct3D, face-culling such as this can be enabled and used for rendering without any additional effort on the part of the game developer other than specifying geometry in a clockwise or counterclockwise order. Face culling can be used to cull geometry that is visible even further to avoid the processing of unnecessary geometry.

The direction the polygon takes in OpenGL or Direct3D depends on the order in which the vertices are specified. By default, in OpenGL counterclockwise order is used to specify front facing polygons, while in Direct3D clockwise order is used. You can change the order the API uses. Changing the order the API uses for determining if a polygon is facing toward or away from the viewer can allow developers to use one common system regardless of the API being used. That way, geometry does not need to be adjusted after being loaded from a file, there is no need for multiple versions of the mesh for that purpose.

Frustum Culling

Frustum culling is a technique that uses planes to determine if objects are visible to the player. In frustum culling up to six planes are created to enclose the entire view volume the player is seeing. This is known as view frustum culling, and the idea is that any object that falls outside of this view volume can be rejected from the rendering process because there is no way it is visible. An example of this is shown in Figure 15.1.

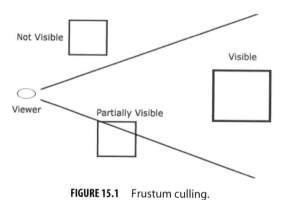

FIGURE 15.1   Frustum culling.

View frustum culling defines a plane for the left, right, top, and bottom of the view volume as well as the near and far planes. If there is no limit to the distance, the far plane can be left out. Together these planes represent a volume where any object that is not in front of all of these planes can be rejected, which can be determined using a plane classification test. As soon as an object fails the test against a plane, the algorithm knows it is not visible and can proceed from there. When testing complex geometry such as character models, it is acceptable and common to use bounding geometry for the culling test instead of the triangles that compose the model. The most common types of bounding geometry are the bounding sphere and box.

ON THE CD

On the CD-ROM in the Chapter 15 folder are demo applications that perform view frustum culling in OpenGL, Direct3D 9, and Direct3D 10 that we collectively call the Frustum Culling demos. The demos create a frustum class that is used for the tests. This class has a function used to create the view frustum and functions used to test if a point, sphere, cube, or box is visible. The list of planes is stored in a Standard Template Library (STL) vector container, and there are helper functions that are part of the class that is used to add a plane to the frustum, get a plane from the frustum, and get the total plane count. The Frustum class is shown in Listing 15.1.

LISTING 15.1 THE Frustum CLASS

```
class Frustum
{
   public:
      Frustum();

      void CreateViewFrustum(float angle, float ratio, float near,
                             float far, Vector3D &camPos,
                             Vector3D &lookAt, Vector3D &up);

      void AddPlane(Plane &pl);
      bool GetPlane(int index, Plane *out);
      int GetTotalPlanes() { return (int)m_frustum.size(); }

      bool isPointVisible(float x, float y, float z);
      bool isSphereVisible(float x, float y, float z,
                           float radius);
      bool isCubeVisible(float x, float y, float z, float size);
      bool isBoxVisible(Vector3D min, Vector3D max);
```

```
    private:
        std::vector<Plane> m_frustum;
};
```

The helper function used to add a plane simply adds the plane object to the container using the push_back() method of the vector object. The function used to get a plane will return the address of the plane object to the caller assuming the index of the desired plane is valid. These two functions are shown in Listing 15.2.

LISTING 15.2 PLANE HELPER FUNCTIONS

```
void Frustum::AddPlane(Plane &pl)
{
    m_frustum.push_back(pl);
}


bool Frustum::GetPlane(int index, Plane *out)
{
    if(out == 0 || index >= (int)m_frustum.size() || index < 0)
        return false;

    *out = m_frustum[index];

    return true;
}
```

The tests to see if a point, sphere, cube, or box is visible are each straightforward. For each of them the functions loop through each of the planes that make up the frustum and perform a classification test. For a point the test makes sure the position is in front of each plane. As soon as that is not true, the function returns false, or else it returns true if all classification tests pass. For the sphere the radius is used in addition to the sphere's position to see if the sphere collides with the plane and if it is in front of it. As long as the sphere penetrates or is completely in front of the planes, it is visible.

For the cube it calls the box's test function since a cube is a box with the same length in size in all directions. The box function tests that each point of the box falls in front of each plane within the volume. The visibility functions are shown in Listing 15.3 for the Frustum class.

LISTING 15.3 THE VISIBILITY FUNCTIONS

```cpp
bool Frustum::isPointVisible(float x, float y, float z)
{
   for(int i = 0; i < (int)m_frustum.size(); i++)
   {
      if(m_frustum[i].GetDistance(x, y, z) < 0)
         return false;
   }

   return true;
}


bool Frustum::isSphereVisible(float x, float y, float z,
                              float radius)
{
   float distance = 0;

   for(int i = 0; i < (int)m_frustum.size(); i++)
   {
      distance = m_frustum[i].GetDistance(x, y, z);

      if(distance < -radius)
         return false;
   }

   return true;
}


bool Frustum::isCubeVisible(float x, float y, float z, float size)
{
   float minX, maxX;
   float minY, maxY;
   float minZ, maxZ;

   minX = x - size; maxX = x + size;
   minY = y - size; maxY = y + size;
   minZ = z - size; maxZ = z + size;

   return isBoxVisible(Vector3D(minX, minY, minZ),
                       Vector3D(maxX, maxY, maxZ));
}
```

```
bool Frustum::isBoxVisible(Vector3D min, Vector3D max)
{
    if(isPointVisible(min.x, min.y, min.z))
        return true;

    if(isPointVisible(max.x, min.y, min.z))
        return true;

    if(isPointVisible(min.x, max.y, min.z))
        return true;

    if(isPointVisible(max.x, max.y, min.z))
        return true;

    if(isPointVisible(min.x, min.y, max.z))
        return true;

    if(isPointVisible(max.x, min.y, max.z))
        return true;

    if(isPointVisible(min.x, max.y, max.z))
        return true;

    if(isPointVisible(max.x, max.y, max.z))
        return true;

    return false;
}
```

The last function is the creation of the view frustum. The function starts by creating three vectors that are used for the calculation of the various planes along with their offsets that are used for plane creation. During the plane creation the plane's CreateFromTri() function is used to create each plane, and the result is added to the frustum list. Since six planes are being created by this function, the vector object reserves six elements to avoid unnecessary allocations and re-allocations in the STL container. Although the function looks long, it is fairly straightforward and can be seen in Listing 15.4. For each plane that is created, a triangle of points are created based on the view volume. These triangle points are used to create each plane that is added to the view frustum list.

LISTING 15.4 CALCULATING THE VIEW FRUSTUM

```
void Frustum::CreateViewFrustum(float angle, float ratio,
                                float near, float far,
                                Vector3D &camPos, Vector3D &lookAt,
                                Vector3D &up)
{
   Vector3D xVec, yVec, zVec;
   Vector3D vecN, vecF;

   Vector3D nearTopLeft, nearTopRight,
            nearBottomLeft, nearBottomRight;

   Vector3D farTopLeft, farTopRight,
            farBottomLeft, farBottomRight;

   float radians = (float)tan((DEG_TO_RAD(angle)) * 0.5);
   float nearH = near  * radians;
   float nearW = nearH * ratio;
   float farH = far    * radians;
   float farW = farH   * ratio;

   zVec = camPos - lookAt;
   zVec.Normalize();

   xVec = up.CrossProduct(zVec);
   xVec.Normalize();

   yVec = zVec.CrossProduct(xVec);

   vecN = camPos - zVec * near;
   vecF = camPos - zVec * far;

   nearTopLeft     = vecN + yVec * nearH - xVec * nearW;
   nearTopRight    = vecN + yVec * nearH + xVec * nearW;
   nearBottomLeft  = vecN - yVec * nearH - xVec * nearW;
   nearBottomRight = vecN - yVec * nearH + xVec * nearW;

   farTopLeft      = vecF + yVec * farH - xVec * farW;
   farTopRight     = vecF + yVec * farH + xVec * farW;
   farBottomLeft   = vecF - yVec * farH - xVec * farW;
   farBottomRight  = vecF - yVec * farH + xVec * farW;

   m_frustum.clear();
   m_frustum.reserve(6);
```

```
        Plane plane;

        plane.CreatePlaneFromTri(nearTopRight, nearTopLeft,
                                 farTopLeft);
        AddPlane(plane);

        plane.CreatePlaneFromTri(nearBottomLeft, nearBottomRight,
                                 farBottomRight);
        AddPlane(plane);

        plane.CreatePlaneFromTri(nearTopLeft, nearBottomLeft,
                                 farBottomLeft);
        AddPlane(plane);

        plane.CreatePlaneFromTri(nearBottomRight, nearTopRight,
                                 farBottomRight);
        AddPlane(plane);

        plane.CreatePlaneFromTri(nearTopLeft, nearTopRight,
                                 nearBottomRight);
        AddPlane(plane);

        plane.CreatePlaneFromTri(farTopRight, farTopLeft,
                                 farBottomLeft);
        AddPlane(plane);
    }
```

Frustum culling is view dependent. This means that any time the view changes, you have to recalculate the view frustum.

A screenshot of the demo application is shown in Figure 15.2. In the demo application 10,000 boxes are rendered to the scene. To avoid rendering boxes that are not visible, the frustum test is used for each object. The use of the frustum can be toggled by pressing the spacebar key on the keyboard. For really high-end PCs it is possible that the machine is so powerful that you'll need to increase the box count to see a difference between using and not using the frustum test.

FIGURE 15.2   Screenshot from the frustum culling demo.

Occlusion Culling

Some scenes have a large depth complexity associated with them. For example, if a city like New York City was modeled in a game, a lot of buildings would block visibility of other buildings and objects behind them. In a game with high depth complexity this can be very common and causes objects that cannot be visible to be drawn and processed as if they were. If the load is great, this can become an unnecessary burden for the gaming hardware.

The avoidance of rendering geometry that is not visible because another object is between it and the viewer is known as occlusion culling. There are many different ways occlusion culling can be performed. One way is to define planes within the 3D scene that represent large objects. During rendering, the geometry of the environment is tested against these planes for classification based on the view, where any objects that have a different classification from the viewer are not rendered. An illustration of this is shown in Figure 15.3.

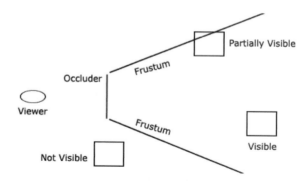

FIGURE 15.3 Occlusion culling.

The difficult part of occlusion culling is knowing where to place planes and how many to place. Placing planes in inefficient areas can prove more wasteful than helpful when rendering a scene. Also, using too many planes can eventually hurt performance instead of improving it. This means, in other words, that creating planes out of all or the majority of polygons in a scene has a severe negative impact on performance. Other types of preprocessed occlusion culling techniques discussed in this chapter include the following.

- Potential visibility sets
- Portals

In game scenes without depth complexity the use of occlusion culling might not be as efficient or worth the effort as with other scenes. Finding an efficient set of locations for occlusion planes can be time-consuming and difficult. Algorithmically, planes can be defined, but their accuracy and efficiency is not always guaranteed. The use of occlusion culling depends largely on the type of gaming environment being used and the types of geometry in the scene. In the case of a large city like New York, well-placed and defined occlusion planes can make a huge difference.

Each graphics API has hardware occlusion culling solutions available. In this chapter we see how it is done manually to get a better understanding of it. The method using the graphics hardware works by first rendering objects with the occlusion feature enabled in the first pass. During the second pass, as the scene is being rendered normally, the graphics API can obtain how many pixels actually made it to the screen for each object during the first pass. This value can be used to determine how visible, if at all, an object is.

In occlusion culling a frustum is created based on the surface that is acting as the occluding object and the view. This means the frustum code created in the previous section can be used for occlusion testing. The only difference is that a new function will need to be added that will specifically create the frustum based on a flat surface.

On the accompanying CD-ROM in the Chapter 15 folder are demo applications for OpenGL, Direct3D 9, and Direct3D 10 that perform occlusion culling manually on the CPU. We collectively call these the Occlusion Culling demos. The demo applications build off of the frustum culling code seen earlier in this chapter and add a function to build the planes used for the occlusion test using the model-view matrix and four points on the surface that are used as the occluding object. The added function is shown in Listing 15.5 and is called CreateOcclusionFrustum(). The occlusion field only needs to create five planes, each of which are added to the planes list of the class. An occlusion volume requires five planes, with the first being the plane of the surface, and the rest being for the left, right, top, and bottom planes that make up the field. The different between the view frustum and the occlusion frustum is that the view frustum encloses the viewing volume, while the occlusion frustum surrounds and extends from an object's surface that is set up to occlude other objects. The test used for view frustum visibility works using the occlusion frustum. The best occluding surfaces are often really large flat surfaces such as the outer walls of a large city building.

LISTING 15.5 THE ADDED FUNCTION TO THE FRUSTUM CLASS FOR OCCLUSION

```
class Frustum
{
   public:
      void CreateOcclusionFrustum(Vector3D p1, Vector3D p2,
                                  Vector3D p3, Vector3D p4,
                                  Matrix4x4 &viewMatrix);
};
```

To set up the occlusion frustum, each of the points that make up the surface used in the occlusion test must be transformed by the model-view matrix. This has to happen because the occlusion test is view dependent, which means the occlusion frustums must be recalculated each time the view or occluding object moves. The cam variable in the function is used as the camera's center position. Since it is an untransformed origin, when combined with transformed data, it can be used as a quick way of representing the camera's center. These positions are used to create each of the planes of the frustum, where the first plane lies parallel to the surface and the remaining planes are created from the center camera position and each of the points of the occluding surface. If the distance of the front plane is less than or equal to 0, the planes for the occlusion must be calculated in the opposite direction. This is assuming that it doesn't matter which direction the occluding object is facing in the game environment. This allows the occlusion frustum to be created correctly regardless of which direction the occluding object is facing. The function used to create the occlusion frustum is shown in Listing 15.6.

 The Vector3D *and* Plane *classes were first discussed in Chapter 3, "Ray Tracing."*

LISTING 15.6 CREATING AN OCCLUSION FRUSTUM

```
void Frustum::SetupOcclusion(Vector3D p1, Vector3D p2,
                             Vector3D p3, Vector3D p4,
                             Matrix4x4 &viewMatrix)
{
   Vector3D world_p1, world_p2, world_p3, world_p4, cam;
   Plane o_plane;

   world_p1 = viewMatrix.VectorMatrixMultiply(p1);
   world_p2 = viewMatrix.VectorMatrixMultiply(p2);
   world_p3 = viewMatrix.VectorMatrixMultiply(p3);
   world_p4 = viewMatrix.VectorMatrixMultiply(p4);

   o_plane.CreatePlaneFromTri(world_p1, world_p2, world_p3);

   if(front.d > 0.0f)
   {
      AddPlane(o_plane);

      o_plane.CreatePlaneFromTri(cam, world_p1, world_p2);
      AddPlane(o_plane);

      o_plane.CreatePlaneFromTri(cam, world_p2, world_p3);
      AddPlane(o_plane);

      o_plane.CreatePlaneFromTri(cam, world_p3, world_p4);
      AddPlane(o_plane);
```

```
        o_plane.CreatePlaneFromTri(cam, world_p4, world_p1);
        AddPlane(o_plane);
    }
    else
    {
        o_plane.CreatePlaneFromTri(world_p3, world_p2, world_p1);
        AddPlane(o_plane);

        o_plane.CreatePlaneFromTri(cam, world_p2, world_p1);
        AddPlane(o_plane);

        o_plane.CreatePlaneFromTri(cam, world_p3, world_p2);
        AddPlane(o_plane);

        o_plane.CreatePlaneFromTri(cam, world_p4, world_p3);
        AddPlane(o_plane);

        o_plane.CreatePlaneFromTri(cam, world_p1, world_p4);
        AddPlane(o_plane);
    }
}
```

Each of the planes is created from a triangle that makes up the points of the occluding object. To create a plane out of a triangle, a new function was added to the Plane class from Chapter 3, called CreatePlaneFromTri(). This function takes three points that make up the triangle and stores the plane result. To create the plane, the triangle is normalized by finding the edge vectors, getting the cross-product between them, and normalizing the results. This normal is used as the plane's A, B, and C values, and D is calculated as 1 minus the dot product of the normal and one of the points on the plane (i.e., any point that makes up the triangle). This added function of the Plane class is shown in Listing 15.7. The normal of the triangle is the normal of the plane, and the distance variable is based on any of those points on the plane. A screenshot from the occlusion demo is shown in Figure 15.4.

LISTING 15.7 CREATING A PLANE FROM A TRIANGLE

```
void Plane::CreatePlaneFromTri(Vector3D &t1, Vector3D &t2,
                Vector3D &t3)
{
    Vector3D e1, e2, n;
```

```
        e1 = t2 - t1;
        e2 = t3 - t1;

        n.CrossProduct(e1, e2);
        n.Normalize();

        a = n.x;
        b = n.y;
        c = n.z;
        d = - (a * t1.x + b * t1.y + c * t1.z);

        // A point on the plane (class member variable).
        point = t1;
    }
```

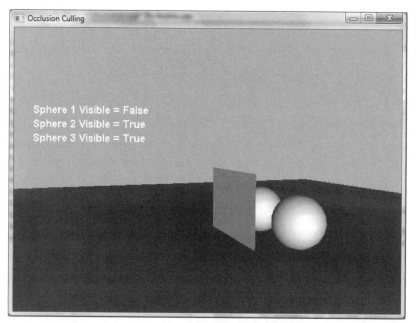

FIGURE 15.4　A screenshot from the occlusion culling demo.

SCENE AND SPACE PARTITIONING

Partitioning is a term used to describe the separation of data. In video game graphics partitioning is commonly used to split space and geometry. In scene and space partitioning, which we refer to as just space partitioning, space is divided into sections. Any object, geometry, and so on that falls within those sections is assigned to those partitioned areas. When it comes time to render the scene, the sections that are determined to be visible are rendered, while the rest are culled out. This is usually done using data structures and recursive algorithms along with frustum culling, where if one section is determined not visible, then all of its child (sub) sections are immediately culled out. The sections that are visible have their child nodes tested for visibility until all nodes have been either rendered or culled. In practice this is a very efficient and fast way to cull geometry, and all major 3D video games use one algorithm or a hybrid of algorithms for the display of their scenes. Figure 15.5 shows an example of splitting up space into different sections.

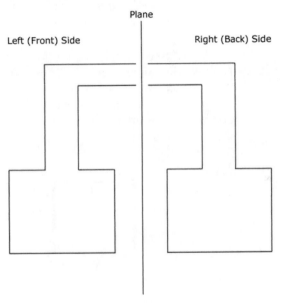

FIGURE 15.5 Splitting space.

BSP Trees

A binary space partitioning (BSP) tree is a binary tree data structure that is used to partition the geometry of a scene to allow for the culling of geometry that is not visible. In a BSP tree it is possible to perform a searching algorithm that renders the scene's polygons in front-to-back or back-to-front order. Culling can be performed on the nodes of the BSP tree to reject geometry that can't be seen from the rendering process. A node is an element within the data structure. BSP trees have been used in many major video games including *Quake*, *Doom*, and *Half-Life*. A BSP tree is often calculated offline by a tool and used in the run-time application to quickly process and render geometry. BSP trees can also be used for other uses such as real-time collision detection and are not just for rendering.

In the beginning of 3D video games a BSP tree was an efficient way to render the polygons of a scene in the correct order before the Z-buffer became standard in graphics hardware. Using a BSP tree for rendering in the manner of early games is less efficient than using the Z-buffer. However, BSP trees can be used for fast collision detection and, with the addition of potential visibility sets, which are discussed later in this chapter, for large-scale culling and fast rendering.

Rendering without using potential visibility sets and the Z-buffer with front-to-back rendering is less efficient than using them in combination. Many games today use BSP trees with potential visibility tests and the Z-buffer to quickly render a scene.

A BSP tree starts by taking in a list of polygons that define a scene. The insertion algorithm that is performed on the tree splits the polygons into convex pieces. A convex shape is essentially a shape where a line segment that lies within the shape cannot cross any of the shape's edges. Concave is the opposite. An example of concave and convex shapes is shown in Figure 15.6.

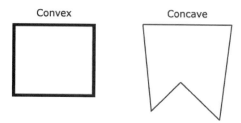

FIGURE 15.6   Convex (left) and concave (right).

When data are inserted into the BSP tree, they are split into two halves, that is, two nodes. The insertion algorithm recursively continues to split each half further and further into more nodes until a certain number of polygons exist in the nodes at the bottom of the tree, a certain recursion depth has been reached within the tree, or some other condition proves true. Geometry is only stored in leaf nodes. A leaf node is a node with no children. In a BSP tree the leaf nodes are the nodes at the bottom of the tree.

As data are inserted in the BSP tree, a partitioning plane is defined. This plane is used to classify on which side the polygons fall. The left node stores polygons that are in front of the partitioning plane, while the right node stores polygons that are behind it. Polygons that span both sides are often split up into multiple pieces so that each piece fits on one side or the other.

The partitioning plane is also known as the splitter plane.

A partitioning plane can be axis-aligned or it can be determined by one of the polygons in the scene. Usually, planes created out of polygons in the scene are chosen to find the best partitioning plane that can be used to divide the scene. Axis-aligned means the planes align to an axis (X, Y, or Z), and planes that are coplanar with the polygons are planes that are created out of chosen polygons from the scene.

The creation of a BSP tree is fairly straightforward. A list of polygons is taken, initially of the entire scene, and is split into two halves. These halves are recursively split further and further until no more splits can be made. Once the condition occurs that causes the insertion algorithm to stop, the BSP tree data structure is created and ready. Pseudo-code for the creation of a BSP tree is shown as follows, where a minimum number of polygons per leaf node is used as the stopping condition:

```
Class BSPNode
{
   BSPNode *frontNode;
   BSPNode *backNode;

   Polygon[] polygonList;
};


function CreateBSPNode(Polygon[] listOfPolygons)
{
   BSPNode *node = new BSPNode();


   // If threshold is met then stop recursion.


   if(listOfPolygon.count <= MIN_NODE_POLY_COUNT)
   {
      node.polygonList = listOfPolygons;

      return node;
   }


   // Else continue.


   Plane splitPlane = GetBestSplitter(listOfPolygons);
   Polygon[] subPolyList1;
   Polygon[] subPolyList2;
```

```
foreach(index i in listOfPolygons)
{
   if(splitPlane.Classify(listOfPolygons[i]) == FRONT)
   {
      subPolyList1.push(listOfPolygons[i]);
   }
   else if(splitPlane.Classify(listOfPolygons[i]) == BACK)
   {
      subPolyList2.push(listOfPolygons[i]);
   }
   else
   {
      // Return two split polygons in p1, p2.

      Polygon p1, p2;

      splitPlane.ClipPolygon(listOfPolygons[i], &p1, &p2);

      subPolyList1.push(p1);
      subPolyList2.push(p2);
   }
}


node.frontNode = CreateBSPNode(subPolyList1);
node.backNode  = CreateBSPNode(subPolyList2);

return node;
}
```

BSP trees are more efficient for indoor scenes because the partitioning planes of those polygons are more efficient for dividing up the scene than what can be created out of a terrain. The planes of a BSP tree are important to the efficiency of the tree. Also, the balance of the tree can affect the tree's performance. Balance in a tree data structure means there are the same number or close to the same number of nodes on each side of the tree. In the case of a BSP tree there are close to the same number of left (front) nodes as there are right (back) nodes. This leads to a tree that can be processed efficiently in the average case.

The partitioning plane is chosen using a scoring algorithm that performs these steps.

1. Loop through all polygons and create a plane for each one.
2. For each plane add up the number of polygons that are on the front and back sides.

3. The plane with the lowest absolute difference (abs[front total − back total]) is the polygon that is the best choice to use for the partitioning plane.

When determining which plane to use for the partitioning plane, the value of the difference between the front and back polygons is known as the partitioning score. The lower the score, the better candidate it makes. Choosing a polygon with a score that is close to 0 means the plane will create a more balanced split than other polygons. This algorithm is fairly simple and is a brute force algorithm. It simply looks for the polygon that comes closest to 0 and uses that. For large scenes this can take some time, which is why BSP compilers exist to create a BSP tree offline and to store the results in a file that can be loaded by the game later on. Pseudo-code for the calculation of the partitioning plane is as follows.

```
function GetBestSplitter(Polygon[] listOfPolygons)
{
    plane = Plane();
    minPlane = Plane();
    minCount = 9999999999, currentCount = 0;

    foreach(element i in listOfPolygons)
    {
        // Create plane out of this polygon.


        plane.Create(listOfPolygons[i]);


        // Determine how many polys are on the front and back.


        for each(element j in listOfPolygons)
        {
            frontCount = 0, backCount = 0;


            // Wouldn't test current (plane) polygon.


            if(i != j)
            {
                if(plane.Classify(listOfPolygons[j]) == FRONT)
                {
```

```
                             frontCount++;
                          }
                          else if(plane.Classify(listOfPolygons[j]) == BACK)
                          {
                             backCount++;
                          }
                          else
                          {
                             // The split polygon would create one on each.


                             frontCount++;
                             backCount++;
                          }
                      }
                  }


                  // Score the current polygon.


                  currentCount = abs(frontCount - backCount);


                  // If current polygon proves to be the smallest so far...


                  if(currentCount < minCount)
                  {
                      minPlane = plane;
                      minCount = currentCount;
                  }
              }

         return minPlane;
     }
```

When processing the BSP tree, whether for rendering or collision detection or something else, a searching algorithm is used. To process from left to right (i.e., front to back) all that needs to happen is to write a recursive function that keeps traversing through the left nodes until it reaches the left-most node. From there it processes the node's data (i.e., render, perform collisions, etc.), moves to the parent node, processes the right child, moves to the parent's parent, and continues until it reaches back to the top of the tree. If rendering from back to front, the same thing occurs, but the algorithm moves to the rightmost node then backs up to the top.

Potential Visibility Sets

A potential visibility set (PVS) is a data structure used specifically for determining which nodes of a partitioned space or scene (e.g., octree, BSP tree, etc.) are visible to each other's nodes. In other words, each node maintains a list of which nodes it can potentially see. This can be represented as a list of node pointers, an array of Boolean flags, and so forth. When building a PVS, it is often performed as an off-line process. Some tools, such as Valve's *Half-Life 2* map editor, called *Hammer*, create the BSP tree and the PVSs for each node.

Generating a PVS can be as simple as using ray tracing by creating a ray from every vertex of a node (as the ray's origin) and pointing to each vertex in every other node and performing intersection tests against the scene. If any ray intersection test passes, then the current node being processed can potentially see the other node it was checking for visibility. When an intersection between two vertices proves that nothing is blocking the path of the ray, the node that can be potentially seen is added to the node that is currently being processed in the PVS list.

During the game the rendering system can use the PVS as a way of only testing and rendering nodes that can potentially be seen. An example of this is determining which node the viewer is in, rendering that node, and frustum culling or rendering the nodes it can potentially see as determined by the PVS list.

Octrees

Octrees and quad trees are types of bounding volume hierarchy (BVH) data structures that can be used for space partitioning. A BVH starts by creating a large bounding box around the entire geometry (i.e., environment), using the insertion algorithm. The insertion algorithm then recursively divides the bounding box into smaller boxes and divides the polygons of the geometry based on which box they fall into. This process continues until some condition is met (i.e., a minimum number of polygons are in a node, recursion depth is met, etc.).

A quad tree is a BVH that splits each node into four equal sections. An octree splits the nodes into 2×2 (two rows and two columns), that is, eight, smaller nodes. As with the BSP tree, the leaf nodes of the quad tree and octree store the geometry information. The octree can be thought of as a 3D version of the quad tree, which is considered 2D. Both can be used on 3D geometry.

The creation of the quad tree uses a straightforward recursive function that is actually more straightforward than the BSP tree. A list of geometry is passed to the insertion function, a bounding box is calculated out of that geometry, the bounding box is split into four sections, and a loop is used to determine which polygons fall within which box. These subboxes are then further broken down until a stopping condition is met. The pseudo-code for the creation of a quad tree is as follows.

```
function CreateQuadNode(Polygon[] listOfPolygons)
{
   QuadNode node = new QuadNode();

   BoundingBox aabb = CalculateBoundingBox(listOfPolygons);
   node.aabb = aabb;


   // Stop recursion once list becomes small.


   if(listOfPolygons.count <= MIN_NODE_POLY_COUNT)
   {
      node.polygons = listOfPolygons;

      return node;
   }


   // Else continue.

   // Divide large bounding box into four areas (quad).
   // In other words SPLIT ALONG X and Y axis.


   frontLeftBox  = CalculateSubBox(aabb, FRONT_LEFT);
   backLeftBox   = CalculateSubBox(aabb, BACK_LEFT);
   frontRightBox = CalculateSubBox(aabb, FRONT_RIGHT);
   backRightBox  = CalculateSubBox(aabb, BACK_RIGHT);


   // Divide main polygon list into sub-lists.


   Polygon[] frontLeftList;
   Polygon[] backLeftList;
```

```
Polygon[] frontRightList;
Polygon[] backRightList;

foreach(element i in listOfPolygons)
{
   if(frontLeftBox.IsPolyIn(listOfPolygons[i]) == true)
   {
      frontLeftList.push(listOfPolygons[i]);
   }
   else if(backLeftBox.IsPolyIn(listOfPolygons[i]) == true)
   {
      backLeftList.push(listOfPolygons[i]);
   }
   else if(frontRightBox.IsPolyIn(listOfPolygons[i]) == true)
   {
      frontRightList.push(listOfPolygons[i]);
   }
   else if(backRightBox.IsPolyIn(listOfPolygons[i]) == true)
   {
      backRightList.push(listOfPolygons[i]);
   }
}

node.frontLeftNode  = CreateQuadNode(frontLeftList);
node.backLeftNode   = CreateQuadNode(backLeftList);
node.frontRightNode = CreateQuadNode(frontRightList);
node.backRightNode  = CreateQuadNode(backRightList);

return node;
}
```

Once the insertion algorithm has finished executing, the entire quad tree is created. This tree can be rendered using frustum culling and a recursive search function. In the case of the quad tree the function starts with the root (top) node and test if it is visible. If so, the function looks to see if there is any geometry in the node. If the node does not have geometry, that means it has children (sub) nodes, or else it means the geometry can be rendered and the function can return. If there are child nodes, then each node is passed to the recursive function until all nodes have been processed. The pseudo-code for this recursive rendering function is as follows.

```
function RenderQuadTree(Frustum frustum, QuadTreeNode node)
{
   if(node == NULL)
      return;


   // Cull (return) if camera cannot see this node.

   if(frustum.isVisible(node.aabb) == FALSE)
      return;


   // Either render the leaf node or must traverse.

   if(node.polygons != NULL)
   {
      foreach(polygon in node.polygons)
      {
         // Render poly using API like OpenGL, Direct3D, etc.
      }
   }
   else
   {
      RenderQuadTree(frustum, node.frontLeftNode);
      RenderQuadTree(frustum, node.backLeftNode);
      RenderQuadTree(frustum, node.frontRightNode);
      RenderQuadTree(frustum, node.backRightNode);
   }
}
```

An octree is essentially a quad tree, but with eight subboxes that are created for each node instead of four.

On the CD-ROM in the Chapter 15 folder are demo applications that create and use an octree, which are collectively called the Octree demos. The demo creates an octree using the pseudo-code shown in this section and uses it to render out a large terrain. A screenshot of the demo application is shown in Figure 15.7.

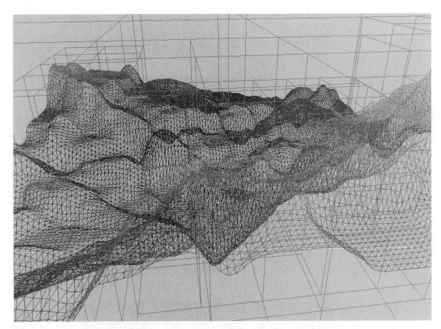

FIGURE 15.7   A screenshot from the Octree demos.

Portals and Sectors

Portal rendering is a technique that was first used in the early days of 3D gaming. One very famous game that used portals was Id Software's *Duke Nuke 'Em 3D*. A portal rendering system can be fairly straightforward when compared to the other data structures described so far in this chapter. Using portal rendering, it was possible for early games such as *Duke Nuke 'Em* to create efficient mirror effects and other special effects that, at the time, would have been extremely difficult to perform otherwise.

In portal rendering the game world is divided up into sectors. Taking an indoor game as an example, each sector can be a different room of the level. Each sector is connected by an invisible portal, which can be anything, even something as simple as a doorway or window opening.

When rendering with portals and sectors, the first step is to render the sector the player is currently in. Then, using frustum culling, the visible portals are determined and the sectors that connect to them are rendered. This process is recursive and continues until all visible portals and the sectors that connect to them are rendered. If the portal rendering system allows for portals to recursively reference themselves or each other, a recursion depth limit must be imposed to prevent infinite rendering loops. An example of this is shown in Figure 15.8.

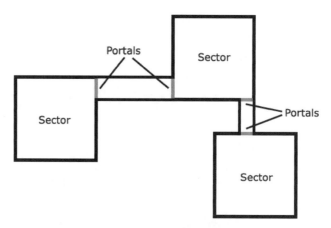

FIGURE 15.8 Portal rendering.

In portal rendering in the early days an occlusion frustum was created out of the invisible portal and the current viewer. Any objects in adjacent sectors connected to the visible portals that could be seen by this occlusion frustum were rendered. In the early days the geometry of the sector (e.g., the walls of the room) were also clipped to this frustum and rendered. This gave the added benefit of avoiding expensive pixel overdraw, but on today's hardware it is more expensive to clip polygons in real time than just render without the clipping, as far as portal rendering goes. Today, a simple portal rendering system only has to render the player's sector, render all sectors that can be seen through visible portals, and use the frustum to render all of the sector's objects (e.g., characters, weapons, props, vehicles, etc.).

Some games use more complex portal rendering systems where a portal is used to connect not only adjacent sectors but sectors that are nowhere near each other or even have no relationship to one another. Portals can also be used to connect to the same sector they are leaving. This can create weird yet cool, almost paradoxical game worlds. In the game *Portal*, which comes bundled in Valve's *Orange Box*, it is possible to manually place portals anywhere in the game world and to not only see through them as if they were real portals but to travel through them in real time. This allows players to place portals in front and behind them and be able to see themselves through one while facing another. In the game *Prey*, on the Xbox 360, it is even possible to shoot yourself in the back through one portal across the game room.

Continuous Level-of-Detail

A continuous level-of-detail (CLOD) algorithm is used to dynamically adjust the level-of-detail (LOD) of a terrain patch in real time as necessary. This allows for patches closer to the viewer to be rendered at a higher detail level than patches that are farther away. This is important because without a CLOD algorithm, the same amount of geometric detail will be used for close patches as for far away patches, which is a waste of processing resources. For terrains that are large in scope it is important to use LOD to get the most performance out of the terrain rendering system. Some CLOD algorithms also add more detail to surfaces that need it and take away detail from surfaces that don't need it. For example, if a patch of terrain is relatively flat, less detail can be used to represent it, regardless of how close it is to the viewer if the detail is not noticeable anyway.

Geomipmapping is similar to the texture mip-mapping discussed earlier in relation to texture mapping, but instead of working with textures, it uses geometry. In Geomipmapping the terrain patches are divided into different levels of detail. During rendering, the patches are assigned an LOD based on their distance from the viewer, and frustum culling on the patches is used to cull out large amounts of geometry. LOD and terrain patches are essentially simple forms of geomipmapping. Real-time optimally adapting mesh (ROAM) is another famous CLOD algorithm. The ROAM algorithm operates on a binary tree data structure known as a binary triangle tree.

The main issue that CLOD algorithms face concerns cracking with the terrain patches. When a patch of a higher LOD is next to a lower-detail patch, the edges of some of the higher-detail patches might not match up with the lower-detail versions. This causes terrain polygons to break off, leaving gaps throughout the terrain. Various algorithms can be used to combat this, each essentially stepping through and testing which patch has geometry that has broken off from the terrain and smoothing it out. This step can add a bit of a burden on the CPU, but it is necessary to avoid the cracking.

When rendering terrains with patches of varying LOD, it is important to deal with the cracking behavior. This includes rendering with quad trees and octrees because using LOD with those data structures can also cause cracking.

Additional Scene Partitioning Techniques

Additional structures can be used to partition a scene or a space in 3D. The data structures and algorithms used are heavily determined by the type of environment and geometric complexity used in the game. In this chapter we've discussed the most common types of data structures used for both indoor and outdoor scenes. A few other data structures that are outside of the scope of this discussion are as follows:

- Beam tracing
- Sphere trees
- *k*d-trees
- ROAM 2.0

GEOMETRY INSTANCING

In video games there are often situations where many similar objects need to be drawn to the screen. Often, these objects differ slightly in their physical properties but are essentially the same. Examples of these objects include asteroids, trees, rocks, and plants.

Drawing many objects separately can be quite expensive. A faster solution is to render out all of the objects with a single draw call rather than one at a time. This eliminates function call overhead as well as having to send data down the pipeline over and over. This technique is known as instancing, and it can be used to tremendously improve the performance of a rendered scene.

In instancing, one version of the object is sent to the GPU. For every instance that is to be drawn, the per-instance data are also passed along as a data stream. In Direct3D 10 up until this point everything that was specified was specified using per-vertex data. Another data creation flag, the D3D10_INPUT_PER_VERTEX_DATA flag, is used to specify the per-instance data. This flag is used during the creation of an input layout object. Examples of pieces of data that can be specified on the per-instance level include the following.

- World transformations
- Colors
- Animations
- Heights
- Scale

Two types of instancing are true instancing and pseudo-instancing. Pseudo-instancing is where per-instance data are sent along a stream, like the texture coordinates, into specially designed shaders. In OpenGL this can be faster than not using instancing at all since glTexCoord() calls are in-lined. Instancing in this manner is tricky and is more of a substitution if true instancing is not available.

True instancing is broken down into four typical techniques: hardware, shader, constant, and stream. In hardware instancing API function calls are used to set up the number of times an object is to be drawn and its per-instance data. In Direct3D 10 this can be set up during the input layout creation; in Direct3D 9 this can be specified using the `IDirect3DDevice9::SetStreamSourceFreq()` function to set the number of instances that need to be drawn with the per-instance data in a second vertex buffer; in OpenGL extensions exist such as `NVX_instance_arrays` and `GL_EXT_draw_instanced`. In OpenGL vertex arrays can be used to specify the object's geometry and per-instance data.

In shader instancing the per-instance data are specified in system memory. During rendering, a batching approach is taken to render out the maximum number of instances that can be copied into the vertex shader's constants. This approach does not use the hardware to perform the instancing but can be efficient if hardware support is not present. Constant instancing is similar to shader instancing without the batching. With constant instancing each object is drawn at one time using a single draw call, but the information is already stored and ready in memory, making it faster than drawing one at a time without the memory being ready.

Stream instancing is similar to hardware instancing, but instead of using shader constants to control how objects are drawn, this is done by offsetting the separate stream used to store the per-instance data.

Instancing a large number of similar objects is a very useful and important technique to modern video game graphics. One very popular game that made use of instancing is *Kameo* by Rare.

ADDITIONAL OPTIMIZATION TECHNIQUES

Other common optimizations are performed in video game graphics in modern and next-generation games. Many of these optimizations focus on completely avoiding the execution of complex code instead of just making the algorithms run as fast as possible. This section discusses a few of these useful techniques.

Dynamic Branching

Shader Model 3.0 introduced the notion of dynamic branching, which allows a shader to quit its execution early based on a specified dynamic condition. In Shader Model 3.0 support for true conditional and looping statements was added to the technology. By using dynamic branching, it is possible to avoid very costly vertex and pixel operations if the situation calls for it. In previous Shader models, such as 2.0, conditional and looping statements were severely limited and not dynamic (i.e., only limited static implementations were allowed). In pre-3.0 versions shaders could not early-out of execution using a loop or a conditional statement. Shader Model 3.0 changed this and allowed for more dynamic control over shader execution.

The effectiveness of dynamic branching has a lot to do with the specific hardware card being used. The efficiency of dynamic branching is increasing with each generation of graphics cards, and utilizing them to their full potential can greatly benefit a game's performance, especially if it uses very complex and expensive shaders to perform various effects. To use dynamic branching, developers can use loops with variable conditions, if statements, and other conditional code to skip shader operations. For example, when performing lighting, if the diffuse contribution is 0, then the specular contribution is 0. If this is placed in a conditional statement, not only can the calculation of the specular component be skipped, but the fragment itself does not even need to be set since there is no light contribution for that pixel. Of course, this depends on the shader and what exactly it is doing.

State Management

Video games require a lot of different resources to be switched for every frame that is rendered. A few of the more common of these resources include the following graphics-related items:

- Geometry buffers (e.g., vertex, index, etc.)
- Shader effects
- Textures
- Effect parameters
- Rendering device states
- Blend states
- Render targets
- Transformations

When switching resources, a cost is associated with that operation. Depending on how many times resources are switched and how expensive each individual switch is, depends on how it affects a game's performance. Traditionally, switching shaders and textures have been among the most expensive state switches that are being used. If these state switches occur enough times in a frame, they can have a noticeable negative impact on the game's performance that often can be unacceptable.

One method that can be used to resolve this issue is state management. The idea behind state management is to reduce the number of state switches as much as possible. For example, let's say an application has six objects, half of which used texture A and half of which used texture B. If the application renders one object for each texture and alternates between the two, the application would be performing the worst-case scenario of texture switches. This can look like the following.

Render: Object (A), Object (B), Object (A), Object (B), Object (A), Object (B),

If state management is used for the rendering of those six objects, all objects that require texture A would be rendered first and then all objects that require texture B. This would give at most two texture switches instead of six. In a game situation there can be many objects that are texture-mapped and have other resources (e.g., different shaders, their own transformations, etc.).

In next-generation video games resources are so complex that it is often very hard or impossible to completely eliminate all unnecessary state switches, but the goal is to reduce them as much as possible. For example, does an application render objects by texture? If so, what about multiple textures? What about shaders and shader parameters? In practice it is sometimes hard for a game to have perfect state management because many of these resources, together, can make the task difficult. For example, every object has its own transformation, but if the objects are rendered primarily using that, then many costly texture and shader switches might occur. If objects are rendered by shader, many other resources might be heavily switched as a result, which might cost more than the shaders.

In a video game developers who use state management often choose a few resources that have the largest expense in their game and sort based on those. For example, a game might render all objects by shader, and then it might subsort each of those by texture or vice versa.

 A scene graph can be used to group objects by their property relationships.

SUMMARY

The optimization of video game graphics is very important to game developers. There are so many different aspects to this topic that an entire book on this one subject would be highly beneficial. As video games become more and more complex, so do the issues that game developers face. These issues require solutions that are often not trivial and require a lot of research and experimenting.

The purpose of this chapter was to give you an idea of some of the many different obstacles you will face as a graphics programmer. Many of these obstacles depend on the hardware and type of video game being developed and have been encountered by developers for many years.

The following elements were discussed in this chapter:

- Back-face culling
- Frustum culling
- Occlusion culling
- Portals

- ROAM
- Continuous level-of-detail (CLOD)
- Binary-space partitioning trees
- Quad trees
- Octrees
- Potential visibility sets
- Instancing
- Dynamic branching
- State management

CHAPTER QUESTIONS

Answers to the following chapter review questions can be found in Appendix A, "Answers to Chapter Questions."

1. Culling is known as what?
   - A. Scene management
   - B. State management
   - C. Hidden surface removal
   - D. None of the above
2. Describe far plane culling and name one limitation and a solution for it.
3. What are the two types of face culling mentioned in this chapter? What are their purposes?
4. What are the two types of frustum culling discussed in this chapter? What are their differences and purposes?
5. How does graphics API occlusion culling work?
6. What is the main purpose of scene and space partitioning?
7. What is a BSP tree? On what data structure is the BSP tree based? Describe how the BSP tree operates in a 3D scene.
8. What are the different ways a splitting plane can be created with a BSP tree? List and describe the two mentioned in this chapter.
9. What is a convex mesh? What is a concave mesh?
10. What are potential visibility sets, and how are they used in games?
11. What is a quad-tree? What is an octree? What types of scenes do they work best with?
12. Why are octrees and quad trees more efficient for outdoor rendering than a BSP tree or portal rendering system?
13. What are portals, and what are sectors? What are their purposes for scene management?
14. Describe instancing. What advantage does it give complex scenes?
15. List the different types of instancing mentioned in this chapter.
16. Describe continuous level-of-detail and its purpose for terrain rendering.

17. Describe ROAM and its purpose for terrain rendering.
18. What is dynamic branching, and how does it affect game graphics? In which shader model was it introduced?
19. Describe state management. What use does it have for video game and graphics developers?
20. What kind of data structure was mentioned that can be used for state management?
   A. Graph
   B. Binary tree
   C. Hash table
   D. None of the above
21. True or false: A quad tree is a 3D data structure.
22. True or false: The Z-buffer is used for visibility determination.
23. True or false: Binary space partitioning trees are more suitable for outdoor environments.
24. True or false: Instancing is used to draw the same instance of a model multiple times with slightly different properties.
25. True or false: BSP tree nodes split geometry into concave pieces.
26. True or false: Dynamic branching was introduced in Shader Model 2.0.
27. True or false: The partitioning plane is also known as the splitting plane.
28. True or false: Occlusion and view frustum culling are view independent.
29. True or false: Dynamic branching allows early-out execution for shaders.
30. True or false: Partitioning a scene into more manageable sections is known as state management.

CHAPTER EXERCISES

Exercise 1: Implement the portal/sector data structure. Also, implement a searching algorithm that can be used to render the data structures in a 3D scene.

Exercise 2: Implement the BSP tree data structure, insertion, and searching algorithms. Implement the front-to-back transversal search.

Exercise 3: Build off of Exercise 2 and implement a back-to-front transversal search.

16

CONCLUSIONS

In This Chapter

- A Look Behind
- A Look Forward
- Final Thoughts

The topic of computer graphics, especially as far as modern video games are concerned, is a vast and complex subject. Modern video game graphics programmers and artists are under a tremendous amount of pressure to create great-looking visuals at great performance rates. Game graphics offer a unique challenge because not only must visuals look as good as they can, but they must also perform at exceptional rates. As new hardware is introduced to the market, this can become very challenging, as developers must learn to use new technology at their highest potential. Because of how fast the hardware industry grows and evolves, this occurs quite often. An example of this can be seen in the video game console market, where new video game consoles offer fresh challenges that developers must overcome to be able to utilize the latest hardware at its fullest potential.

A LOOK BEHIND

Throughout this book we looked at how to perform many different rendering techniques using graphical APIs such as OpenGL and Direct3D and took an introductory look at how to perform ray tracing and software rendering on the CPU. A lot of information was covered, but the completion of this book only marks the beginning of video game graphics. Hardware will change, games will become more complex, and the gamers' expectations will rise with every game that raises the bar for the entire industry.

Some of the topics discussed in this book could have been given their own individual books. Examples of such topics include software rendering, ray tracing, game mathematics, data structures and algorithms, post-processing effects, and global illumination. The knowledge that goes into modern video game graphics is vast and often is composed of many different subject areas such as mathematics, physics, and art. To move forward it is important to have a firm understanding of each of the areas that concern game graphics, even those topics that are not necessarily unique to video game graphics (e.g., data structures).

Game Mathematics

Throughout this book we've seen mathematics used for every aspect of game graphics. Everything from the shading of an individual pixel to the representation of vertices and vectors are based on math. Video games use mathematics extensively in many areas of a game outside of graphics. These areas include the following:

- Game graphics
- Physics

- Collision detection and response, which is considered by some as part of the general game physics
- Artificial intelligence
- Game logic
- Compression
- Encryption
- 3D audio

It is very important that the mathematics code that is part of a game or a game engine be optimized for speed and efficiency. For objects that are calculated hundreds or thousands of times per frame, the speed at which those operations can be carried out is often a major priority. There are a number of ways to make math code faster to process. These methods include:

- Choosing the most effective representation that performs the desired task (e.g., using quaternions for rotations and interpolations is faster than using matrices and uses less memory for its structure)
- Choosing the right operators (e.g., using bit operators appropriately, multiplying by an inverse instead of dividing multiple times, etc.)
- Taking advantage of extended instruction sets supported by the hardware's central processing unit

Taking advantage of extended instruction sets can include using streaming SIMD (single instruction, multiple data) extension SSE instructions. SSE was originally designed by Intel for their Pentium processors and is now also supported by some AMD processors.

Traditionally, processors processed a single data element using a single instruction. By using instruction sets based on SIMD, it is possible to operate on multiple data elements with a single instruction. An example of a multiple data element can be seen with the 3D vector. If you wanted to add two vectors together using an SIMD instruction, you could add them using a single instruction instead of one instruction for each axis, which for a 3D vector would be three instructions. SSE is an instruction set that can operate on floating-point values, whereas some other instruction sets, such as multimedia extensions (MMX), operate only on integer variables. Also, SSE can operate on four data elements at a time, while MMX, for example, can operate on two data elements at a time.

 MMX and AMD's 3DNow are other types of extended instruction sets.

SSE introduces eight new registers in the processor, which are 128 bits long (i.e., can hold four 32-bit single-precision elements). These registers are xmm0, xmm1, xmm2, xmm3, xmm4, xmm5, xmm6, and xmm7. When working with SSE, you use assembly language. In C++ you can use inline assembly using the keyword _asm. If coded efficiently, your math library can run faster than not using SIMD instructions such as SSE. The downside is that you need to be comfortable with assembly language, which is outside the scope of this book.

MMX did not introduce new registers and instead used registers from the FPU. This limited processors because they cannot use MMX and the FPU at the same time.

Ray Tracing

Ray tracing was discussed in this book to introduce you to some of the general techniques and topics that go hand in hand with other popular game graphics techniques such as calculating light mapping and other effects. Although ray tracing wasn't discussed in great detail, enough of the topic was covered to allow you to get a start creating your own ray tracing rendering system. Building your own ray tracing system, even for fun, can be quite educational and enlightening. When compared to rasterization, some ray tracing techniques are actually easier and more straightforward to implement in code.

There are many additional important ray tracing topics if you want to build a highly sophisticated and complex ray tracer. Data structures and algorithms are one of these topics that are used a lot in ray tracing. This topic was first discussed in Chapter 15, "Optimization," for both the rendering and the management of scenes and for optimization for performance benefits. Other techniques are used for rendering realistic scenes. Two popular techniques that were first discussed in Chapter 10, "Global Illumination Techniques," include path tracing and photon mapping, both of which can be used to compute the global illumination of complex scenes.

The biggest issue about ray tracing is that it is traditionally not a real-time technique. By being offline, ray tracing systems are able to compute scenes by using expensive and complex algorithms using extremely highly detailed data and resolutions that are not suitable for real time. The results are scenes that far surpass anything we seen in real-time video games today. The results of ray tracing can be seen in computer-generated movies such as *Shrek* and *The Teenage Mutant Ninja Turtles*. Over the years real-time ray tracing has made enough progress that computer graphics programmers can start to look at it more optimistically for future video games.

Rasterization

Most of this book focused on hardware rendering using the OpenGL and Direct3D graphics APIs. Although graphics API are very good at the tasks given them, developers must put in a lot of effort to get the best performance out of their applications. The key idea with standard APIs is that they can be used by anyone for any kind of graphical application. The downfall is that these APIs are not so high level that they are all that is needed in a video game without additional code and systems being developed.

In Chapter 15 we touched upon the importance of optimizations in video games. Resources and memory are finite, and as gamer expectations increase, so does the complexity of the scenes in cutting-edge games. This trend will not end any time soon, especially with the emergence of high-definition gaming on the newer video game consoles and PCs.

Video game graphics are often about figuring out how to perform a task with the least amount of processing with the best acceptable results. Bump and normal mapping is one such technique where the cost of using a look-up texture to aid in the lighting calculations of surfaces is far cheaper than defining that detail using geometry. Individuals who are good at problem solving and figuring out alternatives to solutions will find a great challenge in video game development, especially game graphics for the next generation of games.

Advancements in Lights and Shadows

Lights and shadows are highly important topics when talking about the realistic rendering of virtual environments. The human eye is very sensitive to lighting and the absence of lights. If a scene is not realistic, the mind can quickly point this out. The more realistic the lighting and shadows, generally the better the scene looks for games that aim for realistic visuals. This can be seen in Chapter 10, where the addition of global lighting and shadows dramatically increases the realism of a scene.

Many topics go into the simulation of realistic lighting and shadows for both dynamic and static geometry. Static geometry allows for the possibility of precomputing a lot of data that can be quickly rendered in real time. Dynamic objects, on the other hand, can be more complex in their implementation. When advancing the look of any scene, a lot of time is often spent in lighting and shadows as well as the geometric detail of the scene and postprocessing effects.

As real-time lighting advances, so does the overall impact developers can have on scenes. Eventually, real-time lighting and shadows will completely replace preprocessing information for most games. One day, with enough technological advancement, real-time lighting and shadows can become the standard for all lighting effects in a scene. Real-time global illumination is already a reality, so this idea might be closer than most people realize.

Rendering People and Nature Realistically

Often, the graphics in video games attempt to be as realistic as possible. Video game graphics have come a long way, but they are still a far cry from reality. This can mostly be seen in the way most video games render characters such as humans and natural environments. Although video game graphics are making progress in these areas, a lot more research can be done.

Rendering people has always been difficult in computer graphics. Many properties of the human skin are hard to duplicate in real time. One method (out of many) that is used for skin rendering is called subsurface scattering. Subsurface scattering is a technique used to simulate the appearance of materials such as skin as light passes through them and scatters. A great example is when you take a bright flash light and place it against one side of your hand. On the other side you can see the light as it scatters through the blood in your hand. When rendering skin, it is little details like this, among many others, that make skin look realistic. Today, most characters are rendered with non-natural materials that often look plastic or rough like a dry rock. Also, rendering the different parts of a character from the skin, eyes, hair, clothes, weapons, armor, and so on ideally would use different materials for each mesh of the object. Some games, especially in the last generation, used one or only a few different materials when detailing characters.

Rendering nature is an equally difficult task. Because nature is composed of so many different objects it is hard to realistically render each one of them in real time. These objects include but are not limited to the following.

- Clouds
- Skies
- Sun and moon
- Water (touched upon in Chapter 14, "Water Rendering")
- Terrain (touched upon in Chapter 13, "Rendering Nature")
- Trees and other plant life
- Grass
- Foliage
- Rocks
- Fog
- Global lighting and soft shadows
- Weather effects such as rain, snow, and heat hazes

In the current generation of video games (e.g., PlayStation 3, Xbox 360, Wii) the detail in rendering nature will increase by leaps and bounds. As these scenes become more complex, so does the physics and collision system and the amount of data required to render the scene, along with increased complexity of rendering systems so that they can manage the data efficiently enough for acceptable performance. In open world games, such as Rockstar's *Grand Theft Auto IV*, this large amount of data has to be streamed off of the disk fast enough to give the impression that the world is consistently live and inhabited.

A Look Forward

This book is only the beginning when it comes to learning about video game graphics and modern game development. Although this book covered a lot of information, there is a lot more to learn when it comes to video game graphics. As time passes, the way we create graphics in video games will change to reflect the times and the technology available. Scenes will grow more complex as game developers push for bigger and better results than were accomplished in previous generations.

When moving forward in video game graphics education, a few topics will surely come up as you progress. In Chapter 15 we shed a little light on one of these topics: data structures and their related algorithms. Another topic is video game engines, as they often have very complex and robust rendering systems inside their architectures.

Data Structures and Algorithms

Computer graphics revolve around the idea of data structures and the algorithms that operate on them. In Chapter 15 we discussed a number of data structures and various algorithms that can be used to manage or speed up the rendering of a scene. The topic is very important to computer graphics and has been since the beginning of video game development.

A data structure is a structure that defines how memory is represented and stored. Data structures are the organizational building blocks that applications use to perform various tasks throughout their executions. These tasks, which are known as algorithms, are code that is executed and uses the data structures to perform something meaningful to the application. The most basic data structure is the array, and one of the most basic algorithms, when dealing with arrays, is the insertion of data in the elements of the container.

The topic of data structures and algorithms can become quite complex and can span multiple books. If you are unfamiliar with data structures and their algorithms, such as graphs, trees, lists, and so forth, we recommend that you read the book *Data Structures for Game Developers*. The book is focused on the C++ programming language and covers a wealth of information useful in general and game development.

Game Engine Design and Architecture

The creation of a 3D game engine is not trivial in any sense. Video games are more than just graphics rendering, and to be able to create a commercial-quality modern 3D video game, developers need to have up-to-date technology and experienced individuals backing the project. Game engines are so important that some companies provide middleware solutions to other development companies. One example is the Unreal 3.0 engine created by Epic Games.

Game engine is another term for a game framework. A game framework is a set of abstract code that is used as the foundation for a gaming project. This framework is composed of many high-level subframeworks, some of which are built on top of existing APIs. Examples of the various subframeworks that make up a video game engine include:

- Rendering system
- Physics system
- Input system
- Sound/audio system
- Networking system
- Memory management routines
- Data loading routines
- Scripting system

Each of these high-level frameworks can be further broken down into smaller subsystems. Using the rendering system as an example, these subsystems can include but are not limited to the following.

- Material system
- Postprocessing system
- Geometry rendering cache
- Animation system
- Particle system

The purpose of a game engine is to create code for systems on a high level so that they can be used to manage and execute the various parts of a game. For example, consider DirectX, which is not as large or high level as a game engine but can be used as the basis of many of a game engine's systems. Using an API such as Direct3D is much easier and higher level than manually writing graphics routines ourselves and trying to implement all of the features we want by hand. If we were to do everything by hand, we would quickly realize that we are writing a lot of redundant code. That redundant code can be placed into an API, and that API can be used in different applications. Game engines are important to the video game industry because a good game engine can be used in multiple types of gaming projects, rather than just one. This allows developers to save time writing code and allows them to focus more on the game project than the technology behind it.

In Chapter 15 we saw a simple set of examples of how important data structures and algorithms are. These are all topics important to game engine design and architecture. Along with data structures and algorithms for graphics, the following are also very common and extremely important to modern game engines.

- Memory management
- Profiling
- Resource management
- Asset creation tools (e.g., level editors, particle editors, etc.)
- Fast math libraries
- Fast asset management
- Artificial intelligence–related data structures and algorithms
- Physics-related data structures and algorithms

FINAL THOUGHTS

This book covered a lot of information. Video game graphics is a large field of study that will continue to grow as computer technology increases in power and complexity and as gamers require better visuals from the products they purchase. This book aimed to give you plenty of information and experience implementing different algorithms in game graphics, many of which are commonly used in modern commercial video games.

The next step after this is to build a graphics engine that can be used as part of a larger video game engine. The creation of a video game engine is no small task and can become quite complex and advanced when implementing features found in many commercial video games, especially "AAA" gaming titles. Fortunately, after reading through this book, you should be equipped with everything you need to start moving toward the next level of video game development.

A

ANSWERS TO CHAPTER QUESTIONS

CHAPTER 1 ANSWERS

1. A. Preprocessed means that it is processed ahead of time. In this case, it means offline, usually during development.
2. C. Post means after. A postprocessed effect is one that is created after a scene has been rendered. Examples include depth-of-field, pixel-based motion blur, tone mapping, and so forth.
3. A real-time effect is an effect that is calculated in real time for each frame or a number of frames.
4. Video games use rasterization as a fast way to render 3D scenes, especially when compared to ray tracing. Rasterization is a technique that is used to render individual surfaces to the screen by determining where on the screen they are and filling in those pixels appropriately.
5. Ray tracing is a ray- and intersection-based technique used to render 3D scenes. It is used throughout computer graphics, most noticeably in computer-animated media such as movies and television.
6. False. Although Direct3D has a software-rendering mode, OpenGL and Direct3D are hardware-rendering APIs.
7. True. Cross-platform in this case technically means between the various Windows operating systems and the Xbox 360 game console (and presumably their successors).
8. True. Ray tracing has traditionally been known to be very expensive to calculate, and it has yet to be used as the basis for a major video game.
9. False. There would not need to be any need to clip polygons when testing for ray or polygon intersection. Polygons are often clipped in rasterization.
10. False. XNA is built on top of DirectX 9.

CHAPTER 2 ANSWERS

1. C. There are 8 bits in a single byte, which is the size of the char data type in C++.
2. B. There are 2 bits in a binary digit.
3. D. There are 32 bits (4 bytes) in an integer.
4. B. There are 4 bytes in an integer.
5. C. There are 1024 kilobytes in a megabyte.
6. A. In an RGB color of 24 bits, there are only three components (red, green, and blue).
7. Base-2 is the base binary values use. There are two max values in each column. In the case of binary, this is either a 0 or a 1.

8. Base-10 is the base we commonly use, and it has up to 10 values for each column.
9. Hexadecimal values are base-16 numbers.
10. D. B (11 * 16 = 176) + A (10 * 1) = 186
11. A polygon is a surface with three or more connected points.
12. A concave mesh is a mesh where all edges are not facing each other. In other words, a line segment inside a concave mesh going from one edge to another might cross a polygon of the mesh. Convex is the opposite.
13. B. A triangle has three edges.
14. A sphere is faster to process because its calculations are less expensive overall.
15. A vector is a mathematical object that represents a direction along n-axes.
16. A vector with a length of 1 is called a unit-length vector.
17. The dot product can be used to get the cosine angle between two unit-length vectors.
18. The cross product, also known as the scalar product, computes a vector that is perpendicular to two vectors.
19. In computer graphics, a matrix is used to represent transformations.
20. The determinant.
21. A ray has an origin and a direction.
22. A plane is an infinitely flat surface that extends infinitely along two axes.
23. A scalar is a floating-point value.
24. D. They are **NOT** commutative operations.
25. The technique of choice for video games where geometry is rasterized to the screen and its pixels are shaded.
26. Ray tracing is a technique used to generate a scene using rays.
27. A quaternion is used to represent rotations. They are more efficient than using matrices for rotations and interpolations.
28. (1) Four floating-point values are required to represent a quaternion instead of up to sixteen for a matrix. (2) A quaternion is faster to interpolate. (3) Quaternions do not suffer from mathematical errors such as the commonly known "gimbal-lock."
29. Linear interpolation interpolates between two values using a percentage.
30. Spherical interpolation smoothly interpolates between two values using a constant motion.

CHAPTER 3 ANSWERS

1. Ray tracing is a technique that uses ray intersections to generate a graphical image.
2. Forward ray tracing traces rays from the light source into the scene.
3. Backward ray tracing (also known as ray casting) traces rays from the viewer into the scene.
4. Backward ray tracing is faster and requires fewer rays, and every pixel is shaded if an object occupies its space.
5. D.
6. (1) Get the sphere-ray vector. (2) Test the cosine angle between them for possible collision. (3) If collision is not found, take the square of the sphere's radius, ray to sphere vector length, and the square of the angle between the two vectors to test if the ray passes through the radius of the sphere.
7. (1) Get the angle between the plane's normal and the ray's direction. (2) Test if the absolute value of the angle is less than 0, meaning there is no intersection because the ray is parallel to the plane. (3) If the previous test passed, we get the ray's distance from the plane using the ray's position with that of the plane.
8. (1) Get two edges from the triangle. (2) Get the vector product (cross) between the first edge and the ray's direction. (3) If the cosine angle between the vector product of the previous test result and the first edge is less than 0, then the ray passes outside of the edge.
9. It is slower, not all rays definitely intersect an object where a pixel is located, and it requires a great deal more rays.
10. It is easy to implement, faster to process than forward ray tracing, and it definitely shades all pixels that should be shaded.
11. Take the ray's origin and move it along the ray's direction as far as the distance of the intersection. That vertex position is the point of intersection.
12. D. Depth-of-field would not increase the number of rays that are traced in a scene.
13. Since rays are independent of one another, multiple rays can be processed by the different cores of a CPU at the same time.
14. B.
15. False.
16. False.
17. True. If a ray from one position to another is obtained, then to test if there is a line-of-sight would be to test if any surface in the scene intersects that ray.
18. False.
19. True.
20. False. Although tricky, it is possible and has been done.

21. True.
22. False. Spheres are faster than boxes and triangles.
23. False. Animated movies offline their rendering.
24. True. Researchers studying this topic have implemented real-time ray tracers.
25. True.

CHAPTER 4 ANSWERS

1. C.
2. In rasterization, geometry is transformed to pixel locations that are shaded one surface at a time. Geometry is clipped to the bounds of the view-port, and the area that makes up the screen-space surface is rendered.
3. To offload the work from the CPU to a dedicated device designed and optimized for the task.
4. They are dedicated devices whose purpose is to offload work from the CPU.
5. Clipping truncates primitives so that they fall only within the screen bounds. When clipped primitives are rendered, only the information necessary to display it is used.
6. B.
7. It stands for frames per-second. The easiest way to calculate it is to count the frames until a second has passed. The resulting value is the FPS.
8. Double buffering creates an additional buffer that is used for rendering. Rendering is alternated between the buffers.
9. Page flipping is where rendering buffers are displayed by switching between them.
10. Double buffering allows for smoother animations, while page flipping builds on that to avoid copying the contents of buffers.
11. Page flipping is more efficient because it doesn't copy data from buffer to buffer.
12. Depth testing is used to determine which pixels are to be rendered to. Depth testing is implemented in a depth buffer.
13. A stencil buffer can be used as a masking buffer to control how pixels are rendered.
14. C.
15. Back-face culling is the culling of faces that are facing away from the viewer. This can speed up rendering because faces that are not seen by the camera are culled out of the scene.
16. It is using three buffers for rendering.

17. If the line crosses the view-port, then it is clipped, or else it is either not visible (ignored) or it is rendered because it is fully visible.
18. The triangle is transformed to screen-space, and the rectangular area making up the triangle is defined. This rectangle is then clipped to the view-port, and the triangle is rendered.
19. Three: the model, the view, and the projection.
20. True.
21. False. Their general purpose is the same, but they are not performed in the same manner.
22. False.
23. True.
24. False. Graphics hardware wouldn't be more efficient at 3D than 2D. If anything, 2D graphics would be less work for modern graphics hardware than 3D.
25. False.

CHAPTER 5 ANSWERS

1. The fixed-function pipeline is generally a set of rendering algorithms and states that are part of the rendering API.
2. Low-level shaders are written in assembly, while high-level shading languages are written in a language similar to C/C++.
3. It is easier to write in a high-level language, it is faster to develop high-level shaders, and they are easier to maintain.
4. OpenGL Shading Language.
5. High-Level Shading Language.
6. C for graphics.
7. A semantic is a keyword used to bind your own variables to the inputs and outputs of a shader, and it tells the HLSL how the variable is used. A technique is an effect. In HLSL, multiple technique effects can be specified in one file.
8. Constant, uniform, temporary, input, and output registers.
9. Type qualifiers allow you to prefix an object with how it is used. These types include default, uniform, varying, and const (constant).
10. False.
11. False.
12. True.
13. False. There are also geometry shaders.
14. True.
15. RenderMan is more than a shading language and is a very powerful renderer.
16. True.

17. False.
18. False. Shaders didn't catch on until the turn of the millennium.
19. False. Just because they are high-level, they don't have to be object-oriented.
20. False. A shader can be part of a material, but they are not synonymous.

CHAPTER 6 ANSWERS

1. D.
2. TGA stands for Targa. DDS stands for Direct Draw Surface.
3. Texture compression reduces the size of the texture. Compression is lossy or lossless.
4. Lossless reduces the size without giving up quality, while lossy does sacrifice quality for size.
5. Lossy allows for great reduction is data size but at the cost of quality. Lossless keeps quality, but the compression ratios are not always as high as with lossy.
6. DDS files use DXTC compression, which stands for DirectX Texture Compression. DXTC is a lossy compression format.
7. A8L8 is a great format to use for normal maps because one of the axes can be generated in the pixel shader. It doesn't compress data other than dropping one of the components, which slightly reduces space requirements.
8. The 3Dc is designed for normal maps and is also a lossy compression.
9. Run-length encoding essentially records how many times a piece of data repeats. This allows the repeated data to be removed, which can save space for images that have a lot of consecutive pixels of the same color. Although the TGA file format supports run-length encoding, the compression type is not supported by graphics hardware.
10. False.
11. False.
12. True.
13. False. Lossy compression is not the best option for normals, because it will hurt the quality of the normals in the file.
14. True.
15. True.
16. False.
17. False. 3Dc is better for normal maps. DXTC is great for color maps.
18. True.
19. True.
20. True.

CHAPTER 7 ANSWERS

1. Alpha mapping allows pixel-level alpha values to be mapped to surfaces. It is implemented using a texture (either the alpha channel or a separate texture).
2. Cube mapping is used to map six images onto a surface, which works great for environment mapping. Cube maps can be accessed by 3D texture coordinates, or the coordinates can be generated.
3. B.
4. Reflection mapping uses cube mapping to perform reflections in a 3D scene.
5. Refraction mapping uses cube mapping to perform refractions in a 3D scene.
6. Render targets are render buffers that can be created and rendered to. They allow games to render scenes to these surfaces for various purposes. They can be used for postprocessing effects, dynamic cube mapping, mirrors, and so forth.
7. An image filter is an algorithm that is executed on the data of an image. Mostly, they can be used to perform special effects on an image.
8. The algorithm executes a dot product on each of the image pixels and the luminance constant to change the image to black-and-white.
9. The sepia filter builds off of the luminance filter but adds a brownish tone to the image and retains some of its original color.
10. It always faces the viewer.
11. In the early days they were used for characters and objects, such as in the original *Doom*. Today, they are mostly used for particle effects.
12. Anti-aliasing attempts to reduce or eliminate aliasing effects in images. This can reduce those artifacts to improve the look of a rendered scene.
13. It occurs because pixels are square, and since they can not be partially rendered to, a staircase effect can be seen. This is especially true if the resolution is low.
14. Super sampling renders at an increased resolution and then downsamples the results to the resolution you want displayed. You can eliminate the appearance of jagged edges. There is adaptive, random, and grid super sampling.
15. Dynamic cube mapping uses render targets to dynamically create the cube map that is used for the objects. Dynamic cube mapping is often used for real-time reflections.
16. False.
17. True.
18. False.
19. True.
20. True.

CHAPTER 8 ANSWERS

1. It is an algorithm used to light a surface.
2. A material describes how a surface is to appear and interact with lighting, if any is present.
3. Color map, diffuse light, emissive, specular light, and ambient light.
4. A directional light is light that comes from a direction but has no specific origin. In computer graphics this is used to model global lights that do not need a position but come from a general direction.
5. A point light is a light that shines in multiple directions over a specific distance. In computer graphics these types of light sources are modeled to look like most real-life lights.
6. A spot light is light that shines through a cone. In computer graphics it is used to model light types such as flashlights.
7. Ambient light is global light. It is used in game graphics as a simple way to approximate this light.
8. Diffuse light is light that has reflected off of a rough surface. It is used in graphics to model rough surfaces.
9. Specular light is a shiny highlight that appears on objects. In computer graphics it can be used to model such materials.
10. Lambert diffuse lighting is determined by the dot product between the normal and the light vector. This value is multiplied by the color, which causes the lighting effect.
11. The Phong model uses the reflection vector and incident vector to calculate the specular reflectance.
12. The Blinn-Phong model builds off of the Phong model and calculates the specular reflectance using a faster operation than the original Phong.
13. Bump mapping is a technique used to define the normals at a pixel level so that the lighting can create details that would be difficult to model.
14. Normal mapping is used to make a low-resolution model look like a higher-resolution model by using bump mapping to simulate the detail.
15. Parallax mapping builds off of bump mapping to add the illusion of depth to the surface. It allows for a greater level of detail when mapping to flat surfaces so that they appear complex and 3D.
16. Lens flare is an artifact that appears as light hits the camera lens. In games it is usually done as 2D elements rendered to the screen based on if a really bright light is visible.
17. A light shaft is a shaft of light coming through objects such as sunlight through leaves. It is used in *Crysis*.
18. Blooming creates a halo around bright points. It is usually done by blurring bright values.

19. Similar to a bump map, but a height map is an image that stores heights, not colors. A height map just has heights, while a displacement map has vectors that are used to displace geometry.

20. False. The view vector is not needed for the Lambert diffuse algorithm.

21. False. Blinn-Phong uses the half vector.

22. True.

23. False. Attenuation is used in point lights to cause the fall-off effect, not visibility.

24. True.

25. True. It extends on bump mapping, which extends on per-pixel lighting.

26. True.

27. False.

28. True.

29. False. It is used to add a bright halo around bright objects, not to brighten the scene.

30. True.

CHAPTER 9 ANSWERS

1. Shadow projection as described in this book essentially draws an object with a matrix that is designed to flatten it and project it in a specific direction. The matrix creation can take the following form:

```
function CreateShadowMatrix(Plane plane, Vector4D lightPos)
{
  float dp = plane.Dot(lightPos);
  float matrix[16] = 0;
  matrix[0] = dp - lightPos.x * plane.a;
  matrix[4] = 0 - lightPos.x * plane.b;
  matrix[8] = 0 - lightPos.x * plane.c;
  matrix[12] = 0 - lightPos.x * d;
  matrix[1] = 0 - lightPos.y * plane.a;
  matrix[5] = dp - lightPos.y * plane.b;
  matrix[9] = 0 - lightPos.y * plane.c;
  matrix[13] = 0 - lightPos.y * d;
  matrix[2] = 0 - lightPos.z * plane.a;
  matrix[6] = 0 - lightPos.z * plane.b;
  matrix[10] = dp - lightPos.z * plane.c;
  matrix[14] = 0 - lightPos.z * d;
  matrix[3] = 0 - lightPos.w * plane.a;
```

```
    matrix[7] = 0 - lightPos.w * plane.b;
    matrix[11] = 0 - lightPos.w * plane.c;
    matrix[15] = dp - lightPos.w * d;
    return matrix;
}
```

2. To render the shadow on a nonflat surface, the stencil buffer or clipped polygon can be used. Instead of rendering a complex model a lower-resolution version of the mesh, another mesh that approximates its general shape or a simplified shape such as a circle can be used for the shadow creation.

3. Some pros are their ease of implementation, that they don't require special hardware, and that they are fairly cheap to process. Some cons are that they are not realistic, they don't allow objects to self-shadow themselves, and they can't be used to shadow other scene objects.

4. A shadow volume is extruded silhouette geometry that creates a volume. This volume is often used with the stencil buffer to mask shadowed areas of a scene so that the rendering can detect where shadows are and are not. Carmack's reverse generally switches the volume counter and order for front- and back-facing polygons to remove artifacts that can appear, such as if the camera is already in a shadowed area.

5. An edge is part of the silhouette if it is part of one polygon that is facing the camera while the rest of the polygons that it is attached to are facing away from it. To determine if an edge is part of the outline, you have to check if the previous condition is true.

6. Some pros are they can allow objects to self-shadow, they allow objects to shadow all surfaces within a scene, and they are more realistic than projection shadows. Cons include the overhead in creating volumes for every object in the scene, the requirement of a stencil buffer if stencil shadow volumes are used, and the fill-rate cost associated with them.

7. A soft shadow has soft edges, whereas a hard shadow is sharp and solid across its surface. Soft shadows are more realistic, and they are caused by light bouncing around the environment, where some points receive more light than others.

8. The main difference is that hard shadows are sharp, while soft shadows soften as their areas reach their outer edges. In video games, since realism is often the goal, soft shadows are a better solution even though they are harder to compute with some algorithms.

9. In shadow mapping, the scene's depth is rendered from the point of view of the light source. When the scene is rendered for the final pass, the depth values in the shadow map are projected onto the scene and are used to determine if a point is in shadow or if it is unshadowed.

10. Aliasing artifacts can be minimized by increasing the resolution of the shadow map and by blurring the shadow map.

11. Cascading shadow mapping is a technique in which the view frustum is split into multiple sections and a different shadow map is assigned to each section. Usually, the sections farther from the viewer are larger. This allows quality to be kept for shadows throughout the view volume, whereas one shadow map would have to stretch across the entire scene, which could compromise quality.

12. A simple solution is to blur the contents of a shadow map to create the approximation of a soft shadow.

13. Deferred shading is shading that is postponed until after the scene has been initially rendered. Its main advantage is that it allows the lighting and other shadings to occur cheaply by only rendering where the light's influence surrounds. Its main disadvantage is that it is difficult to work with different materials in one pass, such as velvet and silk.

14. The G-buffer is a rendering target or a series of targets used to store all the information necessary to shade the scene in a later step. Today, it is usually created using MRTs (multiple rendering targets).

15. Using multiple rendering targets.

16. A light map is a texture that is often preprocessed with the necessary information to display lighting and shadowing information on a surface. In video games, light maps have always been used to display lights and shadows that would have been difficult or impossible to compute in real time for the target hardware.

17. Usually, a set of light map texture coordinates is created, and the light map image is created by using the interpolated surface vertices and other attributes (such as normals) to calculate the lighting and, optionally, the shadowing information. The developer choose the lighting and shadowing algorithms used for the light map's image based on what they decide is the best option.

18. The images can be placed in a larger texture atlas and batched together instead of having one for each surface.

19. Lumels.

20. Planar texture projection essentially projects the vertices of an object onto an axis plane and then uses this information to generate a texture coordinate.

21. False. Shadows are not free in computer graphics and do not occur as a side effect of lighting.

22. False. This is known as shadow mapping.

23. True.

24. True.

25. True. The projection shadowing technique described in this book would not allow for self-shadowing. Shadow volumes and shadow mapping would allow for it.

26. False. Soft shadows are shadows with a hard edge.
27. True.
28. False.
29. True.
30. True. Technically, a developer would need to write a different shader for each lighting algorithm (for example, Lambert diffuse, Phong for specular, and so forth).

CHAPTER 10 ANSWERS

1. Global illumination is lighting that has bounced around a scene a number of times so that surfaces are lit not only directly from light sources but also from other nearby surfaces.
2. Global illumination in computer graphics is a general simulation of how light appears in nature. This leads to more realistic renderings.
3. Direct lighting is light that comes directly from a light source, such as the sun or a light bulb.
4. Indirect lighting is light that has come indirectly from nearby surfaces after the light has bounced off of it.
5. Ambient occlusion is a value that represents the visibility percentage of a point or a pixel in the scene.
6. It can be used to shadow an object realistically and is usually multiplied by the ambient value. This allows soft shadows to appear during a scene.
7. *Crysis* uses what the developer calls screen-space ambient occlusion, which is a real-time screen-space technique for quickly approximating ambient occlusion for the pixels of a rendered scene.
8. Radiosity divides the scene into a number of patches. While lighting the patches, energy is transferred throughout the scene for a specified number of bounces.
9. Path tracing extends ray tracing. In path tracing, new rays are created and traced for the point of intersection to account for the indirect lighting of nearby surfaces.
10. In ray tracing, without any global illumination algorithms applied, the lighting used is direct light. Path tracing attempts to account for indirect light to create global illumination.
11. Photon mapping extends ray tracing. In photon mapping, a special data structure called a photon map is created. This photon map stores the accumulated direct and indirect illumination of intersected points. When rendering the scene using normal ray tracing, the photon map is used as a look-up table to determine what the color for the point of intersection should be. If using a *k*d-tree, the

point of intersection's position can be used in the tree to look up the illumination for that point.

12. A *kd*-tree is usually used because it is very fast to look up an element with *k*-dimensions.

13. Precomputed radiance transfer is used to compute the radiance of all points (vertex-level or pixel-level) of a scene. This radiance information is used to shade these points to account for the entire rendering equation (i.e., global illumination).

14. Spherical harmonics.

15. Light maps.

CHAPTER 11 ANSWERS

1. C.

2. C.

3. It keeps the precision of the colors, and a higher range of colors can be used. This is important when rendering a scene with quality and displaying it correctly with that quality.

4. B.

5. B. Tone mapping converts the HDR data into a form that can be displayed.

6. Quality in computer graphics has always been important. HDR allows for a higher quality rendered image, which is important for games.

7. Tone mapping takes the HDR data and maps it to the LDR range so that it can be displayed. This must happen because monitors and TV screens are designed for a specific range of colors.

8. Dynamic tone mapping adjusts the contrast based on the lighting conditions, which can be useful when you are trying to simulate the eye's response to changes in light. This is used in video games for that very purpose.

9. Light blooming blurs the bright parts of the scene and blends them on top of the rendered scene to create the blooming effect.

10. Light streaks are similar to blooms with the exception that the blurring occurs multiple times in different directions.

11. True. It can be done, but its quality is not the same as with HDR data.

12. False. Light streaks are a separate technique and are not a free result of tone mapping.

13. True. This can be done using higher bits with integer formats. Floating-point formats allow for larger precision, though.

14. True. Only the bright parts will be in the buffer since the HDR values are the bright parts.

15. False. The quality is better with HDR, but it is not technically impossible to use LDR.

CHAPTER 12 ANSWERS

1. Gaussian, radial, and motion blur.
2. Depth-of-field blurs are based on the focal range. Objects outside this range are blurred, while objects inside the range are not. Blurring occurs gradually as the objects move closer to the edge of the focal range and beyond. Depth of field is used to add cinematic quality to games.
3. Objects outside of it are blurred fully, while objects inside of it are not.
4. *Acceptable circle-of-confusion* is a term used to describe a circle that is indistinguishable from a point. As this circle gets gradually bigger, more blurriness is seen on the rendered result. Therefore, depth of field is not a sharp change from normal to blurred, although such a simple method could be used if its results were acceptable.
5. Motion blur blurs the scene based on camera and object motion. It is used to add cinematic quality to games.
6. Geometry-based motion blur extrudes geometry and accumulates blur based on that. Its main advantage is that it does not require special hardware support. Its main disadvantage is that it is difficult to implement and is not efficient.
7. Pixel-based motion blur uses rendering targets to specify the direction of the blur. Its main advantage is that it can create some impressive blur results. Its main disadvantage is that blur bleeding needs to be resolved and managed.
8. *Particle system* is a name used to describe an object that manages a list of particles. This chapter discussed sparks, fire, smoke, and weather effects.
9. *Point mass* is a physics term used to describe an object whose orientation is irrelevant. When you are calculating point masses, only the linear translation is taken into consideration. Since particles are tiny and their orientation would not mean much to the application, point masses are a great choice. A rigid body has its orientations calculated.
10. Force equals mass times acceleration.
11. To allow the system to be able to create any type of effect that is desired. It also makes specifying effects with an external editor a great idea.
12. They allow images to be placed dynamically on the surface of other objects, such as bullet holes in walls. Decals can be used for bullet holes, burn marks, blood, foot prints, tire marks, and so forth.
13. The decal can be aligned with the surface if the surface is flat. If it is not flat, the decal has to be clipped to each of the surfaces it touches.
14. Using elements together along two axes, with transparency, can give effects a 3D appearance.
15. False. It blurs based on where objects appear in the focal range.

16. False. A simple example of motion blur was used with the accumulation buffer.
17. True.
18. False.
19. True.

CHAPTER 13 ANSWERS

1. In this book we discussed sky planes, boxes, and domes.
2. Multiple layers of textures.
3. A sky box allows depth in the distant scenery to be represented easily. Its main disadvantage is its shape, which cannot appear as realistic or natural as a sky dome.
4. Fog can be used to help hide the horizon.
5. A disadvantage is that it requires more geometry. Advantages include that it looks realistic, has smooth transitions into the horizon, and has smooth day-to-night transitions in real time.
6. As textures that are part of the sky geometry and as billboards.
7. It takes a volumetric approach and uses billboards.
8. Brute force rendering means rendering out the entire mesh without consideration for optimizations such as culling. Terrains are often far too complex to render using a brute force approach in video games.
9. A terrain patch is a small section of terrain. Many patches can be used together to form the entire terrain.
10. The midpoint displacement algorithm creates a line between two points that lie on the edge of a square. This square initially is the edges of the entire terrain model.
11. The fault formation algorithm starts off with a grid for the terrain. This grid can be flat or have initial height values, as is also the case for the midpoint displacement algorithm. The algorithm creates a random line from one edge of the terrain to the other. The heights of every vertex on one side of the terrain are lowered, while the heights on the opposite side are raised.
12. Tiles are blended together to smoothly texture a surface based on some factor, such as height. If a different tile was used for a different elevation, then height could be used as the blending factor.
13. ROAM, BSP-tree, Octree, Quad-tree.
14. This is known as displacement mapping, and it means a texture can be used to store heights, which can be added to vertices to change their positions.
15. Box filtering is used to smooth the terrain. It essentially averages each of the heights of the terrain to smooth it out.

CHAPTER 14 ANSWERS

1. The water in *Goldeneye 007* used a simple textured surface, such as a rectangle, as its water. In *Perfect Dark*, the movement of the texture changed over time rather than remaining constant like it did in *Goldeneye 007*.

2. In *Dragonball Z Budakai Tenkaichi 2*, the water had transparencies, and its surface animation used multiple images.

3. *Half-Life 2* used much more realistic rendering techniques for water. These include rendering water with reflections, refractions, Fresnel, and bump mapping.

4. The water in *Crysis* used some of the most advanced water rendering techniques used in video games. The water was an animated mesh that used very complex equations for its movement, which was based on wave and wind directions.

5. *BioShock* rendered water as its main element for both visuals and game-play. Water in games was traditionally limited, mostly due to limited hardware. Today, games have many more resources, and *BioShock* took advantage of this by implementing water in a game at a level that was not previously done.

6. Fresnel combines reflections and refractions based on the viewing angle of the camera to the surface. This is used in water rendering to give it a more natural and realistic appearance.

7. Bump mapping is used as a cheap method of rendering small animated waves. If the surface is completely flat, using bump mapping can give it a nonflat appearance.

8. In *Far Cry*, a game by Crytex, the water was initially a simple disk mesh that followed the player around. This mesh used reflections and transparencies to get more of a water feel, but the mesh itself was fairly simple. The game used screen-space tessellation as well.

9. Caustics describe an envelope of reflected and refracted light as it strikes a curved surface, or in this case, the water's surface. This can cause light to be more concentrated in some directions than others.

10. Shorelines appear on large bodies of water where the terrain meets the water. In a game, it is possible to choose shallow areas (i.e., where the water surface is close to the terrain underneath it) for shorelines, which can be done using multi-texturing.

CHAPTER 15 ANSWERS

1. C. Removing geometry that can not be seen is known as culling, which is hidden surface removal.

2. Objects that are farther away from the viewer than the far plane are not rendered. This can cause far away objects to pop in and out of the scene.

3. Front-face culling culls all faces that are facing the viewer, while back-face culling culls faces that face away from the viewer.

4. View frustum culling culls geometry that is not within the view volume, while occlusion culling culls objects that are blocked by other surfaces.

5. Objects need to be rendered with the occlusion on so that when the scene is rendered, the hardware will test which pixels are occluded and which are not.

6. To organize a scene so that it can be quickly managed and processed. Examples include speeding up and increasing the efficiency of rendering, collision detection, physics, and so on.

7. A BSP tree is a binary data structure that is used to sort the polygons of a scene in order from front to back. The data can be rendered in front to back or back to front order. Sorting the geometry of a level into a BSP tree can speed up some operations, such as collision detection.

8. A splitting plane can be axis aligned or it can be created from a polygon within the scene, which is usually chosen using a scoring algorithm.

9. A convex mesh is one where all faces can see all other faces, with no occluding faces. A concave mesh is the opposite.

10. A potential visibility set, also known as PVS, is a list used to inform which nodes of a data structure can see which other nodes.

11. A quad-tree is a data structure that partitions the scene into four sections. Each section is recursively partitioned until some condition is met. An octree is the same, but it partitions in eight sections. Also, an octree is the 3D version of a quad tree.

12. A BSP tree's efficiency depends on many occluding surfaces, for which outdoor terrains are not suited. A portal rendering system's efficiency depends on the portal locations, which would be difficult to place for an outdoor setting.

13. A sector is a section of a game world, while portals are invisible regions that connect sectors.

14. Instancing allows multiple objects with varying attributes (such as position) to be rendered with a single draw call. Rendering in one large batch can lead to performance benefits, which is great for complex scenes that can take advantage of it.

15. Hardware, shader, constant, and stream instancing.

16. Continuous level-of-detail renders geometry at a high level of detail the closer it is to the camera. Using terrains as an example, this allows geometry in the distance to be rendered with less detail, which is more efficient.

17. ROAM is a technique used to render a large terrain more efficiently. ROAM, which stands for real-time optimally adapting mesh, is a very famous CLOD algorithm. The ROAM algorithm operates on a binary tree data structure known as a binary triangle tree.

18. Dynamic branching was introduced in Shader Model 3.0, and it uses conditional statements to control the execution of operations within a shader. This can allow some operations to be avoided, thus possibly improving performance for complex shading effects.

19. State management attempts to manage the state changes of a graphics API. Some state changes can be expensive, so limiting them can lead to performance benefits.

20. A graph data structure.

21. B. Although it can be used on 3D data, it is considered a 2D data structure.

22. True. The Z-buffer is used to test if a pixel that is being rendered is closer to the viewer than a pixel that was already rendered. If so, it is visible; otherwise, it is not.

23. False. BSP trees are better suited for indoor areas than outdoor areas.

24. True.

25. False. They are split into convex pieces.

26. False. It was introduced in Shader Model 3.0.

27. True.

28. False. Both occlusion culling and view frustum culling require the view information.

29. True.

30. False. State management attempts to minimize API state changes.

B

COMPILING THE SAMPLE SOURCE CODE

In This Chapter

- Compiling on Win32
- Compiling on Mac
- Compiling on Linux

In this book we've used OpenGL for Windows, Mac, and Linux and Direct3D for Windows operating systems. To compile and execute the sample source files on the CD-ROM, it is important to have the necessary tools and files set up and available. If using the same tools as the sample projects on the CD-ROM, you can open the projects on the platform of your choice and compile, build, and execute the sample applications. The Direct3D 10 samples assume that you are using Windows Vista and DirectX 10–compatible graphics hardware.

COMPILING ON WIN32

Compiling Win32 applications with Direct3D requires the DirectX SDK. This can be downloaded from Microsoft's DirectX Web site at http://www.microsoft.com/downloads and search for the DirectX SDK. Once the SDK is installed, you can begin creating DirectX-based applications. If you are using Visual Studio 2003, 2005, or 2008, the extensions for the tools are installed during the DirectX SDK installation. This allows Visual Studio to know where the SDK is installed so that it can access its header files and libraries. The DirectX SDK comes with all of the necessary files for development using DirectX 9 and DirectX 10. To code with DirectX 10, you need Windows Vista and optionally (but highly recommended) a DirectX 10–compatible graphics card.

In this book, we used Microsoft's Visual Studio 2005 Express for the integrated development environment. It can be downloaded for free from http://www.microsoft.com/express/. At the time of writing this appendix, Visual Studio 2008 Express is available for download from the Express Web site and, if you choose, you can use that tool instead of Visual Studio 2005.

When you install a Visual Studio tool, the OpenGL headers and libraries are also installed. In this book, we used the OpenGL extension library known as GLee and the OpenGL utility toolkit. GLee is used to allow for easy loading of OpenGL extensions, such as the GLSL extensions, and can be downloaded from http://www.opengl.org/sdk/libs/GLee/. The OpenGL utility toolkit (GLUT) can be downloaded from http://www.opengl.org/resources/libraries/glut/ and allows for cross-platform OpenGL window creation on Windows, Mac, and Linux.

COMPILING ON MAC

We used GLee and GLUT (mentioned in the previous paragraph) for the OpenGL window creation and extension loading in Mac. For the programming integrated development environment, we used XCode, which can be downloaded for free from Apple's developer Web site at http://developer.apple.com/tools/xcode/. Once XCode is installed, it comes with the necessary header files and libraries for OpenGL application development.

COMPILING ON LINUX

For Linux, we used GLee and GLUT for the OpenGL rendering performed in this book. For development, we used KDevelop. KDevelop is a free and highly recommended integrated development environment for the various Linux operating systems. It can be downloaded for free from http://www.kdevelop.org/.

RECOMMENDED RESOURCES

In This Chapter

- Recommended Tools
- Recommended Books
- Recommended Web sites

RECOMMENDED TOOLS

Throughout this book, we used several free tools for the development of the sample source code. These tools are highly recommended to you and include the following.

- Visual Studio 2005/2008: A Windows XP/Vista integrated development environment (http://www.microsoft.com/express/)
- Xcode: A Mac OS X integrated development environment (http://developer.apple.com/tools/xcode/)
- Kdevelop: A Linux integrated development environment (http://www.kdevelop.org/)
- OpenGL Extension Library (http://www.opengl.org/sdk/libs/GLee/)
- OpenGL Utility Toolkit (http://www.opengl.org/resources/libraries/glut/)
- DirectX SDK (http://msdn2.microsoft.com/directx)
- NVIDIA's Melody (and other useful tools) (http://www.developer.nvidia.com/)

RECOMMENDED BOOKS

The books in this section are a few titles that can be of some use to anyone wanting to expand their knowledge on the different areas of game development. Reading these books is recommended for those looking for more detailed knowledge about many of the topics discussed in this book.

- *Mathematics for 3D Game Programming and Computer Graphics*, 2nd edition. Charles River Media (2003)
- *Data Structures for Game Developers*. Charles River Media (2007)
- *Ultimate Game Engine Design and Architecture*. Charles River Media (2006)
- *Ultimate Game Programming with DirectX*, 2nd edition. Charles River Media (2008)

RECOMMENDED WEB SITES

The Web sites in this section can be useful to anyone wanting to expand their knowledge on the different areas of game development. For additional Web sites and Web articles, visit UltimateGameProgramming.com.

- Finding Next Gen—CryEngine 2 (http://delivery.acm.org/10.1145/1290000/1281671/p97-mittring.pdf/)
- The Official OpenGL Web sites (http://www.OpenGL.org/)
- Microsoft Developer Network (MSDN) (http://msdn.Microsoft.com/)

OBJ LOADER

In This Chapter

- The File Format
- Loading Tokens
- Loading the OBJ File
- Generating Tangents

M any samples in this book used more complex models than simple shapes and objects for the scene geometry. These samples loaded geometry from a text file format known as OBJ (extension .obj). OBJ files are easy to load, and they are a supported export option in many 3D modeling and animation packages.

In this appendix, we will examine the files used to load the geometry in the sample applications from this book and discuss the files' formats. The geometry file format used is a matter of personal preference for this book but it helps to understand how to load OBJ models if you want to load the models on the CD-ROM.

THE FILE FORMAT

OBJ files are very common in 3D modeling and animation packages. The file is text based and can easily be parsed in code. Usually, only a subset of information is needed to be loaded from the OBJ model, but this depends on the application and its use. In this book, we only needed to load the geometric information and not any object materials. We focus here on what is known as the Wavefront OBJ. Although all OBJ formats are similar, some can have slight differences that make parsing them different between the formats. Most editors place the word *Wavefront* in a comment at the top of the file so you know it is a Wavefront OBJ model that is being loaded.

In an OBJ file, each line has a different piece of information dealing with the model. Each line starts with a keyword followed by a set of information, depending on what the beginning keyword is. Some of the keywords followed by the data that follows them include:

- `mtllib` (string)
- `usemtl` (string)
- `v` (float, float, float)
- `vn` (float, float, float)
- `vt` (float, float)
- `f` (int, int, int) or (int/int, int/int, int/int) or (int/int/int, int/int/int, int/int/int)
- `g` (string)
- `s` (int)
- `#`

Additional keywords can be found in the OBJ file dealing with freeform curves, but for this book, those are not explored. In this book, we only deal with polygone-based information.

The keyword # marks the start of a comment. Any line that starts with this symbol can be ignored by the code parsing the file.

The keywords s and g are for smoothing groups, which are not necessary for this book. The keywords mg and o are also part of the smooth group set, but, again, this book doesn't have a use for those. In the samples, we assumed that the models loaded were of one mesh. If you want to separate models into meshes, the files will need to be loaded so that g marks the name of the mesh, and the faces that follow it are its polygons until the end of the file or until another g (another mesh) is encountered.

The keywords mtllib and usemtl are material keywords. usemtl represents the use of a material, whose name follows the keyword. The material information, including names, is found in a material file, which is specified following the keyword mtllib. mtllib represents the name of the material file, while usemtl is a name of a material in that file. The material file for an OBJ model is also a text file that is easy to parse. These files store diffuse, specular, texture file names and so forth. In this book, we did not need those external files since it was easier to specify any textures and lighting information that was needed for an effect in code instead of in a separate file. It also made reading the code easier since users will not need to navigate multiple files to find the material information a specific object uses. With that said, the material keywords were not used in this book, although you can easily extend the OBJ loader that will be discussed in this appendix to load them if you want.

The polygonal information is represented by the keywords v, vn, and vt. The keyword v represents a single vertex and is followed by three floating-point numbers for the X, Y, and Z axes. vn is the vertex normal followed by the normal's vector, and vt is the vertex texture coordinate. Each of these elements appears on their own lines, and usually all the vertices of a model appear first followed by the normals and then the texture coordinates. When loading these pieces of information, we will create a list for each as we parse the file, which you'll see later in this appendix.

The last keyword, f, specifies a polygon face (i.e., a triangle). The face specifies index values for which vertex, normal, and texture coordinate each point of the triangle uses. Therefore, if v, vn, and vt have been loaded into separate arrays, the keyword f specifies the array index for the attributes each point of the triangle uses. Each f that is encountered specifies all three points of a triangle, although some OBJ formats allow for four-point polygons.

If the model does not use any texture coordinates or normals, f is followed by three integers that index the vertex positions of each of the triangle's points. If vertex positions and normals are specified, there will be two integers in the form of (int/int, int/int, int/int), or if all three attributes are found in the file, then (int/int/int, int/int/int, int/int/int) is used. Some 3D applications that export to the OBJ format specify a single default texture coordinate and normal vector and index those even if the model does not use any.

This book assumes only three-point triangles, so when creating models to load using the code found in this book, it is important to ensure that the OBJ models you create are Wavefront OBJ models and that they are exported as triangles, not quads. It is also assumed that the model file's faces are specified as (int/int/int, int/int/int, int/int/int), which most editors conform to. An example OBJ model of a cube can be seen in the following:

```
# Wavefront OBJ exported by MilkShape 3D

v -10.000000 9.500000 10.000001
v -10.000000 -9.500000 10.000001
v 10.000000 9.500000 10.000001
v 10.000000 -9.500000 10.000001
v 10.000000 9.500000 -10.000000
v 10.000000 -9.500000 -10.000000
v -10.000000 9.500000 -10.000000
v -10.000000 -9.500000 -10.000000
# 8 vertices

vt 0.000000 1.000000
vt 0.000000 0.000000
vt 1.000000 1.000000
vt 1.000000 0.000000
# 4 texture coordinates

vn 0.000000 0.000000 1.000000
vn 1.000000 0.000000 0.000000
vn 0.000000 0.000000 -1.000000
vn -1.000000 0.000000 0.000000
vn 0.000000 1.000000 0.000000
vn 0.000000 -1.000000 0.000000
# 6 normals

g Box01
s 1
f 1/1/1 2/2/1 3/3/1
f 2/2/1 4/4/1 3/3/1
s 2
f 3/1/2 4/2/2 5/3/2
f 4/2/2 6/4/2 5/3/2
s 1
f 5/1/3 6/2/3 7/3/3
f 6/2/3 8/4/3 7/3/3
s 2
```

```
f 7/1/4 8/2/4 1/3/4
f 8/2/4 2/4/4 1/3/4
s 3
f 7/1/5 1/2/5 5/3/5
f 1/2/5 3/4/5 5/3/5
f 2/1/6 8/2/6 4/3/6
f 8/2/6 6/4/6 4/3/6
# 12 triangles in group

# 12 triangles total
```

LOADING TOKENS

The OBJ file format is fairly straightforward. Each line has a different attribute that makes up the model, and within each line the information is separated by a white space or a "/", as in the case of the polygon faces. When parsing the information of an OBJ file, all that needs to occur is to load each line one at a time and then break those lines down into individual tokens.

A token is essentially a piece of information. The vertex v, for example, is followed by three tokens: one for the X, one for the Y, and one for the Z. When loading the OBJ file, we can read each line and read the first token. For a vertex, the first token is v. The first token, which is the keyword, always tells you what type of information is being loaded.

Once a line is loaded and its first token is read, the keyword type determines how many tokens follow and what you are to do with them. To make this easy, the OBJ loading code uses a class called TokenStream, which was created to take as input the contents of an entire file and to return each token one at a time. The class declaration is shown in Listing D.1.

LISTING D.1 CLASS DECLARATION FOR THE TokenStream CLASS

```
class TokenStream
{
    public:
        TokenStream();
        ~TokenStream();

        void ResetStream();
```

```
        void SetTokenStream(char *data);
        bool GetNextToken(std::string *buffer);
        bool GetNextToken(std::string *token, std::string *buffer);

        bool MoveToNextLine(std::string *buffer);

    private:
        int m_startIndex, m_endIndex;
        std::string m_data;
};
```

The class has a function that is used to move to the start of the data, to set the data to the class as one large string, to move to the next line in the text, and to get the next token. The class has as member variables index values for the start and end read position of the data being parsed and the data as a string object.

For resetting the token stream, this essentially means setting the start and end index to 0, which marks the front of the data buffer. The function used to set the data to the stream takes in a character buffer and sets it to the member object's string. This character buffer can be all the data of a text file loaded and passed all at once, which is what the samples perform when using this class. The constructor, destructor, resetting, and setting functions are shown in Listing D.2 along with a helper function called isValidIdentifier(). The helper function is used to determine if a character is a character between ! and ~. Anything outside this range includes white spaces, tabs, new-line and return markers, and so forth. When parsing the OBJ file, we can treat any character outside this range as a delimiter, which means we can read characters that make up a token until we see either a space, new line, or some other character that would act as a delimiter.

LISTING D.2 THE FIRST FEW FUNCTIONS FROM THE TokenStream CLASS

```
        bool isValidIdentifier(char c)
        {
            // Ascii from ! to ~.
            if((int)c > 32 && (int)c < 127)
                return true;

            return false;
        }
```

```
TokenStream::TokenStream()
{
    ResetStream();
}



TokenStream::~TokenStream()
{

}



void TokenStream::ResetStream()
{
    m_startIndex = m_endIndex = 0;
}



void TokenStream::SetTokenStream(char *data)
{
    ResetStream();
    m_data = data;
}
```

Two functions are used to get a token from the file. The first function takes a buffer that stores the resulting token and returns true or false if a token was able to be read. If we were at the end of the file, the GetNext-Token() function would fail since it can't get the next token (or if a data buffer was never set). This function starts by reading delimiters until a valid character is found. This way, if the parsing starts by reading a bunch of white spaces, for example, those spaces can be skipped until we reach the start of the next token's information.

The function then reads each character starting from the starting index until it reaches a delimiter such as a white space or new line. Every valid character that is read moves the ending index one position down. Once a delimiter is read, the loop in the function ends, and the string between the start and ending indexes represent the token. This token is then set to the buffer object. To avoid a situation where a string is specified with quotes, the first character in the data that is being parsed is tested before the loop that is used to extract the token is executed. Thus, as long as the code considers the data to be part of the string, it won't stop reading until it sees another quote. If testing for quotes were not done, information meant to be read as one string might be broken up when it should not. This is not necessary since the OBJ file does not specify strings with delimiters (i.e., spaces between words), but if this class were being used for other purposes, the functionality could come in handy. The GetNextToken() function is shown in Listing D.3.

LISTING D.3 THE GetNextToken() FUNCTION

```
bool TokenStream::GetNextToken(std::string *buffer)
{
   bool inString = false;
   m_startIndex = m_endIndex;
   int length = (int)m_data.length();

   if(m_startIndex >= length)
      return false;

   while(m_startIndex < length &&
         isValidIdentifier(m_data[m_startIndex]) == false)
   {
      m_startIndex++;
   }

   m_endIndex = m_startIndex + 1;

   if(m_data[m_startIndex] == '"')
      inString = !inString;

   if(m_startIndex < length)
   {
      while(m_endIndex < length &&
            (isValidIdentifier(m_data[m_endIndex]) ||
            inString == true))
      {
         if(m_data[m_endIndex] == '"')
            inString = !inString;

         m_endIndex++;
      }

      if(buffer != NULL)
      {
         int size = (m_endIndex - m_startIndex);
         int index = m_startIndex;
```

```
            buffer->reserve(size + 1);
            buffer->clear();

            for(int i = 0; i < size; i++)
            {
                buffer->push_back(m_data[index++]);
            }
        }


        return true;
    }


    return false;
}
```

The overloaded `GetNextToken()` function is used to search for a specific token and to return the token immediately after it. Again, if this class were being used for other purposes, the overloaded `GetNextToken()` function could come in handy. It is in Listing D.4.

LISTING D.4 THE OVERLOADED `GetNextToken()` FUNCTION

```
    bool TokenStream::GetNextToken(std::string *token, std::string
*buffer)
    {
        std::string tok;

        if(token == NULL)
            return false;

        while(GetNextToken(&tok))
            {
                if(strcmp(tok.c_str(), token->c_str()) == 0)
                    return GetNextToken(buffer);
            }

        return false;
    }
```

The last function is `MoveToNextLine()`, and it is used to move to the next line of text in a file's character buffer. The purpose of this function is to skip all data in the token stream until a new line or the end of the file is reached. This function is particularly useful in the OBJ loader because if a comment line marked by # is found, the entire line can be skipped. The MoveToNextLine() function is shown in Listing D.5. If this function was being used for a different application and if the information that made up the line was wanted, the information could be returned to the parameter buffer.

LISTING D.5 THE MoveToNextLine() FUNCTION

```
bool TokenStream::MoveToNextLine(std::string *buffer)
{
   int length = (int)m_data.length();

   if(m_startIndex < length && m_endIndex < length)
   {
      m_endIndex = m_startIndex;

      while(m_endIndex < length &&
            (isValidIdentifier(m_data[m_endIndex]) ||
            m_data[m_endIndex] == ' '))
      {
         m_endIndex++;
      }

      if((m_endIndex - m_startIndex) == 0)
         return false;

      if(m_endIndex - m_startIndex >= length)
         return false;

      if(buffer != NULL)
      {
         int size = (m_endIndex - m_startIndex);
         int index = m_startIndex;

         buffer->reserve(size + 1);
         buffer->clear();

         for(int i = 0; i < size; i++)
         {
            buffer->push_back(m_data[index++]);
         }
      }
   }
```

```
        else
        {
            return false;
        }

        m_endIndex++;
        m_startIndex = m_endIndex + 1;

        return true;
    }
```

LOADING THE OBJ FILE

Now that we have a way to load the file and break its contents down into individual tokens, we are ready to load the OBJ model. The models in this book loaded the vertex positions, normal vectors, and texture coordinates as one triangle list. The code also calculated the tangents used for bump mapping, which is discussed later in this appendix. The OBJ loader's class is shown in Listing D.6.

LISTING D.6 THE OBJ LOADER'S CLASS

```
class ObjModel
{
    public:
        ObjModel()
        {
            m_vertices = NULL;
            m_normals = NULL;
            m_texCoords = NULL;
            m_tangents = NULL;
            m_totalVerts = 0;
        }

        ~ObjModel()
        {
            Release();
        }
```

```
                    void Release();
                    bool LoadOBJ(char *fileName);


                    float *GetVertices()   { return m_vertices; }
                    float *GetNormals()    { return m_normals; }
                    float *GetTexCoords()  { return m_texCoords; }
                    float *GetSTangents()  { return m_tangents; }
                    int    GetTotalVerts() { return m_totalVerts; }

                private:
                    float *m_vertices;
                    float *m_normals;
                    float *m_texCoords;
                    float *m_tangents;
                    int m_totalVerts;
            };
```

The `ObjModel` class has functions for deleting the class's dynamic memory allocations, loading a file, and accessing the member variables. When an OBJ file is loaded, the face information is used to create one large triangle list. This is easier because OpenGL and Direct3D require indexes to index array elements for a vertex and all its elements, not to index each element separately. Although you can generate a compatible index list, it is more work and is not necessary for the samples in this book. In the OBJ file, each attribute has its own index list, while the common APIs assume that each vertex, normal, and texture coordinate uses the same index. Since the only dynamic information is the vertices, normals, and texture coordinates, they are required to be released at some point. This is done in the class's `Release()` function, which is shown in Listing D.7.

LISTING D.7 THE CLASS'S Release() FUNCTION

```
        void ObjModel::Release()
        {
            m_totalVerts = 0;

            if(m_vertices != NULL)
            {
                delete[] m_vertices;
                m_vertices = NULL;
            }
```

```
if(m_normals != NULL)
{
   delete[] m_normals;
   m_normals = NULL;
}

if(m_texCoords != NULL)
{
   delete[] m_texCoords;
   m_texCoords = NULL;
}
}
```

The loading of the OBJ file is the largest function because of all the necessary string parsing that is used. The function, called LoadOBJ(), starts by loading all the characters of a file and setting the file to a token stream object. Once the information is loaded, the data that was read can be deleted since a copy of it exists inside the class. This is shown in Listing D.8 in the first section of the LoadOBJ() function.

LISTING D.8 THE FIRST SECTION OF THE LoadOBJ() FUNCTION

```
bool ObjModel::LoadOBJ(char *fileName)
{
   std::ifstream fileStream;
   int fileSize = 0;

   fileStream.open(fileName, std::ifstream::in);

   if(fileStream.is_open() == false)
      return false;

   fileStream.seekg(0, std::ios::end);
   fileSize = fileStream.tellg();
   fileStream.seekg(0, std::ios::beg);

   if(fileSize <= 0)
      return false;

   char *buffer = new char[fileSize];

   if(buffer == NULL)
      return false;
```

```
TokenStream tokenStream, tempStream;
std::string tempLine, token;

fileStream.read(buffer, fileSize);
tokenStream.SetTokenStream(buffer);

delete[] buffer;

tokenStream.ResetStream();
```

Once the token stream has been created, we are ready to load the data. To make this easier, we actually have two token streams: one to get each line of the file and the other to further parse those individual lines. The next section of the LoadOBJ() function starts by calling a while loop that executes until no more lines can be read from the file. Inside this loop, for every line that is read, a new token stream is set with its contents.

Along with the token streams, four std::vector array objects are created to temporarily hold the parsed information from the file. Once set, the second token stream gets the first token, which is the keyword that tells us what information is stored on the line. If it is v, the three tokens after it are read and added to the temporary vector array list for the positions. If it is vn, the three tokens that are read are added to the normal vector array and so forth. The second section of the LoadOBJ() function is shown in Listing D.9. When a face is encountered, another loop is used to separate each index that is added to the face vector array.

LISTING D.9 THE SECOND SECTION OF THE LoadOBJ() FUNCTION

```
std::vector<float> verts, norms, texC;
std::vector<int> faces;

while(tokenStream.MoveToNextLine(&tempLine))
{
   tempStream.SetTokenStream((char*)tempLine.c_str());
   tokenStream.GetNextToken(NULL);

   if(!tempStream.GetNextToken(&token))
      continue;

   if(strcmp(token.c_str(), "v") == 0)
   {
      tempStream.GetNextToken(&token);
      verts.push_back((float)atof(token.c_str()));
```

```
      tempStream.GetNextToken(&token);
      verts.push_back((float)atof(token.c_str()));

      tempStream.GetNextToken(&token);
      verts.push_back((float)atof(token.c_str()));
   }
   else if(strcmp(token.c_str(), "vn") == 0)
   {
      tempStream.GetNextToken(&token);
      norms.push_back((float)atof(token.c_str()));

      tempStream.GetNextToken(&token);
      norms.push_back((float)atof(token.c_str()));

      tempStream.GetNextToken(&token);
      norms.push_back((float)atof(token.c_str()));
   }
   else if(strcmp(token.c_str(), "vt") == 0)
   {
      tempStream.GetNextToken(&token);
      texC.push_back((float)atof(token.c_str()));

      tempStream.GetNextToken(&token);
      texC.push_back((float)atof(token.c_str()));
   }
   else if(strcmp(token.c_str(), "f") == 0)
   {
      int index = 0;

      for(int i = 0; i < 3; i++)
      {
         tempStream.GetNextToken(&token);
         int len = (int)strlen(token.c_str());

         for(int s = 0; s < len + 1; s++)
         {
            char buff[12];

            if(token[s] != '/' && s < len)
            {
               buff[index] = token[s];
               index++;
            }
            else
            {
```

```
                        buff[index] = '\0';
                        faces.push_back((int)atoi(buff));
                        index = 0;
                    }
                }
            }
        }

        token[0] = '\0';
    }
```

The first function of the LoadOBJ() function allocates the memory of the class member variables to store the information as if it were a triangle list. Once the memory is allocated, it loops through the total number of faces and uses the face index information to place the vertices, normals, and texture coordinates in the member variables. Once done, the temporary vector arrays are no longer needed, and the geometry is loaded as a triangle list and is ready to use. The third section of the LoadOBJ() function is shown in Listing D.10.

LISTING D.10 THE THIRD SECTION OF THE LoadOBJ() FUNCTION

```
int vIndex = 0, nIndex = 0, tIndex = 0;
int numFaces = (int)faces.size() / 9;
m_totalVerts = numFaces * 3;

if(m_totalVerts != 0)
   m_vertices = new float[m_totalVerts * 3];

if((int)norms.size() != 0)
   m_normals = new float[m_totalVerts * 3];

if((int)texC.size() != 0)
   m_texCoords = new float[m_totalVerts * 2];

if(m_totalVerts != 0)
   m_tangents = new float[m_totalVerts * 3];

for(int f = 0; f < (int)faces.size(); f+=3)
{
   m_vertices[vIndex + 0] = verts[(faces[f + 0] - 1) * 3 + 0];
   m_vertices[vIndex + 1] = verts[(faces[f + 0] - 1) * 3 + 1];
   m_vertices[vIndex + 2] = verts[(faces[f + 0] - 1) * 3 + 2];
   vIndex += 3;
```

```
    if(m_texCoords)
    {
      m_texCoords[tIndex + 0] = texC[(faces[f + 1] - 1) * 2 + 0];
      m_texCoords[tIndex + 1] = texC[(faces[f + 1] - 1) * 2 + 1];
      tIndex += 2;
    }

    if(m_normals)
    {
      m_normals[nIndex + 0] = norms[(faces[f + 2] - 1) * 3 + 0];
      m_normals[nIndex + 1] = norms[(faces[f + 2] - 1) * 3 + 1];
      m_normals[nIndex + 2] = norms[(faces[f + 2] - 1) * 3 + 2];
      nIndex += 3;
    }
  }
}
```

The last section of the LoadOBJ() function generates the tangents that are used for the bump mapping samples. Since the OBJ file format does not specify attributes for tangents, these are generated manually by the LoadOBJ() function. The tangent generation is shown in Listing D.11. Tangents are created for each triangle with the CalculateTangent() function, which is discussed in the next section.

LISTING D.11 THE FOURTH AND LAST SECTION OF THE LoadOBJ() FUNCTION

```
int triVert = 0;

for(int v = 0, t = 0; v < m_totalVerts * 3; v+=3, t+=2)
{
  int nextV, nextT, prevV, prevT;

  if(triVert == 0)
  {
    nextV = v + 3;
    prevV = v + 6;
    nextT = t + 2;
    prevT = t + 4;
  }
  else if(triVert == 1)
  {
    nextV = v + 3;
    prevV = v - 3;
```

```
                    nextT = t + 2;
                    prevT = t - 2;
                }
                else if(triVert == 2)
                {
                    nextV = v - 6;
                    prevV = v - 3;
                    nextT = t - 4;
                    prevT = t - 2;
                }

                CalculateTangent(&m_vertices[v],
                                 &m_vertices[nextV],
                                 &m_vertices[prevV],
                                 &m_normals[v],
                                 &m_texCoords[t],
                                 &m_texCoords[nextT],
                                 &m_texCoords[prevT],
                                 &m_tangents[v]);

                triVert = (triVert + 1) % 3;
            }

        verts.clear();
        norms.clear();
        texC.clear();
        faces.clear();

        return true;
    }
```

GENERATING TANGENTS

As mentioned in Chapter 8, "Lighting and Materials," tangents are used to create a tangent matrix. The tangent matrix is used to transform vectors into tangents, also known as texture space. The tangent matrix is made up of the s-tangent, bi-normal, and normal vectors. The normal can be the vertex normal, which our OBJ model has. The bi-normal is the cross-product between the normal and the s-tangent. This means the bi-normal can be calculated inside a shader to reduce the amount of bandwidth that is used for objects. The only term that needs to be calculated ahead of time is the s-tangent, which is done using the helper function CalculateTangent() in the source file for the OBJ loading class.

The s-tangent represents the change in direction of the TU texture coordinate, while the bi-normal represents the change in TV. This means that to calculate tangents for a model, the model has to have texture coordinates. Texture coordinates are floating-point values that are used to map an image onto a surface along the U and V axes for a 2D texture.

The `CalculateTangent()` function takes the vertices of a triangle, the normal of the first vertex (or face normal if they all share the same normal), and the texture coordinates for the triangle. The function outputs the tangent vector in its final parameter, which was used in the `LoadOBJ()` function to create the tangent list.

The calculation of the s-tangents starts by getting the edges between the triangle's vertices and scaling them by the dot product between them. The dot product is calculated between the edge and the normal. Once the vertex edges are calculated, the same is done for the texture coordinate edges, which is followed by a simple test to make sure the edges are moving in the right direction so that the following code can be executed on edges that move in either direction instead of having to have versions for both cases. Once this is done, the tangent is calculated. The tangent that is created is used for the first vertex in the function's parameter list. Each vertex has to have its tangent calculated, which is done in the `LoadOBJ()` function.

If you are unfamiliar with the mathematics of tangents, we recommend reading up on them in a mathematics book, which you can find in Appendix C, "Recommended Resources." The `CalculateTangent()` function is shown in Listing D.12.

LISTING D.12 THE `CalculateTangent()` FUNCTION

```
void CalculateTangent(float *v1, float *v2, float *v3,
                      float *n1,
                      float *t1, float *t2, float *t3,
                      float *tangent)
{
    float edge1[3], edge2[3];

    edge1[0] = v2[0] - v1[0];
    edge1[1] = v2[1] - v1[1];
    edge1[2] = v2[2] - v1[2];

    float dp;

    dp = n1[0] * edge1[0] + n1[1] * edge1[1] + n1[2] * edge1[2];
```

```
edge1[0] = edge1[0] - n1[0] * dp;
edge1[1] = edge1[1] - n1[1] * dp;
edge1[2] = edge1[2] - n1[2] * dp;


edge2[0] = v3[0] - v1[0];
edge2[1] = v3[1] - v1[1];
edge2[2] = v3[2] - v1[2];

dp = n1[0] * edge2[0] + n1[1] * edge2[1] + n1[2] * edge2[2];

edge2[0] = edge2[0] - n1[0] * dp;
edge2[1] = edge2[1] - n1[1] * dp;
edge2[2] = edge2[2] - n1[2] * dp;


float tcEdge1[2], tcEdge2[2];

tcEdge1[0] = t2[0] - t1[0];
tcEdge1[1] = t2[1] - t1[1];

tcEdge2[0] = t3[0] - t1[0];
tcEdge2[1] = t3[1] - t1[1];

if((tcEdge2[0] * tcEdge1[1]) > (tcEdge1[0] * tcEdge2[1]))
{
   tcEdge1[0] = -tcEdge1[0];
   tcEdge2[0] = -tcEdge2[0];
}

float d = tcEdge1[0] * tcEdge2[1] - tcEdge2[0] * tcEdge1[1];

tangent[0] = 1; tangent[1] = 0; tangent[2] = 0;

if(!(d > -0.0001f && d < 0.0001f))
{
   tangent[0] = (edge1[0] * tcEdge2[0]) -
                (edge2[0] * tcEdge1[0]);

   tangent[1] = (edge1[1] * tcEdge2[0]) -
                (edge2[1] * tcEdge1[0]);

   tangent[2] = (edge1[2] * tcEdge2[0]) -
                (edge2[2] * tcEdge1[0]);
```

```
        dp = (float)sqrt(tangent[0] * tangent[0] +
                         tangent[1] * tangent[1] +
                         tangent[2] * tangent[2]);

    if(!(dp > -0.0001f && dp < 0.0001f))
    {
        dp = 1 / dp;

        tangent[0] *= dp;
        tangent[1] *= dp;
        tangent[2] *= dp;
    }
}
}
```

INDEX

C

C++ code

    data type names in, 24

    use of, 15

`CalculateTangent()` **function, using with OBJ loader,** 616–619

calculations, speeding up, 437

Carmack's reverse, explanation of, 407

caustics technique, use in *Crysis***,** 517

Cg shader, features of, 211–212

char data type, bits in, 26

circle of confusion, using with Poisson-disk filter, 468

clamping data, effect of, 454–455

`Clear()` **function**

    using in Direct3D, 120

    using with Blank Window demo, 122, 127

`ClipLine()` **function, using,** 131–134

clipping

    applying to dynamic decals, 483

    of lines, 131

    polygons, 10

    process of, 128

    in rasterization, 117–118

CLOD (continuous level of detail), using, 555

clouds, rendering, 495–496

code samples. *See* pseudo code

collision detection

    testing for, 41

    for triangles, 41–42

    using convex geometry in, 39

    using planes in, 57

color buffers, updating, 146

color class, using with CPU backward ray tracer, 90–91

color detail, preserving, 31

color formats, using with texture maps, 219–220

color maps

    noncompressed example of, 258

    texture compression of, 257–258

color ranges

    (HDR) high-dynamic-range, 29–31

    (LDR) low-dynamic-range, 29

    8-bit values in, 450

color rendering buffers, support for, 140

color values

    specification of, 28

    tone mapping, 455

Color3 class, using with Blank Window demo, 123

color-key transparency, using, 271–272

colors

    bleeding, 423

    converting to luminance values, 323

    describing as gray-scale, 323

    setting for pixels, 128

    using image filters with, 322–323

comments

    using in assembly source code, 178

    using in GLSL, 185

compressing images, 221–223. *See also* texture compression

compression, lossless versus lossy, 257–258

computer graphics

    in movies and TV, 5

    in video games, 6–13

computer-generated imagery, types of, 114

concave polygons, using, 39

const type qualifier, using in GLSL, 188

constant buffer, using in Shader Model 4.0, 254

constructive solid geometry editor, example of, 17

continuous level of detail (CLOD), using, 555

convex polygons

    considering as brushes, 43

    using, 39

coordinate spaces

    representing, 49

    significance of, 48

cosine angle, calculating for vectors, 46–47

CPU backward ray tracer

    cleaning up after, 98

    Color3 class for, 91

    features of, 85–86

    plane class for, 89–90

    ray class for, 88

License Agreement/Notice of Limited Warranty

By opening the sealed disc container in this book, you agree to the following terms and conditions. If, upon reading the following license agreement and notice of limited warranty, you cannot agree to the terms and conditions set forth, return the unused book with unopened disc to the place where you purchased it for a refund.

License:

The enclosed software is copyrighted by the copyright holder(s) indicated on the software disc. You are licensed to copy the software onto a single computer for use by a single user and to a backup disc. You may not reproduce, make copies, or distribute copies or rent or lease the software in whole or in part, except with written permission of the copyright holder(s). You may transfer the enclosed disc only together with this license, and only if you destroy all other copies of the software and the transferee agrees to the terms of the license. You may not decompile, reverse assemble, or reverse engineer the software.

Notice of Limited Warranty:

The enclosed disc is warranted by Course Technology to be free of physical defects in materials and workmanship for a period of sixty (60) days from end user's purchase of the book/disc combination. During the sixty-day term of the limited warranty, Course Technology will provide a replacement disc upon the return of a defective disc.

Limited Liability:

THE SOLE REMEDY FOR BREACH OF THIS LIMITED WARRANTY SHALL CONSIST ENTIRELY OF REPLACEMENT OF THE DEFECTIVE DISC. IN NO EVENT SHALL COURSE TECHNOLOGY OR THE AUTHOR BE LIABLE FOR ANY OTHER DAMAGES, INCLUDING LOSS OR CORRUPTION OF DATA, CHANGES IN THE FUNCTIONAL CHARACTERISTICS OF THE HARDWARE OR OPERATING SYSTEM, DELETERIOUS INTERACTION WITH OTHER SOFTWARE, OR ANY OTHER SPECIAL, INCIDENTAL, OR CONSEQUENTIAL DAMAGES THAT MAY ARISE, EVEN IF COURSE TECHNOLOGY AND/OR THE AUTHOR HAS PREVIOUSLY BEEN NOTIFIED THAT THE POSSIBILITY OF SUCH DAMAGES EXISTS.

Disclaimer of Warranties:

COURSE TECHNOLOGY AND THE AUTHOR SPECIFICALLY DISCLAIM ANY AND ALL OTHER WARRANTIES, EITHER EXPRESS OR IMPLIED, INCLUDING WARRANTIES OF MERCHANTABILITY, SUITABILITY TO A PARTICULAR TASK OR PURPOSE, OR FREEDOM FROM ERRORS. SOME STATES DO NOT ALLOW FOR EXCLUSION OF IMPLIED WARRANTIES OR LIMITATION OF INCIDENTAL OR CONSEQUENTIAL DAMAGES, SO THESE LIMITATIONS MIGHT NOT APPLY TO YOU.

Other:

This Agreement is governed by the laws of the State of Massachusetts without regard to choice of law principles. The United Convention of Contracts for the International Sale of Goods is specifically disclaimed. This Agreement constitutes the entire agreement between you and Course Technology regarding use of the software.